THE NUCLEAR NON-PROLIFERATION REGIME

Also by Raju G. C. Thomas

DEMOCRACY, SECURITY AND DEVELOPMENT IN INDIA

ENERGY AND SECURITY IN THE INDUSTRIALIZING WORLD (*co-editor*)

INDIAN SECURITY POLICY

PERSPECTIVES ON KASHMIR

THE GREAT POWER TRIANGLE AND ASIAN SECURITY (*editor*)

THE SOUTH SLAV CONFLICT (*co-editor*)

The Nuclear Non-Proliferation Regime

Prospects for the 21st Century

Edited by

Raju G. C. Thomas
Professor of Political Science
Marquette University
Wisconsin

First published in Great Britain 1998 by
MACMILLAN PRESS LTD
Houndmills, Basingstoke, Hampshire RG21 6XS and London
Companies and representatives throughout the world

A catalogue record for this book is available from the British Library.

ISBN 0–333–68964–X

First published in the United States of America 1998 by
ST. MARTIN'S PRESS, INC.,
Scholarly and Reference Division,
175 Fifth Avenue, New York, N.Y. 10010

ISBN 0–312–21042–6

Library of Congress Cataloging-in-Publication Data
The nuclear non-proliferation regime : prospects for the 21st century
/ edited by Raju G.C. Thomas.
p.   cm.
Includes bibliographical references and index.
ISBN 0–312–21042–6 (cloth)
1. Nuclear nonproliferation.   I. Thomas, Raju G. C.
KZ5675.N83 1997
341.7'34—dc21   97–37889
                                                          CIP

Selection, editorial matter and Chapters 1 and 14 © Raju G. C. Thomas 1998
Chapters 2–13, 15, 16 © Macmillan Press Ltd 1998

All rights reserved. No reproduction, copy or transmission of this publication may be made
without written permission.

No paragraph of this publication may be reproduced, copied or transmitted save with
written permission or in accordance with the provisions of the Copyright, Designs and
Patents Act 1988, or under the terms of any licence permitting limited copying issued by
the Copyright Licensing Agency, 90 Tottenham Court Road, London W1P 9HE.

Any person who does any unauthorised act in relation to this publication may be liable to
criminal prosecution and civil claims for damages.

The authors have asserted their rights to be identified as the authors of this work in
accordance with the Copyright, Designs and Patents Act 1988.

This book is printed on paper suitable for recycling and made from fully managed and
sustained forest sources.

10   9   8   7   6   5   4   3   2   1
07   06   05   04   03   02   01   00   99   98

Printed in Great Britain by
The Ipswich Book Company Ltd
Ipswich, Suffolk

Contents

List of Tables   vii

List of Figures   viii

Acknowledgements   ix

Notes on the Editor and Contributors   x

1   The Renewed NPT: Old Wine in New Bottles?
    Raju G.C. Thomas   1

Part I   Global Perspectives   **23**

2   Nuclear Proliferation Following the NPT Extension
    George Rathjens   25

3   A Treaty Reborn? The NPT after Extension
    Joseph F. Pilat and Charles W. Nakhleh   41

4   The NPT and Power Transitions in the International
    System
    T.V. Paul   56

5   The Causes of Nuclear Proliferation and the Utility of
    the Non-proliferation Regime
    Bradley A. Thayer   75

6   Chemical, Biological, and Missile Proliferation
    Kathleen C. Bailey   130

7   The NPT: Coping with the Best and Worst Cases
    Zachary S. Davis   140

Part II   Regional Perspectives   **157**

8   Proliferation and Non-Proliferation in Ukraine:
    Implications for European and US Security
    Stephen Blank   159

9   Japan's Nuclear Policy: Reflections on the Immediate
    Past, Prognosis for the 21st Century
    Ryukichi Imai   183

10 Nuclear Imbalance of Terror: The American Surveillance
    Regime and North Korea's Nuclear Programme
    Bruce Cumings   207

11 Is the Nuclear Option an Option for South Korea?
    Tong Whan Park   243

12 South Asia's Nuclear Revolution: Has It Occurred Yet?
    Peter R. Lavoy   260

13 The Indian and Pakistani Nuclear Programmes: A Race
    to Oblivion?
    Sumit Ganguly   272

14 Should India Sign the NPT/CTBT?
    Raju G.C. Thomas   284

15 Iran's Nuclear Quest: Motivations and Consequences
    Haleh Vaziri   310

Part III   Retrospect   **331**

16 The Realities of Nuclear War: Memories of Hiroshima
    and Nagasaki
    James N. Yamazaki   333

Index   351

List of Tables

1.1	Tests and Treaties of Weapons of Mass Destruction	3
1.2	Known Nuclear Tests Worldwide, 1945–96	5
1.3	The Nuclear Scorecard (December 1996)	6
6.1	Selected Ballistic Missile Capabilities (≥ 300 km Range)	135
6.2	Selected Cruise Missile Capabilities (≥ 300 km Range)	136
9.1	Primary Energy Requirements in China by 2010	200
9.2	Energy in China in 2010	200
9.3	Nuclear Power in China (Proposed Installed Capacities)	200
12.1	Four Possible Scenarios for the Nuclear Competition in South Asia	266

List of Figures

9.1 Long-term Energy Supply and Demand Forecast
    of Japan   189
9.2 Nuclear Power Plants in Japan (August 1994)   191
9.3 Nuclear Power Stations near Japan   201

Acknowledgements

In May 1994, a symposium on the prospects for the 1970 Non-Proliferation Treaty in the forthcoming NPT Renewal negotiations in 1995 was organized at Marquette University. About 30 academics and practitioners representing various viewpoints were invited to take part in the discussions. The symposium was sponsored and funded by the joint Center for International Studies of the University of Wisconsin at Milwaukee and Marquette University, one of 16 such National Resources Centers set up by the US Department of Education; and by the Allis-Chalmers visiting professors programme of Marquette University. The discussion and debates were conducted over two full days, extending from 9 a.m. to 10 p.m. on each day. Following the NPT Renewal Conference held at the United Nations in New York in 1995, participants at the 1994 symposium as well as other specialists were invited to submit chapters examining the prospects for the nuclear non-proliferation regime into the next century.

Several students and other personnel at Marquette University assisted in the organization of the symposium or helped prepare the manuscripts. They included the previous Marquette Director of the Center for International Studies, H. Richard Friman, and the then Programme Assistant, Maureen Walsh. Others who contributed to the symposium and the later book project included some of our political science graduate Research Assistants: Amrita Shetty, Bernard Kearney and Dengming Chen.

The editor would also like to acknowledge sections of various chapters that were adapted from, or parts previously published by the contributors in books by the Plenum Press and Duke University Press, and in journals that include *The Irish Studies Quarterly, The Washington Quarterly*, and *Security Studies*.

T.M. Farmiloe, Publishing Director, Annabelle Buckley, Senior Commissioning Editor, and John M. Smith, Senior Book Editor, all of the Macmillan Press in Britain, and Deborah Bennett, the copy-editor, also in Britain, were helpful and patient while I brought this volume to its completion.

RAJU G.C. THOMAS
Marquette University

Notes on the Editor and Contributors

Raju G.C. Thomas is Professor of Political Science at Marquette University in Milwaukee, Wisconsin. He is the Co-Director of the joint Center for International Studies of the University of Wisconsin-Milwaukee and Marquette University, one of 16 National Resource Centers set up by the US Department of Education. Professor Thomas was a Visiting Scholar/Research Fellow at the Center for Science and International Affairs at Harvard University (1980–81, 1988–89); the Center for International and Strategic Affairs at the University of California–Los Angeles (1982–83); the Defense and Arms Control Studies Program at the Massachusetts Institute of Technology (1988–89); the International Institute for Strategic Studies, London (1991–92); and the University of Wisconsin–Madison (Summer 1994). He has lectured at or consulted with various agencies of the US Department of Defense, the Foreign Service Institute of the US State Department, the Royal College of Defense Studies and the Royal Naval College of the British Ministry of Defence, and at several Universities in the US, Britain, Sweden, India, Pakistan, Sri Lanka, Australia, Canada, South Korea, Malaysia and Singapore. Between 1965 and 1969, he worked for British multinational corporations in India.

His books include *The Defence of India* (1978); *Indian Security Policy* (1986); *South Asian Security in the 1990s* (1993); and *Democracy, Security and Development in India* (1996). He is the contributing editor or co-editor of *The Great Power Triangle and Asian Security* (1983); *Energy and Security in the Industrializing World* (1990); *Perspectives on Kashmir* (1992); and *The South Slav Conflict: History, Religion, Ethnicity and Nationalism* (1996). He is currently editing a book entitled *Comparative Reforms in China and India*. He has published over 20 articles in professional journals such as *World Politics, Orbis, World Affairs, Asian Survey, Pacific Affairs, Survival, Mediterranean Quarterly, Washington Quarterly, Journal of Strategic Studies*, and *Harvard International Review*, over 25 chapters in edited books, and over 50 editorial articles in leading newspapers such as the *New York Times, Los Angeles Times, Christian Science Monitor, Chicago Tribune, St. Louis Post Dispatch, Times of India, Hindustan Times, Indian Express*, and *India Today*. Professor Thomas was educated at Bombay University, the London School of Economics, the

University of Southern California, and the University of California at Los Angeles from where he obtained his PhD in Political Science.

Kathleen C. Bailey is a Senior Fellow on the staff of the Director of Lawrence Livermore National Laboratory, where she conducts research on national security, arms control, and proliferation issues. From 1990 to 1992, Dr Bailey was Vice-President and Director of Arms Control Studies at National Security Research, Inc., and taught courses on national security policy at George Mason University. From 1987 to 1990, she was Assistant Director of the US Arms Control and Disarmament Agency, with policy responsibilities on nuclear, chemical, missile and conventional arms proliferation. She was appointed to this position by President Reagan and was confirmed by the US Senate. She was a Deputy Assistant Secretary in the US Department of State's Bureau of Intelligence and Research, 1986–87; headed the Office of Research in the US Information Agency, 1983–85; and she served as president of a political risk consulting firm in San Francisco, 1981–83. She also worked earlier at Lawrence Livermore National Laboratory, 1976–81. Her last position there was Associate Division Leader responsible for intelligence assessments of nuclear proliferation, technology transfer and foreign energy programmes.

In addition to many articles and book chapters, Dr Bailey's publications include *Doomsday Weapons in the Hands of Many: The Arms Control Challenge of the 90s* (1991); *Strengthening Nuclear Nonproliferation* (1993); and *The UN Inspections in Iraq: Lessons for On-Site Verification* (1995). She has also authored a fiction novel about biological weapons use by terrorists, *Death for Cause* (1995). Kathleen Bailey received her PhD in Comparative Politics with emphasis on South Asia and the Middle East from the University of Illinois in 1976. Her dissertation on the National Iranian Oil Company was written after a year of research in Tehran.

Stephen Blank is the Douglas MacArthur Professor of Research at the Strategic Studies Institute of the US Army War College. He was appointed an Associate Professor of National Security Affairs at the Strategic Studies Institute in 1989. Prior to this appointment, Dr Blank was Associate Professor for Soviet Studies at the Center for Aerospace Doctrine, Research, and Education of Air University at the Maxwell Air Force Base.

He has published numerous articles on Soviet/Russian military and foreign policies, and is the author of *The Sorcerer as Apprentice: Stalin's Commissariat of Nationalities* (1994); and the co-editor of *The Soviet Military and the Future* (1992). He is also the editor, with Professor Alvin Rubinstein of the University of Pennsylvania, of the forthcoming book on

Russian policy in Asia and the Far East, *Russia in Asia: Imperial Decline* (1997). Professor Blank's MA and PhD are in Russian History from the University of Chicago.

Bruce Cumings is John Evans Professor of International History and Politics, Departments of History and Political Science, and Director of the Center for International and Comparative Studies, Northwestern University. Earlier, he taught in the Department of Political Science at Swarthmore College, 1975–77; at the Jackson School of International Studies, University of Washington, 1977–86, and in the History Department, University of Chicago, 1987–94.

He is author or co-author of eight books, including the two-volume study of *Origins of the Korean War* (1981, 1990), *War and Television* (1992), and *Korea's Place in the Sun: A Modern History* (1997). He has published more than 50 articles in various journals. Professor Cumings is the recipient of National Endowment for the Humanities and MacArthur Foundation research fellowships. He was the principal historical consultant for the Thames Television and Public Broadcasting System's six-hour documentary *Korea: The Unknown War*. He received his BA from Denison University in 1965, and his PhD from Columbia University in 1975.

Zachary S. Davis is an analyst of international nuclear policy at the Congressional Research Service in Washington, DC. He maintains a series of widely circulated issue papers on the nuclear programmes of various countries, tracks executive and legislative branch activity in nuclear non-proliferation policy, and reports to members of Congress and Congressional committees on non-proliferation issues. His recent reports to the US Congress (monographs) include: *Nonproliferation Issues for the 104th Congress*; *Counter-Proliferation Doctrine: Issues for Congress*; *Nuclear Nonproliferation Strategies for South Asia*; *Nonproliferation Regimes*; *Policies to Control the Spread of Nuclear, Chemical and Biological Weapons, and Missiles*; *US Plutonium Policy*; *The Nuclear Nonproliferation Treaty*; *International Atomic Energy Agency: Strengthen Inspection Authority?*; *A Nuclear Weapons Free Zone in the Middle East*; *The South Pacific Nuclear Free Zone Treaty*; *Nuclear Proliferation from Russia: Options for Control*. He has also authored several issue briefs on nuclear developments in North Korea, Iran, Iraq, South Africa, Pakistan, and India. Among his recent scholarly publications, he was guest editor of a special issue of the journal *Security Studies* on international relations theory and nuclear proliferation.

He received his MA and PhD degrees in Political Science from the University of Virginia. He earned his BA in Politics from the University of California, Santa Cruz. His doctoral thesis examined the nuclear strategy and arms control policies of President Eisenhower, including the Atoms for Peace programme. Dr Davis has lectured extensively on non-proliferation issues, taught courses on US foreign policy, and served as a consultant on arms control to grant-making foundations.

Sumit Ganguly is a Professor of Political Science at the Graduate School and Hunter College of the City University of New York. He is also an Adjunct Professor of Political Science at Columbia University. A specialist in ethnic conflict and regional security in South and South East Asia, he is the author of *The Origins of War in South Asia: The Indo-Pakistani Conflicts since 1947* (2nd edition, 1997) and *The Crisis in Kashmir: Portents of War, Hopes of Peace* (1997). He has also co-edited four other books, the most recent with Michael E. Brown, *Government Policies and Ethnic Relations in Asia and the Pacific* (forthcoming). Professor Ganguly has published in *Asian Survey, Asian Affairs, The Bulletin of the Atomic Scientists, Current History, Foreign Affairs, The Journal of International Affairs, International Security, The Journal of Strategic Studies, Survival* and *The Washington Quarterly*. He is currently at work on a book that attempts to explain political quiescence and ethnic violence in Malaysia and Sri Lanka. Professor Ganguly received his PhD from the University of Illinois.

Ryukichi Imai is Ambassador Extraordinary and Plenipotentiary of Japan. He was formerly Ambassador of Japan to Kuwait and to Mexico. He was the Permanent Representative of Japan to the Conference on Disarmament in Geneva. He has served as General Manager, Engineering, Japan Atomic Power Co.; Counsellor, Atomic Energy Commission of Japan; Senior Advisor, Japan Atomic Industrial Forum; Distinguished Scholar and Member of the Board of the Institute for International Policy Studies, Tokyo; Professor of Social Sciences, Kyorin University; and Visiting Professor, Sophia University, Tokyo. He was also at one time a Science Reporter for *Asahi Shimbun*. He is currently member of the Governing Board, Stockholm International Peace Research Institute.

His books include: *Science and Nation* and *Science and Diplomacy; Nuclear Safeguards; Nuclear Power and International Politics; Nuclear Energy and Nuclear Proliferation;* and *Disarmament II*. He is also the author of *Nuclear Energy and Post-Cold War Management of Nuclear Weapons; Memoirs of a Non-Career Ambassador;* and *The United Nations at the Crossroads.* Ambassador Imai received his MS in Mathematics and DrEng. in Nuclear Engineering from the University of Tokyo; and MA degrees from both Harvard University and the Fletcher School of Law and Diplomacy.

Peter R. Lavoy is Assistant Professor in the Department of National Security Affairs at the US Naval Postgraduate School in Monterey, California. Prior to taking this position in 1993, he worked as a Research Fellow at the Center for Security and Technology Studies at Lawrence Livermore National Laboratory, 1992–93; and at the Center for International Security and Arms Control at Stanford University, 1991–92.

Professor Lavoy's publications include 'Nuclear Arms Control in South Asia', in *Arms Control toward the Twenty-First Century*, edited by Jeffrey A. Larsen and Gregory J. Rattray (1996); 'Arms Control: The Neglected Object of Nuclear Diplomacy', in *Nuclear Proliferation in South Asia*, edited by Ishtiaq Ahmad (1996); 'Avoiding Nuclear War' (with C. Raja Mohan) in *Crisis Prevention, Confidence Building, and Reconciliation in South Asia*, edited by Michael Krepon and Amit Sevak (1995); 'Civil–Military Relations, Strategic Conduct, and the Stability of Nuclear Deterrence in South Asia', in *Civil–Military Relations and Nuclear Weapons*, edited by Scott D. Sagan (1994); and 'Nuclear Myths and the Causes of Nuclear Proliferation', in *Security Studies* (Spring/Summer 1993). He is the editor of the monograph *The Future of Foreign Nuclear Materials* (1995).

Professor Lavoy has travelled extensively in South Asia. He speaks and reads Hindi and Urdu. He conducted a three-week lecture tour in Pakistan for the US Information Agency in 1997, and has participated in several regional confidence-building workshops with Indians and Pakistanis, including the biannual US–Pakistan Joint Symposium in Washington; and 'Traveling Seminar V: US Foreign Policy in South Asia', a USIA-sponsored forum in which he acted as the conference mediator in Karachi, Pakistan, and New Delhi, India, 1994. Peter Lavoy received his BA from Oberlin College, and his PhD from the University of California at Berkeley. His dissertation is entitled 'Learning to Live with the Bomb: India and Nuclear Weapons, 1947–1974'. He also attended the Berkeley Urdu Language Program in Lahore, Pakistan (1989–90), and the Graduate Institute of International Studies in Geneva, Switzerland (1981–82).

Charles W. Nakleh is a technical staff member in the Safeguards Systems Group at the Los Alamos National Laboratory. His research interests include the applications of environmental monitoring to international safeguards, safeguarding of advanced nuclear fuel cycles, and policy and technology issues related to the Fissile Material Cutoff Treaty (FMCT), and the Treaty on the Nonproliferation of Nuclear Weapons (NPT). He has published articles in scholarly journals on environmental monitoring and high-energy physics. He received his PhD in Physics from Cornell University in 1996.

Tong Whan Park is Associate Professor of Political Science and Director of the Forum on Korean Affairs at Northwestern University, Evanston, IL. He is also Adjunct Research Fellow at the Korea Institute for Defense Analyses in Seoul.

Over the years Professor Park has been developing research and teaching connections with many Korean institutions including a two-year Fulbright professorship at Seoul National University, a three-year visiting research fellowship at the Sejong Institute, and a short-term research appointment at the Institute of Foreign Affairs and National Security. Before starting his academic career, he had served as a reporter for *The Hankook Ilbo* (Daily) in Seoul. Dr Park's research interest centres on international relations and Northeast Asian politics. His work in both English and Korean has appeared in many scholarly journals on both sides of the Pacific as well as chapters in edited volumes. In particular, his thoughts on the security of the Korean peninsula can be found in his book entitled *U.S. Forces in Korea and Their Strategic Missions* (1990). He is currently working on Korea's foreign policy, with emphasis on political security issues. He received his MA and PhD in Political Science from the University of Hawaii; an MA in International Law from Choong-Ang University in Seoul; and an LLB from Seoul National University.

T.V. Paul is Associate Professor of Political Science at McGill University, Montreal, Canada, and specializes in international and regional security issues. He is the author of *Asymmetric Conflicts: War Initiation by Weaker Powers* (1994); and co-editor (with Richard Harknett and James Wirtz) of *The Absolute Weapon Revisited: Nuclear Arms and the Emerging International Order* (forthcoming 1997). He is currently writing a book entitled *Power versus Norms: Why Nations Forbear Nuclear Weapons*. He has written extensively on security issues, especially relating to war and nuclear proliferation. He is a member of the International Institute of Strategic Studies (IISS, London) and also the Assistant Editor of *Canadian Journal of Political Science*. He holds an MPhil degree from Jawaharlal Nehru University in New Delhi, and subsequently received his MA and PhD degrees from the University of California, Los Angeles.

Joseph F. Pilat is with the Nonproliferation and International Security Division of Los Alamos National Laboratory. He previously served in the Center for National Security Studies and the Strategic Analysis Group at Los Alamos. He was a special adviser to the Department of Energy's representative at the Third Review Conference of the Nuclear Non-Proliferation Treaty, served as representative of the Secretary of Defense to the Fourth NPT Review Conference, and as an adviser to the US Delegation at the 1995 NPT Review and Extension Conference. He has been Special Assistant to the Principal Director and Assistant for Nonproliferation Policy in the Office of the Deputy Assistant Secretary of Defense for Negotiations Policy, and a Senior Research Associate in the Congressional Research Service.

Dr Pilat has taught in the Department of Government, Cornell University, and the Department of History, Georgetown University. He has been a visiting Fellow at Cornell's Peace Studies Program and a Philip E. Mosely Fellow at the Center for Strategic and International Studies in Washington, DC. He has lectured widely, including at Harvard University, UCLA, the RAND Corporation, and the Naval Postgraduate School. He has written extensively for US and European scholarly journals. He is the author or editor of numerous books, including *Ecological Politics: The Rise of the Green Movement* (1980); *The Nonproliferation Predicament* (1985); *Atoms for Peace: An Analysis after Thirty Years* (1985); *The Nuclear Suppliers and Nonproliferation: International Policy Choices* (1985); *Beyond 1995: The Future of the NPT Regime* (1990); and *1995: A New Beginning for the NPT?* (1995).

George Rathjens was Professor of Political Science at the Massachusetts Institute of Technology from 1968 to 1996 and is now Professor Emeritus. He is affiliated with MIT's Center for International Studies. His recent publications include contributions to *A Nuclear-Free-World* edited by Joseph Rotblat, Jack Seinberger and Balchandra Udgaonker (also published in *Foreign Affairs*); to *Nuclear Weapons after the Cold War* (with Carl Kaysen and Robert McNamara); and a chapter, 'Energy and Climate Change' to *Preserving the Global Environment*, edited by Jessica Tuchman Mathews. He has also contributed 'Nuclear Proliferation after the Cold War' to *Technology Review* (with Marvin Miller); 'Environmental Change and Violent Conflict' to the *Scientific American* (with Thomas F. Hormer-Dixon and Jeffrey H. Boutwell); 'Rethinking Nuclear Proliferation' to *The Washington Quarterly*; and 'Military Intervention in Intrastate and Ethnic Conflict' to *Racism, Xenophobia and Ethnic Conflict* edited by

Simon Belsker and David Carlton. He is also a co-author, with Carl Kaysen, of 'Peace Operations by the United Nations: The Case for a Volunteer UN Military Force', published by the American Academy of Arts and Sciences (and in abbreviated form as 'Send In the Troops: A UN Foreign Legion' in *The Washington Quarterly*).

Dr Rathjens was on the staff of President Eisenhower's science adviser, George Kistiakowsky, from 1959 to 1960; Chief Scientist and then Deputy Director of the Advanced Research Projects Agency, Department of Defense, from 1960 to 1962; Deputy Assistant Director for Science and Technology and then Special Assistant to the Director, US Arms Control and Disarmament Agency, 1962–65; and Director of the Systems Evaluation Division of the Institute for Defense Analyses, 1965–68. In 1979–80, he was with the Department of State on partial leave of absence from MIT, serving in a dual capacity as chairman of the management group for US participation in the International Nuclear Fuel Cycle Evaluation; and as deputy to Gerard Smith, President Carter's Ambassador-at-Large for Nuclear Non-Proliferation Matters. In addition to his appointment at MIT, he has held visiting professorships at Marquette University, the University of California at Irvine, and Wellesley College. He is a Fellow of the American Academy of Arts and Sciences; and served as chairman of the Massachusetts Commission on Nuclear Safety. He has been a consultant to the Department of Energy, the Environmental Protection Agency, Office of Technology Assessment of the US Congress, and Sandia National Laboratory.

He holds a BS degree in Chemistry from Yale University and a PhD in Chemistry from the University of California at Berkeley. He taught Chemistry at Columbia University from 1950 to 1953 and was a Research Fellow in Chemistry at Harvard University from 1958 to 1959.

Bradley A. Thayer is a PhD candidate in the Department of Political Science at the University of Chicago and a predoctoral fellow at the Center for Science and International Affairs, Harvard University. His articles include 'Nuclear Weapons as a Faustian Bargain', *Security Studies* (Autumn 1995), and 'The Risk of Nuclear Inadvertence: A Review Essay', *Security Studies* (Spring 1994). He is presently finishing his dissertation, 'Creating Stability in New World Orders: Why Collective Security and Concert Systems Fail, Why the Balance of Power Works'. He also has been a consultant for the Rand Corporation in Santa Monica, California (Summer 1993) where he worked on developing regional deterrence strategies for the US Air Force and Army.

Haleh Vaziri received her PhD in International Relations from Georgetown University's Department of Government in 1995. She is presently a post-doctoral research fellow at Harvard University's Center for Middle East Studies as well as visiting Professor of Political Science at Averett College's Northern Virginia International Program. She has presented numerous papers and written articles on Iranian foreign policy, state–society relations in the Middle East, and women's human rights. She is the co-author (with Mahanaz Afkhami) of *Claiming Our Rights: A Manual for Women's Human Rights Education in Muslim Societies* (1996).

James N. Yamazaki, a medical doctor, is a native of Los Angeles, and has been Clinical Professor at the Children's Hospital of the University of California at Los Angeles (UCLA) from 1951 to 1997. He served with the US Army Batallion Surgeon 106th Infantry Division POW, Germany, during the Second World War; and later worked for the US Atomic Bomb Casualty Commission (ABCC) of the National Academy of Sciences–National Research Council between 1949 and 1951. He was the Physician-in-charge of the US Atomic Bomb Casualty Commission Laboratory, Nagasaki, assigned to establish the clinical and laboratory facilities, and to develop relationships with the people and the Nagasaki University Medical School Faculty. Here he conducted the investigation into the long-term effects of the atomic bomb survivors, focusing on the effect on the foetus and children. He initiated an interdisciplinary study of the radiation effects on early development with members of the UCLA Laboratory of Nuclear Medicine and Radiation Biology, and the Brain Research Institute, American Academy of Pediatrics (1957–70) and used this position to convey to physicians the implication of atomic warfare and radiation to children and to the environment. Yamazaki participated on national and international symposia and review panels, including those sponsored by the US Atomic Energy Commission, the US Department of Energy, the International Congress of Pediatrics, and the World Health Organization, serving on an Advisory Panel to study the effect of radiation on intrauterine brain damage from the Chernobyl accident (Moscow, 1992).

He is the recipient of the Distinguished Service Award from the Children's Hospital of Los Angeles, 1989; the Merit Award from the Marquette University Alumni Association, 1991; the Professional Achievement Award for Excellence from the UCLA Alumni Association, 1996; and the Third Order of the Sacred Treasure of Japan (the highest award given to a foreigner by the Japanese Government), 1996.

Professor Yamazaki has published over 40 articles relating to effects of the atomic bomb on children, and laboratory investigation of the effects of radiation on the developing brain. He is the author (with Louis B. Fleming) of *Children of the Atomic Bomb: An American Physician's Memoir of Nagasaki, Hiroshima, and the Marshall Islands* (1995). The book was translated and released in Japan as *Genbaku No Ko* by Professor M. Aiki (1996). He received his BA in 1939 from UCLA and his MD in 1943 from Marquette University's School of Medicine (now the Medical College of Wisconsin).

1 The Renewed NPT: Old Wine in New Bottles?

Raju G.C. Thomas

1 THE SIGNIFICANCE OF THE PROBLEM

The Nuclear Non-Proliferation Treaty (NPT) was opened for signature in 1968 and came into effect in 1970 following ratification by the required number of states. The NPT was to remain in force for 25 years and accordingly the original treaty expired in 1995. Following a meeting at United Nations headquarters in New York in April 1995, the NPT was renewed indefinitely without change to the text. The membership of the renewed NPT is now nearly unanimous with only three states of significance remaining outside: India, Pakistan and Israel. Although there were earlier predictions about the NPT's imminent collapse, especially after India tested an atomic device in 1974, the Treaty has survived. Indeed, the NPT's prospects at the beginning of the 21st century may be argued to be much less gloomy than in the early 1960s when predictions were made that by the turn of this century there would be more than 30 nuclear weapons states in the world. With the exception of India in 1974, no new states have conducted nuclear tests, and even India has refrained from further tests.

The Future of the NPT

However, there are also doubts as to whether the renewed NPT would hold indefinitely beyond 2000. Proliferation, even among signatory states, is likely to be covert as in the case of Iraq and North Korea in the 1980s and early 1990s. Or, proliferation may be diverted into grey areas not covered by the Treaty as in the case of India which is seeking to develop and deploy nuclear-powered submarines. Prognosis for the renewed NPT is further clouded by India's refusal to sign the Comprehensive Test Ban Treaty (CTBT) in 1996 unless a timetable for the elimination of all nuclear weapons was introduced into the proposed treaty.[1] India's main concern was that the nuclear 'haves' and especially China would continue to possess nuclear weapons that have been tested successfully. Among the advanced industrialized states, there is

1

now the technological prospect for simulated laboratory testing, a method which may be as good as the real thing and which is not covered by the CTBT. The procedure adopted at the Conference on Disarmament in Geneva required unanimous agreement on the CTBT by all of its 44 members. India's refusal to sign it in August 1996 therefore amounted to a veto of the CTBT in Geneva. In an alternative procedural move, Australia then introduced the CTBT in the UN General Assembly which required only a two-thirds majority for the Treaty to be passed. This draft resolution on the CTBT was passed by the 185 member UN General Assembly on September 10, 1996, by a vote of 158 to 3, with five abstentions.[2] There were 19 states that did not vote for a variety of reasons including failure to pay its UN dues. Only Bhutan and Libya joined India in opposing the CTBT resolution. Cuba, Lebanon, Mauritius, Syria and Tanzania abstained. Iran which was expected to oppose the Treaty decided to support it on the day of the vote.

The Biological Weapons Convention (BWC) and the Chemical Weapons Convention (CWC) were successfully concluded in 1972 and 1993 respectively, but the clandestine production of biological and chemical weapons (the 'poor man's bomb') continues to remain worrisome. At the end of 1996 the CWC had not yet been ratified by at least 65 of the signatories and therefore had not yet gone into effect. The 62 states that initially ratified the Treaty included India but not the United States whose Senate rejected the convention in September 1996 on the grounds that it did not provide foolproof verification and was likely to be ineffective against nations that ignored it.[3] Meanwhile, there is no universal treaty or convention on missile proliferation that will halt the production and deployment of delivery systems for nuclear, biological and chemical weapons. The American-sponsored Missile Technology Control Regime (MTCR) remains a set of guidelines among seven Western industrialized countries (US, UK, France, Germany, Italy, Canada and Japan) not to transfer missile and rocket technology to those countries aspiring to develop missiles. The MTCR does not carry the same legal constraint as the NPT which is a multilateral and near-universal treaty.

No doubt significant strides have been made in controlling and eliminating nuclear weapons missile capabilities in the US and Russia, and in the European regional theatre. The LTBT, SALT-I, the TTBT, SALT-II, the INF, START-I, START-II and the CTBT, all represent gains in the struggle against nuclear weapons capabilities and missile delivery systems among the nuclear weapons states. (See Table 1.1.) The Biological and Chemical weapons conventions banning these other weapons of mass destruction are also indicators of significant gains in making the world a safer place. But there are as yet no moves or even serious discussions among the formal nuclear powers about moving towards comprehensive nuclear disarmament.

Table 1.1   Tests and Treaties of Weapons of Mass Destruction

---

1945:   First atomic test conducted by the US at Alamogordo, New Mexico.

1945:   US drops atomic bombs on Hiroshima and Nagasaki, Japan.

1949:   Soviet Union conducts its first atomic test in Kazakhstan.

1963:   Limited Test Ban Treaty. Banned nuclear tests in the atmosphere, in outer space and under water. The LTBT is signed by the nuclear powers United States, Britain and France but not by France and China. India is also a signatory to the LTBT.

1964:   China conducts its first atomic test.

1968:   The Nuclear Non-Proliferation Treaty is finalized and opened for signature. Following ratification by the required number of states, the NPT went into effect in 1970.

1972:   The Strategic Arms Limitation Talks Agreement (SALT-I) including the Anti-Ballistic Missile Treaty is concluded between the United States and the Soviet Union.

1972:   The Biological Weapons Convention is finalized and opened for signature. The BWC went into effect in 1974 following the required number of ratifications.

1974:   The Threshold Test Ban Treaty is signed by the US and the Soviet Union. The TTBT limits underground nuclear testing by the two superpowers.

1974:   India conducts its first and only atomic test in the Rajasthan desert. The test is conducted underground and is not in violation of the LTBT which India signed.

1979:   The Strategic Arms Limitation Talks Agreement (SALT-II) is signed by the United States and the Soviet Union. In 1981 the US Senate rejected ratification of the treaty.

1991:   The Strategic Arms Reduction Talks (START-I) is concluded between the United States and the Soviet Union. Both sides agree to reduce their nuclear weapons by one-fifth to 8–9,000 warheads.

1993:   The Strategic Arms Reduction Talks (START-II) is concluded between the United States and Russia. Both sides agreed to reduce the number of nuclear warheads to 3,500.

1993:   The Chemical Weapons Convention is finalized and opened for signature. The CWC requires 65 states to ratify in order to go into effect. The CWC went into effect in May 1997, following its ratification by more than 100 states, including the US.

1995:   The Nuclear Non-Proliferation Treaty is renewed indefinitely without revision. India, Pakistan and Israel did not sign.

1996:   In August, India vetoes the Comprehensive Test Ban Treaty in the 44-member Conference on Disarmament in Geneva. In September, the United Nations General Assembly passes the CTBT by a vote of 158 to 3, with 5 abstentions, and 19 states not participating. India, Bhutan and Libya voted against the treaty.

The Nature of the NPT Debate

There are differences among policymakers and analysts on the eventual status of the nuclear non-proliferation regime beyond the year 2000. Basically, these differences may be grouped together under two opposing viewpoints.

According to the supporters of the NPT who represent the overwhelming majority viewpoint mainly promoted by the United States, the Treaty has met all or most of its basic objectives. Renewal without revision was expected to promote the prevailing satisfactory (if not ideal) state of affairs into the foreseeable future. After all, almost all the 185 states represented at the United Nations had signed and ratified the Treaty since 1968 with the notable exceptions of India, Pakistan and Israel. Even if some key states have not signed, there have been no additional nuclear weapons states beyond the existing five. Following the Indian test of an atomic device in May 1974, India's stockpile went from one to zero. Certainly, the earlier fears of more than 30 nuclear weapons states existing by the year 2000, as envisaged during the Kennedy administration, did not materialize and appears unlikely to happen in the next decade. The policy attitude of this group is simply a case of 'leave well enough alone'. To have tinkered with the old NPT in 1995 with the purpose of devising a new treaty to cover all the problems that emerged during the 25-year period would only have opened the floodgates of controversy leading to no agreement and no renewal. It is not the precise clauses of the NPT that matter whatever its weaknesses, as much as the Treaty's well understood overall prohibition against the spread of nuclear weapons among additional states. Thus, North Korea may have been within its legal rights to invoke Article X of the NPT in March 1994 allowing it three months' notice and withdrawing from the Treaty. But international pressures led by the US prevented it from invoking this clause and going nuclear.

According to the opponents of the NPT, which is the marginal minority viewpoint argued mainly by India, the Treaty has failed to meet its objectives. Unlike non-discriminatory multilateral treaties such as the BWC and the CWC whose terms apply equally to all its signatories, the NPT is a discriminatory treaty that creates an exclusive club of nuclear 'haves' and a permanent mass membership of nuclear 'have-nots'. Moreover, throughout the original NPT's existence, states that should have signed it, such as India, Pakistan, and Israel (and at one time, South Africa, Brazil and Argentina), had refused to sign the Treaty. Moreover, there are at least four NPT signatory states – Iraq, Iran, Libya, and North Korea – who signed the treaty but at one time or another engaged (and may still be engaged) in clandestine nuclear weapons programmes. And there are at least three other signatory states – Japan, South Korea and Taiwan – who are engaged in developing major civilian nuclear energy programmes with the capacity to divert to nuclear weapons programmes if sufficiently motivated by security concerns. These concerns arise from the continuing growth of Chinese nuclear weapons capabilities and uncertainties about North Korea's nuclear ambitions. With the end of the Cold War and with US alliance relationships in Asia ending or in decline, the industrialized and technologically advanced states of Japan, South Korea and Taiwan may perceive the need to develop independent nuclear deterrents to meet future security needs. For India in particular, Chinese nuclear capabilities and Pakistan's clandestine nuclear weapons and missile programmes aided by China, remain a major security problem.

Until 1992, two nuclear powers, France and China, had not signed the Treaty. Even after these two states signed the NPT, they continued to conduct nuclear weapons tests until 1996 in anticipation of the moratorium that would be imposed on all nuclear testing by the Comprehensive Test Ban Treaty (CTBT) that was concluded in September 1996. This state of affairs suggests that the majority of states which do not need to sign the Treaty because they lack nuclear ambitions have signed it. On the other hand, a handful of states with nuclear ambitions which need to sign the Treaty have not signed it, or have signed it in bad faith, or may change their minds about their Treaty membership as new security circumstances emerge.

Even if the first and more optimistic viewpoint is likely to prevail beyond 2000, to assume the second and more pessimistic viewpoint may be useful in order to anticipate and resolve some of the problems that may arise in the future. It is important to note that 'Going Nuclear' may well be a function of both technological capabilities in the making of nuclear weapons and perceptions of security threats to a state. So long as states

Table 1.2   Known Nuclear Tests Worldwide, 1945–96

	USA	USSR	France	Britain	China	India
Atmosphere	215	219	50	21	23	0
Underground	815	496	159	24	22	1
Total	1030	715	209	45	45	1

Source: United Nations Physicians for Social Responsibility (Reproduced in the *New York Times*, September 11, 1996.)

Table 1.3   The Nuclear Scorecard (December 1996)

- 70 000 nuclear weapons in the world in 1986
- 40 000 nuclear weapons in the world today, but these equal 700 000 Hiroshima bombs
- 3% of these 40 000 weapons are in the UK, France and China
- 97% of these weapons belong to Russia (24 000) and the US (15 000)
- By treaty and unilateral cuts, nuclear weapons will fall to 21 000 by 2003
- Russia and the US will each keep 10 000 deployed and stored nuclear weapons
- South Africa, Ukraine, Kazakhstan and Belarus gave up their nuclear weapons
- Israel, India and Pakistan have not signed the NPT and can make and deliver nuclear weapons if they want

---

Source: *The Defense Monitor*, Center for Defense Information, Washington DC, December 1996.

do not possess the needed nuclear weapons technology (for example Nigeria), or possess the technological capability but do not perceive serious threats to itself (for example Canada), the NPT will remain an acceptable but irrelevant treaty. On the other hand, perceptions of security threats to a state may be the outcome of technological capabilities to produce nuclear weapons. If two antagonistic states are capable of developing nuclear weapons, there will be a tendency for each state to assume that the other will do so thereby justifying it own attempt to pre-empt the other in acquiring such weapons. What operates here is the classic 'security dilemma' and the so-called 'mad military momentum', namely, that if we can do it, then they can do it too, therefore we must do it before they do it. Such external nuclear threat projections by one state become self-fulfilling prophecies. Whatever the compulsions, the present nuclear weapons proliferation tendencies point to somewhat uncertain prospects for the non-proliferation regime in the 21st century.

Some Issues Not Addressed by the NPT

No technological methods exist as yet to prevent the diversion of peaceful nuclear energy programmes to nuclear weapons programmes. The acquisition and absorption of peaceful nuclear technology and the ability to build civilian nuclear facilities also provide that state with military nuclear capabilities. Thus Articles I and II of the NPT which prohibits nuclear 'haves' from giving nuclear weapons or its technology to 'have-nots', and 'have-nots' from seeking to acquire them, stand in contradiction to Articles IV and V which promote peaceful nuclear research and commercial activity. Article IV states:

> 1. Nothing in this Treaty shall be interpreted as affecting the inalienable right of all Parties to the Treaty to develop research, production and use of nuclear energy for peaceful purposes without discrimination and in conformity with articles I and II of the Treaty.
> 2. All the Parties to the Treaty undertake to facilitate and have the right to participate in the fullest possible exchange of equipment, materials and scientific and technological information for the peaceful uses of nuclear energy.

Likewise, Article V states:

> Each Party to the Treaty undertakes to take appropriate measures to ensure that, in accordance with this Treaty, under appropriate international observation and through appropriate international procedures, potential benefits from any peaceful applications of nuclear explosions will be made available to non-nuclear weapons States Party to the Treaty on a non-discriminatory basis and that the charge to the such Parties for the explosive devices used will be as low as possible and exclude any charge for research and development.

Needless to say, the problem of civilian–military dual-use technologies applies to 'peaceful' chemical and biological research and industrial activities, and to space rocket and satellite development programmes. Indeed, nearly all technological research, development and production carry dual-use purposes. They include the areas of electronics, computer hardware and software, automotive engineering, aircraft, and shipbuilding. Most major states have comparatively easy technological access to biological and chemical weapons which could serve as a substitute for nuclear weapons either for deterrence or war-fighting purposes. The acquisition of missile technology which may be a spin-off from civilian space rocket and satellite development programmes provide delivery systems for nuclear, biological and chemical weapons to distant targets. Treaties and informal multilateral agreements such as the BWC, the CWC and the MTCR are not guarantees against covert programmes and operations. The NPT has proved not to be so either.

Throughout the Cold War, Article VI – the only article in the Treaty that addressed the issue of vertical proliferation – remained a dead letter. Even after the end of the Cold War, there is no indication that this article will be fulfilled in the foreseeable future. Article VI states:

Each of the Parties to the Treaty undertakes to pursue negotiations in good faith on effective measures relating to the cessation of the nuclear arms race at an early date and to nuclear disarmament, and on a treaty on general and complete disarmament under strict and effective international control.

Article X of the Treaty seems to contradict the whole purpose of the NPT by providing an easy escape clause. Article X states:

1. Each Party shall in exercising its national sovereignty have the right to withdraw from the Treaty if it decides that extraordinary events, related to the subject matter of this Treaty, have jeopardized the supreme interests of its country. It shall give notice of such withdrawal to all other Parties to the Treaty and to the United Nations Security Council three months in advance. Such notice shall include a statement of the extraordinary events it regards as having jeopardized its supreme interests.

In 1993 North Korea gave three months' notice citing extraordinary events having jeopardized its supreme interests but was prevented by the United States from withdrawing from the NPT.

Other problems with the NPT may be found in old problems that remain unresolved, and newer problems that have emerged since the Treaty was drawn up in 1968. Three problems, in particular, call for special attention.

(a) The clauses of the NPT have failed to cover the acquisition of nuclear-powered submarines and carriers and, indeed, any other weapon system that may be propelled by nuclear power. While it was one thing to develop peaceful nuclear energy reactors which may also provide weapons capabilities, it was quite another thing to use such nuclear power to propel weapon systems intended for war. This is a grey area of nuclear weapons proliferation that had not been envisaged in 1968 when the Treaty was drawn up. It was not addressed in 1995 when the NPT was renewed without change.

(b) One American strategic writer has projected a scenario whereby civilian nuclear energy facilities in one state may be used as potential weapons by an adversary state.[4] By attacking an enemy state's nuclear reactors, whether through conventional air bombing, a terrorist attack with bombs or dynamite, or foreign-sponsored internal sabotage at the power plant, a non-nuclear state may produce almost the same desired physical catastrophe as the launching of a nuclear attack. Merely the threat to attack such civilian nuclear facilities may represent a nuclear deterrent capability without the actual possession of nuclear weapons. The Israeli attack on

Iraq's Osirak nuclear power plant in 1981 could have produced an explosion with radioactive fallout if the Iraqi reactor had been critical at the time. Accidental Chernobyl-type nuclear meltdowns could be staged through conventional attacks, or acts of terrorism and sabotage. Perhaps with such dangers in mind, India and Pakistan signed an agreement in 1988 (and later formalized in a treaty in 1991) not to attack each other's nuclear facilities in the event of armed conflict.

(c) Technological advances now indicate that miniature nuclear tests may now be simulated in the laboratory. This will be an advantage that advanced industrialized states will possess over the less developed states. Detection would be difficult if not impossible, motivating states with such technological capabilities to move in this direction for fear others may be doing the same. Indeed, India had argued that it was because the United States and other advanced Western industrialized states had reached this technological frontier that they were now so willing to sign the CTBT.

If these unresolved problems and trends continue into the next millennia, the purpose and effectiveness of the renewed NPT would remain ambiguous, and the near universality and indefinite extension of the renewed NPT of 1995 would appear meaningless. What we have essentially is old wine in new bottles, or perhaps even old wine in old bottles with new labels. The general global security climate following the end of the Cold War may have undergone substantial transformation, but this transformation presents a mixed and uncertain picture of the future of the nuclear non-proliferation regime beyond 2000.

2   THE NON-PROLIFERATION REGIME AFTER THE COLD WAR

Perhaps American efforts to stem the spread of nuclear weapons would appear more likely to succeed in the post-Cold War era. Without the nuclear stand-off based on mutual assured destruction between the United States and the former Soviet Union, Western nuclear guarantees to non-nuclear weapons states facing potential regional nuclear threats may now be brought under a credible Western nuclear umbrella – unless these states feared nuclear threats from the US-led West itself. For example, Iraq, Iran and Libya would hardly be interested in such nuclear protection. With the West having achieved undisputed military supremacy, one American anti-proliferation watchdog even suggested that the United States should think not just in terms of containing nuclear weapons proliferation, but should attempt now to 'win' the war against proliferation.[5] Such optimism may be premature.

Vertical and Horizontal Proliferation Threats

The old NPT was largely aimed at preventing 'horizontal' nuclear weapons proliferation. Indeed, the only clause in the Treaty that attempted to contain 'vertical' nuclear weapons proliferation was Article VI. Even Article VI which called upon the 'haves' to move towards nuclear disarmament was intended to strengthen the remaining clauses that sought to prevent 'have-nots' from acquiring nuclear weapons capabilities. If the United States, the Soviet Union and Great Britain, who were mainly responsible for successfully drawing up the NPT in 1968, made no political gestures toward eliminating their own nuclear weapons, they would have carried no credibility in demanding that other states not acquire nuclear weapons either. Despite its clear demand for comprehensive nuclear disarmament, the intention and practice of Article VI as framed by the nuclear powers at the time would appear to be directed at the nuclear 'have-nots' rather than the nuclear 'haves' themselves. Article VI was a deliberately intended false promise in order to lure the 'have-nots' into signing the NPT.

As noted earlier, throughout the Cold War, Article VI was never fulfilled. Vertical proliferation continued until the late 1980s by branching into newer areas of weapons development not restricted by arms control agreements. Thus, the Strategic Arms Limitation Talks (SALT I signed in 1972 and the unratified but largely fulfilled SALT II signed in 1979) essentially provided for a *controlled* Soviet–American nuclear arms race. It was only the INF treaty of 1988 that for the first time eliminated a whole class of intermediate-range nuclear weapon delivery systems of the two superpowers in Europe, without however touching those of Britain, France and China. The Strategic Arms Reduction Talks showed some genuine inclinations towards nuclear weapons reductions but only became more of a reality after the end of the Cold War when the disintegration of the Soviet Union in 1991 ended the threat to the Western world. START-I was signed in 1991 and START-II in 1993 which was expected to reduce the nuclear warhead stockpiles of the United States and Russia to 3,500 by the close of the 20th century.

But there is no indication that the existing five nuclear powers have any intention of moving towards total nuclear disarmament in the foreseeable future. The reason is that comprehensive nuclear disarmament may actually tempt several threshold nuclear weapons states to acquire nuclear weapons. With the complete nuclear disarming of the existing five nuclear weapons states, other current non-nuclear weapons states who acquire a few bombs would become immediate superpowers, not unlike the situation in the late 1940s and early 1950s when the US and the USSR possessed just a handful of atomic and/or hydrogen bombs. Comprehensive nuclear disarmament among the existing 'haves' may actually advance horizontal nuclear proliferation among the 'have-nots.' This dilemma is not easily resolved.

The end of the Cold War significantly halted and reversed the upward spiral of vertical nuclear weapons proliferation between the United States and Russia, the successor state to the Soviet Union. Britain and France have largely kept their nuclear weapons development on hold although Britain is still considering the continuation of its SSBN Trident submarine programme. The exception among the nuclear 'haves' is China which continued with its nuclear weapons and missile development programmes. However, France and China – two nuclear NPT 'hold out' states – signed the Treaty in 1991 and 1992. Whether the NPT is now strengthened with the inclusion of the remaining two nuclear weapons states will remain somewhat dubious. It did not stop France and China from going on testing nuclear weapons until 1996 before adhering to the CTBT. Some of these tests were conducted above ground contravening the 1963 Limited Test Ban Treaty which neither China or France had signed.

The end of the Cold War directly or indirectly contributed to the cessation of horizontal nuclear weapons proliferation tendencies in Southern Africa and Latin America. Among the professed 'have-nots' who had earlier refused to adhere to the NPT, South Africa has since signed the NPT in 1991. In 1992, Argentina and Brazil accepted full-scope safeguards under the 1967 Treaty of Tlatelelco, an NPT substitute that sought to maintain Latin America as a nuclear-weapons-free zone.[6] Of the nuclear weapons states that emerged from the breakup of the Soviet Union in 1991, Belarus and Kazakhstan signed the NPT in 1993, Kazakhstan signing only after considerable pressure was put on it by the United States. In January 1994, after considerable resistance against American and Russian pressures, Ukraine agreed to give up its nuclear weapons and adhered to the NPT. However, having become independent nuclear weapons states briefly following the disintegration of the Soviet Union, it should not be too difficult for these three ex-Soviet republics, especially Ukraine, to return to a major nuclear weapons capability in the future. Similar to Pakistani fears of a reabsorption into a Greater India, Ukrainian fears persist about being reabsorbed into a Greater Russia, although Russian–Ukranian relations are not as hostile as Indo-Pakistani relations.

These post-Cold War developments seemed to indicate that the three remaining major 'hold-out' states – India, Pakistan and Israel – would soon follow the others thereby making the membership of the renewed NPT universal. This has not yet happened. There have been other developments in the world that indicate somewhat gloomy prospects for containing proliferation.[7] For example, efforts by NPT signatories, Iraq and North Korea, to move close to nuclear weapons capability, suggest not only that IAEA safeguards are insufficient, but that the Treaty may be a good cover for a nuclear weapons programme. The revelation by South Africa following the end of the apartheid regime that it had produced six nuclear bombs, is again a further indication that international nuclear safeguards against covert nuclear weapons development are insufficient. Even after the signing of the Israeli–Palestinian accords in 1993, Israel's decision not to sign the NPT may be linked to some early hesitations on the part of some significant Arab states not to sign the 1991 Chemical Weapons Convention (CWC). The CWC was ratified by a sufficient number of states and went into effect in 1997. However, verification to prevent the diversion of civilian chemical facilities to weapons capabilities by signatories to the CWC would prove to be even more difficult than is the case of the NPT. It was for this reason that the US Senate postponed ratification of the CWC in 1996. Only when it became clear that the CWC would go into effect anyway did the Senate ratify the convention in April 1997. So long as a covert chemical weapons programme is easily undertaken by Arab states whether they have signed the CWC or not, Israel will be reluctant to to give up its nuclear weapons option. Alternatively, all sides may sign the CWC and the NPT, but this may not prevent covert programmes in the Middle East and elsewhere.

In particular, the outlook for containing nuclear weapons proliferation in South Asia has not changed much since the end of the Cold War. The impetus to 'go nuclear' in India and Pakistan continues to arise largely from potential nuclear threats perceived from each other. The growth of Chinese nuclear weapons capabilities complicates the nuclear threat environment in Asia. Thus, the international security environment may have undergone a positive change for the West in many ways, but for India these changes have made little difference to its nuclear threat perceptions. The end of the Cold War has produced no new attitudes and policies in India in favour of advancing the nuclear non-proliferation regime.[8] Indeed, the mood in India for not giving up its nuclear weapons option may have strengthened in the mid-1990s generating even greater resistance to the Comprehensive Test Ban Treaty (CTBT) as well. For India, signing the CTBT would be tantamount to signing the NPT and giving up its nuclear weapons option.

In sum, whereas the growth of nuclear weapons capabilities among the existing nuclear weapons states ('vertical' proliferation) may have been substantially reversed, the potential spread of nuclear weapons among some states on the brink of nuclear weapons capabilities ('horizontal' proliferation) has shown mixed tendencies. Towards the close of the 20th century, the situation has been transformed in Latin America and Southern Africa. It has improved marginally in the ex-Soviet republics and East Asia. But the situation has changed little in the Middle East and has worsened in South Asia and the Korean peninsula with potential ramifications for the rest of Asia and the world.

Regional and Global Proliferation Assessments

South Asian security was largely unaffected by the end of the Cold War because the earlier motivations to acquire nuclear weapons in this region had little to do with that East–West global confrontation. The end of Soviet–American competition to supply arms to the region has only made conventional arms procurement more uncertain. Compulsions to go nuclear in South Asia were mainly due to the prevailing regional security relationships among India, Pakistan and China based on territorial disputes and regional political rivalries. This situation remains largely unchanged between India and Pakistan. The Sino-Indian border dispute may have been resolved de facto along the line of actual control but the growth of Chinese nuclear and naval power continue to cause security apprehensions in India.

Three newer evolving conditions, two external and one internal, tend to promote the continuing Indian resolve not to sign the Non-Proliferation Treaty. The first condition is the political uncertainty that exists between the end of the Cold War and whatever the 'New World Order' may shape up to be in the years to come. The rising tide of Islamic nationalism in West, Central and South Asia, and nuclear ambitions in these regions as well as elsewhere in Eastern Europe and East Asia, are developments that sustain India's nuclear 'option' policy. The second condition is the smuggling of nuclear fissile materials out of the former Soviet Union, and especially reports of Pakistani efforts to acquire these materials. This development lends support to the position of the pro-bomb lobby in India that the government must now proceed swiftly towards a full-fledged nuclear weapons programme. The third condition is the rise of Hindu nationalism in India currently reflected in the growing power of Hindu nationalist parties such as the Bharatiya Janata Party (BJP), the Shiv Sena and the Vishwa Hindu Parishad. The Hindu nationalist parties, and nationalist Indians in general, favour tougher policies on issues concerning Pakistan and the Muslim world, and demand the immediate development of nuclear weapons. These trends add pressure on successive Indian governments, of whatever political party, to embark on a nuclear weapons programme.

Two aspects of the earlier 'vertical' proliferation question had contributed to the South Asian nuclear impasse. First, India had argued that the global proliferation of weapons of mass destruction among the 'haves' constituted a threat to world security affecting all nations. Secondly, especially if the first Indian argument were to be dismissed as unconvincing (since all other non-nuclear states face the same problem but have signed the NPT), India also argued that it could not risk signing the NPT so long as the growth of Chinese nuclear weapons across its northern borders could not be contained, let alone eliminated.

Meanwhile, despite repeated denials by Islamabad, Pakistan was alleged to have reached weapons capability by the mid 1980s and may have even stockpiled one or two bombs by the early 1990s. In response, India periodically threatened to proceed with a weapons programme of its own – that is, if it had not already undertaken a covert programme. Indeed, Pakistan has claimed on many occasions that India was the instigator of the nuclear arms race when it tested an atomic device in 1974 and that Pakistan was merely responding. Under these circumstances, Cold War or no Cold War, neither India nor Pakistan seemed ready to sign the NPT. In the mid 1990s, both India and Pakistan remain on the brink of nuclear weapons capability as they had done for over a decade. However, both continue to protest publicly that they do not have nuclear weapons. At the same time, both have declared that they will not sign the NPT.

Since both India and Pakistan claim that the other has nuclear weapons, analysts in South Asia have suggested that it may be too late to establish a 'nuclear weapons *free* zone'. Instead, they propose that discussions should centre on how to establish a 'nuclear weapons *safe* zone'. The former Indian Chief of Army Staff, General K. Sundarji, stated in August 1991: 'We must stop repeating the mantra of universal nuclear disarmament. We must not knock the theory of regional non-proliferation for South Asia on the grounds that only a global approach makes sense; but on the grounds that proliferation has occurred beyond the point of no return: the Chinese, Indian and Pakistani genies cannot be put back into the bottle'.[9]

Following the end of the Cold War, India's first argument for not signing the NPT (vertical nuclear proliferation) would appear to have weakened since the global nuclear arms race among the four 'White' nuclear 'haves' is winding down rapidly. The second Indian argument (regional horizontal proliferation pressures) would also appear to have weakened. Sino-Indian relations have improved considerably. In September 1993, subject to a final settlement, India and China agreed to maintain the lines of actual control along their Himalayan borders where they had fought a war in 1962.[10] The exchange of visits at the level of president and prime minister paralleled by growing trade have further normalized relations between India and China. However, such an optimistic assessment of the global nuclear condition in the post-Cold War era would be somewhat misleading. New developments show both positive and negative signs for the nuclear non-proliferation regime. India's 'global' arguments for not signing the NPT may be taking on newer and perhaps even more credible dimensions. Meanwhile, India's 'regional' arguments for maintaining the nuclear weapons option or for joining the nuclear weapons club have not necessarily lessened in intensity.

Proliferation tendencies in the Middle East, Central Asia and Northeast Asia add to the proliferation pressures in South Asia.[11] Conversely, it could be argued that if South Asia is nuclearized, holding back the proliferation tide elsewhere in the world would become more difficult as well.

North Korea's efforts in the late 1980s and early 1990s to build the bomb at its Yongbyon nuclear complex may carry no direct or immediate security implications for South Asia except to demonstrate the failure of the Non-Proliferation Treaty to check the spread of the bomb among the Treaty's signatories.[12] A worst case scenario might envisage a South Korean response in kind to North Korean nuclear weapons production, followed by similar responses in Taiwan and Japan triggering a complex nuclear arms race among these countries and with China. A regenerated and active Chinese nuclear arms build-up within the new and expanded Asian strategic nuclear context would then call for an Indian nuclear response. A Pakistani nuclear arms build-up would almost certainly follow the Indian decision. By early 1996, US efforts to get North Korea to open its nuclear installation for inspection appear to have succeeded although this success may have much to do with the lowering of American demands on the terms of inspection of North Korean atom sites. Therefore, whether these inspections can effectively prevent a clandestine nuclear weapons programme in North Korea under its paranoid communist regime have yet to be demonstrated.[13] If Iraq, a more open society and signatory to the NPT, could have managed a successful clandestine nuclear weapons programme before 1991, then North Korea, a more closed society and also signatory to the NPT, should be able to evade discovery. Periodic IAEA inspections have proved to be unreliable in the past and may prove to be unreliable in the future.[14]

Relatively more serious proliferation tendencies are to be found in the Middle East and Central Asia. Previous Indian concerns arose from possible Libyan–Pakistani connections in the development of an 'Islamic bomb'. India had alleged in the early 1980s that various Libyan holding companies were set up in Pakistan to channel Libyan petrodollars and uranium ore from Niger (channelled through Tripoli) for the Pakistani nuclear weapons programme.[15] Indirect financial assistance for the bomb through regular economic aid channels was also alleged to have come from Saudi Arabia. The construction of the uranium enrichment plant at Kahuta was facilitated by such indirect Arab financial backing. Whatever the veracity of such earlier Indian reports, there are no further allegations of Arab–Pakistani connections in the 1990s, perhaps because the Pakistani programme has become self-sufficient. Pakistan has now stockpiled weapons grade enriched uranium at the Kahuta plant and further efforts in this direction continue.[16]

Iraq's experience during the 1990–91 Gulf crisis and war may provide some dangerous lessons for would-be proliferators elsewhere including states in the subcontinent. Irrespective of the rights and wrongs of the Iraqi invasion and annexation of Kuwait, one lesson that may be learnt by the near-nuclear weapons states is that if Iraq had possessed even a small arsenal of crude nuclear devices before it annexed Kuwait, the course of events in the Gulf might have been different. Either the threatened attack by the US-led coalition might have been deterred; or the punitive Western military retaliation might have been deferred until the security of Iraq's neighbours, especially Israel and Saudi Arabia, was assured; and until probable casualties to Western forces from Iraqi chemical and nuclear weapons attacks could be avoided. Thus, the possession of a few crude nuclear bombs may be perceived by near-nuclear weapons states in the less industrialized world either to deter attacks, or to raise the threshold of external military intervention by the industrialized West with their advanced high-tech conventional weapons.[17]

Iran, for example, declared its right to obtain nuclear weapons following the Gulf War and called upon other Muslim nations to match Israel's capabilities.[18] Iranian Vice President, Ayatollah Mohajerani, declared in October 1991: 'Because the enemy has nuclear facilities the Muslim states too should have the same capacity. Muslims should try to go ahead...[until] the atomic capacity of Muslims and Israel should be [are] at par'.[19] Iran has made unsuccessful attempts thus far to develop gas centrifuges for enrichment, to purchase a small plutonium-production reactor from China, and to buy a research reactor from India.[20] Towards the end of the Bush administration, the CIA assessed that by the year 2000 Iran would be a nuclear weapons state, although there is no evidence in the mid 1990s that this dire prediction would materialize.[21] In the autumn of 1992, the US Congress Republican Research Committee Task Force on Terrorism and Unconventional Warfare came up with an even more disturbing report than that of the CIA. According to this Committee's report (largely unconfirmed though), Iran had already acquired four nuclear weapons from the former Soviet Muslim republics. Other reports in late 1993 indicated that Iran had obtained weapons grade uranium from Kazakh scientists, and was now dividing up its nuclear programme into small segments in order to continue work on a nuclear weapons programme without arousing Western suspicions.[22] The report further stated that in November 1991, Iran and Pakistan had concluded an agreement on uranium enrichment, with Iran providing the funding and Pakistan the scientific personnel.[23] Whatever the authenticity of these claims, there is a major nuclear research programme underway in Iran which Iran claims is for peaceful purposes only. Much of this is a legacy of the Shah who had built up a large reservoir of skilled nuclear personnel by promoting their education in nuclear technology in the West.

Both Iran and Syria have obtained various versions of the Scud missile from North Korea. In particular, the Scud Mod-D missile known as the Nodong, is capable of reaching a range of 1,000 kilometres and capable of being fitted with chemical or nuclear warheads. Syria has also contracted with China for the purchase of a nuclear research reactor, for medium range M-9 missiles, and chemical ingredients for missile fuel.[24] That nuclear weapons may constitute the 'great equalizer' among unequal conventional military powers, is a lesson that has not been lost on the states of the Middle East and South Asia.

Until 1994, the continued possession of nuclear capabilities in Ukraine, Belarus and especially Kazakhstan may have increased the determination in India and Pakistan not to give up their nuclear weapons option. But since that time, Belarus and Kazakhstan signed the START-I Treaty and agreed to give up all its nuclear weapons.[25] Belarus and Kazakhstan also signed the NPT in 1993. After a great deal of hestitation, Ukraine reluctantly agreed in principle to give up its nuclear weapons and also adhered to the NPT.[26] However, their earlier arguments for not giving up their weapons, and their demands for monetary compensation if they are to give up their weapons, will continue to motivate them and other hold-out states to retain or seek weapons in the future.

For example, along with Russia, Kazakhstan claimed at one point that it was part of the original nuclear weapons states who were parties to the NPT that was finalized in 1968. The sentiments expressed within

Kazakhstan in 1991 for not giving up its nuclear weapons will strike sympathetic chords in South Asia and the Middle East. Referring to the 'respectful' visits of US Secretary of State James Baker, British Foreign Secretary Douglas Hurd, and French Foreign Minister Roland Dumas to the capital Almaty during 1991–92, Scitkazy Matayev, a spokesman for President Nursultan Nazarbayev, declared: 'If we didn't have nuclear weapons, they wouldn't have bothered.'[27] Matayev continued: 'A state with nuclear bombs has a decisive voice in world affairs'. However, under pressure from the United States, President Nursultan Nazabayev agreed in May 1992 to scrap all nuclear weapons systems on its soil and to sign the NPT as a non-nuclear weapon state.

Likewise, Ukraine initially backtracked on its commitments to get rid of its nuclear weapons.[28] Ukraine was expected to transfer its 176 long-range nuclear missiles and 37 long-range bombers to Russia. At the end of 1992, Ukraine possessed 1,656 warheads which it inherited from the total stockpile of 10,909 nuclear warheads of the former Soviet Union. Despite being a party to the START-I Treaty, the Ukrainian President, Leonid M. Kravchuk, was nevertheless reluctant to give up the country's nuclear weapons capabilities. As the *New York Times* put it, Kravchuk 'fears that without the status symbol of nuclear weapons, his country will be treated as just another Third World basket case, lucky to get phone calls returned from the White House, let alone any foreign aid. Moreover, the idea of transferring weapons to Russia for safekeeping is not exactly the Ukrainians' idea of safety, given the history of colonization by Russia.'[29] However, during President Clinton's visit to Kiev in January 1994, President Kravchuk promised to give up Ukraine's nuclear weapons provided Ukraine was compensated. Ukraine claimed that it needed between $2.8 billion and $5 billion just to dismantle its nuclear weapons.[30] The US had offered $175 million for dismantling the weapons and $155 million for economic development.

The Ukrainian terms for giving up its nuclear weapons raise another problem which may encourage more states to acquire nuclear weapons. US negotiations with North Korea, Ukraine, Belarus, Kazakhstan and Pakistan have demonstrated that the possession of, or the ability to acquire nuclear weapons is an effective tool for demanding monetary compensation or some other form of foreign aid. In a statement entitled, 'Extortion and the Bomb', Senator John Glenn of Ohio pointed out that the use of the diplomatic strategy of 'Give us aid...or we'll proliferate' may become quite commonplace in the post-Cold War era.[31] According to Glenn, the Ukrainian posture was 'Give us aid or we will be forced to inherit a nuclear deterrent.' In Pakistan, where a US aid embargo was enforced in response to Pakistan's development of nuclear weapons, the posture was 'Resume aid, or we'll just become more dependent on our nuclear option.' North Korea's posture, according to Glenn was 'ante up, or we'll leave the NPT', the North Korean 'ante' being a demand for nuclear reactors, economic aid and diplomatic recognition. Glenn concluded:

> If today, three countries are asking to be paid off for supporting nonpro-liferation, who will seek to be paid tomorrow? Will Iran hold its NPT membership hostage to new nuclear technology transfers from the West? What will be China's price for continued membership? Will our friends make such demands? With the US foreign aid budget already in decline, America will not long be able to sustain a policy of paying off countries to join, or stay in, the nuclear regime...
>
> The global nuclear regime will survive if, and only if, its members believe that membership enhances security. If regime violaters are disciplined rather than rewarded, confidence grows. If technologies that are recognized as unsafeguardable are banned globally, confidence grows. If safeguards are strengthened so that inspectors will be able to detect violations instantly, confidence grows. None of these requires the payment of tribute.[32]

Indian and Pakistani proliferation motivations are linked to the above conditions elsewhere in the world – more directly with conditions in West and Central Asia, and somewhat indirectly with conditions in Europe and East Asia. Proliferation in West and Central Asia would constitute a positive trend for Pakistan but a disturbing development for India. In the early 1990s, some Indian reports claimed the possibility of nuclear collaboration between Pakistan and Kazakhstan, and the possible transfer of enriched uranium from Tajikistan to Pakistan in the future.[33] Such claims were never confirmed and the probability of such an occurrence may be low, but more speculation of this kind (the classic security dilemma) may provide the basis for a change in India's nuclear policy.

For Pakistan, the existence of more friendly Muslim nuclear weapons states would reduce the relative strategic nuclear power of India in the region. Therefore, Pakistan would favour such developments. Faced with multiple deployments of nuclear weapons in China, Pakistan and in some of the Muslim countries further west, the credibility of an Indian nuclear deterrent posture would become more complex, and perhaps ineffective. Israeli reactions to such trends would further complicate the delicate balance of mutual deterrent relationships in West, Central and South Asia. If such a scenario were to come about, the net outcome would be unstable nuclear relationships in the more extended and wider region of Central, West and South Asia. On the other hand, the spread of nuclear weapons in parts of the ex-Soviet Union and Eastern Europe and in East Asia would essentially encourage and facilitate decisions in South Asia to go nuclear with less fear of Western political and economic sanctions.

Of course, these are all pessimistic secenarios. From an optimistic standpoint, the non-utility and the sheer futility of nuclear weapons are becoming increasingly evident among both nuclear 'haves' and 'have-nots.' If nuclear weapons can never be used, then why possess them? Is there any conflict scenario where nuclear weapons several times the destructive power of Hiroshima and Nagasaki may be justifiably used? When will the nuclear powers ever learn? But what may be obvious in the abstract and at a general level may not be so evident at the practical and regional level. Whether for prestige or for genuine deterrence and war-fighting purposes, nuclear weapons and especially the knowledge to make them cannot be wished away so easily.

3   THEMES AND PERSPECTIVES

The two-part organization of this book provides global and regional perspectives. In Part One, George Rathjens, Joseph Pilat and Charles Nakhleh examine the conditions and prospects for the renewed NPT in the next century. T.V. Paul and Bradley Thayer examine the theory and practice of the prevailing nuclear proliferation regime. Kathleen Bailey points out that the proliferation of chemical and biological weapons and missile capabilities cannot be separated from nuclear weapons proliferation. Zachary Davis evaluates some optimistic and pessimistic scenarios for the NPT regime in the 21st century. In Part Two, regional assessments are made by Stephen Blank, Ryukichi Imai, Bruce Cumings, Tong Whan Park, Sumit Ganguly, Peter Lavoy, Raju Thomas and Haleh Vaziri about the prospects for containing the spread of nuclear weapons in Eastern Europe, East and South Asia, and the Middle East. Finally, in retrospect, James Yamazaki portrays the real terror of atomic warfare, something that is forgotten in state policies and abstract theories that are discussed in a vacuum by policymakers and academics. He narrates his personal experience in dealing with the death and destruction caused by the bombing of Hiroshima and Nagasaki, in treating the Japanese survivors of the atomic bombing, and the long-term radiation effects on future generations.

NOTES

1. See *India's Role in the United Nations*, Monograph issued by the Ministry of External Affairs, Government of India, May 1996, p. 13 (no publication source or date). For full statement enunciating the reasons for India's rejection of the CTBT, see *Times of India*, June 21, 1996.
2. *New York Times*, September 11, 1996.
3. See *New York Times*, September 13, 1996.
4. See Bennett Ramberg, *Nuclear Power Plants as Weapons for the Enemy: An Unrecognized Military Peril*, Berkeley: University of California Press, 1984.
5. See Thomas W. Graham, 'Winning the Nonproliferation Battle', *Arms Control Today*, vol. 21, no. 7, September 1991, pp. 8–13.
6. See 'Stopping the Spread of Nuclear Weapons: Still Time to Act,' *The Defense Monitor* (Washington DC), vol. 21, no. 3, 1992.
7. See special report entitled 'The Nuclear Epidemic', in the *U.S. News and World Report*, March 16, 1992.
8. See, for instance, Manoj Joshi, 'Nuclear Bomb Doctrines in a Changed World Scenario', *New India Times* (New York), December 31, 1993.
9. General (Retired) K. Sundarji, 'Nuclear Realpolitik', *India Today*, August 31, 1991.
10. See Reuter's news report entitled, 'China, India Sign Landmark Border Agreement', September 7, 1993. The agreement was signed in Beijing by Chinese and Indian prime ministers, Li Peng and P.V. Narasimha Rao. The Indian Embassy in Beijing issued the following statement: 'Pending a boundary settlement, India and China have agreed to respect and observe the line of actual control' (which separated their troops since the 1962 border war.) 'The two countries have agreed to undertake a series of confidence-building measures, including the reduction of military forces deployed along the India–China border. India and China have agreed to keep their military forces in areas along the border in conformity with the principle of mutual and equal security.'
11. Some parts of this section are taken from Raju G.C. Thomas, *South Asian Security in the 1990s*, Adelphi Paper No. 278, London: Brasseys/International Institute for Strategic Studies, 1993.
12. For various reports of developments in North Korea, see *Programme for Promoting Nuclear Non-Proliferation*, no. 24, 4th Quarter 1993; *The International Herald Tribune*, October 28, 1991; *Far Eastern Economic Review*, November 7, 1991; *Financial Times* (London), November 14, 1991; and *The Independent* (London), November 20, 1991. For an argument against military strikes to take out the Yongbyon nuclear research reactor, see the leader article by William J. Taylor and Michael Mazarr, 'Defusing North Korea's Nuclear Notions', *New York Times*, April 13, 1992.
13. See Richard K. Betts, 'Outlaw With a Bomb', *New York Times*, December 31, 1993.
14. See David A.V. Fischer, 'The Future of the IAEA', *Programme for Promoting Nuclear Non-Proliferation: Issue Review*, No. 2, December 1993. Fischer argues that 'the failure in Iraq was chiefly a failure by leading governments to acquire and share the findings of intelligence. It was not the

failure of the NPT safeguards system as it was drawn up by 45 countries in 1970–71 and is set forth in the ISEA document INFCIRC/153....The 1971 system was not designed to detect the existence of a wholly independent, clandestine nuclear fuel cycle – such as Saddam Hussein's...'.

15.   See Raju G.C. Thomas, 'India's Perspective on Nuclear Proliferation in South Asia', in Neil Joeck, Ed., *The Strategic Consequences of Nuclear Proliferation*, London: Frank Cass, 1986, 67–79.

16.   See Manoj Joshi, 'Nuclear Questions', *Frontline* (Madras), December 20, 1991.

17.   Jessica Mathews' advice in her article entitled, 'Kick Baghdad Out and Strengthen the Nonproliferation Treaty', is not likely to help. See *International Herald Tribune*, October 18, 1991.

18.   See 'Stopping the Spread of Nuclear Weapons: Still Time to Act', *The Defense Monitor* (Washington, DC), vol. 21, no. 3, 1992.

19.   *The Nation* (Lahore), October 24, 1991.

20.   'Stopping the Spread of Nuclear Weapons: Still Time To Act', *The Defense Monitor*, vol. 21, no. 3, 1992.

21.   'Iran: Quest for Security and Influence', in *Jane's Defence Weekly* (International Edition), vol. 5, no. 7, July 1, 1993, p. 311.

22.   See *Proliferation Watch*, US Senate Committee on Governmental Affairs, vol. 4, no. 5, September–October 1993, p. 4.

23.   *Jane's Defence Weekly*, July 1993.

24.   *New York Times*, January 10, 1993.

25.   See editorials of the *New York Times* and the *Washington Post* entitled 'Ukraine and the Bomb', 'Ukraine's Nuclear Arms', and 'Targeting the Bomb' in the *International Herald Tribune*, December 5 and 7–8, 1991. An assessment of the situation following the START II agreement in January 1993 is provided by Thomas L. Friedman, 'Beyond START II: A New Level of Instability', *New York Times*, January 10, 1993.

26.   See *New York Times*, January 11 and 12, 1994.

27.   See Andrew Higgins, 'Deadly Secrets for Sale', in 'The Sunday Review' of *The Independent* (London), April 19, 1992.

28.   *Independent*, July 6, 1992.

29.   *New York Times*, January 10, 1993.

30.   *Programme for Promoting Nuclear Non-Proliferation*, no. 24, 4th Quarter 1993.

31.   Senator John Glenn, 'Extortion and the Bomb', in *Proliferation Watch* (US Senate Committee on Governmental Affairs), vol. 4, No. 5, September–October, 1993, p. 1.

32.   *Ibid.*

33.   *Hindustan Times*, January 25, 1992; and *Hindu*, January 13, 1992.

Part I
Global Perspectives

2 Nuclear Proliferation Following the NPT Extension
George Rathjens

Surprise that Iraq had made as much progress toward acquiring nuclear weapons as it had before the Persian Gulf war and the more recent concerns about North Korea's nuclear programme have meant that nuclear weapons proliferation has recently gained attention in the US Government – and in others – to a degree unknown since the Carter years. The Clinton administration is supporting the policies developed during those earlier years to deny potential proliferators access to materials and technology relevant to weapons acquisition – and delivery – and it made vigorous and successful efforts to get an indefinite extension of the Nuclear Non-Proliferation Treaty of 1970 when it came up for review in 1995. It is also developing, within the Department of Defense, new 'counter-proliferation' initiatives.

It is unlikely, however, that either the administration's commitment to old policies or its new efforts will be very successful and they may, in some respects, be counter-productive. If one believes that the nuclear proliferation problem is serious, more will be required; in particular, a determined and sustained commitment to an international collective security regime, however distant its realization may now seem.

1 THE OLD REGIME

Following the discovery of nuclear fission in 1938, scientists and the world's political leaders sought to prevent the spread of nuclear weapons through secrecy, through proposing that all of the world's nuclear activities be placed under the control of a single international agency, through attempting to ban all nuclear weapons tests, and through trying to limit access to critical materials and technologies by placing constraints on international trade and nuclear power facilities. In 1968, after 30 years of effort, the best hope seemed to lie in a treaty that would require:

(1) that the nuclear weapon states not assist others to acquire weapons,
(2) that the non-nuclear weapon states agree not to acquire them; and
(3) that facilities in the latter states capable of producing fissionable materials that might be used in weapons be subject to surveillance by the International Atomic Energy Agency (IAEA) to assure that they were not being so used.

The result was the Nuclear Non-Proliferation Treaty of 1970. Its conclusion – and the fact that the vast majority of states, 178, have acceded to it – has been widely hailed as a great arms control achievement. Indeed, for many, it has been viewed as *the* cornerstone of the international nuclear weapons non-proliferation regime and, when the Treaty came up for review and possible extension in 1995, it was still widely considered an indispensable element of the regime.

But the Treaty has proved to be inadequate in important respects.

(a) Some of the states of greatest concern, notably Israel, India, Pakistan, Argentina, Brazil, South Africa and North Korea refused for many years to accede to the Treaty. The first five still do; and efforts to get North Korea to honour NPT obligations to forgo efforts to acquire nuclear weapons capabilities and to accept measures that would permit high-confidence verification that it is not engaged in such efforts have been fraught with difficulties. The main burden was borne by the United States, with no evident help from China – the country in the best position to provide it–and North Korea succeeded in getting the United States and South Korea to pay an extortionate price for an only marginally satisfactory resolution of its differences with United States and the IAEA relating to these matters.

(b) There is no provision in the Treaty itself for sanctions. (In the event of discovery of a violation, the IAEA can bring the issue to the attention of the Secretary General of the United Nations [UN], but the imposition of sanctions must be decided by the Security Council.)

(c) Nothing in the Treaty prohibits a state from developing indigenous capacities for the production of fissionable materials or producing and stockpiling such materials or other components that might be used in nuclear weapons. These lacunae are particularly troublesome because the development of facilities for uranium enrichment and spent fuel processing and the acquisition of stockpiles of plutonium and enriched uranium can be rationalized, albeit with greatly varying degrees of credibility, as being consistent with non-military nuclear power aspirations.[1] Thus, there is the possibility that a non-nuclear weapon state, party to the Treaty, might legitimately stockpile plutonium and/or enrich uranium, only to withdraw from it – as is permitted with three months' notice – to rather suddenly acquire a significant stockpile of nuclear weapons.

Appreciation of these inadequacies in the NPT has meant that increasingly there has been emphasis, particularly by the advanced industrial states, on preventing nuclear weapons acquisition through policies of denial extrinsic to the Treaty. These have involved national and multinational controls on the export of critical technologies; economic and political pressure on many nations to forgo the development of indigenous uranium enrichment and spent fuel reprocessing facilities; and efforts, particularly by the United States, going back to the Ford and Carter administrations, generally to discourage the transport and stockpiling of plutonium and its use for power reactors.[2]

A fuller characterization of the nuclear non-proliferation regime of the 1970s and 1980s must also take account of two important features of the Cold War:

(1) In their worldwide competition for influence, support and bases, the Soviet Union and the United States entered into alliances with other countries and, in some cases, intervened broadly in their politics and military policies, generally discouraging the independent acquisition of nuclear weapons by these states. The quid pro quo was that the superpowers guaranteed, explicitly or implicitly, the security of these countries, some of which might otherwise have acquired nuclear weapons of their own for defence against a variety of real and imagined threats. The effect of the division of much of the world into the two great blocs was thus to constrain greatly the impetus to nuclear proliferation within them. Acquiring nuclear weapons seemed neither politically feasible nor militarily necessary in countries such as Italy and Poland.

(2) At the same time, the intensity of the US–Soviet competition was so great that many other issues of concern in the two societies were treated with relatively low priority, and this included nuclear weapons proliferation. Thus, when the Soviet Union invaded Afghanistan the United States subordinated its efforts to dissuade Pakistan from going ahead with its nuclear weapons programme to the higher priority of securing Pakistani support in thwarting Soviet advances in Afghanistan. At the same time, it backed off in trying to induce India to accept IAEA inspection safeguards on all its nuclear facilities because of concern that if it did not back off, Soviet influence in India might increase.

2   CHANGES

Now though, the nuclear weapons proliferation problem must be considered in a new light. Although the collapse of the Soviet empire brought freedom, relief and hope to many of what had been its constituent peoples, concern is increasing about possible Russian efforts to re-establish influence and control. It is this fear that has underlain the interest of the Viségrad and the Baltic states in becoming members of the European Union and in getting the security guarantees of membership in the North Atlantic Treaty Organization (NATO). And this is the basis for Ukrainian pleas for guarantees of its security as a quid pro quo for giving up control over nuclear weapons on its soil that might serve as deterrent to Russian irredentism. Although Russian economic pressure, coupled with Western economic carrots, have induced Ukraine to yield on the nuclear weapons question, it remains to be seen whether NATO collectively, or the United States unilaterally, will soon extend security guarantees to any of the countries of eastern Europe – or to any others – as it did to its NATO partners and to Japan and South Korea in the days of the Cold War. Moreover, in the light of recent experience in Bosnia, it is by no means clear that US or NATO security guarantees would have much credibility, even if offered. Thus, the impetus to acquisition of nuclear weapons by states around the periphery of Russia is likely to be a potential problem for some years, and this may be true in other areas as well where states with hostile neighbours may no longer feel, as they could in the past, that they could rely with some confidence on US – or Soviet – protection.

The demise of the Soviet Union has also brought to the fore questions of effective control of nuclear weapons and stocks of fissionable material, both in Russia and in what were the other Soviet republics. Moreover, it is now feared that skilled and experienced people who were formerly employed in the Soviet nuclear weapons programme might sell their services to other states that have an interest in acquiring nuclear weapons.

Although the threat of war on a global scale, involving the use of many thousands of Soviet and US nuclear weapons – along with perhaps hundreds from other countries – has certainly receded with the collapse of the Soviet Union and the end of the Cold War, these developments have also led, then, to the at least partially offsetting effect of an augmented impetus for diffusion of nuclear weapons to an even greater number of states and possibly to an increase in the likelihood of their use in small numbers.

The other most significant development of recent years affecting perceptions about the proliferation problem has been the Gulf War. The reader may recall that persuading the US Congress and public that the United

States should use military force against Saddam Hussein was not easy. The Bush administration offered a series of rationales for such use: that it should be done to signal that deliberate aggression across frontiers would not be tolerated in the new world order; that the Iraqis had to be ejected from Kuwait, and control of the country had to be restored to its legitimate rulers; that the prospect that Iraq might acquire control over the bulk of Middle East oil was an intolerable threat; that Saddam Hussein was another Hitler; and even that US jobs were at stake. Yet, none of these appeals proved to be as effective as the contention that Iraq might soon acquire nuclear weapons. That possibility really did seem to trouble Americans, at least according to opinion polls.

With the allied military victory, it became clear that Western (including Israeli) intelligence had seriously underestimated the scope and scale of the Iraqi nuclear weapons programme. Although Iraq had been a party to the NPT and had accepted IAEA inspection of its *declared* nuclear facilities, its very large nuclear weapons programme had escaped IAEA notice. Moreover, after its military defeat, ascertaining the full scope of that programme proved to be extraordinarily difficult, even with unprecedentedly intrusive searches. The lesson of this experience is that a nation determined to acquire nuclear weapons can go very far toward its goal without discovery, despite being a party to the NPT and accepting traditional IAEA surveillance. Even if, as expected, the IAEA will be more insistent on inspection of undeclared but suspect facilities in the future, and even if it has Security Council backing in doing so, there must be grave questions about the adequacy of the system and procedures. It is most unlikely that the Security Council would actually mandate the use of military force, and then, if necessary, that it would be used effectively to back up demands for unrestricted and unimpeded inspection, as the imbroglio over North Korea's nuclear programme illustrates.

That problem prompts another observation about the 'old regime'. The existence of facilities in North Korea for the production of militarily significant quantities of plutonium, or its separation and stockpiling, was judged to be so unacceptable by the United States that it was willing to incur considerable costs, both financial and diplomatic, to induce North Korea to terminate its efforts. Yet, Japan has gone much further in acquiring reprocessing capacity, and although a number of governments have found this in some measure objectionable, it has not provoked anywhere near as vehement a response. This illustrates a major difficulty of trying to build a truly universalist nuclear non-proliferation regime or even one based on dividing the countries of the world into discrete classes, as in the case of the NPT, where the division is based solely on whether or not states had conducted an overt nuclear weapons test by the time the Treaty entered into force.

In addition to these distinct events of recent years that bear so significantly on the proliferation problem – the demise of the Soviet Union, the end of the Cold War, and the Gulf War – important evolutionary changes should be noted.

The technical wherewithal for getting into the weapons business has become dramatically more accessible since the initiation by the United States of its 'Atoms for Peace' programme over 40 years ago. That initiative led to the release of a great deal of previously classified information and the training of many students from Third World countries in nuclear science and engineering.

Advancements in uranium enrichment technologies and the spread of those technologies is a particularly noteworthy development. At the beginning of the nuclear age, gaseous diffusion emerged as the enrichment technology of choice. It was, however, so difficult and so dependent on economies of scale that for some years the Soviet Union and the United States maintained an effective duopoly in the provision of enrichment services for commercial purposes. The prospect that other nations would pursue a weapons option based on highly enriched uranium was accordingly generally discounted. It seemed cheaper and easier for them to produce weapons-grade plutonium. But with the development of gas centrifuge and other technologies including, prospectively, laser-based enrichment, not to mention the Iraqi resurrection and improvement of the World War II calutron method, would-be proliferators have more enrichment options to consider.

Even more dramatic are the developments in computer capacity that make capabilities that are far beyond those available to the United States and the Soviet Union when they designed their first nuclear weapons available to virtually any state interested in weapons.

These and other technical developments are doubly troublesome from a non-proliferation perspective. It will be increasingly easy for would-be proliferators to design bombs and to acquire fissionable materials and other components for them; and it will be increasingly unlikely that the United States and other advanced countries will have positions in uranium enrichment and other weapons-usable technologies that are so dominant that they can be used effectively as leverage to induce other states to eschew weapons programmes.

An additional point about uranium, albeit a relatively unimportant one because the amounts required for a modest weapons programme are small: because prospects for nuclear power generation have sharply declined since the 1970s, and because there is essentially no demand in the nuclear weapons states for uranium for weapons, it has become a glut on the market. There is now a surfeit of potential suppliers, and the cost of uranium required to make a bomb has fallen drastically: from between roughly $200,000 and $400,000 15 years ago (in 1979 dollars) to perhaps a tenth of that today.

It should be noted that, although it is not directly relevant to the acquisition of nuclear weapons, access to missiles capable of reliably delivering them can also be expected to increase.

One is left with the unsettling conclusion that trying to stem nuclear weapons proliferation mainly through policies of denial, that is, through the imposition of export controls on critical materials and the threat of sanctions against states that will not accede to and comply with the NPT, is not likely to be adequate and will be of diminishing utility. Yet, as the consequences of the end of the Cold War – chaos and the diminished willingness of the great powers to guarantee the security of other states – become more apparent, the interest of nations in acquiring nuclear weapons for deterrence may increase.

3   ON NEW APPROACHES – OR AT LEAST CHANGES IN EMPHASIS

Given the dramatic changes of the last few years, it is clearly a time for some rethinking about national and international nuclear non-proliferation policies. This has begun, at least in the United States, where it has found its most notable expression in the Department of Defense. The emphasis has its basis in three observations.

(1) Attempts to prevent the spread of nuclear weapons through export controls and other efforts at denial of critical materials and technology are likely to be of diminishing utility, as suggested here.

(2) With control over nuclear weapons spreading to increasing numbers of countries – and with possible erosion of control in the former states of the Soviet Union – the likelihood of their unauthorized or accidental launch is likely to increase.

(3) The spread may result in control being vested in the hands of some persons or regimes that cannot be deterred from using nuclear weapons by the threat of the use of force, nuclear or otherwise.

The result has been much talk about a new, or at least enhanced, counter-proliferation effort by the US Department of Defense to complement non-proliferation efforts. Although the rhetoric includes references to such things as enhanced intelligence collection efforts and targeting and attack capabilities, the most – perhaps only – tangible commitment is to theatre-based ballistic missile defence. The emphasis is perhaps understandable – or at least explainable. With the demise of the Soviet Union, the United States faces few direct military threats to either its territory or its forces abroad with which it cannot easily cope: the exception is those involving use of weapons of mass destruction. Putting aside for the moment the possibility of forcing a change in regime through military conquest, the US military establishment has conceptually three options for dealing with threats of this last kind: deterrence, counterforce attack, and active defence. Having conceded that deterrence may not be effective in all cases, and recognizing the political difficulties of counterforce attacks, particularly of those involving pre-emption, the military must give active defence high priority. The alternative from the Department of Defense's perspective is to concede that this mission is beyond its reach – as it has been ever since the development of nuclear weapons. Making such a concession may be especially difficult considering that very strong claims – that were, as it turns out, wildly exaggerated ones – were made for the effectiveness of the US Patriot air defence missile system against modified Soviet Scud missiles in the Gulf War. But the concession must be made. Nuclear weapons are so powerful and cities – and deployed troops – are so fragile that a defence that is less than, say, 90 per cent effective is not very interesting, and 90 per cent success is probably just not on the cards, given the multiplicity of means of delivery of nuclear weapons, including particularly the possibility of the use of cheap, but effective, decoys in the case of delivery by ballistic missiles.

What is needed now is a broad reconsideration of the nuclear proliferation problem, one unencumbered by constraints of past thinking, particularly by the dichotomization of the world's nations, as exemplified in the NPT, into nuclear weapon and non-nuclear weapon states, and by the almost exclusive emphasis on denial as the means of preventing the spread of nuclear weapons.

As to the first point, instead of classifying states as either nuclear weapon states or non-nuclear weapon states, it might be useful to think in terms of the following classes:

(1) those with no nuclear weapons and no apparent interest in them;
(2) those holding such weapons who do not appear to have a real need for them;
(3) those who might reasonably rationalize acquisition of nuclear weapons for deterrence of attack by others; and

(4) those whose interest in nuclear weapons would seem to be mainly for coercive or aggressive use against others.

Most states clearly belong in the first category the United States, Britain, and France, but probably no others, in the second. The third category might be usefully subdivided. There are states, such as Israel, that might have a perceived need for nuclear weapons to cope with conventional attack by an adversary. There are others, of which India might be an example, that might, in the event of a major conventional war, reasonably want nuclear weapons to deter an opponent's use of them. Or, again in the event of a conventional war, a state might hope to deter intervention by third parties. With conventional war in Korea having been a real possibility for many years, and a continuing one, this could have been an important motivation for North Korea's apparent nuclear weapons programme, although probably not the only one. There are several states, such as China, Pakistan, Russia and Ukraine, that might reasonably want nuclear weapons to hedge against both conventional and nuclear attacks. Libya and Iraq are examples of states that might belong in our fourth category, although the main motivation in the case of either or both could well be to deter third party intervention in conventional conflict initiated by them.

In exploring non-proliferation policy options, it would be wrong simply to dismiss the first class of states as of no concern. The world community ought to be sensitive to the possibility that attempts to impose universalist constraints on international trade in technology and materials that might be used for nuclear weapons programmes can adversely affect the interests of these states even if it is other states' possible nuclear weapons aspirations that motivate such policy initiatives.

Turning to the second category, the United States, Britain and France are not now directly threatened by any significant power, nor are they likely to be in the near term – or to be more precise, they are not likely to be subject to any direct threats to which nuclear weapons would be a remotely reasonable or even plausible response. Nor are nuclear weapons in the hands of these three Western powers likely to be either necessary or credible – much less both – for deterrence or actual use in dealing with likely threats to their interests abroad or to allies or friendly third parties. It is perhaps worth noting in this connection that none of the three, as far as is known, seriously contemplated the use of nuclear weapons against Iraq in 1990–91 when Saddam Hussein clearly threatened their access to Gulf oil, even though it is hard to imagine a more serious threat to their interests, especially those of France, which, without any oil of its own, is more dependent than the others on imports from the Middle East. Western nuclear weapons are, therefore, essentially useless and ought, accordingly, to be of little concern to anyone except their own citizenry, who are burdened with the cost of their maintenance.[3]

Two slight caveats should perhaps be considered. It is argued that nuclear weapons may have symbolic and even some diplomatic value. Certainly this perception was a factor in the British decision in the late 1940s to acquire them, when it was argued that having them would enable Britain to play a larger role in international affairs than it otherwise could. Now though, with a better appreciation of their limited military utility, their symbolic significance is much diminished. To the extent it is of residual importance, elimination of the US, British and French weapons, or even just large reductions in their numbers, not to mention consummation of a comprehensive nuclear test ban treaty and agreements on the cessation of production of fissionable materials for weapons purposes, might have some salutary effect in inducing others to give up nuclear weapons or to forgo their acquisition. In the present environment, these last effects are probably more important to the United States, Britain, and France than the symbolic effects of retention – and continued weapons testing.

There are also the possibilities of accidental or unauthorized use, or of some weapons falling into the hands of other nations or even terrorists. Although these risks can be easily reduced to almost arbitrarily low levels, given that there is no real need for maintaining Western nuclear weapons in any state of readiness, they cannot be totally dismissed.

For the above reasons, it would be good if the US, British and French weapon stockpiles could be reduced or destroyed, but what might be done with them is really not of *first order* importance in consideration of nuclear weapons non-proliferation policies.

The real problems lie in the instances in which nuclear weapons may have perceived utility for either coercive or deterrent purposes. Whatever the rationale, questions will arise as to what might be done to prevent or dissuade would-be proliferators from pursuing weapons options and how to neutralize capabilities should they be developed.

Efforts at denial have not been totally ineffective. Pakistan's acquisition of nuclear weapons was no doubt delayed as a result of the imposition of constraints by the United States and other industrial countries on exports to it. But it is not obvious that delay in this case has made much difference. In others, it may have. Where there were changes in domestic politics, motivations to acquire weapons may have dissipated before ambitions could be realized. Difficulties in access to technology may have had this effect in Argentina and Brazil. Although there are no obvious cases, there may also have been instances involving a difficult call where impediments to access, or the existence of the NPT and accession of neighbours to it, might have tipped the balance against a nation's going ahead with a weapons programme. But with evidence that at least half a dozen states have made substantial progress toward acquiring nuclear weapons, notwithstanding efforts to impede their access to critical materials and technology, one cannot be very optimistic about the future of these approaches.

Counter-proliferation efforts are not likely to be any more successful, assuming the focus is mainly on active defence. If, however, one includes the possibility of pre-emptive destruction of nuclear capabilities, at least short-term success cannot be dismissed on purely technical grounds. The world has seen two examples of such destruction – the Israeli attack on Iraq's Osirak reactor in 1981 and the allied attacks against a broader range of Iraqi nuclear facilities a decade later. But it is noteworthy that these have been the only successful attempts so far, that the Israeli attack was successful only in a tactical sense – its main effect may have been to rein-force Iraqi determination to acquire nuclear weapons, reflected in its sub-sequent efforts – and both these attacks were carried out when a state of war existed between Iraq and the attacking parties. The Israeli attack was noted with considerable opprobrium in many parts of the world, and the US-led attacks were politically possible only in the context of much wider military operations sanctioned by the Security Council. It is most unlikely that such attacks would have been initiated had Iraq not invaded Kuwait, even as it has seemed most unlikely that the United States or another power would have pre-emptively attacked North Korea's nuclear facilities had it continued with its nuclear programme, as long as it did not also attack South Korea – or Japan.

We are left to conclude that continuing to try to deal with nuclear weapons proliferation through relatively easy, supply-side options is likely to be of limited utility. There will undoubtedly be benefits in the extension of the NPT, in the selective use of constraints on the transfer of technology and critical materials, and maybe even in the Department of Defense's counter-proliferation approaches, but such benefits must be weighed against the costs: in the case of active defence by the United States, the waste of many billions of dollars, with perhaps emulation to some degree by other countries, and possible undercutting of the Anti-Ballistic Missile Treaty; and in extension of the NPT and in otherwise selectively con-straining access to critical materials and technology through export con-trols, the political reaction to behaviour that will be widely seen to be discriminatory. But the greater costs will arise from misleading people about the efficacy of such measures. The result is likely to be that people will discount the importance of reducing nations' motivations to acquire weapons. Thus, to continue nearly exclusive focus on policies of denial will be diversionary; quite possibly, critically so.

There are three possible options for reducing motivations: the resolution of basic differences between adversarial states, one or both of which may fear attack by the other; the provision of security guarantees to states that feel threatened; and military conquest of would-be proliferators, followed by occupation to establish new regimes with no interest in nuclear weapons.

The United States has made serious efforts to catalyse the settlement of the Arab–Israeli conflict, and in the case of Egypt and Israel with some success, albeit at very considerable cost. The Camp David accords have meant that roughly 50 per cent of US foreign assistance has gone to those two countries. But other efforts, for example in trying to help in the resolution of Indo-Pakistani differences, have had little success. Realistically, in the world political environment of today, most of the impetus for the resolution of differences between adversarial states will almost certainly have to come from those states themselves. 'Good offices' roles played by other states are likely to contribute only marginally, particularly if those other states are unwilling, as will generally be the case, to incur large political or economic costs.

Security guarantees have met with more success. It is indisputable that the US guarantee of South Korea, exemplified by the stationing of 40,000 troops in that country for 40 years, has been an important factor in dissuading South Korea from proceeding with an overt nuclear weapons programme or even with the construction of a spent fuel reprocessing plant for its commercial reactor fuel – a plant that could have facilitated its getting into the weapons business. But while South Korean restraint has been an important consequence, it was not the primary *reason* for the US guarantee. The main motivation was rather the containment of communism. The same can be said of guarantees by the United States to its NATO allies and Japan. As noted earlier though, the world is now a very different place. It is now unbelievable that the United States would guarantee the security of, say, India or Pakistan, much less that of Ukraine, and beyond the wildest fantasy to believe that it would be willing to deploy large numbers of troops for decades in any of these countries, even if they were wanted. And no other major powers are likely to be eager to play that role either.

As to conquest and occupation, the record of the United States has been mixed. After World War II, it nurtured the development of governments in Germany and Japan that could be trusted to use military power, if at all, only for purposes of which it would generally approve, but the US record in the Caribbean and Central America has been quite the opposite. And it has to be noted that notwithstanding two attempts by Saddam Hussein to acquire nuclear weapons, the United States chose, after military victory in the Gulf, not to follow through with his removal and the establishment of conditions such that the possibility that Iraq would acquire nuclear weapons during, say, the next two decades could be safely dismissed.

Scepticism about the immediate prospects for reducing demand through a hegemonical approach would then seem to be warranted. Although Russia and China might conceivably play this role abroad – the former with respect to its 'near abroad' and China in East Asia – for many years, the United States would be the only conceivable candidate for such a role on a world scale, and while it just might serve as a mediator, arbiter or catalyst in the resolution of disputes underlying the interest of some states in acquiring nuclear weapons, and might even be able and willing to use force to cause the replacement of political authorities who aspire to get nuclear weapons by others clearly not interested in them, it is most doubtful that it could, within the next few decades, acquire the requisite strength, confidence of others, and support of its own people to meet the more fundamental objective of a truly effective non-proliferation regime: guarantee of the security of all states that might otherwise feel a need for nuclear weapons for deterrence or self-defence.

4   HOPE FOR THE FUTURE

The best, albeit not very immediate, hope of meeting this last objective must lie in a collective approach to security. This was, of course, the great challenge for a fleeting moment at the time when the United Nations was organized and before the Cold War supervened. Now, the world has another chance: the possibility of restructuring the UN and related international institutions, and generating broad support for them and confidence in them, so that they can play the role – and more – envisaged for them when they were formed.

The challenges are different and in important respects more difficult than when the UN was being organized. Then, the main issues were to prevent the resurgence of the kinds of militarism demonstrated by Germany and Japan during the preceding decade and to cope with aggression across frontiers. Now there are, in addition, the more immediately troublesome problems of proliferation of weapons of mass destruction and of ethnic conflict, affronts to human rights, and chaos. These new challenges arise at a time when respect for the UN is low and when, accordingly, there is great resistance to the surrender of sovereignty to it and little willingness to provide financial support for its operations; when, indeed, there appears to be widespread objection in nations throughout the world to incurring large costs, military or otherwise, to deal with threats that do not seem *immediately* serious to vital national interests.

Thus, the very idea of strengthening the UN so that it can be instrumental in dealing with ethnic strife and civil conflict and in guaranteeing the security of states against external threats is understandably seen by many as little more than a will-o-the-wisp or, at best, a very distant prospect. But the fact that there have been such dramatic – and not widely predicted – changes in the world as the demise of the Soviet empire, the sudden reunification of Germany, a so-far generally peaceful revolution in South Africa, and the glimmerings of hope for a resolution of Arab–Israeli differences and now between Catholics and Protestants in Ireland, all in the last several years, suggests that such cynicism may well be unwarranted. Surely in a time of such flux, it should be the part of statesmanship to approach the future with optimism about possibilities for changes in world governance and to resist both isolationism and go-it-alone approaches to security.

One's first impulse is to suggest that the lead in doing so will have to come largely from the United States; and for a brief instant, when Iraq threatened Kuwait in 1990, it seemed that President George Bush might commit himself – and, to the extent he could, the United States – to providing that lead. But it soon became clear that that was not to be the case. Notwithstanding glowing remarks about establishing a 'new world order' and the impressive mobilization of broad international support for Desert Shield and Desert Storm, the administration displayed no initiative in trying to strengthen the UN so that it might deal more effectively with crises. On the contrary, it seemed more interested in using the UN than in strengthening it. Moreover, after its military victory over Iraq, it acceded to the protection of the Kurds in northern Iraq and to intervention in Somalia only after considerable pressure, it resisted making commitments that might require the stationing or use of US military forces abroad, particularly if the commitments might be of extended duration, and, in policy statements, it made it clear that the United States would intervene militarily in areas of crises only when it was in the US national interest, very narrowly defined, and then, only under severely circumscribed conditions. It was not long before references to Bush's 'new world order' began to carry derisive connotations.

Coming to the presidency as Bill Clinton did with only a minority of the popular vote, with virtually no experience in foreign affairs and with no apparent sense of the need and opportunity for fundamental changes in world order, it is hard to imagine a president less well equipped than he to take up the challenge with which Bush at least flirted: namely, that of trying to change the international system in fundamental ways from what Americans have known since the United States emerged as a world power almost a century ago. Instead, Clinton's approach to international issues has been essentially reactive, and such initiatives as his administration has attempted have been almost exclusively in the domestic arena – or responsive to domestic pressures. Although disappointing, it is hardly surprising that the overall tenor of its May 1994 policy statement on multilateral peace operations is one of constraint and retrogression, notwithstanding diplomatic obeisance in the document to collective approaches to international security and to hope for the UN. The sad reality is, then, that we are not likely to see, for at least the next year and a half, much, if any, presidentially inspired movement toward the development of a world order based on the rule of law and on collective security that seems needed if demands for nuclear weapons are to be largely eliminated.

Yet, if one looks to the next century, the case for such development seems overwhelming. The nuclear proliferation argument alone would seem sufficient if one believes, as Albert Einstein argued, that 'the unleashed power of the atom has changed everything save our modes of thinking, and thus we drift toward unparalleled catastrophes.'[4]

NOTES

1. Those not familiar with nuclear technology should understand that ordinary uranium cannot be used *directly* for fabricating nuclear weapons. For weapons purposes, the concentration of the isotope with a mass number of 235 must be greatly increased, typically from the natural concentration of 0.71 per cent, to greater than 90 per cent, by a process called 'enrichment'. (Uranium enriched to this degree is also used to fuel most naval propulsion reactors and some research reactors. Most electricity generating reactors require fuel enriched to about 3 per cent U-235.) Alternatively, weapons can use plutonium as the fissionable material. It is produced in reactors from the much more abundant uranium isotope, 238. After removal from the reactor, it must be separated chemically from the residual uranium and fission products in what is commonly referred to as spent fuel reprocessing. The Hiroshima bomb was made from highly enriched uranium; the Nagasaki weapon, and most others, from plutonium.

2. Some of these efforts can be, and have been, construed to be contrary to both the spirit and letter of the NPT. In addition to the features described above, the Treaty specifies, as a concession to the interests of the non-nuclear weapons states, that nothing in it should be interpreted as 'affecting

the inalienable right of all the Parties to the Treaty to develop research, production and use of nuclear energy for peaceful purposes.' Indeed, the Treaty requires that 'parties in a position to do so shall cooperate in contributing to the further development of the applications of nuclear energy for peaceful purposes, especially in the territories of non-nuclear-weapon States Party to the Treaty.' The conflict inherent in trying to both limit nuclear weapons proliferation *and* realize the benefits of the 'peaceful atom' is also reflected in the dual mandate – and in the budget – of the IAEA.

3.   'Executive Summary: The Clinton Administration's Policy on Reforming Multilateral Peace Operations', Presidential Decision Directive 25, unclassified document, Washington, DC, May 3, 1994.

4.   Quoted in Ralph E. Lapp, 'The Einstein Letter that Started It All', *New York Times Magazine*, August 2, 1964.

3 A Treaty Reborn? The NPT After Extension

Joseph F. Pilat and Charles W. Nakhleh

The indefinite extension of the Treaty on the Non-proliferation of Nuclear Weapons (NPT) on May 11, 1995, a decision widely hailed in policy and academic circles both within the United States and abroad, confirmed the Treaty's central role among international efforts to prevent the spread of nuclear weapons and to regulate global nuclear commerce. The Review and Extension Conference (RevExCon), the meeting of the NPT's parties that took the decision on indefinite extension, provided a unique forum for the post-Cold War international debate on the entire spectrum of nuclear matters, ranging from nuclear weapons and testing to peaceful uses of nuclear energy. The debate revealed large divergences of opinion among the Treaty's parties on many of these issues.

The NPT, of course, reflects the international views on nuclear issues that prevailed at the time of the Treaty's negotiation and entry-into-force. Yet those views have evolved, in some cases extensively, during the Treaty's first 25 years, and particularly since the end of the Cold War. How have nations' attitudes and policies towards nuclear weapons and energy changed over the years? What implications do these changes have for the political agreement that underlies the Treaty? And how might changes in attitudes affect the Treaty's ability to influence and regulate nuclear activities in the future?

Coming as it does at the end of the Cold War, and 50 years after Hiroshima and Nagasaki, the RevExCon provides a useful context for an exploration of some of the questions raised above. The following discussion begins by recalling the political conditions and assumptions that were essential to the Treaty's form and content at its inception and contrasts them with those that now obtain. This is followed by an analysis of the debate at the RevExCon, with a view towards discerning underlying areas of political consensus and disagreement concerning military and peaceful nuclear issues. Finally, we summarize some of the nuclear issues that the NPT will have to contend with in the future, offering some speculations on how the NPT might affect, and be affected by, these longstanding or emerging issues.

1   THE CHANGING NUCLEAR CONTEXT

The NPT was negotiated and concluded during the Cold War and inevitably reflects national interests and expectations formulated in that context. In that framework, the NPT was a bold attempt to use multilateral means to balance international concerns for global security with emerging national ambitions in the civil and military nuclear arena. It reflected US and Soviet interests in securing a degree of stability in their confrontational Cold War relationship and in ensuring their ability to influence developments in sensitive regions of the globe. It reflected the desires of developed industrial nations, especially the European nations and Japan, to exploit what appeared to be a promising technology for commercial use and advantage. And it reflected the hopes of key developing nations that the transfer of this important scientific and technological capability would have the potential to ameliorate their serious socioeconomic problems and to enhance their political stature.

The objectives embodied in the resulting Treaty involved non-proliferation, the promotion of peaceful uses of nuclear energy, and the encouragement of arms control. The fundamental objective of the Treaty is to prevent the spread of nuclear weapons to states that do not possess them. The obligations of states parties to the NPT established in the first three articles of the Treaty are designed to ensure the realization of this objective. Pursuant to Article I, each nuclear weapon state party undertakes not directly or indirectly to transfer nuclear weapons or other nuclear explosive devices or the control over such weapons or explosive devices to any other state whatsoever. Furthermore, the weapon states are not to assist, encourage, or induce any non-nuclear weapon state to manufacture or otherwise acquire nuclear weapons or other nuclear explosive devices or the control over such weapons or explosive devices. Article II enjoins the non-nuclear weapon states parties to the Treaty not to receive the transfer or direct or indirect control of nuclear weapons or other nuclear explosive devices, and not to manufacture or otherwise acquire nuclear weapons or other nuclear explosive devices, and not to seek or receive any assistance in their manufacture. Article III provides that each non-weapon state party to the NPT is to accept international safeguards, as set forth in agreements to be negotiated with the International Atomic Energy Agency (IAEA), to be applied to all source or special fissionable material in all peaceful nuclear activities within its territory, under its jurisdiction, or carried out under its control anywhere, to verify Treaty obligations by preventing the diversion of nuclear energy from peaceful uses to nuclear weapons or other nuclear explosive devices.

Articles IV and V address the then-widespread interest in the peaceful uses of nuclear energy by providing a framework for peaceful nuclear cooperation. All parties to the Treaty undertake, in accordance with Article IV, to facilitate the fullest possible exchange of equipment, materials, and scientific and technological information for the peaceful uses of nuclear energy. Those parties to the Treaty with an advanced nuclear capability are to cooperate in contributing to the further development of the peaceful applications of nuclear energy, particularly in the territories of non-weapon states parties to the Treaty and with due consideration for the needs of the developing world. Article V affirms the principle that potential benefits from peaceful nuclear explosions – which never materialized in any significant way – should be made available to non-weapon states on a non-discriminatory basis. This article is now a dead letter.

A third objective of the NPT is to encourage arms control efforts in the nuclear and non-nuclear arenas. Accordingly, under Article VI, each of the parties undertakes to pursue 'good faith' negotiations on effective measures relating to cessation of the nuclear arms race at an early date, to nuclear disarmament, and to the achievement of a Treaty on general and complete disarmament under strict and effective international control. In this vein, Article VII states that nothing in the Treaty affects the right of any group of states to conclude regional treaties to ensure the total absence of nuclear weapons in their respective territories.

These objectives constituted, however bold for the times, a compromise – a Cold War compromise. This compromise is apparent in the language as well as the negotiating history of the Treaty. The original Irish proposal adopted unanimously by the General Assembly in 1961 contained only a prohibition against the transfer of ownership or control of nuclear weapons from a state possessing them to one that did not, as well as a pledge by states not possessing these weapons to abstain from manufacturing or acquiring them. It contained no mention of the provisions regarding peaceful uses of nuclear energy or nuclear disarmament that later made their way into the Treaty, provisions that reflected primarily the desires of the non-weapon states to minimize discriminatory aspects of the Treaty and of the world it reflected. Another issue that proved to be a stumbling block in the negotiations for several years was Western collective defence. NATO, of course, depended on the American nuclear guarantee, supplemented by the then-developing British and French nuclear forces. At that time, NATO nuclear-sharing arrangements, particularly the Multilateral Nuclear Force (MLF) and the Atlantic Nuclear Force (ANF) proposals, were being discussed within the alliance. The Soviets were adamantly opposed to such proposals, particularly to any initiative that would seem to give West

Germany actual control over nuclear weapons. The eventual Treaty, which permitted the deployment of US-owned and controlled nuclear weapons on the territory of NATO allies, including West Germany, struck a balance between competing concerns but ultimately did nothing to affect the collective defence arrangements of the day.

The NPT's environment clearly played a key role in influencing the final form of the Treaty. This political environment, which appeared to many as reflecting the only possible world, included the following:

- stable but confrontational US–Soviet relations in which nuclear weapons played a central role;
- global US and Soviet power and influence, along with security guarantees to allies and varying degrees of influence or control over allies and client states;
- a strong Cold War consensus between the United States and the Soviet Union on the adverse strategic implications of proliferation;
- the secondary role of other states, including other nuclear powers;
- the centralization of nuclear technology – especially sensitive weapon-related technology – in a few supplier states, and the existence of little indigenous capability in the developing world;
- the emergence of a large number of developing nations from decolonization with little power, and correspondingly little influence on global security issues; and
- high expectations for peaceful uses of nuclear technology.

The end of the Cold War has changed the international environment in the following fundamental ways:[1]

- the unexpected collapse of the Soviet Union has ended the global US–Soviet rivalry as well as the Soviet domination of eastern Europe;
- the US global presence is diminishing, and its Cold War security guarantees are coming into question both in the United States and abroad;
- the resulting strategic environment is extremely uncertain;
- American and Russian views and influence are not nearly as decisive as they used to be;
- there are widespread doubts about the utility of nuclear weapons in warfare, these weapons are no longer as central to international relations, and their devaluation and delegitimization is occurring, but there are divergent views on the proliferation threat and its implications;
- the United States and Russia have achieved unprecedented reductions in nuclear arms, however, as denuclearization proceeds, the attitudes and policies of the United Kingdom, France, and China are steadily gaining in importance;

- the nuclear weapon policies of the three unacknowledged weapon states – Israel, India, and Pakistan – have also gained in importance;
- regional conflicts among developing (and developed) nations have displaced the global US–Soviet confrontation as the primary sources of tension and hostility in the world;
- both peaceful and weapon-related nuclear technologies are widely disseminated throughout the world; and
- immediate interest in nuclear power is waning, with important exceptions in Asia and Europe.

These post-Cold War changes have altered the very foundations — political and technological – of the NPT. Neither nuclear proliferation nor nuclear power has had the appeal that was expected at the time of the NPT's creation. The relatively small number of states that contributed significantly to the negotiations over the NPT – mainly the United States and the Soviet Union – has been replaced by a much larger number of politically important and technologically capable states – the other three nuclear weapon states, the three threshold states, the advanced non-weapon states, and several important emerging regional powers – with far less mutual agreement on the goals and means of non-proliferation, nuclear energy, and arms control. Were negotiations on a non-proliferation Treaty to be held today, it is unlikely that any Treaty would be agreed to, and almost certainly not a Treaty similar in form to the NPT. The number of important actors and the divergences in political interest would simply be too great.

And yet the NPT is a part of the heritage left to us by the Cold War. It is the principal international instrument that codifies the non-proliferation regime. Its indefinite extension indicates that many countries still find that regime to be consonant with their political interests, at least on the surface. However, the conference left several controversial issues unresolved, and whether its decisions ultimately ameliorate or exacerbate differences over nuclear issues in the future depends in part on the level of political consensus among the Treaty's parties.

2   PAST AS PROLOGUE?

The RevExCon was in many ways a microcosm of the current debate on nuclear weapon issues. As the first review conference to reflect to some degree the end of the Cold War, it provided a window on how the politics that shape the dynamics of proliferation have changed in recent years. In

New York, new actors emerged to claim their places on the non-proliferation stage, while some older, more familiar actors assumed newly important roles. Still others that were previously important revealed they were fading from the spotlight. Despite these differences, the conference largely focused on old issues, which were sometimes debated in a new context, although a few new ones did rise to prominence during the debate.

Security Issues at the RevExCon

The United States and other states have called the indefinite extension of the NPT a victory for the principle of non-proliferation, and non-proliferation was clearly victorious by the conference's end. However, it is equally clear that broader nuclear-weapon and disarmament issues were in the foreground of the RevExCon. Perhaps foremost in the minds of many delegates was the unresolved question of the future of nuclear weapons. According to the document entitled 'Principles and Objectives for Nuclear Nonproliferation and Disarmament' adopted at the RevExCon, all future nuclear arms control arrangements should be part of 'the determined pursuit by the nuclear weapon States of systematic and progressive efforts to reduce nuclear weapons globally, with the ultimate goal of eliminating those weapons.'

While consistent with the Treaty's preambular language, this statement goes beyond the NPT's language in Article VI. Although the commitments undertaken in the principles and objectives document are not legally binding, they do embody the substantive consensus of the parties in New York. They are clearly a measure of the political expectations of the non-weapon states and reflect the view that their interests lie in the reduction of existing arsenals. Despite this declaration on ultimate goals, there is little or no consensus among the weapon states on the nature, scope, and timing of further nuclear arms reductions, let alone on complete nuclear disarmament. Indeed, it is not obvious that all nuclear weapon states share this view of the end point of arms control, despite their assent to the principles and objectives document. Some of the difficulties that will be encountered in the future are perhaps foreshadowed by the Chinese nuclear test a few days after the conference as well as by France's resumption of nuclear testing in the Pacific, on the one hand, and the international reaction to them on the other. This fundamental difference of interests creates tensions between those states who would use the NPT as a springboard to future disarmament and those who see it as a codification of a limited agreement on non-proliferation that will be felt in the future, perhaps as early as 1997, when the preparatory work for the Review Conference in 2000 formally begins.

Even the more limited, albeit more concrete, steps envisioned in the principles and objectives document – the achievement of a Comprehensive Test Ban Treaty 'no later than 1996', and the 'immediate commencement and early conclusion of negotiations' on a Treaty banning the production of fissile material for explosive purposes – are encountering substantial difficulties at the Conference on Disarmament (CD). That either agreement, especially a cutoff, will be achieved is not clear. In any event, these difficulties suggest that a consensus on the difficult questions of nuclear weapon policies after the Cold War has not yet been achieved. They also indicate that dealing with the nuclear weapon legacy of the Cold War will be extraordinarily difficult in political, technical, and environmental terms.

Another issue left unresolved by the RevExCon that may prove divisive in the future is the question of security assurances. In the wake of the Cold War, many have argued that the weapon states should enhance their security assurances, perhaps through an international legally binding instrument. Some states, especially China, have also urged the nuclear powers to conclude an agreement not to initiate the first use of nuclear weapons in any conflict. With the exception of China, which has given a no-first-use pledge, the nuclear weapon states have been unwilling to take this step. Although the nuclear weapon states did enhance their security assurances through UN Security Council Resolution 1984 prior to the conference, this action was widely regarded as insufficient. These issues were raised at the RevExCon and provoked contentious debate, but the most that could be agreed was that 'further steps should be considered to assure non-nuclear weapon states party to the Treaty against the use or threat of use of nuclear weapons. These steps could take the form of an internationally legally binding instrument.' This is best interpreted as a deferral of a difficult decision rather than as a reconciliation of widely differing national interests. The issue will undoubtedly prove to be contentious at the review conference in 2000.

Peaceful Nuclear Issues at the RevExCon

Several debates over peaceful uses of nuclear energy and nuclear cooperation arose before or during the RevExCon, including the following:

- debates over the 'inalienable' right to peaceful cooperation, with the United States and Iran at the centre of these arguments;

- disputes, which were largely played out at the margins of the conference, between the United States and Russia and China over nuclear assistance to Iran;
- questions about the future form and content of export controls as weapon-relevant technologies spread ever further; and
- debates over the appropriate authority to decide non-compliance with non-proliferation undertakings.

Other matters that were apparent in the debates included differences over plutonium use and management, both for materials released from weapons by disarmament activities and for materials in civil programmes. The differences between the United States and Russia on the one hand, and between the United States and the advanced industrial powers on the other, were potentially explosive but were not openly divisive at the conference.

One thread that ran through the conference's debates on the peaceful uses of nuclear energy was the increasing decentralization of nuclear technologies, expertise, and supply. Western Europe and Japan have displaced the United States as the centres of commercial nuclear research and development. Russia and China (with India perhaps not far behind) are poised to enter the commercial nuclear market heavily – should it revive – and their assessments of the non-proliferation costs and benefits of nuclear assistance could well differ from those of the United States. The disputes over Iran clearly illustrate these divergent cost-benefit analyses.

As was pointed out above, the NPT was based on certain assumptions about the availability and desirability of nuclear technologies. The ongoing debates about who should or should not supply what to whom show that these assumptions no longer hold true today. Although it is widely known that peaceful nuclear aid can in principle help a clandestine weapon programme, this is not the only factor in nations' supply calculations. Commercial and security incentives also play a prominent role. These basic factors – the dissemination of nuclear technologies, the rise of multiple competing suppliers with differing interests, and economic interests in a potentially lucrative international nuclear trade – appear likely to continue to spark debates in the future. The RevExCon did not, and could not, resolve them definitively.

Continuing Divergences

The results of the RevExCon seem to indicate that the essential provisions of the NPT – a prohibition on the acquisition of nuclear weapons by the non-weapon states, the establishment of a regulated nuclear supply regime, and a commitment by the nuclear powers to pursue nuclear arms control and disarmament – continue to be widely supported throughout the international community. US policymakers in particular have emphasized the Treaty's continuing importance in the formulatlon and implementation of military and civilian nuclear policy.

But the extreme effort to avoid an outright vote on the NPT exerted in New York by Jayantha Dhanapala, the Sri Lankan conference president, indicates strongly that basic differences in national interests – in particular those between the weapon states and the developing regional powers – were not fundamentally reconciled as much as they were managed. For the time being, the states involved agreed to disagree on much of the NPT's broad nuclear agenda. Although very few states appeared to find undermining the Treaty, or worse, in their immediate national interest, many did not desire indefinite extension either. The brief political analysis presented above indicates some of the reasons why and further suggests that the basic political support necessary to the NPT's continued relevance is far more fragile than has been commonly acknowledged.

As new nuclear issues and controversies arise in the future, political support for the NPT will depend on these national interests and on the coalitions and marriages of convenience they may engender. Nations will continue to honour and support the Treaty in the long term only if they continue to find it to be in their national interests. But how will they react if, for example, allegations about Iran's nuclear activities are proven to be true? Or if some key regional powers withdraw from the Treaty as an act of political protest? How could this political consensus be challenged in the future?

3   CHALLENGES OLD AND NEW

As noted above, the NPT was an attempt to provide some order to the international nuclear endeavour as it stood in the 1960s. Throughout the intervening decades, however, the fundamental political bases of the Treaty have changed dramatically. The extension of the NPT means that it will have to address military and civilian nuclear issues in the changed political context. Chief among these issues are the future of nuclear weapons, non-compliance with Treaty obligations, the NPT holdout threshold states, conflicts over the development of closed nuclear fuel cycles, and conflicts over nuclear cooperation with states such as Iran.

Non-proliferation, Disarmament, and the NPT

The NPT embodies the important but limited international consensus on
non-proliferation that now exists. Today's dynamic and decentralized international political environment strongly suggests that no other major international agreements dealing directly with nuclear proliferation are likely to
come along for the foreseeable future. The only likely agreements will be
regional in scope, most notably nuclear-weapon-free zones. In this climate,
will states continue to view the NPT as fulfilling a useful function? If the
proliferation problem spirals out of control, the NPT will be judged to have
failed. Perhaps it could not survive the end of the Cold War. Most states
have made a no-weapons pledge by now and would presumably disavow it
in this event; it would not be possible or perhaps even desirable to save the
Treaty in the midst of a nuclear-armed crowd. If the problem remains
limited to the hold-out states and a few parties, the NPT will not have
failed. It would remain useful as a norm, a confidence-building measure
and, depending on safeguards improvements and other issues, as a partially
enforceable, limited legal instrument, with great political value.

The latter best characterizes the current situation, especially after the
decision on the indefinite extension of the Treaty and the RevExCon's
demonstration of support for the IAEA's efforts to strengthen international
safeguards, but the proliferation situation is not stable and could worsen.
Although the technical barriers to proliferation have eroded dramatically
and are not a significant obstacle to a determined proliferator, there are
still considerable political impediments to a decision to acquire nuclear
weapons, and most states remain sceptical about the benefits of such a
decision. Widespread withdrawals from the Treaty seem unlikely for political reasons, but a few nations have sought to develop a weapons capability without overtly withdrawing. Over the years, experts and officials have
warned that such states could use adherence to the NPT as a source of
political cover and of technical aid. However, the number of states that
have pursued such a course has remained small. It seems reasonable to
expect that proliferation will not worsen dramatically in the next decade or
so; however, it is also unlikely that the problems confronting us today will
disappear or be resolved in that time frame.

Beyond proliferation, there is little reason to expect that the arms reductions of the immediate post-Cold War years will be accelerated in the
future. The fate of START-II is uncertain. There is not much consensus in
the United States and Russia over START-III and even less in China,
Britain and France over reductions in their arsenals. Yet the RevExCon
made commitments to progress in nuclear arms control, in both specific

and general terms, as never before. There are high expectations for continued dramatic reductions in weapons throughout the developed and developing world. This presents a potential problem for the NPT because high expectations, when disappointed, inevitably bring in their train bitter resentment, for which the NPT would be an obvious target.

Can the NPT Deal with Non-Compliance?

Non-compliance has become one of the NPT's most pressing problems over the last five years. The revelations of safeguards violations in Iraq and North Korea, and suspicions about the intentions of Iran, have raised serious questions about the credibility of the NPT in its non-proliferation role. The international debate over Iran's behaviour has further raised the question of the appropriate authority for determining when and where non-compliance has occurred. Is it the IAEA? Or the permanent members of the Security Council? This was a subject of some controversy between Iran and the United States at the RevExCon. Although the conference reaffirmed that the IAEA is the 'competent authority...to verify and assure...compliance with its safeguards agreements with States parties undertaken in fulfillment of their obligations under Article III(1) of the Treaty, with a view to preventing diversion of nuclear energy from peaceful uses to nuclear weapon or other nuclear explosive devices', the larger point of the authority to determine compliance with the Treaty was not resolved there and will undoubtedly crop up again in the future.

It could be argued that Iraq, at least, has paid some price for its violations of its Treaty commitments. This is true to some degree but fails to capture the essence of the problem. The United States and others initiated the Gulf War for reasons that were unrelated to Iraq's nuclear weapon programme or to its violation of the NPT's provisions. Indeed, it was only after the Gulf War, and in the euphoria of the coalition victory, that a non-proliferation mandate for the United Nations was created and that the actual extent of Iraq's weapon programme was discovered. Although hopes for the United Nations and collective enforcement of international law ran unrealistically high after the successes of the Gulf War, they have declined somewhat since then as a result of United Nations difficulties in Somalia, Bosnia, and elsewhere. The situation in Iraq is very unlikely to be repeated in other proliferous nations, as the history of developments in North Korea since the Gulf War suggests.

For their part, North Korea and Iran have not yet been subject to any substantive punishment. A lack of political agreement on how to define and how to respond to non-compliance is a key factor in both cases.

However, the cases are very different in nature, which is perhaps responsible for the differences in treatment to date. Indeed, North Korea has received financial and technical rewards for its recognized non-compliance. Policymakers apparently felt that their options in North Korea came down to a choice between financial incentives for good behaviour – bribery – or war. This example is particularly distressing in light of the fact that North Korea is a poverty-stricken state with virtually no allies and few or no friends. Yet even in this situation, the permanent members of the Security Council were not willing to risk the mild stick of economic sanctions, let alone resort to the forcible measures employed during the Gulf War. Clearly, the prospect of a new conflict on the Korean peninsula was not acceptable to the United States and its regional allies, and China held that diplomacy offered a better chance of resolving the issue.

With respect to Iran, there is no clear-cut case of non-compliance with safeguards or other formal agreements, but a pattern of acquisitions that suggests the pursuit of nuclear weapons. However, there is no agreement within the international community on whether or how to deal with these concerns.

Divergent judgements of risk and reluctance to accuse states of misbehaviour are likely to obtain in future situations and cast severe doubt on the NPT's ability to deal with future non-compliance. There are no good political reasons to expect more political unity among the most powerful of the Treaty's parties in future cases of non-compliance than was shown in these three cases. Proliferation will probably be seen as too distant a problem to warrant immediate risks, especially any risks of war.

However, as suggested above, it is not a foregone conclusion that there will be a flood of cases of non-compliance in the future. There may well be; but in the past proliferation has always proceeded slower than was expected. If there are new cases of non-compliance, however, the NPT will be hard pressed to respond. Its future may be at stake.

Addressing the Threshold States

The main obstacles to the threshold states' joining the NPT have been much discussed over the years. They spring from fundamental political assessments within these states as to their security requirements. It is far beyond the purview of the NPT to address these political concerns directly, although they are reflected in NPT debates. In recognition of this, several proposals have recently been put forward in an attempt to address proliferation within the two regions primarily involved: the Middle East and South Asia. Proposals for increased transparency and other confidence-building measures regarding the nuclear programmes of India and Pakistan and various proposals for limiting or otherwise managing unsafeguarded fissile-material production in South Asia and the Middle East have been at the forefront of these attempts.

So far, they have met with little success, but even if they were to succeed, they could create conflicts with the NPT. The main problem is one of legitimization of the nuclear arsenals of these three countries. A good example of this is the global ban on fissile-material production for nuclear explosives called for in the principles and objectives document of the RevExCon and currently under discussion at the CD. If such a ban is eventually agreed, and if the threshold states accede to it – two conditions that are by no means certain – then the existence of their nuclear arsenals, or at least the status of unsafeguarded nuclear materials, will for the first time be implicitly acknowledged and sanctioned by an international agreement. In other words, they will be implicitly recognized as weapon or quasi-weapon states. However, such an acknowledgment is not consistent with the definition of a nuclear weapon state given in the NPT. Other agreements that attempt to address nuclear weapon issues could potentially create similar conflicts.

The problem is the NPT implications of dealing with states that already are nuclear weapon states but have not acceded to the NPT. Regional attempts at arms control may prove to be desirable in some cases, particularly if they are based on a viable set of incentives and disincentives, and thereby have some prospect of being realized. But even in these cases, the outcome may have undesirable effects on the NPT regime. These issues are difficult, but the main point of this discussion is to point out that there are potential conflicts between traditional universal approaches to non-proliferation and the more novel regional approaches. These conflicts are most likely manageable and are certainly not as large a problem as non-compliance. In the worst case, they could cast some doubt on the credibility of the NPT's provisions in today's world.

Conflicting Nuclear Energy and Supply Policies

The NPT's nuclear cooperation provisions, as argued above, rest on assumptions about the appeal of nuclear energy and the existence of a few dominant supplier nations that no longer hold true. During the 1960s, the United States and the Soviet Union dominated the nuclear-supply arena in their respective political blocs. There was agreement between the United States, the major western European states, and Japan on peaceful fuel cycle strategies, including the eventual use of reprocessed plutonium to provide power, and little dissemination of nuclear technologies among the developing nations.

This situation no longer obtains. The number of potential suppliers has grown dramatically since the 1960s, and the United States no longer occupies the dominant position it once did. Particularly important is the entry of Russia and China into the world nuclear market in the last few years. While Western supply policies were largely harmonized through the establishment of the Nuclear Suppliers Group (NSG) – though not without difficulties – these two countries pose challenges. Russian export behaviour in the aftermath of the Soviet Union's breakup threatens the NSG consensus. China is not a member of the NSG and is not likely to be integrated into that structure in the foreseeable future, given that Chinese views on nuclear supply and its underpinnings are to some degree different (perhaps unbridgeably so) from those of the United States and other key Western supplier nations. The conflicts between the United States and Russia, and the United States and China, over nuclear cooperation with Iran illustrate the emerging situation clearly.

The growing technological capability of the developing nations, and the budding interest in nuclear power and cooperation in Asia, are also new factors facing the NPT and its safeguards system. If other Asian nations begin to increase their dependence on nuclear power, and start to seek outside cooperation, both the IAEA's safeguards system and the strained consensus on supply policies will be tested even further.

Moreover, the old consensus on the backend of the nuclear fuel cycle no longer obtains. Ever since the middle 1970s, the United States has forgone reprocessing civil spent fuel and has, through its supply and cooperation agreements, attempted to encourage others to follow its example. This has led to difficulties between the United States and its western European and Japanese allies. While these differences faded in the 1980s, they are now reemerging, and the current US–EURATOM negotiations on a renewal of the nuclear cooperation agreement are encountering difficulties on precisely these issues.

These questions did not loom large at the RevExCon, but they will certainly be important in future deliberations of the Treaty's parties. As the basis for international nuclear cooperation, the NPT must accommodate these developments. If the NPT, either through a failure of safeguards or through political inaction, fails to prevent further proliferation as nuclear cooperation spreads ever further, it will be severely weakened.

4 A FUTURE IN THE MAKING

While confirming the Treaty's central role in international non-proliferation efforts, the indefinite extension of the NPT also suggests the wisdom of reassessing the strength of political support for the Treaty's basic provisions. Implicitly and explicitly, this question is linked to the broader question of the future of nuclear weapons and nuclear energy. The NPT envisions a world ultimately free from nuclear weapons. This view was explicitly stated in the principles and objectives document adopted concurrently with the decision on indefinite extension. Despite this, however, debates on these issues are continuing in many capitals throughout the world; they were not resolved or otherwise brought to a close by the indefinite extension of the Treaty.

The conclusions nations reach will be based first and foremost on calculations of national interest that can and will change over time. In the past, the NPT has influenced national decision-making processes.[2] Will it continue to do so in the future? The NPT was concluded nearly 30 years ago, in a world very different from ours today. It would be surprising if at least some important nations do not change their views of the utility of the Treaty, both for good and for ill. South Africa, Iraq, and North Korea offer illustrations, with very different implications, that this is already occurring. The impact of the political changes in the last few years on the NPT and its Cold War structure remains ambiguous. Global and regional political environments are in a state of great flux. Nations' current attitudes towards nuclear weapons are ambivalent. A good many will continue to abstain from nuclear weapons in the future. Their confidence in the NPT's ability to verify the non-proliferation pledges of other nations will be enhanced if some outstanding issues such as non-compliance are dealt with firmly and effectively. However, these positive results in this and other areas are certainly not inevitable and will not be attained without effort and vigilance.

NOTES

1. For a fuller discussion, see Joseph F. Pilat, 'Rethinking the NPT Model', a paper delivered at a Nonproliferation Policy Education Center seminar, Washington, DC, November 18, 1994.
2. See Lawrence Scheinman, 'Does the NPT Matter?' in Joseph F. Pilat and Robert E. Pendley, eds, *1995: A New Beginning for the NPT* (New York: Plenum, 1995), pp. 217–33.

4 The NPT and Power Transitions in the International System

T.V. Paul

The renewal of the Nuclear Non-proliferation Treaty (NPT) in perpetuity in May 1995 was driven partly by a desire on the part of the nuclear weapon states (NWS) to permanently legitimize their positions as major powers in the international system. Fortuitously for the NWS, the opposition to the Treaty had declined substantially by 1995 with the joining of a number of erstwhile opponents to its ranks, especially South Africa and Argentina. Brazil, another longstanding opponent of the NPT, had initiated regional and bilateral non-proliferation initiatives along with Argentina, effectively agreeing to behave like an NPT signatory state.[1] The success of the US-led coercive diplomacy toward North Korea and Iraq in capping their nuclear weapon programmes, at least in the short run, also strengthened the NPT by the time the extension conference was held in New York.

This chapter asks the question as to whether maintaining a discriminatory NPT permanently is possible or not. I argue that the probable long-term changes in the international system in the 21st century are likely to affect the great power consensus behind the Treaty and the future of the regime. This, however, may be prevented under two conditions: first, nuclear weapons are delegitimized on a global basis through the creation of a more effective and non-discriminatory international regime, and second, the possession of nuclear weapons becomes unnecessary to achieve great power status.[2] These conditions could result from technological breakthroughs which may make nuclear weapons no longer the ultimate source of destructive power in the international system, especially in a deterrent sense.

The arguments of this chapter are drawn from power transition theories embodied in several accounts of change in the international system. What these theories point out is that in the five hundred years since the modern state system has come into being, power distributions have rarely been static, and that new great powers emerged at regular intervals after a given system entered its mature stage and degradation. Weapons of the highest calibre were sought by potential challengers to an existing international order who tended to imitate the capabilities of their opponents in their attempt to overtake the status quo powers of a given epoch.

The chapter also asks: given the inequities of power in the international system and the possibilities of renewal of structural competition in the future in one form or another, can the NPT and the larger nuclear non-proliferation regime survive the challenges of a system with self-help as its dominant characteristic? What are the major threats to the Treaty's future? What strategies can avert the collapse or gradual weakening of the non-proliferation regime?

1 SYSTEMIC CONSENSUS AND THE EMERGENCE OF THE NPT

The NPT was indeed a product of the superpower consensus that emerged in the non-proliferation area in the 1960s.[3] A number of potential nuclear weapon states – especially Japan, Germany and other technologically capable states in the West – were co-opted to the NPT after assurances were made regarding nuclear protection against possible attacks by their enemies and the untrammelled supply of nuclear materials for their civilian energy needs. Several smaller states adhered to the Treaty voluntarily because it provided international legitimacy to their non-nuclear status. The NPT served their interests as it constrained their larger neighbours from going nuclear. The Treaty also made it morally difficult for the nuclear weapon states to use their weapons against the non-nuclear signatory states as the NWS had made conditional no-first-use pledges to such states.

For the nuclear weapon states, the legalization of the monopoly rights of their capability provided the key incentive to pursue the Treaty. The legitimization has been embodied in Article IX, which defines a nuclear weapon state as a country that has manufactured and exploded a nuclear weapon or other nuclear device prior to January 1, 1967. While Article I of the Treaty forbids NWS from transferring weapons to a non-nuclear-weapon state (NNWS), Article II prevents the NNWS from accepting nuclear devices from countries or manufacturing their own nuclear weapons. No corresponding obligations are set on the NWS rights to manufacture a nuclear device.[4]

Thus the unusual coincidence of interests of the NWS and a large number of NNWS facilitated the creation of the NPT. In addition, the NWS, through Article VI of the Treaty, promised to conduct negotiations in earnest to reduce and finally eliminate nuclear weapons. This side of the bargain was haphazardly pursued. In the immediate years after the Treaty was signed, the pace of the nuclear arms race increased as the Cold War rivalry began to manifest in larger proportions. For instance, in 1968 the nuclear powers had a total of 6,737 warheads which by 1990 increased to 31,718.[5] Although the superpower nuclear arms control agreements such as the Strategic Arms Limitation Treaty (SALT) were intended to slow down the arms race, they had the reverse effect as both Moscow and Washington attempted to obtain the maximum qualitative and quantitative limits set by the Treaty.

The major incentive on the part of the nuclear weapon states to pursue an unequal Treaty was the desire to maintain their structural power and their ability to determine the security policies of regional states. This rare systemic cooperation among competing major powers, especially the superpowers, occurred due to their realization of the special capacity that nuclear weapons possession could endow non-great-power states in constraining the ability of major powers to intervene in regional theatres. Regional states, armed with nuclear weapons, could create enough uncertainty regarding their intention to use these weapons and this could put tremendous pressure on the great powers not to intervene against the smaller nuclear states. Some regional states might also loosen their dependency ties with the superpowers, diminishing their prominence as alliance leaders. Nuclear proliferation could affect the systemic stability built around a bipolar structure. These fears continued beyond the Cold War era as evident in the increased great power cooperation to achieve nuclear non-proliferation. The end of the Cold War helped to remove the remaining hurdles to major power cooperation in this realm as they no longer needed to placate regional states that were likely to pursue nuclear weapons programmes. The NPT was renewed in perpetuity due to the lack of serious opposition by major power actors in the international system and the divisions among the ranks of the NNWS on the issue. Both France and China, earlier opponents of the Treaty, joined it in 1991 and 1992 respectively, after realizing that it would not affect their nuclear programmes and that the non-spread of nuclear weapons would assure them major power status for a long period to come. They proved that the Treaty would not in any way constrain their nuclear modernization programmes by conducting nuclear tests days or weeks after the Treaty was extended.

The negotiating strategy of the nuclear weapon states and their allies at the NPT renewal conference clearly showed the determination of these states to maintain the nuclear status quo and monopoly rights of the five declared states. The NWS were not willing to offer any major concessions to NNWS demands for attaching conditions for extending the Treaty.

Differing positions introduced by various NNWS such as Venezuela, Indonesia and Mexico had called for the extension of the Treaty for another 25-year term or indefinite extension based on several commitments and periodic review conferences. Instead, the NWS succeeded in dividing the NNWS by influencing some core members of the group such as South Africa and Argentina and thereby reducing the support for the non-aligned group. At the Foreign Ministers conference of the non-aligned movement in Jakarta, divisions had already begun to surface on the issue of a 25-year rolling extension option. The New York conference witnessed some intense parleying by the NWS and their allies, especially Canada, South Africa and Australia. A final position proposed by South Africa, linking enhanced review process and the acceptance of principles covering non-proliferation, universality, safeguards, peaceful uses, nuclear disarmament and nuclear free zones, and a resolution on the Middle East were pivotal to extending the Treaty indefinitely. The principles were intended as yardsticks, not as definite conditions that several NNWS had demanded.[6] In other words, NWS are not bound by any of these principles, evidenced in the quick resumption of nuclear testing by China and France.

2   SYSTEM CHANGE AND THE NPT

The extension of the NPT in perpetuity was thus a victory of sorts for the nuclear weapon states who joined ranks in pressuring the NNWS who were campaigning against a permanent unconditional extension. Although the renewal of the NPT for an indefinite duration was possible partly due the end of the Cold War, long-term systemic changes, unless managed carefully, are likely to weaken the Treaty. The NPT could be particularly vulnerable to systemic changes as it does not have room for a new great power emerging with nuclear weapons. Additionally, if and when medium-sized states in conflict zones realize the utility of nuclear weapons in deterring their rivals or in constraining the coercive power of nuclear weapon states, they could pursue weapons programmes clandestinely. This would be a second major source of challenge to the NPT's future.

The NWS that clamoured for the permanent extension of the Treaty assume that the nuclear status of the five states can be maintained for a long time to come and that new challengers are unlikely to emerge if the regime becomes embedded. Additionally, it is assumed that if the present five nuclear states reduce their nuclear capability progressively, new great powers will have less incentive to acquire nuclear weapons, claiming no progress in disarmament negotiations.

These assumptions ignore the systemic imperatives of the rise and fall of great powers. A major consequence of the Treaty's permanent maintenance of five great power states with nuclear status is that it does not mandate the orderly exit of a declining great power from the ranks of the privileged nuclear weapons club. The existing five nuclear weapon states are also UN Security Council members and they are generally considered as great powers, although it is debatable whether Britain and France still belong to that category. The Treaty assumes that the present number of great powers will remain the same. It does not provide for a future great power acquiring nuclear weapons, nor does it make it possible for Britain and France to become non-nuclear weapon states, other than through unilateral action.[7] What will happen when: (1) one or more of the present five are no longer great powers or system leaders? And, (2) one or more new great powers, other than the present five, emerge in the international arena with significant military and economic capability to influence events outside their region?

In the past, when a rising major power actor found the system unsympathetic to its aspirations for a leadership role, it resorted to breaking treaties meant for keeping it in the lower ranks and eventually opted for war in order to change its position in the international system. On some occasions, status quo states attempted to curb the power of their rising challengers through unequal arms control agreements.[8] An important example was the naval arms control treaties during the inter-war period. Faced with a burgeoning arms race involving battleships, the three principal naval powers of the 1920s, the United States, Britain and Japan, signed the Washington Naval Treaty of 1922 freezing the naval strength then prevalent among the three states at a ratio of 5:5:3 respectively. The Treaty parties agreed to scrap nearly half their existing battleships and not to build new battleships for a decade or so. In terms of qualitative restrictions, the Treaty limited new battleships to 35,000 tons and cruisers to 10,000 tons (with 8-inch guns). The subsequent London Treaty of 1930 placed several restrictions on the numbers of other types of ships.[9] 'The overall tonnage agreements provided for parity between the US and Great Britain, whereas Japan received only a 6/10 ratio *vis-à-vis* each of the Anglo-Saxon countries.'[10]

Contrary to expectations of the parties, the Treaty did not last too long partly because it could not take into account the changing political circumstances. Although the UK and US perceived the Treaty to be an assurance for maintaining their superiority, they failed to authorize building new warships, owing to domestic economic constraints. During the 1930s Japan, however, accelerated the naval arms production and reached 80 per cent of the US strength, 20 per cent more than it was allowed by the 1930 Treaty. Tokyo used several methods to get around the Treaty limits, including laying down submarine tenders that could be quickly converted into aircraft carriers and cruisers. In 1936, Japan formally abrogated the Treaty. In the domestic politics of Japan also the treaties caused the coming into dominance of the Fleet faction over the Treaty faction in the Navy in 1934 with repercussions for the rise of militarism and Japan's march towards war in the coming years.[11]

The naval arms control failed largely because the treaties did not take into account the rapidly changing political and economic conditions of major powers in the international arena. During the mid-1930s Japan was experiencing substantive economic and technological growth relative to Britain and the United States and the naval treaty's ratio of 5:5:3 'inevitably presented itself to many Japanese as the symbol of an inferior position in the international community that no longer corresponded to realities.'[12] The naval arms limitation treaties thus became a source of intense hostility and conflict in the international system in the 1930s. The rising great power, Japan, felt discriminated against while the status quo states believed that the legitimacy of their superiority was legalized through the treaties, and that Japan was infringing upon an accepted international treaty of great importance. Military leaders in Japan used the naval treaties to gain legitimacy for their aggressive policies *vis-à-vis* China and the Western Allies.

Similar to the Japanese sense of grievance against the naval treaties of the 1930s, a future rising power could feel the effects of the NPT as a negative, discriminatory instrument meant to curtail its ambitions and could make serious efforts to undermine it. Believing that the Treaty is a legitimate international instrument, the status quo states would oppose such efforts, causing hawks to emerge internally in the rising states. The NPT, supposedly meant for maintaining international peace, could become a source of conflict in the international system. This is the systemic consequence of maintaining a highly unequal and discriminatory treaty.

Most international relations theories of change point to the futility of attempts to permanently legalize the monopoly rights or superiority of some states over others. Changes in the power capabilities of the actors who engineered the creation of a regime could undermine its maintenance. Realists argue that regimes can decline when 'either the balance of bargaining power or the perception of national interest (or both together) change among those states who negotiate them.'[13] This is particularly relevant in the non-proliferation realm. To structural realists especially, the demise of the bipolar system has profound implications for nuclear proliferation. With the end of bipolarity, superpower guarantees which have been the most effective instrument to moderate the effects of systemic anarchy will be reduced and weakened and, as a result, the international system is likely to 'revert to a more unvarnished form of anarchy in which systemic attributes such as security dilemma and self-help will be accentuated. The accelerated proliferation of weapons of mass destruction will be an early and noticeable consequence of this change.'[14] According to this perspective, erstwhile partners in alliances in extended deterrence could arm themselves as the demise of the central threat is likely to weaken the solidarity of the alliance system and the protective umbrella that the superpowers, especially the US, had provided.

Although this structural realist account may be plausible, it is critical to examine when and how erstwhile alliance partners may opt for nuclear weapons. What role does the regime play in reducing the security of the allies? Under what conditions would the NPT and the non-proliferation regime falter? Although regime legitimacy could be eroded if a number of smaller adherents defect, to me, the most crucial challenges to the regime would come from the emergence of new great powers such as India, and the re-militarization of defeated states such as Japan. To a lesser extent the challenge could also come from regional actors in protracted conflict zones who are also signatories of the NPT, such as Iraq, Iran, and North Korea, who desire to maintain their independence and status in the international arena through the possession of national nuclear weapons capabilities.

3   POWER TRANSITIONS

Theorists on change posit that the international system witnesses periodic changes in power distributions caused by differential growth rates in economic and military capacities of states. Power transition and power cycle theorists contend that new challengers to the established status quo states arise at some regular intervals. Although the preponderance of the status quo power could prevent wars, challengers would arise due to changes in their internal economic and political conditions.[15] The dominant power transition theorist, Organski, argues that the changes in economic productivity and the capacity and the efficiency of a political system to extract and aggregate human and material resources for national purposes result in conflict outcomes in the long run. The differential growth rate allows a growing nation to reach almost parity with the system leader. At this time, it may feel dissatisfied with the system rules that do not allow it to obtain a leadership role. In order to hasten its passage, the challenger is likely to engage in a war.[16] Although Organski's model has been criticized for its limited number of historical cases, it is a generally accepted theoretical position that dissatisfied states could militarily challenge an existing international order as Germany and Japan did in the 1940s.

Other historical-structural theorists also maintain that major power actors change over time. Diplomatic historian Paul Kennedy believes in the inevitability of the rise and fall of great powers.[17] He shows that although relative decline takes place often as a result of war, it happens during peacetime as well. This occurs largely because of uneven rate of economic growth among different countries and the technological and organizational breakthroughs that bring higher advantages to some *vis-à-vis* others. Great powers could also decline in peacetime if they spend a large portion of their economic resources for military purposes and overextend themselves strategically beyond their original capacity and means. The five hundred year span of historical record that Kennedy covers provides a number of examples of the rise and fall of empires – Spain, the Netherlands, France and Britain.[18] Kennedy had also predicted the relative decline of the US, but its main opponent the USSR declined more rapidly. Although the US has re-adapted to the systemic changes of the 1990s fairly well, its own relative decline in the longrun is still a possibility.

Robert Gilpin argues that the differential growth in the capabilities of various states in the international system results in redistribution of power, followed by war and an eventual change in the system itself. States tend to expand their interests corresponding to the growth in their relative power positions. To Gilpin, social and political arrangements of a given period tend to reflect the interests of the most powerful members of the international system.

> Over time, however, the interests of individual actors and the balance of power among the actors do change as a result of economic, technological, and other developments. As a consequence, those actors who benefit most from a change in the social system and who gain the power to effect such change will seek to alter the system in ways that favor their interests.[19]

Similarly, long cycle theorists have argued that, although the long cycle process determines who will be the leading state controlling global affairs, in the long run, that power will decline. This will happen as rivals begin to challenge the authority of the world power as it starts to lose its monopoly over power resources that allowed its preponderance. 'Initially unipolar concentration of resources gives way to multipolarity, and the rivalries among the global powers increasingly take on the characteristics of oligopolistic competition.'[20] Modelski's historical–structural analysis posits that since 1,500 AD, four states played dominant roles in the management of global affairs, Portugal, the Netherlands, Britain and the US. In a somewhat regular and well-spaced out pattern, three of these world powers had been succeeded by another world power similar to the 'long-term succession of political regimes in a political system lacking regularized elections.'[21]

Structural realists like Waltz contend that the international system has begun to see such a transition in the aftermath of the end of the Cold War. To him, the increased international activity of Japan and Germany in the 1990s represents the changing structure of international politics. When a country's economic capabilities increase to the great power level, it places itself at the centre of regional and global affairs, and if it does not possess the capabilities of a great power it may become vulnerable to other states that possess them.[22] Waltz further argues: 'For a country to choose not to become a great power is a structural anomaly. For that reason, the choice is a difficult one to sustain. Sooner or later, usually sooner, the international status of countries has risen in step with their material resources. Countries with great power economies have become great powers, whether or not reluctantly.'[23]

These systemic factors have been disregarded or denied in the present efforts to maintain US dominance in the security realm and the decision to extend the NPT in perpetuity. Christopher Lane contends that the US efforts to keep its unipolar position as long as possible by 'persuading Japan and Germany that they are better off remaining within the orbit of an American security and economic system than they would be if they become great powers' will not last long. He believes that the 'unipolar moment' is a 'geopolitical interlude that will give way to multipolarity between 2000–2010.' Eligible states are under tremendous pressure to acquire military and economic capabilities, for 'if they do not acquire great power capabilities, they may be exploited by the hegemon.'[24] Other analysts, such as Avery Goldstein, argue that the reluctance of Germany and Japan to acquire nuclear weapons stems from the restrictions imposed by the victors of World War II as well as from domestic political constraints, reflecting sensitivity to the lessons of the war. In addition, the US security guarantees have reduced the incentives for these states to go nuclear. However, 'as the legacy of World War II fades, and as familiar doubts about the compatibility of allied interests develop, one should expect a wider array of alternatives to be considered. Over time, the incentive to field an independent nuclear deterrent is likely to rise.'[25]

The current nuclear non-proliferation regime was established in the 1960s with the presumption that these changes will not occur at least in the near future. But major systemic changes did occur within two decades of the establishment of the regime. The system was transformed dramatically in the early 1990s when the Soviet Union collapsed and thereby lost its superpower status. Its fragmentation also resulted in the dispersion of nuclear weapons to three additional independent states. Although the regime, due largely to the initiatives of the US and Russia, managed to get the three Soviet successor states to accept the NPT and declare themselves as non-nuclear weapons states, it has little room to adjust to such major alterations in the system. A fragmented Russian state can still hold on to nuclear weapons and claim great power status for itself. A declining great power does not have to bow out of the great power contest gracefully or to transform itself into a non-nuclear state.[26]

The international system has begun to show changes in the power capabilities of leading actors. Going by a leading structural indicator of great power status – GNP as percentage of world gross product – the power positions of Russia, England and France have declined relative to Germany and Japan. Other states such as India, despite serious inequities in the division of their internal wealth and problems of national integration, are likely to emerge in the future as great powers with several attributes of a leading actor.[27] Yet, the NPT would retain the nuclear status of Russia, England and France but would not grant that status to Japan, Germany or India.

If these three states emerge as the next great powers, how will the Treaty prevent them from becoming full-fledged nuclear states? India possesses nuclear weapons capability as evident in its 1974 nuclear explosion while Japan has the latent capability to build nuclear weapons and may be experiencing some pressures to do so. Among these states, only Germany remains at the moment fully committed to the regime although Japan officially behaves as a regime supporter. However, the German commitment is contingent on how the European security system would emerge in the next decade or so. If the US presence in Europe declines, while the Russian threat resurfaces, and if there is still a reliance on nuclear weapons for European security, Germany could acquire nuclear weapons.[28]

More than Germany, Japan is likely to emerge as the major challenger to the NPT regime if its security environment worsens. Although Tokyo signed the Treaty in 1970, it delayed the ratification until 1976, mainly due to domestic debates about the 'unequal international order recognized and sanctioned by the Treaty in exchange for the benefits to be derived from enhanced regional security and the greater opportunities for expanding nuclear power as a source of energy.'[29] Japan questioned the need for extension of the Treaty in perpetuity prior to changing its position on this issue. During the 1993 Tokyo summit of the seven leading industrial nations, Japan expressed opposition to an unconditional extension of the NPT. While the then Prime Minister Morihiro Hosakawa sounded more positive about the extension and an 'ultimate abolition of nuclear weapons', three members of the seven party coalition expressed opposition to an indefinite extension of the Treaty.[30]

The opposition to NPT was followed by reports that Japan had acquired all the components necessary for a nuclear weapons programme as North Korea refused to stop its nuclear and missile programmes.[31] In February 1994, Japan also launched its first large rocket, built solely with its own technology, a capability necessary for an ICBM or IRBM programme in the future.[32] In the end, Japan supported the extension of the Treaty due largely to concerns about its relations with Southeast Asia and the US. In some sense, the NPT provides a cover for Japan not to acquire nuclear weapons. In the short run, the cost of breaking the NPT would be higher than the benefits that it would gain from it. But these short term constraints may disappear as the world enters the next century.

Waltz predicts that population, national product, institutions and behaviour strongly suggest that Japan will be next in line for great power status.[33] It is possible that even if Japan accepts the NPT's extension, it may pursue an 'opaque' or 'bomb in the basement' strategy if the security situation in East Asia erodes or if the relations with the US deteriorate over trade issues.[34] The current system leaders would oppose Japan violating the Treaty, and at that point it will have to withdraw from it or pursue an opaque strategy.

Japan faces several systemic and sub-systemic challenges in the decades ahead. At the systemic level, Japan's trade frictions, and continuing threats from Washington to impose sanctions against Tokyo and a possible trade war, could considerably weaken the political and security relationship between these two states. Under such conditions, Japan's reliance on the US for its security, especially through the nuclear umbrella, would decline.[35] Japan will then have to assume more responsibility for its protection. If nuclear weapons continue to be the leading source of security in the great power system, Japan may pursue the nuclear path. The second challenge for Japan in this respect comes from regional actors like China, North Korea and South Korea. China's expansion of military strength, especially naval power in the Pacific, would put pressures on Japan to develop countervailing forces. The escalation of China–Taiwan conflict could also put pressures on Japan to acquire more defensive and deterrent capabilities. More than anything else, the North Korean acquisition of nuclear weapons could place the Japanese leaders under tremendous strain and an opportunity to discard their nuclear opposition.[36]

Some analysts have also speculated that the increasing political and economic clout of Germany could also put pressure on Bonn to acquire nuclear weapons, especially if the US withdraws its security commitment to Europe. 'Given that Germany would have greater economic strength than Britain or France, it might therefore, seek nuclear weapons to raise its military status to a level commensurate with its economic status.'[37] However, the re-militarization of Germany seems a somewhat remote contingency in the short and medium terms.[38] There are major institutional and political constraints in this regard. The most significant one is institutional. The European integration has already provided Germany the necessary key role of a great power and security *vis-à-vis* most of its erstwhile enemies. Its reunification has further strengthened its bargaining power *vis-à-vis* UK and France. The most crucial change, though, is the removal of the Soviet threat and the democratization of Eastern Europe. The Russian threat to Germany is remote as it is buffered not only by Eastern Europe but by several new post-Soviet states. The unilateral German nuclear acquisition, not as part of a NATO programme, could undermine the German position *vis-à-vis* its European neighbours. Opposition could be strong, especially from Russia and Germany's neighbours who were victims of German aggressions in the past.

However, the fact that no similar institutional constraints exist in East Asia makes Japan a more likely candidate for nuclear acquisition in the mediumterm. While only Germany has a remote chance of Russia still emerging as a major nuclear threat, Japan has already two existing nuclear weapon states – China and Russia – as potential enemies and, maybe, in the long run the US as well. In addition, Germany does not confront a regional nuclear challenge as Japan faces with respect to North Korea. Germany's trade conflict with the US is not so significant as that of Japan as the US has not shown a similar assertiveness in trade *vis-à-vis* Germany. These disincentives could change if the pace of institution-building in Europe slows down and nationalism resurfaces again. The continued nuclear modernization of France and Britain could also pressure Germany to rethink its nuclear status in the longer term.

A third potential system challenger is India which has been a leading opponent of the NPT ever since it came into being in 1968. The Indian opposition is largely a result of its belief that the Treaty discriminates against non-nuclear states while allowing no control over vertical proliferation among nuclear weapon states.[39] But behind the Indian opposition lies a larger concern driven by systemic factors. It can be argued that the Indian aversion to the NPT stems largely from its fear that, by signing the Treaty, a major constraint would be imposed on India from achieving great power status.[40] Indian leaders of different political persuasions have viewed that their country has the potential – population, continental size, economic and military resources – to become a major power in the 21st century international system.[41] India challenged the NPT by conducting a nuclear test in 1974 although it did not continue with further tests.

The emergence of these three actors as full-fledged nuclear weapon states may occur not only due to systemic changes, but due to the behaviour of their smaller regional adversaries. When smaller regional states like Pakistan or North Korea acquire nuclear weapons, they nullify somewhat the military and economic advantages of their bigger neighbouring states.[42] In such conditions, the regional power could have a major incentive to acquire nuclear weapons primarily to deter their smaller adversaries. Such acquisitions would have wider systemic implications than merely in the immediate regional context. When a leading actor acquires nuclear weapons, it will not be perceived as a simple effort to deter its regional adversary but as part of the effort to carve out a larger systemic role for itself.

4   AVERTING COLLAPSE OF THE NON-PROLIFERATION REGIME

The likelihood of the aforementioned long-run changes occurring may be controlled or in some cases precluded if existing nuclear powers undertake major changes in the governance of international affairs in general and the perceived utility of nuclear weapons in particular. Although I concur with realists that system change could result in the rise of new challengers, I disagree with the argument that new nuclear powers are bound to emerge and that strategies to avert such an occurrence are futile. In the first place, challengers in the past arose to a certain extent because they were excluded from the benefits of the international order. From the challenger's perspective, a small number of status quo states divided up the advantages of the existing system. The perceived injustice caused to a certain extent the militarization of challengers and the outbreak of wars.

The major change that occurred in the post-war international order has been the inclusion of the key actors in international governance in one sphere or other. Despite the intensity of the Cold War, the challenging great power, the USSR, played a significant role in the UN and in the arms control process, receiving a higher profile in the management of international affairs than previous revisionist great powers such as Germany and Japan were able to achieve. Likewise, although Germany and Japan were not key participants in the security realm, they could compensate for that deficiency by gaining a major share in the international economy and playing a leading role in the management of international economic affairs. They also had important roles in the security management of Europe and Asia respectively as key allies of the US. This situation worked well during the Cold War when the US provided them with security guarantees in the form of a nuclear umbrella.

The end of the Cold War has changed the way security threats are perceived by the leading actors. Global governance is now conducted largely by the US through the UN Security Council which does not include Germany and Japan, and emerging powers like India and Brazil. From a systemic perspective, therefore, it is imperative that these states are given permanent seats in the UN Security Council as a way to co-opt them as states that want to preserve the existing international order rather than challenge it. Their non-nuclear or unacknowledged nuclear status should not stand in the way of their playing a larger constructive role in the international arena.

A welcome consequence of this change would be the delinking of nuclear status and permanent membership in the Security Council. Thus non-nuclear Germany and Japan and an undeclared nuclear state like India could be embraced as key actors without the nuclear factor providing them with any additional status. The continued non-use of nuclear weapons, the conclusion of the CTBT, and the drastic reductions in US–Russian nuclear arsenals could further depreciate nuclear weapons as a power currency in international politics. Emerging great powers would then view possession of nuclear weapons not as a necessary ingredient in obtaining or maintaining their power status. Additionally, their security should be maintained through assured guarantees by other states through both military and institutional means.

5   CONCLUSIONS

The main conclusion of this chapter is that, although imperfect in several respects, the NPT and the non-proliferation regime are likely to continue to exist in the short and medium terms due to the interests of leading actors and smaller states in its preservation. It is a considerable fortune for the Treaty's supporters that all the major powers of the post-war period acquired nuclear weapons before it came into force in 1970. This allowed these states to cooperate in the nuclear realm even when their Cold War rivalries continued. Although two nuclear states – China and France – refused to join the NPT initially, they mounted no active opposition to it. In fact, France behaved almost like an NPT signatory state, and in 1991 it joined the NPT as a nuclear weapon state. In the initial post-Cold War era also the distribution of power in terms of nuclear capacity remained somewhat similar, except that the security environment of three or four emerging major states has changed to a certain extent. Two of them, Germany and Japan, have been within an alliance relationship with the US and their future nuclear behaviour will depend considerably on the continuation of this alliance. The remaining great power candidate, India, opposes the Treaty because it closes the door for India to join the great power club. The Indian test in 1974 was one of the most direct challenges to the Treaty and the regime to date.

The semi-unipolar structure of the international system and the somewhat effective operation of the NPT and the regime will prevent serious challengers from emerging in the short run. In the long run, however, the regime may be challenged as new great powers are likely to emerge in the system with different security concerns. Although non-discrimination is not always necessary for a regime to survive, discrimination against leading actors and potential great powers could hurt the regime in the long run. Some middle ranking actors with serious security challenges may opt for nuclear weapons if they perceive that these weapons provide them with effective deterrent. Regional rivalries constitute the main reasons for their nuclear acquisition but any new acquisition will have an adverse impact on the Treaty and the regime. Neighbouring states will be pressured to acquire countervailing capabilities. Rising major powers in their vicinity would then have a greater incentive to obtain nuclear weapons. The present NWS also would want to maintain their capabilities as insurance against new nuclear challengers as well. All these imply the medium-term persistence of an imperfect regime.

The permanent extension of the NPT, without parallel reforms in international governance by way of inclusion of all major powers in it, may not guarantee that the Treaty will survive in the long run. A major danger of the extension of the NPT in perpetuity is that it has frozen the nuclear status of the present five while disallowing future great powers from acquiring these weapons. The rising great powers would then clandestinely pursue nuclear weapons programmes if they view that the possession of such weapons is essential for their security and status in the international power hierarchy and an effective deterrent against potential attacks by other major powers and minor powers. If one or more powerful state pursues the opaque route, it would effectively scuttle the legitimacy, effectiveness and credibility of the regime. In this sense, a powerful state's pursuit of opaque nuclear capability has wider systemic implications than that of a smaller states. A way thus has to be found for the regime to incorporate future great powers in its purview and thereby adapt to changing systemic and structural conditions. If an effective way is not found, the regime could face the fate of the pre-World War II naval arms control treaties. Violations by the rising challenger, Japan, not only destroyed the treaties but also caused considerable tension in the international system during the 1930s.

NOTES

1. Brazil has signed and ratified the Tlateloco Treaty that forbids nuclear weapons in Latin America, agreed to full-scope IAEA safeguards on all its nuclear facilities in addition to inspections by the Argentine–Brazilian bilat- eral accounting and control system and the administrative machinery called ABACC. For these policy changes, see John R. Redick, 'Nuclear Illusions: Argentina and Brazil', *Occasional Paper* 25 (Washington, DC: The Henry L. Stimson Center, December 1995).

2. This condition is gradually emerging as the depreciation of nuclear weapons as a source of power has accelerated with the end of the Cold War. The prominence that non-nuclear Germany and Japan hold in the international arena also suggests that nuclear possession may not be necessary to acquire major power status. For a discussion of these themes, see T.V. Paul, 'The Paradox of Power: Nuclear Weapons in a Changed World', *Alternatives*, 20(4), November 1995:479–500.

3. Joseph S. Nye, 'US–Soviet Cooperation in a Non-proliferation Regime', in Alexander L. George, Philip J. Farley, and Alexander Dallin, eds, *US–Soviet Security Cooperation: Achievements, Failures, Lessons* (New York: Oxford University Press, 1988), p. 342. See also William C. Potter, 'Nuclear Proliferation: US–Soviet Cooperation', *Washington Quarterly*, 8(4), Winter 1985:141–54.

4. Copy of the Treaty is reprinted in *Status of Multilateral Arms Regulation and Disarmament Agreements*, 4th edn (New York: United Nations, 1992), pp. 110–16.

5. *SIPRI Year Book 1991: World Armaments and Disarmament* (Oxford: Oxford University Press, 1991) p. 25.

6. For the NPT extension conference, see Berhanykun Andemicael, Merle Opelz and Jan Priest, 'Measure for Measure: The NPT and the Road Ahead', *IAEA Bulletin*, 37(3), September 1995:30–8; *New York Times*, May 12, 1995:A1&A10.

7. According to Waltz, great power status is achieved when states are ranked high on the following criteria: size of population and territory, resource endowment, economic capability, military strength, political stability and competence. Kenneth N. Waltz, 'The Emerging Structure of International Politics', *International Security*, 18(2), Fall 1993:44–79.

8. These efforts are somewhat comparable with the attempts by dominant social classes to limit the accessibility of a new weapon to lower classes. For example, in 15th and 16th century Europe, the knightly class and the ecclesiastics supported a ban on siege weapons in order to control the behaviour of mercenaries. For a comparison of these attempts and the

72 *The Nuclear Non-Proliferation Regime*

contemporary efforts by the nuclear states to deny the nuclear capability to lower-ranking states, see James Turner Johnson, *Can Modern War be Just?* (New Haven and London: Yale University Press, 1984), p. 90.

9. Charles S. Fairbanks, 'The Washington Naval Treaty, 1922–1936', in Robert J. Art and Kenneth N. Waltz, eds, *The Use of Force*, 2nd edn (Lanham: University Press of America, 1983), p. 473.

10. Stephen E. Pelz, *Race to Pearl Harbor* (Cambridge: Harvard University Press, 1974), p. 1.

11. Pelz, *Race to Pearl Harbor*, p. 14. See also, T.V. Paul, *Asymmetric Conflicts: War Initiation by Weaker Powers* (Cambridge: Cambridge University Press, 1994), pp. 78–9; Emily O. Goldman, *Sunken Treaties: Naval Arms Control between the Wars* (University Park, Pa: The Pennsylvania State University Press, 1994).

12. Fairbanks, 'The Washington Naval Treaty, 1922–1936', pp. 473–7.

13. Susan Strange, '*Cave! Hic Dragones*: A Critique of Regime Analysis', in Krasner, ed., *International Regimes* (Ithaca: Cornell University Press, 1983), pp. 337–54.

14. Benjamin Frankel, 'The Brooding Shadow: Systemic Incentives and Nuclear Weapons Proliferation', *Security Studies*, 2 (3/4), Spring/Summer 1993:37–78.

15. For the power transition theory, see A.F.K. Organski, *World Politics*, 2nd. edn (New York: Alfred A. Knopf, 1968), ch.14; Organski and J. Kugler, *The War Ledger* (Chicago: Chicago University Press, 1980).

16. Organski, *World Politics*, pp. 19–28.

17. See Paul Kennedy, *The Rise and Fall of the Great Powers: Economic Change and Military Conflict from 1500 to 2000* (New York: Random House, 1988).

18. *Ibid*, p. xvi.

19. Robert Gilpin, *War and Change in World Politics* (Cambridge: Cambridge University Press, 1981), pp. 9 & 86.

20. William R. Thompson, *On Global War: Historical–Structural Approaches to World Politics* (Columbia: University of South Carolina Press, 1988), p. 50. For long cycle approaches, see George Modelski, *Long Cycles in World Politics* (Seattle: University of Washington Press, 1987); Joshua S. Goldstein, *Long Cycles: Prosperity and War in the Modern Age* (New Haven and London: Yale University Press, 1988); Charles F. Doran and Wes Parsons, 'War and the Cycle of Relative Power', *American Political Science Review*, 74, December 1980: 947–65.

21. George Modelski, 'The Long Cycle of Global Politics and the Nation State', *Comparative Studies in Society and History*, 20(2), April 1978:214–35.

22. Waltz, 'The Emerging Structure...', 64.

23. *Ibid.*, 66.

24. Due to differential growth rates among leading actors, the relative power of Japan and Germany has increased dramatically, placing them as eligible states to great power status. 'As their stakes in the international system deepen, so will their ambitions and interests. Security considerations will cause Japan and Germany to emulate the US and acquire the full spectrum of great power capabilities including nuclear weapons.' Christopher Lane, 'The Unipolar Illusion', *International Security*, 17(4), Spring 1993:5–51.

25. Avery Goldstein, 'Robust and Affordable Security: Some Lessons from the Second-Ranking Powers During the Cold War', *Journal of Strategic Studies*, 15(4), December 1992:475–527.

26. It could be argued that for a declining great power actor nuclear possession provides an insurance against unwanted infringements by other states. In political terms, however, this means that the imbalances in nuclear possession will continue irrespective of major changes in the distribution of power in the international system.

27. It is assumed that, in the Indian case, the pace of economic reforms and the push for expanding the Indian share of total global trade would enhance considerably its possibility for becoming a great power in the first two decades of next century. For an earlier analysis of India's power potential, see Baldev Raj Nayar, 'Treat India Seriously', *Foreign Policy*, 18, Spring 1975:133–54; John W. Mellor, ed., *India: A Rising Middle Power* (Boulder, Colo: Westview Press, 1979).

28. Germany took five years to ratify the NPT in 1975. The German opposition to the Treaty partly sprang from the political leadership's aversion to legitimizing permanently the power distribution in the international system. Opponents of the Treaty argued that the NPT would place the five nuclear weapon states at a higher pedestal in international relations and the 'oligopoly of the nuclear five will submit to no corresponding restrictions, will lock in their present superiority and will be increasingly able to make life and death decisions regarding all other states.' Catherine M. Kelleher, 'The Issue of German Nuclear Armament', *Proceedings of the Academy of Political Science*, 29(2), 1968:95–107. German politicians of all persuasions opposed the Treaty in the early stages of its conclusion. Chancellor Konrad Adenauer described it as a 'Morgenthau Plan', while Defence Minister Franz Josef Strauss considered it as a 'new Versailles of cosmic dimensions'. Even Chancellor Helmut Schmidt regarded the NPT as 'questionable even if it was desirable.' Mathias Kuntzel, *Bonn & the Bomb* (London, Pluto Press, 1995), p. xvi.

29. Ryukichi Imai, 'The NPT and Nuclear Proliferation in East Asia: Views toward the 1990s', in J. Pilat and R. Pendleyl, *Beyond 1995: The Future of the NPT Regime* (New York, Plenum Press, 1990), pp. 107–16.

30. Charles Smith, 'Unclear Signals: Nuclear Weapons Policy Shrouded in Ambiguities', *Far Eastern Economic Review*, 30 September 1993:24.

31. These reports were based on a British Ministry of Defence Intelligence communication to Prime Minister John Major. Japan, however, subsequently denied them. See *Sunday Times*, London: January 30, 1994:1& 15.

32. Andrew Pollack, 'Japan Launches Rocket, Cutting Reliance on US', *New York Times*, February 4, 1994:A17.

33. Waltz, 'The Emerging Structure...', 55.

34. The characteristics of nuclear opacity include: no nuclear tests, denial of possession, absence of direct nuclear threats, absence of open military doctrine, no open deployment, no open debate, and the insulation of nuclear weapons activities from foreign and defence policy domains. Avner Cohen and Benjamin Frankel, 'Opaque Nuclear Proliferation', *Journal of Strategic Studies*, 13(3), 1990:14–44.

35. 'Economic competition is often as keen as military competition, and since nuclear weapons limit the use of force among great powers at the strategic

level, we may expect economic and technological competition among them to become more intense.' Waltz, 'The Emerging Structure...', 59. On the relevance of US security guarantee for Japan's continued nuclear abstinence, see William Overholt, 'Nuclear Proliferation in Eastern Asia', in Overholt, ed., *Asia's Nuclear Future* (Boulder, Colo: Westview Press, 1977), pp. 133–59. On the US–Japanese economic competition, especially in foreign direct investments and trade, see Dennis J. Encarnation, *Rivals beyond Trade: America versus Japan in Global Competition* (Ithaca: Cornell University Press, 1992).

36. On the North Korean nuclear programme, see Paul Bracken, 'Nuclear Weapons and State Survival in North Korea', *Survival*, 35(3), Autumn 1993: 137–53; Andrew Mack, 'North Korea and the Bomb', *Foreign Policy*, 83, Summer 1991: 87–104. It is, however, possible that North Korea's full compliance with the NPT can be achieved, especially if reunification of the Koreas takes place peacefully, following the collapse of the communist regime.

37. John J. Mearsheimer, 'Back to the Future: Instability in Europe after the Cold War,' *International Security*, 15(1), Summer 1990:5–56. On differing perspectives on Germany's foreign policy in the post-Cold War era, see Paul B. Stares, ed., *The New Germany and the New Europe* (Washington, DC, The Brookings Institution, 1992); Gregory F. Treverton, *America, Germany, and the Future of Europe* (Princeton: Princeton University Press, 1992).

38. According to one analyst, the German elite and the public have internalized Germany's multilateral role within Europe, and the lessons of history are firmly embedded in the normative context of foreign policymaking and in the institutional decisionmaking structure of the country. These factors are likely to have an enduring effect on Germany's nuclear options. Cathleen D. Fisher, *Correspondence with the Author*, June 7, 1994.

39. The Indian opposition springs from a belief that adherence to the Treaty would obstruct India's political and strategic independence and economic and technological development. T.V. Paul, *Reaching for the Bomb: The Indo-Pak Nuclear Scenario* (New Delhi: Dialogue Publications, 1984), p. 24. See also, T.T. Poulose, ed., *Perspectives of India's Nuclear Policy*, (New Delhi: Young Asia Publications, 1978); Ashok Kapur, *India's Nuclear Option: Atomic Diplomacy and Decision Making* (New York: Praeger, 1976).

40. For the Indian position on the NPT, see Raju G.C. Thomas, 'India and the NPT after the Cold War', in Pilat and Pendley, eds, *Beyond 1995*, 133–50; K. Subrahmanyam, 'India: Keeping the Option Open', in Robert M. Lawrence and Joel Larus, eds, *Nuclear Proliferation Phase II* (Lawrence: University Press of Kansas, 1974).

41. An important Indian politician in the 1970s, Krishan Kant asked rhetorically: 'Should India Place Itself in the Position of Pakistan, Bangladesh and Indonesia and Determine its Role?', *IDSA Journal*, 14(3), January–March 1982:307–28.

42. Some such states are signatories to the NPT. When states such as North Korea, Iraq, and Iran pursue nuclear weapons programmes clandestinely they are undermining the credibility of the regime and its safeguards system. The ineffectiveness of the regime to prevent these states' nuclear buildup could add further incentives to rising great powers to develop their own countervailing systems.

5 The Causes of Nuclear Proliferation and the Utility of the Non-proliferation Regime

Bradley A. Thayer

Many scholars and policymakers have focused their attention on the nuclear Non-Proliferation Treaty (NPT) Extension and Review Conference which was held in New York City in April and May, 1995.[1] Most of the debate about the NPT review conference centred on two questions. First, will the NPT be extended in perpetuity, as the United States and the other nuclear weapon states (NWS) want, or will it be renewed for a fixed period, or periods, of time, as many non-nuclear weapon states (NNWS) desire?[2] Second, what is the price that the US will have to pay for the renewal, either in perpetuity or for a fixed time, of the Treaty. There was concern that the price would include consenting to a complete ban on nuclear testing, which might be codified in a Comprehensive Test Ban Treaty (CTBT);[3] agreeing to a complete cut-off of the production of fissile materials; or making further reductions in the strategic nuclear arsenal of the United States. In addition, there was apprehension that the United States would face demands from many of the NNWS to pressure Israel to surrender its nuclear capability, at a maximum, or at least to require Israel to cap its production of fissile material.[4] The result of the Extension and Review Conference was what the US wanted: the NPT was extended in perpetuity.[5]

Despite the importance of these questions for policymakers and scholars, three more fundamental questions ought to be addressed as well because they serve as the theoretical foundation for the issues that were addressed at the NPT Review Conference. The first question is, do the NPT specifically, and the nuclear non-proliferation regime generally, accomplish their intentions; that is, do the NPT and the non-proliferation regime stop or mitigate nuclear proliferation?[6] The second question is what value or benefit does the nuclear non-proliferation regime provide the

75

United States, for example, does it further the interests of the United States; and the international system, does it promote international stability – the absence of major wars and crises. I will also address a third question, what are the costs of the nuclear non-proliferation regime to the United States and to the international system.[7]

My intention is to address these questions. In answering the first question, I will argue that the NPT and the nuclear non-proliferation regime fail in their primary goal, they cannot stop nuclear proliferation for states that are determined to acquire nuclear weapons. This is because the cause of nuclear proliferation is the insecurity of states and the regime does nothing to address this insecurity. It attempts to stop nuclear proliferation through supply-side measures, by preventing the transfer of nuclear technology to non-nuclear states. As a result, the regime does increase the costs that a state must incur to become a nuclear state, although the cost is not necessarily a prohibitive one.

With respect to the second question, the nuclear non-proliferation regime does benefit the security interests of the United States because it complicates the process of acquiring nuclear capabilities. Continued nuclear proliferation is not in the interests of the US for four reasons. First, nuclear proliferation increases the risk that nuclear weapons may be used against the United States itself or against US allies. Secondly, nuclear proliferation jeopardizes the ability of the United States to project power into regions where there are nuclear powers, e.g. the Gulf, if Iraq's and Iran's nuclear programmes were to come to fruition; or to South Korea, if North Korea's nuclear programme is not halted and its nuclear weapons destroyed.[8] The maintenance and growth of North Korea's nascent arsenal poses great problems for the United States due to the possibility of a nuclear attack against South Korea, Japan, or even the United States.[9] Thirdly, nuclear proliferation increases the risks of starting a chain of proliferation as other adversaries strive to duplicate the capabilities of the original nuclear state, as Japan may presently be considering the acquisition of nuclear weapons in order to match proliferation by North Korea.[10] Fourthly, nuclear proliferation increases the risks of nuclear inadvertence, that is, the possibility that nuclear weapons may be used accidentally, without authorization, or by third parties, such as terrorists.[11]

The nuclear non-proliferation regime has positive effects on the international system as well because it makes nuclear proliferation harder. By increasing the costs of nuclear proliferation, fewer states will acquire nuclear weapons and therefore, in general, the risk of nuclear war will be reduced. Concerning the third question, the nuclear non-proliferation regime is beneficial to the United States and all established nuclear powers because it makes proliferation more difficult. The regime is therefore worth its principal costs, the requirements of Article IV and Article V of the NPT to provide information, materials, and technology for the peaceful use of nuclear energy to the non-nuclear signatories; and, under Article VI of the Treaty, to pursue nuclear disarmament.[12]

However, the principal deleterious effect of the non-proliferation regime is found in its harm to the international system. The regime may not promote international stability because it requires states to proliferate opaquely, that is, to hide their proliferation from other states. Opaque proliferation has seven characteristics: first, there are no nuclear weapons tests by the state; second, the possession of nuclear weapons is denied by the state; third, the state makes no explicit nuclear threats; fourth, it has no declared nuclear doctrine; fifth, there is no open military deployment of nuclear weapons by the state although it may deploy nuclear weapons covertly; sixth, there is no public debate, either amongst the people or the élite, concerning the development of nuclear weapons and the strategic posture adopted by the state; and seventh, the nuclear programme is insulated as an organization from the foreign policy and defence organizations.[13] The nuclear programme may be labelled as a research and development programme to avoid hostile scrutiny by domestic critics. Opaque proliferation entails substantial risks for the state, and for other states as well, because opaque proliferation may incur a greater risk of nuclear war through a failure of deterrence or through nuclear inadvertence, than does visible proliferation. Therefore, the promotion of opaque nuclear proliferation may be a malign effect of the regime because opaque proliferation can be damaging to international stability.

Before I address these questions in detail, it is necessary to determine why states acquire nuclear weapons. Once we know the answer to this question, then it is possible to determine if the NPT and the nuclear non-proliferation regime can be effective in stopping states from acquiring nuclear weapons; the value of the regime to the United States and to the international system; and if the value is worth the costs of the regime.

1   THE CAUSES OF NUCLEAR PROLIFERATION

There are four competing theories concerning the causes of nuclear proliferation. The first is prestige: states acquire nuclear weapons for grandeur and stature. The second is bureaucratic politics: individuals or bureaucracies foist proliferation upon the state in order to increase their own power. The third explanation of nuclear proliferation is technological pull: there is a technological imperative that causes states to develop nuclear weapons. The fourth is that states acquire nuclear weapons to increase their security. In this section I briefly will explain the logic behind each theory and describe the principal flaws of the first three explanations. I conclude that the principal cause of nuclear proliferation is the desire of states to gain increased security from external attack in an anarchic world. The other theories are complementary explanations of proliferation. They are useful for explaining why nuclear proliferation occurred in the manner that it did in each state; but none of the complementary theories, solely or in combination, is sufficient to explain why states acquire nuclear weapons.

Prestige as a Cause of Nuclear Proliferation

The argument that nuclear proliferation is caused by prestige is based on the perception that all great powers must have nuclear weapons.[14] This perception has been vocalized by many political leaders who have a unique conception about the place of their country in the world. One of the most famous political leaders to evince this perception is Charles de Gaulle, who argued that France, in order to be a great power, must develop nuclear weapons.[15] De Gaulle repeatedly emphasized the importance of nuclear weapons for France: 'no country without an atom bomb could consider itself properly independent' and, moreover, 'A great state that does not possess [nuclear weapons], while others have them, does not command its own destiny.'[16] The development of nuclear weapons by France provided the capability and the legitimation for de Gaulle to act in his own perception as an independent actor, a 'third force', independent from the United States and the Soviet Union.[17]

Other Gaullists voiced similar sentiments. Prime Minister Michel Debré asserted that acquiring nuclear weapons was a prerequisite for achieving national objectives, 'including "all influence in international life"'.[18]

In Great Britain, the argument that British prestige required nuclear proliferation was made as well. 'That Britain should cease to play a leading role in international affairs was unthinkable, not only among the country's political leaders but among her people as well, for the nation had long been instinct with a sense of power. Failure to accept the challenge of atomic energy would have been interpreted as a retreat from greatness, an abandonment of power.'[19]

McGeorge Bundy reinforces these arguments with his claim that the objective of British and French proliferation was to gain prestige.[20] The governments of both states believed that nuclear capability was necessary to maintain their status as great powers:

I am persuaded that the basic objective, historically, for both the British and French governments, has been to have a kind of power without which these two ancient sovereign powers could not truly be themselves. This requirement has been clear for each government at every moment of choice from 1945 onward, and it is not a matter of deterrent strategy as such. It is rather a matter of what Britain and France must have, as long as others have it, in order to meet their own standards of their own rank among nations....De Gaulle certainly exaggerated the international political influence that a French bomb would confer but....It is not easy for a foreign observer to be confident that France would still be France, or Britain still be Britain, without their bombs. What is historically clear is that so far their governments have not thought so.[21]

Prestige is not only important to declining great powers but to potential great powers, such as India, as well.[22] Peter Lavoy notes that after China exploded its first nuclear device in October 1964,[23] some Indians believed that India must match Chinese capabilities for reasons of prestige: 'India has to have the bomb if it is to hold sway in the world. Not to make it would betray a lack of will to live – to survive – in this jungle of international strife. Not to make it would be to let the whole world treat us as some third-rate country.'[24] Prestige may be important factor in Ukraine's debate whether or not to keep its strategic nuclear weapons or to return them to Russia. So long as Ukraine has nuclear weapons, it has the attention of the United States because, first, the weapons still may be aimed at the United States; and, second, there is the danger that Ukrainian nuclear technology or material may be acquired by emerging nuclear states. It is not evident that the US would be concerned with Ukraine if it did not have nuclear weapons. Were Ukraine to surrender its nuclear weapons as it is obligated to do, the Ukrainians fear they may be treated as 'some third-rate country' by the West.[25]

In the case of Britain, France, and India, arguments have been advanced that prestige is the most important factor in a state's decision to acquire nuclear weapons. It is now necessary to examine the validity of the argument as well as the empirical evidence in order to determine if prestige is a cause of nuclear proliferation.

Flaws in the Logic of Prestige as a Cause of Nuclear Proliferation

Prestige is neither a necessary nor sufficient cause of proliferation. At best, it is an incidental or complementary cause of nuclear proliferation. This is so for three reasons, first, the validity of the argument is flawed; second, production of nuclear weapons for reasons of prestige alone incurs a great opportunity cost that few states can bear; and third, the argument does not accord with the empirical record.

First, the logic of the theory is flawed because it assumes that nuclear capability confers upon a state great power status when this is not the case. Military capabilities are the most important but not the sole criterion of great power status.[26] Great power status is grounded in more than just nuclear weapons. Traditionally it has been based on the economic, military, and political capability to sustain the projection of power abroad to defend the national interests of a great power or the interests of its allies.[27] Germany and Japan do not have nuclear weapons and yet, since the 19th century in the case of Germany, and the early 20th century in the case of Japan, these states have been considered great powers due to their great economic and conventional military strength. China has nuclear weapons and yet the conception of China as a great power is problematic because it has difficulty projecting power. Israel and Pakistan have nuclear weapons but are not great powers. South Africa's possession of nuclear weapons did not make it a great power; and North Korea will not become a great power if it continues to develop its nuclear weapons capability. Were Britain and France, as well as the United States and Russia, not to have nuclear capabilities, they would still have the conventional and unconventional capability, i.e. biological and chemical weapons, to defend their interests abroad, although the ability to defend those interests against the depredations of a nuclear state would be severely circumscribed. Thus, while the possession of nuclear capabilities is the most important criterion of great power status in a nuclear world, it is not the sole criterion.

Second, nuclear proliferation for reasons of prestige is extremely unlikely because it is difficult for any country to undertake the development, production, and maintenance of nuclear weapons merely for the status that these weapons bestow, if only because the pecuniary and opportunity costs at each stage of the acquisition of the arsenal are too great to warrant acquiring nuclear weapons for prestige alone.

Third, the empirical evidence does not support prestige as a cause of proliferation. In each case of proliferation – attempted proliferation by Germany,[28] proliferation by the United States,[29] the Soviet Union,[30] Great Britain, France, China, Israel, India, Pakistan,[31] and South Africa[32] – prestige is only mentioned as a cause of proliferation in three cases discussed above – Britain, France and India – and in no others. As it will be shown below, these states acquired nuclear weapons because of security concerns, not for reasons of prestige.[33] The opaque nuclear states – India, Iraq,

Iran, Israel, North Korea, Pakistan, and until 1989, South Africa – did not acquire nuclear weapons because of prestige. Quite the contrary. These states have concealed their nuclear weapons programmes with great care. Simply put, the logic of prestige theory does not fit any of these cases. Therefore, lacking theoretical validity and supporting empirical evidence, prestige is neither a necessary nor sufficient cause of proliferation. However, prestige may be a complementary cause of proliferation. Richard Betts illuminates the complementary nature of prestige when he writes with respect to the Indian nuclear explosion of 1974: 'The prestige incentive for nuclear weapons can...be seen as *compensatory*; the 1974 explosion shows that despite the modesty of industrial and economic progress, in the nuclear field India is first class.'[34] Nuclear weapons are sought to make states secure. Any increase in international status or gain in prestige that results from the development of nuclear weapons are additional benefits.

Bureaucratic Push as a Cause of Nuclear Proliferation

Bureaucratic politics theory also offers an explanation of nuclear proliferation – bureaucratic push.[35] The classic works of Graham Allison and Morton Halperin provide a framework for analysing why states make the decisions they do.[36] Allison's model of governmental or bureaucratic politics demonstrates how the individuals who control bureaucracies have their own conceptions and ideas about the problems the state faces and how these problems best may be solved. 'Men share power. Men differ about what must be done. The differences matter. This milieu necessitates that government decisions and actions result from a political process. In this process, sometimes one group committed to a course of action triumphs over other groups....'[37] At other times, however, 'different groups pulling in different directions produce a result,...distinct from what any person or group intended. ...In both cases, [what matters is] the power and skill of proponents and opponents of the action in question.'[38]

In addition to the importance of individuals in bureaucracies, bureaucracy itself affects political decisions as a result of the desire of bureaucracies to have influence with decisionmakers. Bureaucracies want influence with decisionmakers so that they may better pursue the objectives of the bureaucracy. The interests of organizations like bureaucracies largely are determined by the organization's conception of its essence, the organization's conception of what its roles and missions are.[39] A bureaucracy is likely to favour governmental policies and strategies which its members believe will make it more important with decisionmakers and promote the bureaucracy's organizational essence. Similarly, a bureaucracy will contest governmental policies that weaken or take away those functions viewed as necessary to the essence of the organization.[40] As Halperin has argued, the goals of bureaucracies:

> tend to be that of gaining influence in pursuit of ideological concerns. ...Stands on issues are affected by the desire to maintain influence. This could lead to support for certain policies which will require greater reliance on the organization. Participants prefer courses of action which will require information from them or which they will be asked to implement. They recognize that they will gain in influence if such decisions are made.[41]

Using the arguments of Allison and Halperin, bureaucratic theory argues that the decision to proliferate is made by key individuals within the scientific or defence bureaucracies of states. These individuals advocate proliferation in order to enhance or increase the power of their bureaucracy. Key individuals within the bureaucracy of the state push the state into nuclear proliferation. The development and deployment of nuclear weapons should be supported by the bureaucracies that will build the weapons – in most countries this is a civilian nuclear agency – and by the bureaucracies who use the weapons, the military of the country. These bureaucracies will proffer and support the decision because both civil and military bureaucracies will gain in influence with policymakers because policymakers must rely on the civilian nuclear agency and the military to develop, produce, maintain and conduct nuclear weapons operations. If the bureaucratic politics theory is correct, then evidence should exist that the civilian and military bureaucracy pushed for the development of nuclear weapons in the absence of concerns for prestige, or the threat of proliferation from an adversary.

Bureaucracies have played an important role in the development of all states' nuclear weapons. Arguments have been advanced demonstrating the pivotal roles played by leaders of bureaucracies; by Homi Bhabha in the case of India and, in France, by Pierre Guillaumat, Administrator-General of the Commissariat à l'Energie Atomique (CEA),[42] and Pierre Taranger, Industrial Director of the CEA, at the time of the development of the French nuclear arsenal.

Mitchell Reiss argues that the responsibility 'for [India's] nuclear development can be traced to one individual, Homi Bhabha.'[43] This is due to Bhabha's central role in the genesis and growth of India's civil and military nuclear programme, from the initial acquisition of research reactors, to the initial deployment of a Canadian-built reactor, the development of plutonium reprocessing facilities at Trombay and, ultimately, to Bhabha's 1965 attempt to pressure Prime Minister Lal Bahadur Shastri into developing nuclear weapons.[44] Peter Lavoy also argues that Bhabha was essential in causing Shastri's consent to the initiation of a nuclear weapons programme. 'Bhabha's well-timed interventions helped encourage and empower India's bomb lobby, which eventually managed to carry the day...Shastri authorized Bhabha and other scientists to develop a capability for producing nuclear weapons.'[45]

In the case of France, Lawrence Scheinman argues that administrators like Guillaumat and Taranger had a greater effect on the development of the French nuclear weapons than in the case of United States or Britain.

> France under the Fourth Republic would appear to represent the most striking example of minimal political leadership and maximum technocratic direction [from administrators like Guillaumat and Taranger] in the orientation of atomic policy. ...Guidance and direction for nuclear policy came not from the French Government or the French Parliament, but from a small, dedicated group of administrator-technocrats, politicians and military officers whose activities centered on and emanated from the CEA.[46]

The influence of individuals like Bhabha and bureaucracies like the CEA were instrumental in developing nuclear weapons in the case of India and France. The actions of Bhabha and the CEA accord with the bureaucratic politics' explanation of the causes of nuclear proliferation.

Flaws with Bureaucratic Push as a Cause of Nuclear Proliferation

The arguments of bureaucratic push as a cause of nuclear proliferation are not valid. While bureaucracies undoubtedly play an important role in the development of a state's nuclear weapons programme, the argument that bureaucracies or certain individuals within bureaucracies are requisite for nuclear proliferation to occur is incorrect. A counterfactual argument can demonstrate the flaw in this argument. If Homi Bhabha, Pierre Guillaumat, or Pierre Taranger had never existed, India and France would still have developed nuclear weapons. Of course the development of nuclear weapons might have taken more or less time in the absence of these individuals. Yet, these states would still be nuclear states because the states still would face threats to their security. Similarly, the empirical evidence demonstrates that a specific bureaucracy like the CEA, charged with its own interests, is not needed for nuclear proliferation to occur. The need to acquire nuclear weapons as a result of a threat is anterior to the bureaucracy created to build and maintain those weapons. Therefore, the bureaucracy could not be responsible for the decision to obtain nuclear weapons. The US developed nuclear weapons before any bureaucracy like the Atomic Energy Commission existed, as did the Soviets, the British, the Chinese, and other nuclear states.

Recognizing that particular individuals or bureaucratic interests are not necessary for proliferation to occur, the cause of proliferation must lie not with particular individuals or particular bureaucratic interests, but with the threatening conditions that states face.

Technological Pull as a Cause of Nuclear Proliferation

The causal logic of the technological pull theory is a technological deterministic argument: technology can compel decisionmakers to undertake an action that they would not have in the absence of that technology. Once the technology to acquire nuclear weapons is invented, all states capable of acquiring nuclear weapons must do so. Ralph Lapp captures the determinism of this argument when he argues that 'the unremitting buildup of the atomic arsenal [of the US] represents just another example of the technological imperative – when technology beckons, men are helpless.'[47] Another prominent proponent of this argument, Herbert York, similarly exemplifies the deterministic logic of this theory when he writes:

> Every nation that might plausibly have started nuclear weapons programmes did so: Germany, Great Britain, the United States, the Soviet Union, France, and we now know, Japan. So the case has been weakened for those who have argued that governments, or more precisely, generals, emperors, and presidents can hold back from the decision and say 'No'. The decision to develop nuclear weapons is not a fluke of certain governments, but a general technological imperative.[48]

Advocates of technological pull make a strong claim. The argument is not the weak claim that technology nudges decisionmakers into making a decision, or that the interaction of technology and decisionmaker cause changes in behaviour. These weaker claims certainly are true but are not relevant to the causes of proliferation. Clearly, technology has the power to induce changes in the decisionmaking of political leaders. One need only consider the changes wrought by a communication medium such as television, which has influenced the substance and style of political behaviour in American politics, and possibly even has compelled US interventions in the Third World.[49] However, the advocates of technological pull make the stronger claim in the case of proliferation: technology causes proliferation and decisionmakers are powerless to halt the inexorable lure of nuclear weapons.[50] If something is technically possible, then it will be done. Robert Oppenheimer captures this logic in his testimony before the Personnel Security Review Board in 1954. Oppenheimer is asked if his concern about developing the hydrogen bomb increased as its development became more feasible:

> I think it is the opposite of true...my feeling about development became quite different when the practicabilities became clear. *When I saw how to do it, it was clear to me that one had to at least make the thing.* Then the only problem was what one would do about them when one had them. The programme in 1949 was a tortured thing that you could well argue did not make a great deal of technical sense. It was therefore possible to argue also that you did not want it even if you could have it. The programme in 1951 was technically so sweet that you could not argue about that.[51]

Oppenheimer's assertion that once the weapon could be developed it had to be developed is empirical evidence that supports the theory of technological determinism.

Flaws of Technological Pull as a Cause of Proliferation

The logic of the theory is flawed. The weaker claim, that technology affects the decisionmaker and decisionmaking, is sustainable. Clearly, technology affects decisionmaking. The stronger claim of the theory, that proliferation is caused by technology, is not a valid argument and the empirical evidence does not support this argument.

The argument is not valid for four reasons. First, there is an important gap in the explanation: the theory does not explain how technology compels decisionmakers to do what is technically possible. Second, the causal logic is not explained explicitly: the theory does not explain why decisionmakers are as helpless to resist developing nuclear weapons as sailors to the call of the Sirens. Third, the mechanism that allows technology to overcome all resistance to proliferation on economic and moral grounds is not explained. Fourth, the reason why technological pull is a better explanation of proliferation than the alternatives, such as prestige, bureaucratic politics and security, is not explained by the theory.[52]

These gaps in the explanation make technological pull an incomplete theory. The fourth reason why the theory of technological pull is flawed deserves to be emphasized. It would advance the debate about the causes of proliferation if the advocates of the theory would address the competing theoretical explanations of proliferation – prestige, bureaucratic push, and security. The advocates of technological pull have not yet done this, and so the debate over the causes of proliferation is needlessly muddled. In sum, the claim that technology is a cause of proliferation is an under-developed theory whose logical validity is questionable.

Empirically, the theory is flawed as well. In no case can the proponents of technological pull demonstrate that technology was the principal cause of proliferation, i.e. that technology compelled a state to proliferate that would not have done so otherwise. As will be demonstrated below, all nuclear states have acquired nuclear weapons due to security concerns, not because nuclear technology compelled them to proliferate. It is also the case that the theory cannot explain the empirical cases of *countries that have the technology to develop nuclear weapons and yet have not done so.*[53] This point is illustrated by examining the numerous countries who have the technological capability to acquire nuclear weapons and yet have not: Argentina, Belgium, Brazil, Germany, Italy, Japan, the Netherlands, Sweden, South Korea and Taiwan. According to the theory, these states should have developed nuclear weapons. The theory cannot explain why these countries have the technological capability to acquire nuclear weapons, most have had the capability for decades, and yet have not done so. The theory of technological pull is not sufficient to explain the cases of nuclear abstinence, nor is it sufficient to explain actual cases of prolifer-ation. Therefore, the theory is deductively and empirically flawed.

Security as a Cause of Nuclear Proliferation

Security is the most important cause of nuclear proliferation. Realism elu-cidates why security is the most important cause of proliferation.[54] Realism makes two important assumptions. The first is that the interna-tional system is anarchic, that there is no final arbiter of disputes in inter-national politics.[55] The result is that the use of force is always possible. The second assumption is that states desire self-preservation, that they want to survive and maintain their sovereignty and independence.

Realism comprises three conditions, or central ideas, that are necessary to explain the behaviour of states and why states acquire nuclear weapons.[56] The first central idea is that all states possess offensive military capability by virtue of possessing any military capability. All military capability is inherently offensive because any military capability may be used to hurt other states. The second central idea is the uncertainty about intentions. A state can never know if its present allies will remain allies or become hostile because all states inherently have the capacity to do so, and it is very difficult to be certain of the intentions of other states. War is always a possibility because states inherently have offensive military capabilities and potentially hostile intentions. The third central idea of realism is that the relative capabilities of states are more important than the absolute capabilities for ensuring the security of the state. Relative capabilities are important because the security of states is provided by the strength of the state *vis-à-vis* competing states. For example, in absolute terms, the military strength of the Great Britain is stronger today than a hundred years ago, but in relative terms it is weaker.[57]

Realist Predictions About State Behaviour

The central ideas of realism illuminate powerful incentives provided by the anarchic international system for states to act in certain ways. Three types of state behaviour may be predicted from these ideas.[58] The first prediction is that states will act as though they are fearful because of anarchy and their desire for self-preservation. The effect of anarchy for states is that no authority is guaranteed to come to the aid of a state attacked. States are cognizant of the effect of anarchy and are fearful of an attack. In addition, states want to survive but are uncertain about the intentions of other states. This concern is accentuated by the fact that all states inherently have offensive capabilities; all are potential threats; and all are concerned with relative and not absolute capabilities. The result of anarchy, the uncertainty about other states' intentions, the inherent offensive capabilities of states, and the concern of states for relative capabilities, is that states act as though they are fearful and are hesitant to trust other states.

The second prediction of state behaviour made by realism is that states will perform in a self-help manner because states exist in a self-help system.[59] States will do what they can do to guarantee their own survival because no other state is certain to assist a state in peril; nor is there a higher authority to come to the aid of a state in jeopardy. States will build arms to defend themselves in an attempt to balance the capabilities of other states. Waltz terms the development of a state's own armament to defend itself 'internal balancing'.[60] Realism argues that it is better for a state to rely on its own arms to defend itself because it does not have to rely on other states as allies.[61] However, most states lack the resources to defend themselves against the numerous threats in the anarchic international system, and so states form alliances in order to match the capabilities of other states. Waltz terms the formation of alliances 'external balancing'.[62] Alliances are problematic for states because they require a coincidence of interest between the alliance partners but there is no certainty that such a coincidence of interest will occur. Reliance on allies for security is risky because allies may betray the state, buckpassing its alliance commitment; or an alliance partner may force, or chain gang, a state into war.[63] Even when states do ally, they are aware that their present allies may become future foes. Recognizing that states operate in a self-help system, they must pursue their selfish short-term interests rather than their long-term interests because the short-term is of greater concern for survival. If states do not act to guarantee their survival in the shortterm, then there is no certainty that they will survive until the longterm.

The prediction that states will behave in a self-help manner is grounded, first, on the assumption of anarchy, the fact that there is no authority to assist a state attacked; second, on the assumption of self-preservation; and third, on the verities captured by the three central ideas of realism: the inherent possession of offensive capabilities by all states; the uncertainty of intentions of other states; and the concern of states for relative gains. The effect of the first and second ideas is that states face real and potential threats against which they must do their utmost to defend themselves. The concern of states for relative gains means that states will be reluctant to cooperate because of concern that cooperation will benefit to a greater extent its partner, a potential aggressor; and as a result the partner may become a larger threat.

The third prediction of state behaviour that realism makes is that states will attempt to maximize their offensive power.[64] States behave in this way to maximize their chances for survival by maximizing their power relative to other states. By striving to maximize their relative power, states seek opportunities to gain at their rivals' expense in order to become more powerful than their rivals. Ideally, a state would want to become a world hegemon because only in this way could it be assured of survival, no other state could threaten its survival. But few states, if any, have the resources to become a world hegemon, so most states seek to ensure that other states do not gain at their expense, i.e. they seek to balance against aggression by building arms and forming alliances.

The causes of the propensity of states to maximize their offensive power are anchored in the characteristics of the international system that realism explains. The assumption of anarchy and the desire for survival require states to defend themselves. The fact that all states inherently have offensive capabilities, and are uncertain of the intentions of other states, means that actual and potential threats to the survival of states always exist and must be addressed if states are to maintain their independence.

The empirical record of nuclear proliferation supports the arguments of realism. A brief examination of each case of nuclear proliferation will demonstrate that states acquire nuclear weapons principally because they are concerned for their security. This does not mean that prestige, bureaucratic politics or the lure of technology are irrelevant causes of proliferation in any particular case of nuclear proliferation. It is to argue, however, that security is the only necessary and sufficient cause of nuclear proliferation. The other theories are complementary causes which help to explain the mechanics of a particular country's decision to acquire nuclear weapons.

The first state to obtain nuclear weapons, the United States, did so because it believed that Nazi Germany was attempting to develop a nuclear weapon. The German programme was not as advanced as Americans feared. However, the threat of German nuclear proliferation, and its probable result, German victory in World War II, drove the United States to develop nuclear weapons. Richard Rhodes describes a meeting on 11 October, 1941, between Franklin Roosevelt and Alexander Sachs, an unofficial adviser to the Roosevelt administration, in which Sachs, who was serving as an intermediary for the physicist Leo Szilard, related the possibility of an atomic bomb and the importance of developing it before the Germans did:

> 'Alex,' said Roosevelt, quickly understanding, 'what you are after is to see that the Nazis don't blow us up.' 'Precisely,' Sachs said. Roosevelt called in [General Edwin M.] Watson. 'This requires action,' he told his aide.[65]

As the fear of a German atomic bomb drove the United States to obtain nuclear weapons, the Soviets initiated their development of the atomic bomb due to their concern that Germany, Britain and the US were developing atomic weapons. The Soviet effort to develop an atomic bomb began in early 1943 when Igor Kurchatov was selected by Stalin to be the director of the Soviet effort. David Holloway describes possible motivations for the Soviet bomb in which Stalin evinces concern that his allies and Germany possess a capability that the Soviet Union did not have:

> Perhaps Stalin had it in mind that after the war the Soviet Union would have to face a nuclear-armed Germany, for at this early period [1942] he may have had only minimum war aims, which did not necessarily include the destruction of the Nazi state. Perhaps he foresaw that even with the defeat of Germany the Soviet Union would come into conflict with Britain and the United States; after all, they were conducting their atomic projects in great secrecy, without informing the Soviet Union. More probably, the decision should be seen as a hedge against uncertainty. Given that Germany, Britain and the United States were interested in the atomic bomb, was it not as well to initiate a Soviet project,

even though the circumstances in which the new weapon might be used could not be foreseen?[66]

In mid-August 1945, after Hiroshima and Nagasaki, Stalin held a meeting with Kurchatov and the Minister of Munitions, B.L. Vannikov: "'A single demand of you, comrades," said Stalin. "Provide us with atomic weapons in the shortest possible time. You know that Hiroshima has shaken the whole world. The balance [between Britain, the United States and the Soviet Union] has been destroyed. Provide the bomb – it will remove a great danger from us.'"[67] At Potsdam, Truman mentioned to Stalin that the United States had developed a powerful new weapon.[68] When Foreign Minister V.M. Molotov heard about Truman's comment, 'he saw it as an attempt to gain concessions from the Soviet Union. The Soviet leaders regarded the use of the bomb in Japan as part of an effort to put pressure on them, as a demonstration that the United States was willing to use nuclear weapons. Soviet security now seemed to be at risk from a new threat.'[69]

Holloway's discussion reveals Stalin's concern that Germany or his wartime allies might possess a capability, a powerful weapon, that the Soviet Union would not and so strove to match the capabilities of his opponent, Germany, and allies, Britain and the United States. Realism would predict the Soviet decision to acquire nuclear weapons, and the empirical evidence supports realist predictions about state behaviour.

The decision by Great Britain to develop nuclear weapons also supports the realist explanation of nuclear proliferation. Great Britain feared the possibility of US isolation after World War II. Britain needed nuclear weapons capability in order to guard against the danger that it would have to face the threat posed by a nuclear armed Soviet Union alone. The British decision to develop nuclear weapons was rooted in the fear of US isolation in the face of the Soviet threat, and in the legacy of 1940 when Britain faced a great threat alone. As Lawrence and Larus write, 'the possibility that at some future time, reminiscent of the dark days of 1940 after France fell, Great Britain could again find herself at war, alone and facing great odds. The real fear was heightened by concern that America might lapse into a new isolationism from which it might emerge too late to benefit England.'[70] Nuclear weapons would give Britain the capability to deter an attack independently of the United States, so that if the United States were to return to its traditional policy of isolationism and refused to support Britain, Britain could still be secure. With nuclear weapons, Britain could deter an attack from even a state as powerful as the Soviet Union without having to rely upon an ally. The legacy of the German invasion in 1940 was even a greater consideration in the French decision to acquire nuclear weapons. Fear of German rearmament, even nuclear rearmament, was an important factor in the French decision to acquire nuclear weapons as Wolf Mendl argues: 'For France the historic anxiety about Germany did not come to an end with the decisive victory of 1945 and Germany's unconditional surrender. Remote as it seemed, the spectre of a revived and vengeful Germany haunted all Frenchmen...'[71] This fear of German aggression was so great, coupled with the French fear that a rearmed Germany would dominate NATO, that it was the principal motivation of Pierre Mendès-France's decision to proceed with a military nuclear programme on December 26, 1954.[72] Irrespective of the threat of Soviet aggression which was also a factor in the French decision to acquire nuclear weapons, the fear of the German threat provided an important impetus for the French nuclear programme; as did de Gaulle's desire to be independent, not to rely on any ally, even the United States, for the defence of France in the event of a Soviet attack. Jean Lacouture summarizes de Gaulle's thinking:

> What destiny has a people whose salvation depends on the good will of another – even if there is not the shadow of a doubt that this other people would come to its aid? From 1940 to 1945, Charles de Gaulle had had [*sic*] to beg his allies for the means to fight. When one examines de Gaulle's motives for establishing an independent French nuclear capability, one may forget those years too easily. Anything was better than having to beg Roosevelt's successors to be so kind as to give him the means of taking Paris, of saving Strasbourg or liberating Royan. For him, anyone who depends on the decision of a foreign power or of a body like NATO, which is totally manipulated by a foreign power, cannot be free. In time of war, of course, powers of coordination have to be conceded to some new Eisenhower, but, in the meantime, he could not bear that the decision to make peace or war, or to live freely, should depend on another power. ...What is one to think of a country that, in order to *survive*, hands itself over to another? What is the point of protecting oneself against invasion, enslavement, annihilation, if, when all is said and done, our life, our freedom, our fate depend on a Senate majority in Washington, on elections in Iowa or North Dakota?[73]

De Gaulle did not trust that the United States would use nuclear weapons for the defence of France in the event of a Soviet invasion of western Europe. Lacouture describes de Gaulle's suspicion of the United States voiced by de Gaulle in conversations with President Eisenhower in September, 1959: 'I, de Gaulle, know that you, Eisenhower, would dare to risk the survival of your country in order to safeguard Europe: you have already proved your devotion. But what of your successors? Will they take the risk of devastating American cities so that Berlin, Brussels and Paris might remain free?'[74]

De Gaulle's suspicion of the United States was fuelled by the tepid response, in his opinion, of the United States to the 1961 Berlin crisis, the Cuban Missile Crisis, and especially the abandonment of the policy of massive retaliation of the Eisenhower years for Robert McNamara's flexible response policy. De Gaulle wondered exactly how 'flexible' the US response to Soviet aggression would be if it were not 'Miami or Washington that were under threat, but only Rotterdam, Milan or Strasbourg?'[75] The concern of Mendés-France that a rearmed Germany might again pose a threat to France and de Gaulle's realization that, in a nuclear world, he could not depend on his ally, the United States, to save France, demonstrate that the causes of French proliferation are anchored in realism.

The Chinese acquired nuclear weapons for the same realist reasons that the French did: fear of attack, and doubts that their ally, the Soviet Union, would come to their aid if China were attacked. The threat by the United States to to end the stalemate in the Korean War is often cited as a principal motivation of the Chinese programme: 'The president-elect [Eisenhower] explicitly warned the Chinese of his intention to escalate the war if the armistice negotiations remained stalemated. He publicly hinted at the possible use of nuclear weapons against Beijing...'[76] In addition to American nuclear threats made during the Korean War, John Wilson Lewis and Xue Litai argue that the impetus of the Chinese programme, which was launched in January 1955, was the Taiwan Straits crisis of 1954–55; the passage by the United States Congress of the Formosa Resolution in January 1955 which gave Eisenhower authority to use force for the defence of Taiwan; and the possibility that the United States considered using nuclear weapons to assist the French in war in Indochina.[77]

The importance that Mao Zedong placed on acquisition of nuclear weapons, increasing the independence of China is clear: 'We are stronger than before and will be still stronger in the future. We will have not only more planes and artillery but atomic bombs as well. If we are not to be bullied in this present-day world, we cannot do without the bomb.'[78] Chen Yi, the Minister for Foreign Affairs in the summer of 1961, also stressed that the development of nuclear weapons was necessary for China to be independent: 'As China's minister of foreign affairs, at present I still do not have adequate backup. If you succeed in producing the atomic bomb and guided missiles, then I can straighten my back.'[79]

There are two principal causes of Israel's acquisition of nuclear weapons. The first cause was the legacy of the Holocaust, which instilled in the Jewish people the realization that they could depend upon no other state to assist them in a time of peril because other states could not or would not assist them. The second cause of Israel's acquisition of nuclear weapons was Israel's desire to nullify the superior conventional capability of its Arab opponents. Being the sole possessors of nuclear weapons in the Middle East, the Israelis could coerce or deter their Arab neighbours by threatening unacceptable punishment if an Arab attack succeeded in endangering Israeli security. This fear of encirclement and destruction by superior Arab forces was most pronounced during the perilous three weeks of the *hamtana* (wait) before the 1967 war, a 'sense of abandonment and solitude that characterized [the Israeli] situation during the three weeks immediately preceding the outbreak of the war.'[80] During the time between 15 May and 6 June, 1967, 'Egypt marched its army into Sinai and blockaded the Straits of Tiran; Syria concentrated its forces on the Golan Heights, overlooking Israel's northern sector; and Jordan allowed Iraqi and Egyptian force to enter its territory and move close to the Israeli border.'[81] Israel's pleas for assistance to France and to the United States were not met. Israel had not been able to attain a security guarantee from a great power or secure membership in a military alliance such as NATO or CENTO. Frankel concludes that 'Israel's decision to build nuclear weapons was thus an expression by Israel of profound skepticism over the international community's willingness to come to its aid in a crisis, and it signalled Israel's determination to rely on its own capabilities instead.'[82]

The central cause of Indian nuclear proliferation is a realist one, it was to match the capabilities of China. A principal effect of the Sino-Indian war of 1962 was to alarm the government of Jawaharlal Nehru at the power of the Chinese military and the inadequacies of the Indian military.[82] 'India's humiliation at its defeat was acute. The country's military weakness was exposed, and the Himalayas no longer were viewed as an impregnable barrier to invasion.'[84] China's nuclear test on October 16, 1964, was an additional shock to India. Until the detonation of the Chinese nuclear device, 'India's security requirements had been defined exclusively in terms of conventional weaponry. ...Yet the prospect of a neighboring Asian power acquiring nuclear weapons, coming so soon after that country's decisive military victory of India, sparked renewed discussion of India's security. ...[there were] widespread calls for India's development of nuclear weapons.'[85] Only India's nuclear capabilities could elevate India to a position where it could not be subject to Chinese nuclear coercion.[86]

In 1972, President Zulfikar Ali Bhutto reportedly ordered Pakistan's scientific community to commence a nuclear weapons programme. There were two reasons for Pakistan's development of nuclear weapons, each reason accords with realism. First, the 1971 war with India demonstrated that India possessed conventional superiority and could use that superiority to pose an existential threat to Pakistan.[87] Second, Pakistan acquired nuclear weapons in order to match Indian nuclear capabilities so that it would not be subject to Indian nuclear coercion.[88] Although India did not detonate an atomic device until 1974, it was known long before then in Pakistan that India was working to develop nuclear weapons. In 1969, Bhutto expressed his fear of Indian nuclear coercion:

> All wars of our age have become total wars...and it will have to be assumed that a war waged against Pakistan is capable of becoming total war. It would be dangerous to plan for less and our plans should include the nuclear deterrent...India is unlikely to concede nuclear monopoly to others...It appears that she is determined to proceed with her plans to detonate a nuclear bomb. If Pakistan restricts or suspends her nuclear programme, it would not only enable India to blackmail Pakistan with her nuclear advantage, but would impose a crippling limitation on the development of Pakistan's science and technology...Our problem, in its essence, is how to obtain such a weapon in time before the crisis begins.[89]

The Pakistani political leaders are worried that only nuclear capability can ameliorate what they perceive to be the existential threat to Pakistan posed by Indian conventional and nuclear capability. As Raju Thomas notes, the present 'Indian military preponderance does not guarantee Pakistan's independence and sovereignty. Pakistani fear of being absorbed back into a "Greater India" remains at the core of its defence doctrines and objectives.'[90]

If India is a status-quo state, then the Pakistani fear of absorption by India is misplaced. However, if India is an expansionist state, then Pakistan is faced with an existential threat.[91] The empirical evidence does demonstrate that India frequently has intervened in the affairs of neighbouring states: the Indian seizure of Goa from the Portuguese in 1961; three wars between India and Pakistan, including the attack on East Pakistan (Bangladesh) in 1971 which was seen by many Pakistanis as a direct threat to the survival of Pakistan; the absorption of Sikkim in 1975; intervention in Sri Lanka from 1987 to 1990; intervention in the Maldives in 1988; continuing trouble with Pakistan and indigenous forces in Kashmir; as well as the maintenance of economic pressure on Nepal.[92] If this view is correct and India is expansionist, then the Pakistani programme is necessary for the deterrence of a premeditated attack from India and for the mitigation of possible nuclear blackmail from India.[93]

South Africa developed nuclear weapons due to the threat to its security posed by the presence of large numbers of Cuban and Warsaw Pact troops in Angola and Mozambique. South Africans feared a Warsaw Pact or Cuban invasion and developed seven nuclear weapons in order to halt or compel American involvement if such an invasion occurred. Pretoria planned to build seven nuclear weapons to get a security guarantee from the US in the face of Soviet expansionism to the north. After the United Nations imposed a global arms embargo on South Africa in 1987, a South African defence official said, 'the thing we fear the most was *totale aanslag* – a Soviet-led invasion south to Capetown. Letting the US and the Soviets know we had a bomb showed them we were desperate.' According to Armscor officials, 'It was decided not to test or make known South Africa's nuclear capabilities unless the country found itself with its back to the wall.'[94]

This fear was first prevalent in the mid-1970s when large Cuban forces were deployed to Angola to assist the government's fight against guerrilla movements. Preparations were taken in 1977 to test a nuclear device at a test site in the Kalahari Desert: '...when preparations were made a few months in advance of the 1977 test, Soviet spy satellites detected the work on the site to install wiring, detection gear, and instrumentation. Washington and Moscow then applied diplomatic pressure. "Due to international reaction to activities at the site," Armscor said, "the site was abandoned and the holes were sealed."'[95]

Again in the mid-1980s, South Africa prepared to test a nuclear device against the backdrop of the perceived threat from the Cubans and Warsaw Pact troops in Angola. Diplomatic sources said that rising tensions in Pretoria's relations with front-line African states – and concern that Warsaw Pact troops might invade South Africa from Angola and Mozambique – led to the decision to test during the mid-1970s. Likewise, [sources] added, the 1987 decision to re-open the test site was also triggered by South African concern for its northern defences. [Prime Minister P.W.] Botha, these sources said, 'acted immediately' on the test site after Soviet air defence systems had been installed in southern Angola, eliminating Pretoria's air superiority.[96] This activity again compelled US and Soviet involvement, and by the end of 1988, South Africa had an agreement that eliminated its external security threat by compelling Cuban and Warsaw Pact withdrawal from Angola.

South Africa's decision to acquire nuclear weapons supports the arguments of realism. South Africa developed nuclear weapons to maintain its security, either by using nuclear weapons against Cuban or Warsaw Pact forces or to compel US involvement, in the face of the increasing capabilities of its adversaries.

Realism also explains the motivations of states who are presently developing nuclear weapons: Iraq, Iran, and North Korea. Each is attempting to acquire nuclear capability to match the conventional or nuclear capability of neighbouring states. Iraq is building nuclear weapons due to Israeli nuclear capability and because of its fear of superior Iranian conventional capability and resources demonstrated during the Iran–Iraq War. Iran's attempt at proliferation is due to the fear of Iraqi conventional and nuclear capability and Israeli conventional and nuclear capability. The attempt of North Korea to obtain nuclear weapons because of, first, South Korean attempts to do the same in the 1970s; and, second, the steady growth in the quality of the South Korean military with military modernization, changes in military doctrine, and increased and more sophisticated training. Thus, conventionally, South Korea poses a much greater danger to North Korea while North Korea's principal conventional advantage, a larger army, has been decreasing in relevance due to the improvements in South Korea's military. Moreover, the conventional and possible nuclear threat from South Korea has only been reinforced by the collapse of North Korea's principal supporter, the Soviet Union, and the estrangement of North Korea from China.[97]

The empirical evidence supports realist explanations of the causes of proliferation. States acquire nuclear weapons to match the capabilities of adversaries. Only by acquiring nuclear capability can states gain security from nuclear coercion and major wars.

Critiques of Security as a Cause of Nuclear Proliferation

No other theory can challenge the validity of realism in explaining proliferation. The other theories are valuable for embellishing each country's particular decision to proliferate. That is, prestige is a factor in the explanation of the British, French and Indian decision to acquire nuclear weapons. Particular administrators, such as Homi Bhabha, are important for explaining the Indian decision to proliferate. Important bureaucracies, such as the CEA, are important for explaining France's decision to obtain nuclear weapons. Individual political leaders or scientists, such as Franklin Roosevelt, Josef Stalin, Leo Szilard, or Igor Kurchatov, played important roles in the decision of the United States and the Soviet Union to develop nuclear weapons. However, the empirical discussion above demonstrates that it is each state's fear for its security that was the principal cause of proliferation in each case. Realism explains the causes of proliferation.

While the empirical evidence appears to support realism the actions of Argentina and Brazil (who recently have signed the Treaty of Tlatelolco, making all of South America a nuclear weapons-free zone) appear to refute realism. However, upon examination, the actions of Argentina and Brazil do not refute the realist argument for three reasons. First, these states do not need nuclear weapons for their security. Argentina and Brazil can deter one another conventionally, and conventional deterrence can obtain as long as neither state has nuclear capability.[98] Second, Argentina and Brazil face little threat of external nuclear or conventional attack from states outside of South America due to the protection from such attacks afforded by the hegemony of the United States.[99] Third, the threat of nuclear attack only could come from the other if each country had developed nuclear weapons capability because no other South American state has attempted to proliferate. By not developing nuclear weapons, they eliminated a greater threat to their security, the threat of societal destruction posed by nuclear weapons. Security is maintained between Argentina and Brazil through their possession of conventional forces sufficient to deter the other state. The acquisition of nuclear weapons by both states would serve to make them less secure since both would face nuclear devastation while providing no benefit, deterrence from external attacks, that is not provided already by conventional deterrent capabilities of each state.

The preceding arguments have demonstrated that states build nuclear weapons to gain security. Now it is necessary to determine the utility of the nuclear non-proliferation regime, its benefits, and its costs.

2   WHY THE NON-PROLIFERATION REGIME CANNOT STOP PROLIFERATION

Recognizing that states acquire nuclear weapons to gain security, the answer to the question posed at the beginning of this chapter – can the NPT and the non-proliferation regime stop proliferation – is that the nuclear non-proliferation regime has great difficulty stopping states with acute security problems (adversaries with conventional superiority or nuclear capability), from obtaining nuclear weapons. In fact, the empirical evidence suggests that the NPT and the nuclear non-proliferation regime cannot stop these states from acquiring nuclear weapons; nor should it be expected that the regime could prevent proliferation. This is because the regime focuses only on the supply side of the proliferation problem by attempting to keep critical technologies from non-nuclear states; it does not address the cause of proliferation, the insecurity of states.

The nuclear non-proliferation regime attempts to arrest the spread of nuclear weapons in three ways.[100] First, it seeks to delay a state's nuclear weapons programme by inhibiting the transfer of the technology to develop nuclear weapons. By inhibiting the transfer of this technology, the state must reverse-engineer critical technologies or develop them using its own resources. To do either of these things will take more time than if the state could freely acquire technology from advanced industrial states.

Second, the nuclear non-proliferation regime increases the financial and opportunity costs that emerging nuclear states must pay to obtain nuclear weapons by making it difficult to acquire the equipment and material necessary to produce nuclear weapons. There are bilateral and multilateral approaches adopted by NWS and other states in the nuclear non-proliferation regime to prevent the transfer of nuclear-related information, equipment and material to a non-nuclear weapon state. A bilateral approach is the use of safeguard agreements to ensure that when nuclear technology is given to a NNWS, it pledges to use that technology only for peaceful purposes. A multilateral approach to the control of nuclear-related technology is also used by the NWS, principally through the Nuclear Suppliers Group, an association of Western and Soviet Bloc countries created during the Cold War to limit exports of sensitive materials and technologies.[101] A second multilateral approach to preventing nuclear proliferation is executed through an international organization, the IAEA. This organization is charged with, among other duties, monitoring the nuclear facilities of the NNWS to ensure that no nuclear weapons are being produced. By making it difficult to acquire the technology necessary to design, produce and maintain nuclear weapons, these bilateral and multilateral approaches to non-proliferation complicate the acquisition of nuclear weapons by a non-nuclear state.

Third, the nuclear non-proliferation regime lowers the information costs among its members and makes it possible to share information about suspected states among the members.[102] The sharing of information among the members makes it more likely that pattern recognition will be possible. Pattern recognition is the attempt of the regime to determine which states are attempting to acquire nuclear-related technologies and to identify the specific technologies proliferators are attempting to acquire from advanced industrial countries. By facilitating information among advanced industrial countries, there is a greater chance that a state can be stopped from acquiring relevant technologies because states attempting to obtain nuclear weapons will not acquire complete technologies from advanced industrial states. To do so would make detection easier. Rather, these states will acquire the components from many advanced industrial states in order to make detection more arduous. The timely sharing of information facilitates the identification of precisely what the state is attempting to acquire, and from whom, which countries and corporations.

However, despite its strengths, the nuclear non-proliferation regime has not prevented states (India, Israel, Pakistan, and South Africa) from acquiring nuclear weapons, and even signatories of the NPT (Iraq, Iran and North Korea) have acquired or are attempting to acquire nuclear weapons. These examples illustrate that there are significant problems with each aspect of the non-proliferation regime.

The first problem is that the regime can at best only delay, not stop, a nuclear weapons programme. This is so for two reasons. The first reason why delay, even significant delay, may not be possible is due to the assistance given by nuclear weapon states to emerging nuclear states. Nuclear states, both visible and opaque, often have cooperated with emerging nuclear states to assist their developing programmes. The United States assisted Great Britain and France with their nuclear programmes; the Soviet Union assisted China; France assisted Israel; Israel may have assisted South Africa; China may have assisted Pakistan; and Pakistan may be assisting Iran with its programme.[103] These examples demonstrate that nuclear weapon states are willing to place their national interests – assistance to allied states – before the interests of the nuclear non-proliferation regime. The recognition of this fact alone does not permit optimism concerning the ability of the regime to delay nuclear proliferation. The second reason why delay is not possible is because technologies and information do not pose barriers to nuclear proliferation, only hurdles over which states as technically advanced as the United States in the 1940s must pass. As Peter Zimmerman notes,

> Given the fact that the basics of nuclear weapon design and construction are now widely known, as is the technology for producing plutonium and enriched uranium, no nation with the technical abilities of the United States in 1941 can ever be said to be more than five years from possessing a nuclear weapon, regardless of the state of its program at any given moment. There are no technical barriers to nuclear proliferation, only hurdles of greater or lesser size which can be leaped over at greater or lesser cost and on time scales commensurate with the budget for the project and the skill of the workers.[104]

The second problem is that the nuclear non-proliferation regime makes proliferation more expensive but David Kay, who was one of the team leaders of IAEA inspections in Iraq, notes that the regime may make proliferation only very modestly more expensive:

One of the critical components for the Iraqi centrifuge program was maraging steel. I often tried to convince the Iraqis to tell us who their supplier was. Once I tried the argument – 'Don't tell me you can't rat on people who have been your friends. They charge you, you pay a risk premium, and everybody knows that you pay a risk premium because there's a risk that the supplier will be exposed. Go ahead and tell us.' Instead, [the scientific head of the Iraqi nuclear program Dr. Jaffar Dhia] Jaffar pulled out the invoice (without the supplier's name on it) and, sure enough, they had only paid a couple of cents per pound over the world market price for maraging steel. That tells you that for a lot of commodities there is, in fact, not much of a risk. And, maraging steel is one of the more strictly controlled.[105]

The third problem with the nuclear non-proliferation regime is that the recognition pattern of nuclear weapon technology facilitated by the regime may be defeated if the states who possess nuclear weapons technology decide to transfer nuclear weapons technology to proliferators in spite of the regime for reasons of national interest, avarice, or because the states are allied.

The empirical evidence provided by the cases of states who have acquired nuclear weapons regardless of the regime suggests that states who face adversaries armed with nuclear weapons capability, or who face an adversary with preponderant conventional capabilities, and for whom the superpowers are unwilling to extend deterrence will proliferate, irrespective of the non-proliferation regime.[106] States will do what they can to guarantee their survival, including breaking international norms to acquire the means to their security.[107]

The recognition of these problems with the nuclear non-proliferation regime suggests that nuclear proliferation is not a difficulty that can be solved on the supply side. There are too many suppliers of nuclear weapons technologies, including the 'second tier suppliers', the nuclear and non-nuclear states such as Brazil, China, Israel, India, Pakistan, and Taiwan, for a coordinated effort to prevent exports, like the effort sponsored by the Nuclear Suppliers Group, to succeed.[108] Undoubtedly, there are sophisticated technologies, like krytrons, high-speed triggers for nuclear weapons, that are extremely difficult to develop because their production requires sophisticated technologies. However, the absence of the sophisticated technologies does not mean states cannot make nuclear weapons, only that they cannot make the most sophisticated, reliable, and safest nuclear weapons.[109]

Nuclear proliferation is a problem that only can be solved on the demand side. If states feel that nuclear weapons are not needed for their security, then they will not seek to acquire them. During the Cold War, many states who might have acquired nuclear weapons (e.g. Federal Republic of Germany, German Democratic Republic, Italy, Japan, and Poland) did not because they had security guarantees from one of the superpowers.[110] Others attempted to obtain nuclear weapons, like Brazil, Egypt and South Korea, but did not, largely due to pressure from US.[111]

With the end of the Cold War, incentives to acquire nuclear weapons will be higher for two reasons. The first incentive is the multipolar international system that is emerging in the wake of the collapse of the Soviet Union and the end of the bipolar Cold War system. Benjamin Frankel has shown that a multipolar international system is more conducive to proliferation than is a bipolar system. The multipolar system that is emerging in the wake of the Cold War is more conducive to proliferation because multipolar systems are prone to instability for three reasons: first, the number of conflictive relationships are greater;[112] second, alliances are more flexible and harder to manage than in bipolarity and are therefore less effective;[113] and third, alliances are more susceptible to miscalculation and misperception.[114] Frankel captures the difficulty of maintaining alliances in multipolarity succinctly when he writes, 'The relatively large number of powers in the system makes it difficult to have confidence in the commitment of allies while it is still too small to allow for ready compensation if an ally defects or shifts alliance.'[115]

The second incentive for nuclear proliferation in the wake of the Cold War is the declining size of the United States strategic nuclear arsenal due to the START-I and START-II arms control treaties, and the reduction in the conventional military capabilities of the United States. These reductions in forces make credible extended deterrence more difficult because the capabilities of the United States to project power in order to defend credibly non-nuclear allies, are reduced. Therefore, the incentives of non-nuclear states allied with the United States to acquire nuclear weapons to ensure their own security increase.[116]

While the incentives to obtain nuclear weapons have increased and the ability of the United States to extend security guarantees has not improved with the end of the Cold War, nuclear proliferation should continue. The non-proliferation regime cannot arrest the spread of nuclear weapons because it cannot address the fundamental causes of proliferation – the insecurity of states in an anarchic international system.

The lessons of Iraq's attempt to acquire nuclear weapons while remaining a signatory of the NPT demonstrate the weakness of the regime. Kay describes the debate that occurred in an Iraqi task force created to review their clandestine nuclear programme in the wake of the Israeli attack on Iraq's Osirak reactor in 1981:

The diplomats said Iraq should stay in the NPT, and go ahead with the clandestine program. They said it would just draw too much attention to the program if Iraq got out. The scientists, being far more upstanding, said no, get out of the NPT; it didn't protect us anyway when the Israelis attacked our reactor, and let's go ahead with our clandestine program as is our right. At the final meeting, Saddam Hussein turned to the individual who eventually became the scientific head of the Iraqi program, Jaffar Dhia Jaffar, and said, 'Dr. Jaffar, if we stay in the NPT, will it in any way hinder the clandestine nuclear program?' Jaffar says his answer was an immediate and unequivocal no; he said it would have absolutely no effect upon Iraq's program.[117]

Hussein then ordered the continuation of the secret programme, while Iraq remained a party to the NPT. There is tacit recognition, at least among American officials, that the non-proliferation regime has failed to prevent or adequately retard the acquisition of nuclear weapons by states such as Iraq. Such tacit recognition of the failure of the regime to arrest proliferation adequately is found in United States Department of Defense initiative to emphasize counterproliferation in United States policy as well as non-proliferation. The counterproliferation initiative, with respect to nuclear proliferation, combines the more traditional elements of non-proliferation policy, prevention, with measures to provide protection in the event that a crisis or war were to occur with an emerging nuclear state, such as Iran or North Korea. Prevention usually has included the following four measures: first, dissuading states from developing nuclear weapons by providing security assistance; second, denial, such as export controls; third, arms control measures such as nuclear-free zones; and fourth, international pressure, such as sanctions. Coupled with prevention are four measures to provide protection from the nuclear threats: first, defusing the threat already posed by nuclear states, such as destroying their nuclear capabilities; second, deterring the state from using or threatening to use its nuclear weapons; third, offence, such as developing capabilities to locate and destroy tactical ballistic missiles like SCUDs or their mobile launchers; and fourth, defence, such as developing theatre ballistic missile defences.[118]

Whether counterproliferation will be more successful than non-proliferation remains to be seen, of course. However, there are reasons to be pessimistic because it is difficult to use force to halt a state's nuclear programme. The example of the United Nations' effort in Iraq demonstrates that nothing short of the occupation of the state is necessary to locate and destroy definitively the material aspects of the nuclear programme.

Recognizing this, there should be little desire in the United States or in other countries to incur the diplomatic and military costs necessary to arrest and reverse nuclear proliferation. In addition, and more fundamentally, counterproliferation does nothing to address the cause of nuclear proliferation, the insecurity of states, and therefore states will continue to acquire nuclear weapons to increase their security, even in the face of the increased counterproliferation capability of the United States. In fact, the counterproliferation policy of the United States will heighten emerging nuclear states' perception of the United States as a threat, and thus such a policy will only increase the incentives to acquire nuclear weapons.[119]

The Benefits of the Non-proliferation Regime

The value of the nuclear non-proliferation regime for NWS, such as the United States, is that the regime exists to prevent the spread of nuclear capabilities to non-nuclear states while preserving the nuclear capabilities of the declared nuclear states. The nuclear states want to keep nuclear capabilities to themselves alone. Realism explains this desire of the nuclear states. Were nuclear capability to spread, the security of the nuclear states would be jeopardized, as would their ability to defend non-nuclear allies, and to project power.

In order to combat the spread of nuclear weapons, the nuclear non-proliferation regime was created by the established nuclear states. The established nuclear states defined the norm, that is, 'the standard of behavior defined in terms of rights and obligations',[120] for the rest of the world: the declared nuclear states had the right to possess nuclear weapons, but no other state has this right. The established nuclear states declared proliferation to be a violation of a norm of international politics; violators were subject to punishment by way of diplomatic, economic, or even military sanctions. The non-proliferation regime is a creation of the great powers. The regime allows the great powers to punish violators, not in the name of power politics, but rather in the name of a more felicitous concept, the maintenance of an international norm. The non-proliferation regime, and its manifestation, the NPT, serve as a veil for power politics.

The first value of the non-proliferation regime for the international system is that, by making proliferation harder, it may reduce the number of states that acquire nuclear weapons, although the regime cannot stop states who are willing to incur the costs of sanctions from violating the non-proliferation norm. In order to punish a state, however, it is necessary to have credible evidence of its nuclear programme. One of the lessons of the Gulf War is that it is difficult to detect nuclear weapons programme if the state takes steps to defeat the intelligence capabilities of the nuclear weapon states:

> We know from the Iraqi program that they had learned to defeat national technical means (NTM), i.e. signal and satellite intelligence. There had been two major routes. There was a major leakage from the US intelligence program on key satellite data. It had been passed to the Soviets by [the American spy for the Soviet Union] Christopher Boyce. For one reason or another, the information had been passed to the Iraqis, and they had learned with great sophistication how to conceal their activities from US satellite detection. Also, during the Iran–Iraq War, the US shared strategic intelligence information with the Iraqis. The Iraqis were able to look at US data, and they could tell from the data how it was obtained. They were smart enough, with the help of the East Germans and others, to devise ways of beating the system. The intelligence community has invested billions of dollars in NTM and doesn't like to hear this. Unfortunately, though, it really is true that NTM is relatively easy to defeat if you can spend the money and you have the skills.[121]

A lesson of the UN effort after the Gulf War to halt Iraq's nuclear programme is that it is very difficult to monitor all aspects of the programme. A second lesson of the UN effort is that, while much of Iraq's equipment is destroyed, the knowledge to create nuclear production facilities and possibly even nuclear weapons still exists among the Iraqi scientists and engineers who developed a complex and sophisticated nuclear weapons programme. This fact alone means that for some time to come, Iraq will be a matter of concern for the UN and the US.

The second value of the nuclear non-proliferation regime for the international system is that it decelerates the pace of nuclear proliferation because it makes nuclear proliferation more difficult. By making nuclear proliferation more difficult, the regime marginally decreases the speed at which states acquire nuclear weapons capability. A slower pace of nuclear proliferation may make nuclear war less likely because the first state to obtain nuclear weapons, the primary proliferator, may develop a secure second-strike capability and therefore, if it is defensively motivated, i.e. only seeking to make itself secure, it will not be threatened by its adversary's, the secondary proliferator's, emerging nuclear capability. However, if the primary proliferator is not defensively motivated, but offensively motivated, then the reverse may be true. The primary proliferator may use its nuclear capabilities to coerce the secondary proliferator.

3   THE COSTS OF THE NUCLEAR NON-PROLIFERATION REGIME

The nuclear non-proliferation regime has important costs to individual states as well as to the international system. There are two costs for the nuclear weapon states. The first is technological. Nuclear weapon states must make available to non-nuclear states peaceful nuclear technology under the conditions of the NPT. The second cost is that the regime promotes opaque proliferation which makes it harder for nuclear weapon states to detect and, in war, to destroy the opaque state's nuclear weapons programme. The cost for the international system is that opaque proliferation may make the international system less stable, it may promote crises and wars.

The Causes of Opaque Proliferation

Opaque nuclear proliferation is the means by which states proliferate today.[122] Visible proliferation is no longer an option for states because further proliferation is not in the interests of the great powers. The great powers have codified the norm of nuclear non-proliferation in the NPT. So states have great incentive to acquire nuclear weapons opaquely in order to avoid violating the norm of nuclear non-proliferation. There are three reasons why states acquire nuclear weapons opaquely and not visibly. The first reason is offensive. States do not want adversaries to acquire nuclear weapons but desire, instead, to be the only state to possess nuclear weapons capability. Two results stem from this: first, opacity allows states to acquire nuclear weapons covertly, before an adversary does, and thus to possess a significant temporary military advantage over the adversary; second, opacity does not compel other states to acquire nuclear weapons as a response because there is no indisputable evidence of nuclear proliferation. In time, evidence will accumulate, and then other states will be pressured to obtain nuclear weapons, but opacity maximizes the period of time when the primary proliferator is the sole state with nuclear weapons capability.

The second reason why states acquire nuclear weapons opaquely is defensive. Opacity minimizes the risks of preventive war because potential initiators of preventive war, regional adversaries, are unable to ascertain where an opaque state's nuclear facilities and weapons are located because it is likely that they lack sufficient intelligence capability.[123] Thus, opacity serves as a powerful deterrent to preventive war due to the uncertainty and the enormous costs of nuclear retaliation if a state initiates a preventive war.

A third reason for opaque proliferation is due to the impact of the nuclear non-proliferation regime. The non-proliferation regime declares nuclear non-proliferation to be a norm of international politics. States who violate the regime incur the risk of sanctions. Opacity helps defeat sanctions because the regime is never violated explicitly and thus there is never sufficient incontrovertible evidence that an opaque state has acquired nuclear weapons.

The Negative Consequences of Opaque Nuclear Proliferation

Opaque proliferation has a detrimental effect on four factors: international stability; deterrence; the opaque state itself; and on the nuclear non-proliferation regime.

The first negative effect of opaque proliferation for international stability is that it, like visible nuclear proliferation, increases the risk of nuclear war. This is simply because as more states acquire nuclear weapons, the chance of nuclear war increases statistically. A second effect of opacity on international stability is that opaque proliferation may heighten crisis instability. In a crisis, a state may attempt to pre-empt the opaque state's nuclear arsenal because it might believe that the opaque state is going to strike first, as it must if it has a vulnerable arsenal. By striking the opaque state first, the state may believe that any retaliation after the first strike would be acceptable. Because all information about the size of the opaque state's arsenal, indeed even its existence, is hidden, a state could come to believe that it could limit significantly the damage it received in retaliation if it struck first, and this belief diminishes crisis stability. A third negative effect of opacity on international stability is that opacity has negative effects on a state's nuclear command and control system and the operations of its nuclear forces, creating an increased danger of nuclear inadvertence. As Peter Feaver has shown, opacity may have a negative effect on a state's nuclear operations because opaque states compartmentalize information about the nuclear programme. As a result, important operational issues regarding the nuclear programme may not be addressed sufficiently and problems may not be solved or even considered until, in the midst of a crisis, when the state is quickly readying its arsenal, operational problems arise.[124] It is at this time, when the state is forced to confront the neglected operational aspects of its nuclear arsenal, such as how to deploy nuclear weapons, that the risk of nuclear inadvertence is heightened. An example of this danger is found in the purported meeting of Israeli officials at the outset of the October 1973 War, where these officials discussed, possibly for the first time, nuclear options to prevent the Egyptian and Syrian advances.[125] Feaver writes, 'If these accounts are credible, Israel confronted serious nuclear operational dilemmas and had very little time to resolve them.'[126] As a result, the risk of nuclear inadvertence in Israel was intensified due to Israel's neglect of nuclear operations. A fourth negative effect of opacity on instability is due to the increased risk of inadvertent nuclear escalation.

Barry Posen elucidates this danger: 'Unpredicted by the political and military leaders who permit or order them, large-scale conventional operations may come into direct contact with the nuclear forces of an adversary and substantially affect the victim's confidence in his future ability to operate these forces [as the victim wanted to].'[127] Conventional attacks are particularly dangerous where there is a degradation of 'the basic nuclear retaliatory capability of the victim – his second-strike capability – for among nuclear powers this capability is the only insurance policy against nuclear coercion or annihilating attack.'[128] The danger of inadvertent escalation is especially acute for opaque nuclear states because an attacker may not believe that the state does not yet possess nuclear weapons, or because the attacker believes that it could strike only conventional forces without harming the opaque state's retaliatory capability. For example, in a conventional conflict between Syria and Israel, Syria may attack Israeli airfields in order to destroy the aircraft and runways. By doing so, Syria may inadvertently jeopardize Israel's retaliatory capability by destroying these aircraft. Local forces may be placed in a 'use them or lose them' situation, where the planes and their nuclear weapons would be destroyed if not used; or Israel may be forced to use nuclear weapons before its nuclear arsenal, specifically its secure second-strike capability, is lost to attrition.[129]

The second negative result of opaque proliferation affects nuclear deterrence. Deterrence of premeditated attacks is unlikely to obtain unless the adversary knows that the opaque state is, in fact, a nuclear state. Therefore, the opaque state must sacrifice some opacity for deterrence, but not too much, because to do so might provoke adversaries, invite sanctions, and increase the risk of preventive war. Thus there is a risk that deterrence will not obtain because too little opacity was sacrificed by the opaque state. The third negative consequence of opaque proliferation affects the opaque proliferators themselves. The knowledge of the ways in which the nuclear revolution has changed international politics may not be instilled in the relevant individuals and organizations in the opaque state to the same degree as they are in the United States and in Russia. These states will have the same debates as the United States and the Soviet Union had on the requirements of deterrence; on the trade-offs between assured destruction and damage limitation; on the disparity between declared nuclear policy and actual nuclear policy; and on the risks of nuclear inadvertence. These debates are best addressed in a public forum where scholars and policymakers can critique the policies and doctrines of the government and military in an effort to expose fallacies; to minimize the danger of crises, and, if they occur, to promote successful crisis management; to encourage the development of carefully reasoned doctrine; to minimize the incongruities between doctrine, the manner in which political leaders think that nuclear weapons will be used, and the nuclear use policies of the military, the manner in which the military intends to use nuclear weapons; and to minimize the risk of nuclear inadvertence. If these issues are not debated openly, then it is more likely that flawed policies will not be recognized and corrected.[130]

The fourth negative consequence of opaque proliferation is its effect on the nuclear non-proliferation regime. The opaque proliferation is a response to the non-proliferation regime because the regime declares proliferation of states who were not nuclear powers as of January 1, 1967 (i.e. the United States, Soviet Union/Russia, Great Britain, France, and China) to be a violation of the international norm of nuclear non-proliferation and subject to diplomatic, economic, and military sanctions if a state persists in its effort to acquire nuclear weapons. The nuclear non-proliferation regime increases the costs of proliferation but the desire of a state to gain the security provided by nuclear weapons will be too tempting for states who face significant conventional or nuclear threats to their security. All of the opaque states, India, Israel, Pakistan, and South Africa, perceived imminent threats to their security, their independence, and even their survival as a state. Faced with the unenviable decision of acquiring nuclear weapons, risking the imposition of sanctions by the established nuclear states for violating a norm of international politics, and jeopardizing their security as a state, all chose the latter. By choosing to develop nuclear weapons, these states increased their security in an anarchic world but incurred the risk of sanctions and possibly even the use of military force by the established nuclear states. Opaque proliferation obviously undermines the non-proliferation regime because it provides states with an avenue to the acquisition of nuclear weapons in spite of the existence of the regime.

The Positive Consequences of Opaque Nuclear Proliferation

Opaque proliferation also has four important benefits as well. With respect to international stability, there are two positive benefits of opaque proliferation.

The first is that it prevents a chain reaction of proliferation where states develop nuclear weapons in rapid succession because an adversarial state did so. With opaque proliferation, reaction to an adversary's acquisition of nuclear weapons will occur because states match the capabilities of adversaries, but it occurs over more time when compared with visible proliferation, and the greater period of time is beneficial for stability. The second positive result of opaque proliferation for international stability is that it reduces the risk of pre-emption or preventive war. Pre-emption or preventive war is extremely risky if the aggressor is not absolutely certain of the capabilities and location of the defender's nuclear weapons and nuclear facilities. This uncertainty is an important disincentive to attack. Such uncertainty is present among visible nuclear states but visible nuclear states have more robust early warning capabilities because they have greater economic and military capabilities in general than opaque states. The uncertainty is a major benefit of opacity because uncertainty is maximized, and this serves to reduce incentive for preventive war. A regional adversary will not have the capabilities to determine the location of nuclear weapons and nuclear weapons facilities. It is also likely that even a superpower will not possess the certainty needed to guarantee that the opaque proliferator could not retaliate, causing an unacceptable level of damage to the superpower or its allies.[131] Opacity may also defeat pressures for preventive war caused by the asymmetrical timing in the development of nuclear capabilities by rival states. Once a state develops nuclear weapons, it will be tempted to wage preventive war before its adversary's nuclear capability comes to fruition. Opacity may be able to defeat this pressure for preventive war, again due to the introduction by opacity of high levels of uncertainty about the capabilities, the nuclear facilities, and the intentions of the state. Thus, opacity provides a significant check on preventive war or incentives to pre-empt caused by crisis instability.

The second benefit of opaque proliferation is that it allows states to acquire nuclear capabilities while avoiding the sanctions of the nuclear non-proliferation regime. States can avoid sanctions because it is not certain to the great powers and the IAEA that a violation of the regime has occurred. It may be known in general terms to the great powers and the IAEA that a state is developing or possesses nuclear weapons capability but empirical evidence is difficult to acquire. In fact, it requires the co-operation of the state, and opaque states clearly are reluctant to cooperate.

A third benefit of opaque proliferation is that, in George Quester's words, it leaves no 'footprints': the nuclear programme is hidden from the public and so it can be reversed or dissolved more easily than a visible programme.[132] The reason why the programme may be reversed or dissolved more easily is explained by Neil Joeck: 'having flexibility [to secretly halt a state's nuclear programme]...would be particularly helpful in South Asia, where public opinion tends to support nuclear weapons. So long as actions which would reverse proliferation were hidden from public view, a leader would not appear to be losing face, nor [would he be able]...to be accused of capitulation, which would be the consequence of an overt reversal.'[133] Also, the reversibility of opaque proliferation leaves no permanent record to embarrass or burden future relations between states if their relations improve.[134]

The fourth benefit of opacity is that it permits great powers to ignore proliferation by allies while still supporting the nuclear non-proliferation regime. For example, in the 1980s, Pakistan's opaque proliferation stance facilitated cooperation between the US and Pakistan in their efforts to assist the *mujahideen* fighting the Soviets in Afghanistan. Had Pakistan openly defied the nuclear non-proliferation regime, it would have been harder for the United States to cooperate with Pakistan in assisting the *mujahideen*. Moreover, Israel's decision to proliferate opaquely did not force the United States to make a decision between pressuring Israel to abandon its nuclear programme or not pressuring Israel, and thus exposing the hypocrisy of the United States, and as a possible consequence, destroying the regime. Israel's opaque stance has facilitated the ability of the United States to ignore Israel's nuclear weapons capability, while the United States supported the nuclear non-proliferation regime.[135] It may be, however, that the relatively comfortable position of the United States is over. As price of NPT extension, non-nuclear weapon states may pressure the United States to coerce Israel to end its nuclear programme in return for diplomatic and military agreements with its Arab neighbours.

Although opaque proliferation has many positive aspects, a matter of central importance for stable nuclear deterrence among opaque states is whether opaque states are able to deter premeditated attacks.[136] If an opaque state cannot deter premeditated attacks, then opaque proliferation is dangerous. This issue cannot be thoroughly analysed here but, nevertheless, the essence of the debate may be defined. It pivots on the perennial question of 'how much is enough', what level of nuclear forces is needed to deter premeditated attacks upon the state itself.[137] If many nuclear forces are needed to deter premeditated attacks, then clearly opaque states will have difficulty deterring attacks as their arsenals, with the exception of Israel, are believed to be very small.[138] However, if few nuclear weapons are needed to deter premeditated attacks upon the opaque state itself, then the effect of opaque proliferation on deterrence of a premeditated attack may not be detrimental. Even under conditions of opaque proliferation, where the existence of the nuclear arsenal is not certain, deterrence of premeditated attacks is likely to obtain. This is due to the logic that McGeorge Bundy noted in 1969, to wit, political leaders become very cautious in matters involving nuclear weapons:

> There is an enormous gulf between what political leaders really think about nuclear weapons and what is assumed in complex calculations of relative 'advantage' in simulated strategic warfare. Think-tank analysts can set levels of 'acceptable' damage well up in the tens of millions of lives. They can assume that the loss of dozens of great cities is somehow a real choice for sane men. They are in an unreal world. In the real world of real political leaders – whether here or in the Soviet Union – a decision that would bring even one hydrogen bomb on one city of one's country would be recognized in advance as a catastrophic blunder; ten bombs on ten cities would be a disaster beyond history; and a hundred bombs on a hundred cities are unthinkable...it is one thing for military men to maintain our deterrent force with vigilant skill, and it is quite another for anyone to assume that their necessary contingency plans have any serious interest for political leaders. The object of political men – quite rightly – is that these weapons should never be used. I have watched two Presidents working on strategic contingency plans, and what interested them most was simply to make sure that none of these awful events would occur.[139]

The research of Marc Trachtenberg on the Cuban Missile Crisis reinforces Bundy's opinion that the existence of nuclear weapons results in the cautious behaviour and utmost concern of political leaders who face nuclear opponents, that nuclear weapons not be used.[140]

An adversary cannot be certain that an opaque state possesses nuclear weapons. However, the risk of nuclear retaliation in the event of an attack is too great to countenance an attack. As Bundy and Trachtenberg argue, political leaders will be extremely cautious and reluctant even to consider launching an attack against a nuclear adversary. For these reasons, deterrence of premeditated attacks is likely to obtain for opaque nuclear states as well as visible nuclear states.

4 POWER POLITICS AND THE NUCLEAR NON-PROLIFERATION REGIME

This chapter has examined the causes of nuclear proliferation; the effectiveness of the nuclear non-proliferation regime; and the benefits and the costs of the regime. Four conclusions are offered. First, the principal reason why states proliferate is to become more secure from attack. Security is increased by matching the capabilities of adversaries. If an adversary has acquired nuclear weapons, the state must match that capability in order to avoid nuclear coercion. If adversaries have not developed nuclear weapons, the state may do so first, as Israel did, in order to gain security from the opponents' overwhelming conventional capabilities.

Second, because states acquire nuclear weapons for reasons of security the attempt by the nuclear non-proliferation regime to stop nuclear proliferation by controlling the exchange of nuclear and dual-use technology, will not be successful because the regime does nothing to address the fundamental causes of proliferation, the insecurity of states. States know that nuclear weapons capability can increase their security by providing deterrence of premeditated attacks and providing protection against nuclear coercion. Extended deterrence from a superpower offsets, to a degree, the pressure to acquire nuclear weapons. However, neither the United States nor the Soviet Union was never willing or able to extend deterrence to all states who faced a precarious security position; pariah states, like Iran, North Korea, South Africa, were left without security guarantees. It is no surprise that these states developed or are developing nuclear weapons. In the post-Cold War world in the absence of the Soviet threat, the United States will be less willing to extend deterrence to states around the world and less able to with the reductions in its strategic nuclear arsenal. Therefore, the incentives for states to acquire nuclear weapons, including great powers like Germany and Japan, should increase.

Third, the nuclear non-proliferation regime provides a great benefit for nuclear weapon states because they are the only states legally permitted to possess nuclear weapons. Furthermore, the regime allows the nuclear states to sanction states that violate its norm and attempt to develop nuclear weapons. The regime provides a veil for power politics. The regime provides a legal fig-leaf for the actions the United States and other nuclear states would take in the absence of the regime to preserve their security; that is, to keep nuclear capability from spreading and endangering their interests.

For the stability of the international system, the benefit of the nuclear non-proliferation regime is less transparent. The regime does slow the pace of nuclear proliferation and for that reason it promotes stability.

However, the fourth conclusion of this chapter is that the nuclear non-proliferation regime promotes opaque proliferation, which may have a detrimental effect on the opaque state itself, and on the international system. The injurious effects include limiting the effectiveness of nuclear deterrence because the opaque state must strike a balance between revealing enough information to make deterrence credible, and yet not too much information because that would invite sanctions; and limiting the public debate about the nuclear doctrine of the state. These factors jeopardize the stability of the international system because these factors make nuclear war more likely. Yet, it is also the case that opaque proliferation provides important benefits to the state and international system as well. Opaque proliferation serves as a guard against preventive war and pre-emption and thus strengthens crisis stability. These factors lower the risk of nuclear war by promoting stable deterrence.

Ultimately, the nuclear weapon states will have to accept, first, the fact that there are more nuclear states than the NPT permits. Second, they will have to accept that the nuclear non-proliferation regime cannot stop, but can only delay, the spread of nuclear weapons. Third, nuclear weapon states will have to realize that their efforts to halt or to delay nuclear proliferation are decaying due to the relatively unsophisticated technology needed to acquire nuclear weapons, the second-tier suppliers, and most importantly, the political incentives that states have to acquire nuclear weapons. Acknowledging these facts does not permit an optimistic conclusion since the capability to produce nuclear weapons will continue to spread to more states. Moreover, with the end of the Cold War more states will have the political incentives to develop nuclear weapons. Given this condition, the utility of the nuclear non-proliferation regime may be questioned. However, a principal benefit of the nuclear non-proliferation regime will remain, the great powers still will be able to insist that their actions to halt nuclear proliferation are done in the interests of an international regime, and not due to their own self-interests, the interests of power politics.

NOTES

1. A slightly different version of this chapter appears in *Security Studies*, 4, no. 3 (Spring 1995): pp. 463–519. The author would like to thank all the participants of 'The Nuclear Non-Proliferation Regime: Post Cold War Perspectives', Symposium, Marquette University, 13 and 14 May, 1994, for their helpful comments; especially Benjamin Frankel, T.V. Paul, and K. Subrahmanyam. The author also would like to thank Theresa Barton, Avner Cohen, Avi Kober, and Paul Zimmerman.
2. For a good synopsis of the debate over the period of extension of the NPT, see Lennon, 'The 1995 NPT Extension Conference', pp. 207–8.
3. For analysis of the issues surrounding a comprehensive test ban and the utility of a CTBT see Frans Berkhout, Oleg Bukharin, Harold Feiveson, and

Marvin Miller, 'A Cutoff in the Production of Fissile Material', *International Security*, 19, no. 3 (Winter 1994/95): 167–202; Jozef Goldblat and David Cox, eds, *Nuclear Weapon Tests: Prohibition or Limitation?* (Oxford: Oxford University Press, 1988); and Steve Fetter, *Toward a Comprehensive Test Ban* (Cambridge, Mass.: Ballinger, 1988).

4. On the Israeli nuclear programme see Shlomo Aronson with the assistance of Oded Brosh, *The Politics and Strategy of Nuclear Weapons in the Middle East: Opacity, Theory and Reality, 1960–1991 – An Israeli Perspective* (Albany, NY: State University Press of New York, 1992); Frank Barnaby, *The Invisible Bomb* (London: I.B. Tauris, 1989); Shai Feldman, *Israeli Nuclear Deterrence: A Strategy for the 1980s* (New York: Columbia University Press, 1982); Seymour Hersh, *The Samson Option: Israel's Nuclear Arsenal and American Foreign Policy* (New York: Random House, 1991); Peter Pry, *Israel's Nuclear Arsenal* (Boulder, Colo.: Westview Press, 1984).

5. See Aabha Dixit, 'West Grabs Victory in NPT', *Defense News*, 15–21 May, 1995, p. 24; Barbara Crossette, 'Treaty Aimed at Halting Spread of Nuclear Weapons Extended', *New York Times*, 12 May, 1995, p. A1; and Michael Littlejohns and Bernard Gray, 'N–Weapons Treaty Made Permanent', *Financial Times*, 12 May, 1995, p. 4. Also see Bernard Gray, 'A Treaty Acclaimed', *Financial Times*, 11 May, 1995, p. 13; and 'A Nuclear Milestone', *New York Times*, 12 May, 1995, p. A18.

6. Stephen Krasner defines a regime as a set '...of implicit or explicit principles, norms, rules, and decision-making procedures around which actors' expectations converge in a given area of international relations.' Stephen D. Krasner, 'Structural Causes and Regime Consequences: Regimes as Intervening Variables', in Stephen D. Krasner, ed., *International Regimes* (Ithaca: Cornell University Press, 1983), p. 2.

7. This study addresses solely the nuclear non-proliferation regime and not the biological, chemical, and missile non-proliferation regimes, although, of course, each of the questions about the nuclear non-proliferation regime addressed by the study may be asked of the other regimes.

8. The danger that nuclear proliferation may cause to the US itself, its interests and allies, is demonstrated by Robert J. Art, 'A Defensible Defense: America's Grand Strategy After the Cold War', *International Security*, 15, no. 4 (Spring 1991): 5–53; and Steven R. David, 'Why the Third World Still Matters', *International Security*, 17, no. 3 (Winter 1992/93): 127–59.

9. The recent agreement between the United States and North Korea has been widely praised in the United States, however, there are several negative aspects of the agreement that must be emphasized. First, North Korea's agreement to end its gas–graphite reactor programme and to close its reprocessing facility may be irrelevant because North Korea may have produced all the plutonium it needs to meet its political goals, such as deterrence of an attack. Second, providing light-water reactors may not stop the North Korean weapons programme because light-water reactors can produce weapon-grade plutonium if the reactors are optimized to do so. Third, the agreement does not obligate North Korea to dismantle its reactors and reprocessing facility, and to send its spent fuel abroad until the light-water reactors are almost complete. As a result, North Korea has the ability to add 4 to 5 nuclear weapons to its nuclear arsenal in a short time. This seriously

complicates any effort by the US to punish North Korea for violating the agreement. Additionally, North Korea could construct, without being detected by the International Atomic Energy Agency (IAEA) or the US, a small reprocessing plant that could reprocess the spent fuel in its possession presently, or that from the light-water reactors. See David Albright and Kevin O'Neill, 'The Price of Non-proliferation', *The Bulletin of the Atomic Scientists* (January/February 1995): 27–9. Also see Michael J. Mazarr, 'Going Just a Little Nuclear: Non-proliferation Lessons from North Korea', *International Security*, 20, no. 2 (Fall 1995): 92–122.

10. Reports concerning Japanese considerations to develop nuclear weapons include Jim Mann and Leslie Helm, 'Japan Shifts Its Stand on Ruling Out A-Bomb', *Los Angeles Times*, 9 July, 1993, p. A9; T.R. Reid, 'Japan's Shift on A-Pact Raises Concerns Abroad', *Washington Post*, 15 July, 1993, p. A22; Naoaki Usui, 'Japanese Move on NPT Spurs Nuclear Worries', *Defense News*, 19–25 July, 1993, p. 36; and Clayton Jones, 'Korea Prompts Japan to Review No-Nukes Policy', *Christian Science Monitor*, 10 August, 1993, p. 1.

11. The risk of nuclear inadvertence is a relatively new issue in the nuclear literature, and many excellent works are beginning to debate this issue. See Bruce G. Blair, *The Logic of Accidental Nuclear War* (Washington, DC: Brookings Institution, 1993); Peter Douglas Feaver, *Guarding the Guardians: Civilian Control of Nuclear Weapons in the United States* (Ithaca: Cornell University Press, 1992); Scott D. Sagan, *The Limits of Safety: Organizations, Accidents, and Nuclear Weapons* (Princeton: Princeton University Press, 1993); Sagan, 'The Perils of Proliferation: Organization Theory, Deterrence Theory, and the Spread of Nuclear Weapons,' *International Security*, 18, no. 4 (Spring 1994): 66–107. I term this new debate in the nuclear literature, the debate over the vulnerability of states to nuclear inadvertence, the third great nuclear debate. The first great debate was over the vulnerability of state's nuclear forces; the second great debate was over the vulnerability of a state's command and control to destruction. See Bradley A. Thayer, 'The Risk of Nuclear Inadvertence: A Review Essay,' *Security Studies*, 3, no. 3 (Spring 1994): 428–93.

12. The cost of the obligation of the US and other nuclear states to disarm is likely to increase because the US and the others will be criticized by the non-nuclear states at the Review Conference for not having disarmed completely. Although the nuclear states are obligated by the Treaty to disarm, nuclear disarmament in the foreseeable future will only promote instability for a host of reasons, including the elimination of an important obstacle to conventional war between great powers. See Charles L. Glaser, *Analyzing Strategic Nuclear Policy* (Princeton: Princeton University Press, 1990), pp. 166–203.

13. The term 'opaque proliferation' was coined by Benjamin Frankel in his 'Notes on the Nuclear Underworld', *The National Interest*, no. 9 (Fall 1987): 122–6. The concept was further defined and elaborated in Avner Cohen and Benjamin Frankel, 'Opaque Nuclear Proliferation', *The Journal of Strategic Studies*, 13, no. 3 (September 1990): 14–44, esp. 21–2. Also see the other essays in this special issue of *The Journal of Strategic Studies* for discussion of different aspects of the opaque proliferation phenomenon.

14. For an argument that political incentives, like prestige, are a cause of nuclear proliferation see Ted Greenwood, Harold A. Feiveson, Theodore B.

Taylor, *Nuclear Proliferation: Motivations, Capabilities, and Strategies for Control* (New York: McGraw-Hill, 1977), p. 50; and Stephen M. Meyer, *The Dynamics of Nuclear Proliferation* (Chicago: University of Chicago Press, 1984), pp. 50–5.

15. On de Gaulle's conception of France as a great power see Philip H. Gordon, *A Certain Idea of France: French Security Policy and the Gaullist Legacy* (Princeton: Princeton University Press, 1993). For histories of the French nuclear programme see Colette Barbier, 'The French Decision to Develop a Military Nuclear Programme in the 1950s', *Diplomacy & Statecraft*, 4, no. 1 (March 1993): 103–13; and Lawrence Scheinman, *Atomic Energy Policy in France Under the Fourth Republic* (Princeton: Princeton University Press, 1965).

16. The first quote is cited in Alexander Werth, *De Gaulle* (Baltimore: Penguin Books, 1967), p. 343. The second quote is cited in Charles de Gaulle, *Discours et messages*, 5 vols., (Paris: Plon, 1970), vol. 3, p. 369. Both quotes are cited in Gordon, *A Certain Idea of France*, p. 42.

17. On de Gaulle's desire to be a nuclear third force see Michael M. Harrison, *The Reluctant Ally: France and Atlantic Security* (Baltimore: Johns Hopkins University Press, 1981), pp. 101–14.

18. Michel Debré is quoted in McGeorge Bundy, *Danger and Survival: Choices About the Bomb in the First Fifty Years* (New York: Random House, 1988), p. 499.

19. Alfred Goldberg, 'The Atomic Origins of the British Nuclear Deterrent,' *International Affairs*, 40, no. 2 (July 1964): 427. Cited in Lawrence and Larus, 'A Historical Review of Nuclear Weapons Proliferation and the Development of the NPT', in Robert M. Lawrence and Joel Larus, eds, *Nuclear Proliferation Phase II* (Lawrence: University Press of Kansas, 1974), pp. 2–3.

20. On the history of British nuclear programme see Margaret Gowing, *Britain and Atomic Energy, 1939–1945* (London: Macmillan, 1964); Gowing, assisted by Lorna Arnold, *Independence and Deterrence: Britain and Atomic Energy*, 2 vols (London: Macmillan, 1974); Gowing, 'Nuclear Weapons and the "Special Relationship"', in William Roger Louis and Hedley Bull, eds, *The 'Special Relationship': Anglo-American Relations Since 1945* (Oxford: Clarendon Press, 1986), pp. 117–28; Norris, et al., *Nuclear Weapons Databook vol. V*; Andrew J. Pierre, *Nuclear Politics: The British Experience with an Independent Strategic Force 1939–1970* (London: Oxford University Press, 1972); Richard Rosecrance, 'British Incentives to Become a Nuclear Power', in Rosecrance, *The Dispersion of Nuclear Weapons*, pp. 48–65.

21. Bundy, *Danger and Survival*, 502.

22. On the Indian development of nuclear weapons see Shyam Bhatia, *India's Nuclear Bomb* (New Delhi: Vikas, 1979); Brahma Chellaney, 'The Challenge of Nuclear Arms Control in South Asia', *Survival*, 35, no. 3 (Autumn 1993): 121–36; Chellaney, 'South Asia's Passage to Nuclear Power', *International Security*, 16, no. 1 (Summer 1991): 43–72; Ashok Kapur, *India's Nuclear Option: Atomic Diplomacy and Decision Making* (New York: Praeger, 1976); Onkar Marwah, 'India's Nuclear and Space Programs: Intent and Policy', *International Security*, 2, no. 2 (Fall 1977): 96–121; Ziba Moshaver, *Nuclear Weapons Proliferation in the Indian Subcontinent* (New York: St. Martin's, 1991); K. Subrahmanyam, 'India:

Keeping the Option Open', in Lawrence and Larus, *Nuclear Proliferation*, pp. 112–48; and Raju G.C. Thomas, 'The Strategic Consequences of Nuclear Proliferation in South-west Asia: India's Perspective', *The Journal of Strategic Studies*, 8, no. 4 (December 1985): 67–79; Thomas, 'India's Nuclear and Space Programs: Defense or Development?' *World Politics*, 38, no. 2 (January 1986): 315–42.

23. Histories of the Chinese nuclear programme include Morton Halperin, *China and the Bomb* (New York: Frederick A. Praeger, 1965); Alice Langley Hsieh, 'Communist China and Nuclear Force', in Rosecrance, *The Dispersion of Nuclear Weapons*, pp. 157–85; John Wilson Lewis and Xue Litai, *China Builds the Bomb* (Stanford, Calif.: Stanford University Press, 1988); and Norris, et al., *Nuclear Weapons Databook vol. V*, pp. 324–56.

24. Anonymous editorial, *Organizer*, 28 December, 1964. Cited in Peter R. Lavoy, 'Nuclear Myths and the Causes of Nuclear Proliferation', *Security Studies*, 2, nos 3/4 (Spring/Summer 1993): 192–212. Quote is from p. 198.

25. R.W. Apple, 'Ukraine Gives in on Surrendering Its Nuclear Arms', *The New York Times*, 11 January, 1994, p. A1; and Jane Perlez, 'Economic Collapse Leaves Ukraine With Little to Trade but Its Weapons', *The New York Times*, 13 January, 1994, p. A5. On the Ukrainian fear of decreasing relevance for the US were it to become a non-nuclear state see Theresa Hitchens and George Leopold, 'US Initiates Thaw in Ukrainian Relations', *Defense News*, 17–23 May, 1993, p. 6.

26. In fact, the possession of nuclear capabilities may threaten the independence and survival of an emerging nuclear state because it becomes a threat to the interests of the great powers or other states, and so they may be willing to use force against it, that is, to wage a preventive war, before it becomes a nuclear state. The Israeli attack on Iraq's Osirak reactor facility illustrates the danger of a preventive strike faced by emerging nuclear states. While it is not clear that the US intervened in the Gulf in 1990 principally to arrest Iraqi nuclear development, Israel certainly struck Osirak to prevent Iraq from becoming a nuclear state.

27. Kenneth N. Waltz, *Theory of International Politics* (Reading, Mass.: Addison-Wesley, 1979), p. 131; and Waltz, 'The Emerging Structure of International Politics', *International Security*, 18, no. 2 (Fall 1993): 50–61. Jack Levy provides a similar definition, great powers are distinguished from other states in the international system by three criteria: first, great powers have a high level of military capability that makes them relatively self-sufficient strategically and capable of projecting power beyond their borders; second, they possess a broad concept of security that embraces a concern with regional and/or global power balances; and third, they have a greater assertiveness than lesser powers in defining and defending their interests. Jack Levy, *War and the Modern Great Power System, 1495–1975* (Lexington: University Press of Kentucky, 1983), pp. 10–19.

28. On Nazi Germany's attempt to acquire nuclear weapons see Alan Beyerchen, *Scientists Under Hitler: Politics and the Physics Community in the Third Reich* (Cambridge: Cambridge University Press, 1977); David Irving, *The German Atomic Bomb: The History of Nuclear Research in Nazi Germany*, 2nd ed., (New York: Da Capo, 1983); Thomas Powers, *Heisenberg's War: The Secret History of the German Bomb* (New York: Knopf, 1993); and

Mark Walker, *German National Socialism and the Quest for Nuclear Power 1939–1949* (Cambridge: Cambridge University Press, 1989).

29. For histories of the US nuclear programme see Thomas B. Cochran, William M. Arkin, and Milton M. Hoenig, *Nuclear Weapons Databook Volume I: US Nuclear Forces and Capabilities* (Cambridge, Mass.: Ballinger, 1984), pp. 2–20; Stephane Groueff, *Manhattan Project: The Untold Story of the Making of the Atomic Bomb* (Boston: Little, Brown, 1967); Leslie M. Groves, *Now It Can Be Told: The Story of the Manhattan Project* (New York: Harper, 1962); Richard G. Hewlett and Oscar E. Anderson, *The New World: A History of the United States Atomic Energy Commission Vol. 1, 1939–1946* (University Park: Pennsylvania University Press, 1962); Lansing Lamont, *The Day of Trinity* (New York: Atheneum, 1965); and Richard Rhodes, *The Making of the Atomic Bomb* (New York: Simon & Schuster, 1986).

30. On the history of the Soviet decision to acquire nuclear weapons see Ulrich Albrecht, 'The Development of the First Atomic Bomb in the USSR', in Everett Mendelsohn, Merritt Roe Smith, and Peter Weingart, eds, *Science, Technology, and the Military*, vol. 2, (Dordrecht, Netherlands: Kluwer, 1988), pp. 349–78; Thomas B. Cochran, William M. Arkin, Robert S. Norris, and Jeffrey I. Sands, *Nuclear Weapons Databook vol. IV: Soviet Nuclear Weapons* (New York: Harper & Row, 1989), pp. 2–19; David Holloway, 'Entering the Nuclear Arms Race: The Soviet Decision to Build the Atomic Bomb, 1939–45', *Social Studies of Science,* 11, no. 2 (May 1981): 159–97; Holloway, *The Soviet Union and the Arms Race* (New Haven: Yale University Press, 1983); Holloway, *Stalin and the Bomb: The Soviet Union and Atomic Energy, 1936–1956* (New Haven: Yale University Press, 1994); Arnold Kramish, *Atomic Energy in the Soviet Union* (Stanford, Calif.: Stanford University Press, 1959); and George Modelski, *Atomic Energy in the Communist Bloc* (Melbourne: Melbourne University Press, 1959).

31. Among the best sources on the Pakistani programme are Akhtar Ali, *Pakistan's Nuclear Dilemma* (Karachi: Pakistan Economist Research Unit, 1984); Chellaney, 'The Challenge of Nuclear Arms Control in South Asia', pp. 122–4, 127–9; Neil Joeck, 'Pakistani Security and Nuclear Proliferation in South Asia', *The Journal of Strategic Studies*, 8, no. 4 (December 1985): 80–98; Rodney W. Jones, *Nuclear Proliferation: Islam, the Bomb, and South Asia*, The Washington Papers, No. 82 (Beverly Hills, Calif.: Sage, 1981); Ashok Kapur, *Pakistan's Nuclear Development* (London: Croom Helm, 1987); Zalmay M. Khalilzad, 'Pakistan', in Jozef Goldblat, ed., *Non-Proliferation: The Why and the Wherefore* (London: Taylor and Francis, 1985), pp. 131–49; Moshaver, *Nuclear Weapons Proliferation in the Indian Subcontinent*; George H. Quester, 'Some Pakistani Problems and a Nuclear Non-Solution', *The Journal of Strategic Studies*, 8, no. 4 (December 1985): 99–109.

32. There are few detailed histories of the South African programme. See Richard K. Betts, 'A Diplomatic Bomb for South Africa', *International Security*, 4, no. 2 (Fall 1979): 91–115; Robert S. Jaster, 'Politics and the "Afrikaner Bomb"', *Orbis*, 27, no. 4 (Winter 1984): 825–51; A.R. Newby-Fraser, *Chain Reaction: Twenty Years of Nuclear Research and Development in South Asia* (Pretoria: Atomic Energy Board, 1979); Mitchell Reiss,

Without the Bomb: The Politics of Nuclear Non-proliferation (New York: Columbia University Press, 1988), ch. 6, pp. 173–203; Leonard S. Spector, *Going Nuclear: The Spread of Nuclear Weapons 1986–1987* (Cambridge, Mass.: Ballinger, 1987), pp. 220–39; J. E. Spence, 'The Republic of South Africa: Proliferation and the Politics of "Outward Movement"', in Lawrence and Larus, *Nuclear Proliferation*, pp. 209–38. Also see David Albright, 'South Africa and the Affordable Bomb', *The Bulletin of the Atomic Scientists* (July/August 1994): 37–47; and J.W. de Villiers, Roger Jardine, Mitchell Reiss, 'Why South Africa Gave Up the Bomb', *Foreign Affairs*, 72, no. 5 (November/December 1993): 98–109.

33. Indeed, there is a considerable literature on India's attempt to obtain a security guarantee from a nuclear state such as Britain or the United States after the Chinese nuclear detonation of 1964. This behaviour is not indicative of a state seeking to acquire nuclear weapons for prestige. See Benjamin Frankel, 'The Brooding Shadow: Systemic Incentives and Nuclear Weapons Proliferation', *Security Studies*, 2, nos. 3/4 (Spring/Summer 1993): 53–4; Raj Krishna, 'India and the Bomb', *India Quarterly*, 21, no. 2 (April-June 1965): 119–37; M.R. Masani, 'The Challenge of the Chinese Bomb–II', *India Quarterly*, 21, no. 1 (January-March 1965): 26–7; A. G. Noorani, 'India's Quest for a Nuclear Guarantee', *Asian Survey*, 7, no. 7 (July 1967): 490–502.

34. Richard K. Betts, 'Incentives for Nuclear Weapons: India, Pakistan, Iran', *Asian Survey*, 19, no. 11 (November 1979): 1053–72. Emphasis original.

35. The *locus classicus* of the bureaucratic politics explanation of state decisionmaking is Graham T. Allison, *The Essence of Decision: Explaining the Cuban Missile Crisis* (Boston: Little, Brown, 1971), pp. 144–84.

36. Allison, *The Essence of Decision*; and Morton Halperin with the assistance of Priscilla Clapp and Arnold Kanter, *Bureaucratic Politics and Foreign Policy* (Washington, DC: Brookings, 1974).

37. Allison, *The Essence of Decision*, p. 145.

38. Allison, *The Essence of Decision*, p. 145.

39. Halperin, *Bureaucratic Politics and Foreign Policy*, pp. 28, 39.

40. Halperin, *Bureaucratic Politics and Foreign Policy*, p. 39.

41. Halperin, *Bureaucratic Politics and Foreign Policy*, p. 27.

42. The CEA, founded on October 18, 1945, is the organization charged with developing atomic weapons, as well conducting most civil and military nuclear research in France. On the development of the CEA see Mendl, *Deterrence and Persuasion*, pp. 18–19, 27–8; and Scheinman, *Atomic Energy Policy in France Under the Fourth Republic*, pp. 3–19.

43. Reiss, *Without the Bomb*, p. 217.

44. Reiss, *Without the Bomb*, pp. 217–22.

45. Lavoy, 'Nuclear Myths and the Causes of Proliferation', 202.

46. Scheinman, *Atomic Energy Policy in France Under the Fourth Republic*, pp. 213, 215.

47. Ralph E. Lapp, *Arms Beyond Doubt: The Tyranny of Weapons Technology* (New York: Cowles, 1970), pp. 177–8.

48. Cited in Deborah Shapley, 'Nuclear Weapons History: Japan's Wartime Bomb Project Revealed', *Science*, 199 (January 13, 1978): 152–57, quote from p. 155.

49. On the political impact of television see Shanto Iyengar, *Is Anyone Responsible? How Television Frames Political Issues* (Chicago: University

of Chicago Press, 1991). The power of television to compel US intervention has been called the 'CNN factor'. 'CNN pushed the boundaries of world news: no longer did the network merely report news, but through its immediate reportage, CNN actually shaped the events and became part of them.' Lewis Friedland, *Covering the World: International Television News Services* (New York: Twentieth Century Fund Press, 1992), p. 2. Quoted in Frank J. Stech, 'Winning CNN Wars', *Parameters*, 24, no. 3 (Autumn 1994): 37–56.

50. For an excellent summary of technology as a cause of proliferation see Peter Lavoy 'Nuclear Myths and the Causes of Nuclear Proliferation', 194–5. For advocates of technological pull in the nuclear weapons context see Hans Bethe, 'The Technological Imperative', *The Bulletin of the Atomic Scientists* (August 1985): 34–56.

Insightful critiques of technological determinism are found in the work of Donald MacKenzie, see MacKenzie, 'Stellar-Inertial Guidance: A Study in the Sociology of Military Technology', in Mendelsohn, et al., eds, *Science, Technology and the Military*, 187–241; MacKenzie, 'The Soviet Union and Strategic Missile Guidance', *International Security*, 13, no. 2 (Fall 1988): 5–54; MacKenzie, *Inventing Accuracy: A Historical Sociology of Nuclear Missile Guidance* (Cambridge, Mass.: MIT Press, 1990), ch. 8, pp. 382–423. MacKenzie argues that technological determinism is not deterministic but is dependent upon social phenomenon. Also see Langdon Winner, *Autonomous Technology: Technics-out-of-Control as a Theme in Political Thought* (Cambridge, Mass.: MIT Press, 1977).

Steven Flank presents an intriguing argument concerning the processes of nuclear proliferation. By utilizing the social construction of technology, Flank argues that a heterogenous alliance occurs among a society of scientists, politicians, technologies, and interests, which unite to support large technical systems. He thus offers important insights into the evolution of the nuclear programmes of states. See Steven Flank, 'Exploding the Black Box: The Historical Sociology of Nuclear Proliferation', *Security Studies*, 3, no. 2 (Winter 1993/94): 259–94.

51. *In the Matter of J. Robert Oppenheimer: Transcripts of Hearings before Personnel Security Review Board and Texts of Principal Documents and Letters* (Cambridge, Mass.: MIT Press, 1971), p. 251. Cited in Lavoy, 'Nuclear Myths and the Causes of Nuclear Proliferation', 195. Emphasis added.

52. Advocates of technological pull must address the arguments of Donald MacKenzie, who argues that technological invention, in MacKenzie's particular case, the invention of missile accuracy, is a social process and a process that permits technologies to be 'uninvented'. The logic of MacKenzie's arguments applies to nuclear proliferation as well as to missile accuracy. See MacKenzie, *Inventing Accuracy*; and MacKenzie, 'Towards an Historical Sociology of Nuclear Weapons Technologies', in Nils Petter Gleditsch and Olav Njølstad, eds, *Arms Races: Technological and Political Dynamics* (London: Sage, 1990), ch. 8, pp. 121–39. Also see Graham Spinardi, 'Why the US Navy Went for Hard-Target Counterforce in Trident II (And Why It Didn't Get There Sooner)', *International Security*, 15, no. 2 (Fall 1990): 147–90. For another argument critically discussing the relationship between science and society see Yaron Ezrahi, *The Descent of Icarus:*

Science and the Transformation of Contemporary Democracy (Cambridge, Mass.: Harvard University Press, 1990).

53. Mitchell Reiss notes that by the end of the 1970s nuclear research or power programmes existed in over 45 non-nuclear weapons states. *Without the Bomb: The Politics of Nuclear Non-proliferation* (New York: Columbia University Press, 1988), p. 23. Joseph Nye estimates there are 'forty odd states that possess nuclear technology.' Joseph S. Nye, Jr, 'NPT: The Logic of Inequality', *Foreign Policy*, no. 59 (Summer 1985): 126. Also see Frankel, 'The Brooding Shadow', 45n41.

54. The principal works of realism are many. They include Raymond Aron, *Peace and War: A Theory of International Relations*, trans. by Richard Howard and Annette Baker Fox (Garden City, NY: Doubleday, 1966); Edward Hallett Carr, *The Twenty Years' Crisis, 1919–1939: An Introduction to the Study of International Relations*, 2nd ed. (London: Macmillan, 1946); Hans Morgenthau, *Politics Among Nations: The Struggle for Power and Peace*, 5th ed. rev.(New York: Knopf, 1978); Kenneth N. Waltz, *Man, the State, and War: A Theoretical Analysis* (New York: Columbia University Press, 1959). Some neorealist works are Gilpin, *War and Change in World Politics* (Cambridge: Cambridge University Press, 1981); and Waltz, *Theory of International Politics*.

55. Waltz, *Theory of International Politics*, pp. 88–93.

56. The central ideas of realism are drawn from John J. Mearsheimer, 'The False Promise of International Institutions', *International Security*, 19, no. 3 (Winter 1994/95): 9–12.

57. The work of Paul Kennedy provides some of the most thoughtful historical analysis of the importance of relative power. See Paul M. Kennedy, *The Rise and Fall of British Naval Mastery* (London: Allen Lane, 1976), chs. 7 and 10; Kennedy, *The Rise and Fall of the Great Powers* (New York: Random House, 1987); Kennedy, 'The Tradition of Appeasement in British Foreign Policy, 1865–1939', *British Journal of International Studies*, 2, no. 3 (October 1976): 195–215; Kennedy, 'Strategy *versus* Finance in Twentieth-century Britain', in Kennedy, *Strategy and Diplomacy, 1870–1945* (London: Fontana Press, 1983), pp. 89–106.

58. The prediction that state behaviour stems from the conditions of realism is drawn from Mearsheimer, 'The False Promise of International Institutions', pp. 10–12.

59. Waltz, *Theory of International Politics*, pp. 91, 105–07.

60. Waltz, *Theory of International Politics*, p. 168.

61. Waltz, among other realists and neorealist, makes this argument. See Waltz, *Theory of International Politics*, pp. 168–70.

62. Waltz, *Theory of International Politics*, p. 168.

63. The problems that buckpassing and chain ganging pose in alliances are discussed in Thomas J. Christensen and Jack Snyder, 'Chain Gangs and Passed Bucks: Predicting Alliance Patterns in Multipolarity', *International Organization*, 44, no. 2 (Spring 1990): 137–68.

64. Not all realists agree that this is a central idea of realism. As John J. Mearsheimer notes, some realists, 'defensive realists', argue that states are interested primarily on maintaining the balance of power and not maximizing relative power as 'offensive realists' argue. See Mearsheimer, 'The

False Promise of International Institutions'. For examples of defensive realism see Joseph M. Grieco, 'Anarchy and the Limits of Cooperation', *International Organization*, 42, no. 3 (Summer 1988): 498–500; Jack Snyder, *Myths of Empire: Domestic Politics and International Ambition* (Ithaca: Cornell University Press, 1991), pp. 10–13, Snyder calls offensive realism, 'aggressive realism'; and Waltz, *Theory of International Politics*, pp. 126–27. Also see Fareed Zakaria, 'Realism and Domestic Politics: A Review Essay', *International Security*, 17, no. 1 (Summer 1992): 190–6.

65. Rhodes, *The Making of the Atomic Bomb*, p. 314. Also Bundy, *Danger and Survival*, pp. 45–48.

66. Holloway, *The Soviet Union and the Arms Race*, pp. 18–19

67. A. Lavrent'yeva in 'Stroiteli novogo mira', *V mire knig*, no. 9 (1970): 4. Quoted in Holloway, *The Soviet Union and the Arms Race*, p. 20.

68. On Truman's comment to Stalin see Winston S. Churchill, *The Second World War: Triumph and Tragedy* (Boston: Houghton Mifflin, 1953), pp. 640, 669–70; Harry S. Truman, *Memoirs: Year of Decisions* (Garden City, NY: Doubleday, 1955), p. 416. Also see John Lewis Gaddis, *The United States and the Origins of the Cold War, 1941–1947* (New York: Columbia University Press, 1972), pp. 244–5.

69. Holloway, *The Soviet Union and the Arms Race*, p. 20.

70. In Robert M. Lawrence and Joel Larus, 'A Historical Review of Nuclear Weapons Proliferation and the Development of the NPT', in Robert M. Lawrence and Joel Larus, eds, *Nuclear Proliferation: Phase II* (Lawrence: University Press of Kansas, 1974), p. 3.

71. Mendl, *Deterrence and Persuasion*, pp. 21–2.

72. Mendl, *Deterrence and Persuasion*, p. 29.

73. Lacouture, *De Gaulle: The Ruler 1945–1970*, p. 421.

74. Lacouture, *De Gaulle: The Ruler 1945–1970*, p. 421.

75. Lacouture, *De Gaulle: The Ruler 1945–1970*, p. 422.

76. Lewis and Xue, *China Builds the Bomb*, pp. 13–14.

77. Lewis and Xue, *China Builds the Bomb*, pp. 16–34. Also see Shu Guang Zhang, *Deterrence and Strategic Culture: Chinese–American Confrontations, 1949-1958* (Ithaca: Cornell University Press, 1992).

78. Lewis and Xue, *China Builds the Bomb*, p. 142.

79. Quoted in Lewis and Xue, *China Builds the Bomb*, p. 130. Chen was a staunch advocate of Chinese nuclear weapons, arguing that China should develop nuclear weapons, 'even if the Chinese had to pawn their trousers for this purpose'. Quoted in Lewis and Xue, *China Builds the Bomb*, p. 130.

80. Frankel, 'The Brooding Shadow', p. 52.

81. Frankel, 'The Brooding Shadow', p. 52.

82. Frankel, 'The Brooding Shadow', p. 53.

83. On the October 1962 Sino-Indian War from the Indian perspective see Brigadier John S. Dalvi, *Himalayan Blunder: The Curtain Raiser to the Sino-Indian War of 1962* (Bombay: Thacker, 1969); Lorne J. Kavic, *India's Quest for Security: Defense Policies, 1947–1965* (Berkeley, Calif.: University of California Press, 1967), ch. 10, pp. 169–91; Neville Maxwell, *India's China War* (Garden City, NY: Doubleday, 1972). From the Chinese perspective see Steve Chan, 'Chinese Conflicts Calculus and Behavior: Assessment from a Perspective of Conflict Management', *World Politics*,

30, no. 3 (April 1978): 391–410; and Allen S. Whiting, *The Chinese Calculus of Deterrence: India and Indochina* (Ann Arbor, Mich.: University of Michigan Press, 1975).

84. Reiss, *Without the Bomb*, p. 206.
85. Reiss, *Without the Bomb*, p. 207. Devin Hagerty also notes that the threat from the Chinese was an important consideration in Indian thinking before 1962, 'During the 1950s, a confidential consensus emerged among a small core of India leaders that New Delhi should reserve its right to develop nuclear weapons if threatened by a future Chinese nuclear weapon capability'. Devin T. Hagerty, 'The Power of Suggestion: Opaque Proliferation, Existential Deterrence, and the South Asian Nuclear Arms Competition,' *Security Studies*, 2, nos. 3/4 (Spring/Summer 1993): 256–83, quote is from p. 261. Even before the 1950s, the possibility of the development of nuclear weapons was considered by Nehru. In 1946, in response to a question about the potential development of Indian nuclear weapons, Nehru, 'stated his hope that India would develop atomic power for peaceful uses but warned that, so long as the world was constituted as it was, every country would have to develop and use the latest scientific devices for its protection.' Kavic, *India's Quest for Security*, pp. 27–28, n. 19.
86. Reiss, *Without the Bomb*, p. 212.
87. On the 1971 war see Richard Sisson and Leo E. Rose, *War and Secession: Pakistan, India, and the Creation of Bangladesh* (Berkeley, Calif.: University of California Press, 1990).
88. Ashok Kapur has suggested a third potential motivation for Pakistani nuclear capability. Nuclear capability would allow Pakistan to reopen the Kashmir question and negotiate with India from a position of military equality. However, while a robust nuclear capability might allow Pakistan to do this, such a policy would be injudicious because it would incur the risks of any game of Chicken, such as the great difficulties of crisis management and the palpable risks of inadvertent escalation. See Ashok Kapur, 'Pakistan', in Goldblat, *Non-Proliferation*, p. 142. On crisis management see Richard Ned Lebow, *Nuclear Crisis Management: A Dangerous Illusion* (Ithaca: Cornell University Press, 1987); Scott D. Sagan, 'Nuclear Alerts and Crisis Management', *International Security*, 9, no. 4 (Spring 1985), 99–139; and Sagan, *Moving Targets: Nuclear Strategy and National Security* (Princeton: Princeton University Press, 1989), ch. 4, pp. 135–75. On the danger of inadvertent escalation see, *inter alia*, Barry R. Posen, *Inadvertent Escalation: Conventional War and Nuclear Risks* (Ithaca: Cornell University Press, 1991).
89. Zulfikar Ali Bhutto, *The Myth of Independence* (Karachi: Oxford University Press, 1969). Quoted in Khalilzad, 'Pakistan', p. 133.
90. Raju G.C. Thomas, *South Asian Security in the 1990s*, Adelphi Paper no. 278 (London: International Institute of Strategic Studies, 1993), p. 58.
91. It is an unfortunate condition of international politics, one that realism acknowledges, that the intentions of other states cannot be known with certainty. Thus, Pakistani fears may be misplaced if India is a status-quo state and the Pakistani attempts to match Indian capabilities, such as by acquiring nuclear weapons, only exacerbate Indian fears. Robert Jervis' spiral model obtains in this situation. See Robert Jervis, *Perception and Misperception in*

International Politics (Princeton: Princeton University Press, 1976), ch. 3, pp. 58–113.

92. Thomas quotes the concerns of Air Commodore Aliuddin, Pakistani Air Force: 'Several South Asian nations and Pakistan in particular are, therefore, wary of the fact that India is not only developing fast as the eminent regional power in South Asia but also views itself as a power destined to influence global affairs...It is this growing Indian militarism and ambition which is a serious concern for Pakistan. The three India–Pakistan wars, the India annexation of Sikkim and Goa, invasion of the Maldives, economic blockage of Nepal, and refusal to withdraw troops from Sri Lanka in 1989 are all viewed as clear manifestations of India's hegemonistic designs'. Air Commodore Aliuddin, 'Pakistan's Nuclear Dilemma', *Seaford House Papers* (London: Royal College of Defence Studies, 1990), p. 7. Quoted in Thomas, *South Asian Security in the 1990s*, 84, n.19.

93. For an excellent exposition on the possibility and utility of nuclear blackmail, or coercion, see Richard K. Betts, *Nuclear Blackmail and Nuclear Balance* (Washington, DC: Brookings, 1987), pp. 212–33.

94. Mark Hibbs, 'South Africa's Secret Nuclear Program: The Dismantling', *Nuclear Fuel*, May 24, 1993, 9.

95. Mark Hibbs, 'South Africa's Secret Nuclear Program: From a PNE to a Deterrent', *Nuclear Fuel*, May 10, 1993, p. 4.

96. Hibbs, 'South Africa's Secret Nuclear Program: From a PNE to a Deterrent', p. 7.

97. The causes of the North Korea nuclear programme and possible US responses to it are analysed in Kathleen C. Bailey, 'North Korea: Enough Carrots, Time for the Stick', *Comparative Strategy*, 13, no. 3 (July–September 1994): 277–82; Paul Bracken, 'Nuclear Weapons and State Survival in North Korea', *Survival*, 35, no. 3 (Autumn 1993): 137–53; Peter Hayes, 'International Missile Trade and the Two Koreas', *The Korean Journal of Defense Analysis*, 5, no. 1 (Summer 1993): 207–39; Young Jeh Kim, 'North Korea's Nuclear Program and Its Impact on Neighboring Countries', *Korea and World Affairs*, 17, no. 3 (Fall 1993): 478–96; Andrew Mack, 'The Nuclear Crisis on the Korean Peninsula', *Asian Survey*, 33, no. 4 (April 1993): 339–59; Kongdan Oh and Ralph C. Hassig, 'North Korea's Nuclear Program', in Young Whan Kihl, ed., *Korea and the World: Beyond the Cold War* (Boulder, Colo.: Westview, 1994), pp. 233–50.

98. The Argentine army has approximately 35,000 active and 250,000 reserve troops. The Brazilian army has approximately 196,000 active and 1,115,000 first-line reserve troops. Following the 3:1 rule (three attacking units are necessary overcome one defensive unit) for conventional deterrence, it is likely that both states can conventionally deter the other because while Brazil has superiority in manpower, Argentina has superiority in mobile forces (Main Battle Tanks, Armoured Personnel Carriers, Self-Propelled Artillery, Close Air Support Aircraft) that greatly would strengthen the defence in a war. In addition, the geography of the border between Argentina and Brazil permits few avenues of attack, making attack harder and further ameliorating the defender's burden because any attack will be canalized at the points of attack permitted by geography. On Argentine and Brazilian forces see *The Military Balance 1992–1993* (London:

International Institute of Strategic Studies, 1992), pp. 167–8, 170–2. On the 3:1 rule see John J. Mearsheimer, *Conventional Deterrence* (Ithaca: Cornell University Press, 1983), pp. 51–2, 167–82.

99. The Falkland/Malvinas Islands War was precisely a war over the Falkland/Malvinas Islands and posed no existential threat to either Great Britain or Argentina. On the Falkland/Malvinas Island War see Anthony H. Cordesman and Abraham R. Wagner, *The Lessons of Modern War Volume III: The Afghan and Falklands Conflicts* (Boulder, Colo.: Westview Press, 1990); and Max Hastings and Simon Jenkins, *The Battle for the Falklands* (New York: Norton, 1983).

100. The nuclear non-proliferation regime comprises formal treaties, the NPT, the Treaty of Tlatelolco and the Treaty of Rarotonga, which made the South Pacific a nuclear weapons free zone, and Convention on the Physical Protection of Nuclear Material; informal agreements and suppliers groups to enforce nuclear non-proliferation, the Zangger Committee, the London Club/Nuclear Suppliers Group; as well as the International Atomic Energy Agency, an international organization which is instrumental in policing the regime.

101. Aaron Karp, 'Controlling Weapons Proliferation: The Role of Export Controls', *The Journal of Strategic Studies*, 16, no. 1 (March 1993): 18–45.

102. The reduction in information costs is one of the principal benefits of regimes. See Robert O. Keohane, *After Hegemony: Cooperation and Discord in the World Political Economy* (Princeton: Princeton University Press, 1984), pp. 244–47; and Kenneth A. Oye, 'Explaining Cooperation under Anarchy: Hypotheses and Explanations', *World Politics*, 38, no. 1 (October 1985): 1–24.

103. On US assistance to Britain and France see Norris, et al., *Nuclear Weapons Databook vol. V*, pp. 43–54, 188–93. On US assistance to France see Richard Ullman, 'The Covert French Connection', *Foreign Policy*, no. 75 (Summer 1989): 3–33. For Soviet assistance to China see Lewis and Xue, *China Builds the Bomb*, pp. 39–45 and *passim*. On French assistance to Israel see Aronson with Brosh, *The Politics and Strategy of Nuclear Weapons in the Middle East*, pp. 86–7, 91, 94–5, 102, 104 and 116–17. Also see Sylvia K. Crosbie, *The Tacit Alliance: France and Israel from Suez to the Six Day War* (Princeton: Princeton University Press, 1974); and Ann Williams, *Britain and France in the Middle East and North Africa, 1914–1967* (London: Macmillan, 1968). On Israeli assistance to South Africa see David Albright, 'South Africa: The ANC and the Atomic Bomb', *The Bulletin of the Atomic Scientists* (April 1993): 32–7; 'Israel Supplied Tritium for South Africa's Nuclear Weapons', *Israeli Foreign Affairs*, April 13, 1993, p. 3; 'Tracking S. Africa's Elusive A-Program', *The Washington Post*, March 18, 1993, p. A1; 'S. Africa Had 6 A-Bombs', *The Washington Post*, March 25, 1993, p. A1. On China's assistance to Pakistan see David Albright and Mark Hibbs, 'Pakistan's Bomb: Out of the Closet', *The Bulletin of the Atomic Scientists* (July/August 1992): 38–43; and Chellaney, 'The Challenge of Nuclear Arms Control in South Asia', 123–4. Chellaney reports that a secret nuclear test in Xinjiang in May 1983, attended by the then-Foreign Minister of Pakistan Yaqub Khan, resulted in speculation that China may have detonated a Pakistani nuclear device. On Pakistani assistance to Iran see Warren H. Donnelly and Zachary Davis, 'CRS Issue Brief', May 20, 1992, 1–11.

104. Peter D. Zimmerman, 'Technical Barriers to Nuclear Proliferation', *Security Studies*, 2, nos. 3/4 (Spring/Summer 1993): 354; and Zimmerman, 'Proliferation: Bronze Medal Technology is Enough', *Orbis*, 38, no. 1 (Winter 1994): 67–82.

105. David A. Kay, 'Iraqi Inspections: Lessons Learned', *Eye on Supply*, no. 8 (Winter 1993): 91–92.

106. Frankel, 'The Brooding Shadow', 51–54.

107. Robert Jervis, 'Security Regimes', *International Organization*, 36, no. 2 (Spring 1982): 189.

108. On the second-tier or emerging suppliers see William C. Potter, *International Nuclear Trade and Non-proliferation: The Challenge of the Emerging Suppliers* (Lexington, Mass.: Lexington Books, 1990); and Potter, 'The New Suppliers', *Orbis*, 36, no. 2 (Spring 1992): 199–210. More generally, on the restructuring of arms production on a transnational scale see Richard A. Bitzinger, 'The Globalization of the Arms Industry: The Next Proliferation Challenge', *International Security*, 19, no. 2 (Fall 1994): 170–98; and David Mussington, *Arms Unbound: The Globalization of Defense Production*, CSIA Studies in International Security No. 4 (Washington, DC: Brassey's, 1994).

109. However, without sophisticated technologies, such as high-speed computers, and mastery of advanced chemical, engineering, metallurgical and physical skills, states have a much more complicated task developing thermonuclear weapons. These barriers are also impediments to the development of reliable delivery systems, like intercontinental ballistic missiles. However, the Indian, Iraqi, Israeli, North Korean and Pakistani missile programmes demonstrate that missiles of less sophistication are well within the grasp of most nuclear nations. On ballistic missile proliferation see W. Seth Carus, *Ballistic Missiles in the Third World: Threat and Response* (New York: Praeger, 1991); Steve Fetter, 'Ballistic Missiles and Weapons of Mass Destruction: What Is the Threat? What Should Be Done?' *International Security*, 16, no. 1 (Summer 1991): 5–42; Aaron Karp, 'Ballistic Missiles in the Third World', *International Security*, 9, no. 3 (Winter 1984–85): 166–95; Thomas L. McNaugher, 'Ballistic Missiles and Chemical Weapons: The Legacy of the Iran–Iraq War', *International Security*, 15, no. 2 (Fall 1990): 5–34; Mark D. Mandeles, 'Between a Rock and a Hard Place: Implications for the US of Third World Nuclear Weapon and Ballistic Missile Proliferation', *Security Studies*, 1, no. 2 (Winter 1991): 235–68; and Janne E. Nolan, *Trappings of Power: Ballistic Missiles in the Third World* (Washington, DC: Brookings, 1991).

110. For a detailed discussion of the role of superpower security guarantees in preventing nuclear weapons proliferation see Frankel, 'The Brooding Shadow', 47–51.

111. On the role that US pressure played in restraining the Brazilian and Egyptian programmes see Michael Joe Siler, 'Explaining Variations in Nuclear Outcomes among Southern States: Bargaining Analysis of US Non-Proliferation Policies Towards Brazil, Egypt, India and South Korea' (Los Angeles: unpublished Ph.D. diss., University of Southern California, May 1992). On the South Korean programme see Young-sun Ha, *Nuclear Proliferation, World Order, and Korea* (Seoul: Seoul National University,

1983); Reiss, *Without the Bomb*, pp. 86–103; Siler, 'Explaining Variations in Nuclear Outcomes among Southern States'; and Joseph A. Yager, 'The Republic of Korea,' in Yager, ed., *Non-proliferation and US Foreign Policy* (Washington, DC: Brookings, 1980).

112. Kenneth Waltz noted this fact in, 'The Stability of a Bipolar World', *Daedalus*, 93, no. 3 (Summer 1964): 882–3. Also see Waltz, *Theory of International Politics*, ch. 8.

113. Glenn H. Snyder, 'The Security Dilemma in Alliance Politics', *World Politics*, 36, no. 4 (July 1984): 461–95. Also see Glenn H. Snyder, 'Alliance Theory: A Neorealist First Cut', *Journal of International Affairs*, 44, no. 1 (Spring/Summer 1990): 112–17; and Christensen and Snyder, 'Chain Gangs and Passed Bucks', 137–68.

114. Glenn H. Snyder and Paul Diesing, *Conflict Among Nations: Bargaining, Decision Making, and System Structure in International Crises* (Princeton: Princeton University Press, 1977), pp. 419–29.

115. Frankel, 'The Brooding Shadow', 43.

116. For an elaboration this argument see Art, 'A Defensible Defense', 28–30; and George H. Quester and Victor A. Utgoff, 'US Arms Reductions and Nuclear Non-proliferation: The Counterproductive Possibilities', *The Washington Quarterly*, 16, no. 1 (Winter 1993): 129–40; and Quester and Utgoff, 'No-First-Use and Non-proliferation: Redefining Extended Deterrence', *The Washington Quarterly*, 17, no. 2 (Spring 1994): 103–14.

117. Kay, 'Iraqi Inspections', 88. Also see David A. Kay, 'Denial and Deception Practices of WMD Proliferators: Iraq and Beyond', *The Washington Quarterly*, 18, no. 1 (Winter 1995): 87–8.

118. On the counterproliferation initiative see Les Aspin, 'From Deterrence to Denuking: A New Nuclear Policy for the 1990s', in *Shaping Nuclear Policy for the 1990s: A Compendium of Views* (Washington, DC: US Government Printing Office, 1993), pp. 1–26; Aspin, *Report on the Bottom-Up Review* (Washington, DC: Department of Defense, 1993), pp. 73–4; Aspin, *Annual Report to the President and the Congress* (Washington, DC: Department of Defense, 1994), pp. 34–41; and *Report on Non-proliferation and Counterproliferation Activities and Programs* (Washington, DC: Office of the Deputy Secretary of Defense, 1994).

119. Christopher Layne argues that there is a danger that the United States will be perceived as a threat after the Cold War if the United States attempts to pursue a grand strategy of preponderance, suppressing the emergence of new powers. Although he does not address nuclear proliferation, the logic of Layne's argument applies to counterproliferation. See Christopher Layne, 'The Unipolar Illusion: Why New Great Powers Will Rise', *International Security*, 17, no. 4 (Spring 1993): 5–51.

120. Krasner, 'Structural Causes and Regime Consequences', 2.

121. Kay, 'Iraqi Inspections', 91.

122. If great powers, such as Germany or Japan, were to acquire nuclear weapons, they may do so visibly because they possess enough power to violate the norm and incur any sanctions that the other great powers might place upon them. Indeed, other great powers may be reluctant to impose such sanctions and offend the great power because to do so would be to risk alienating an important power.

123. However, the Gulf War demonstrates that opaque states may even deceive the intelligence capabilities of the West. See Kay, 'Iraqi Inspections', 91.

124. Peter Feaver demonstrates the effects of opaque proliferation on the management of the state's nuclear operations in his 'Proliferation Optimism and Theories of Nuclear Operations,' *Security Studies*, 2, nos. 3/4 (Spring/Summer 1993): 159–91.

125 Hersh, *The Samson Option*, 225–27; cited in Feaver, 'Proliferation Optimism and Theories of Nuclear Operations', 177.

126. Feaver, 'Proliferation Optimism and Theories of Nuclear Operations', 177.

127. Posen, *Inadvertent Escalation*, pp. 1–2.

128. Posen, *Inadvertent Escalation*, p. 2.

129. I am indebted to Benjamin Frankel for suggesting this point to me.

130. The importance of open debate as means to correcting the propensity of organizations not to evaluate their own policies and beliefs, and dangers of non-evaluation in the nuclear age, are demonstrated in Van Evera, 'Causes of Wars,' 453–99.

131. The value of mobile launchers for ensuring the survivability of an opaque state's retaliatory force was demonstrated during the Gulf War. Despite its intensive effort, there is no evidence that the US destroyed any of the Iraqi mobile Scud launchers. See US Department of Defense, *Conduct of the Persian Gulf War: Final Report to Congress*, (Washington, DC: US Department of Defense, 1992), p. 226.

132. George H. Quester, 'Knowing and Believing About Nuclear Proliferation', *Security Studies*, 1, no. 2 (Winter 1991): 278.

133 Neil Joeck, 'Tacit Bargaining and Stable Proliferation in South Asia', *The Journal of Strategic Studies*, 13, no. 3 (September 1990): 78.

134. Quester, 'Knowing and Believing About Nuclear Proliferation', 278.

135. Cohen and Frankel also note that Israel's opaque stance benefited the Soviet Union and even the Arab states. The Soviets benefited because a visible nuclear Israel would cause the Arab states to pressure the Soviets to supply them with a similar nuclear capability or at least to supply them with security guarantees. Moderate Arabs prefer to ignore Israeli nuclear capabilities lest their calls for agreement with Israel be attributed to fear of Israeli nuclear strength. Extreme Arabs fear that an acknowledgement of Israeli nuclear capability would force them to renounce the goal of eliminating Israel. See Cohen and Frankel, 'Opaque Nuclear Proliferation', 26–7.

136. A comprehensive analysis of whether opaque nuclear states possess survivable nuclear forces, command and control systems, as well as the susceptibility of the nuclear arsenal of each state to nuclear inadvertence, would be beneficial to the study of the risks and benefits of opaque nuclear proliferation.

137. This question is addressed most prominently by Alain Enthoven and Wayne Smith. See Alain C. Enthoven and K. Wayne Smith, *How Much Is Enough?: Shaping the Defense Program, 1961–1969* (New York: Harper & Row, 1971). Robert McNamara's answer to the question for US deterrence of a premeditated Soviet attack was that at a minimum, US retaliatory forces must be able to destroy 20 to 25 per cent of the Soviet population and 50 per cent of Soviet industry. Enthoven and Smith, *How Much Is Enough?* pp. 175, 207.

138. Estimates as to the size of the arsenals of opaque nuclear states may be drawn from David Albright, Frans Berkhout and William Walker, *World Inventory of Plutonium and Highly Enriched Uranium, 1992* (New York: Oxford University Press, 1993).

139. McGeorge Bundy, 'To Cap the Volcano', *Foreign Affairs*, 48, no. 1 (October 1969): 9–10, 12. Also see Bundy, 'The Bishops and the Bomb', *The New York Review of Books*, June 16, 1983, 3–8; and Bundy, 'Existential Deterrence and Its Consequences', in Douglas MacLean, ed., *The Security Gamble: Deterrence Dilemmas in the Nuclear Age* (Totowa, NJ: Rowman and Allanheld, 1984), pp. 3–13.

140. Marc Trachtenberg, 'The Influence of Nuclear Weapons in the Cuban Missile Crisis', *International Security*, 10, no. 1 (Summer 1985): 148.

6 Chemical, Biological, and Missile Proliferation

Kathleen C. Bailey

The proliferation of chemical and biological weapons, together with the capability to deliver them with cruise or ballistic missiles, is increasing at a much more dramatic rate than is nuclear proliferation. Compared with nuclear weapons, chemical and biological agents are technologically easier to develop, significantly less expensive, and the facilities and products are easier to hide. From a military use standpoint, chemical and biological weapons also have advantages – they can kill large numbers of people, but without the collateral damage of nuclear weapons.

This chapter briefly outlines the status of these other 'proliferations', and discusses their possible effects on nuclear non-proliferation.

1 CHEMICAL WEAPONS PROLIFERATION

Chemical weapons (CW) such as phosgene or mustard gas are relatively simple to make, inexpensive, and are technologically within reach of over 125 countries.[1] The more deadly nerve agents are somewhat more difficult to manufacture, but the task can be accomplished even by a small terrorist group, as the Japanese cult Aum Shinrikyo proved in its production and use of sarin nerve agent in 1995. The processes to make chemical compounds used in classical agents – those known and used since the First World War – are well-documented in unclassified literature.

The equipment necessary can be purchased readily on the open market, and is the same as that required for a host of other chemical–industrial activities. Almost all precursor chemicals required for chemical weapons also have legitimate uses in industry and are used in a very wide range of products. As a result, most precursors are readily available and their possession and storage can be explained as civilian, even if the intent is actually military. Furthermore, chemical agent production is inexpensive compared to the costs of nuclear or advanced conventional weapons. A small plant to make phosgene, for example, would cost only about $2 million.

Although there is clear evidence that some nations – such as Libya, Iran, and Iraq – have made CW, there is no way of knowing how many countries actually have such weapons. A chemical agent production facility is relatively easy to hide: it can be small (a 100-ton facility can be as small as 40 ft. by 40 ft.) and without physical features that would distinguish it. Although on-site inspection of a plant might reveal the fact that CW agent is being produced, there are currently no technical means to locate such a plant in the first place. In other words, the only way to find a well-hidden CW facility is to acquire accurate human-source intelligence about it.

Two principal non-proliferation policies intended to limit the spread of chemical weapons are export controls (the Australia Group) and an arms control agreement, the Chemical Weapons Convention (CWC). Neither have been nor can be effective in stopping proliferation. Export controls can slow the acquisition of CW capability by a few nations by preventing their ready import of the requisite chemical compounds. However, any nation dedicated to acquiring CW can either develop its own indigenous production capabilities, just as Iraq did prior to Desert Storm, or can turn to supplier nations that do not rigorously apply export controls.

The effectiveness of the Chemical Weapons Convention *vis-à-vis* proliferation is similarly limited. The CWC has an elaborate, expensive verification regime which requires routine inspections of chemical plants in member states, and allows for challenge inspections of suspect sites. Nevertheless, the problem remains that any nation choosing to hide its CW production and stockpiling is very likely to succeed, a point acknowleded by Former CIA Director Woolsey, who, during the US Senate ratification hearings on the CWC in 1994, testified, 'I cannot state that we have high confidence in our ability to detect noncompliance with this treaty, especially noncompliance on a small scale.' There are simply too many ways for a nation to cheat with little or no risk of getting caught.[2]

2   BIOLOGICAL WEAPONS PROLIFERATION

Biological weapons (BW) are a terrifying threat not only because they can cause unimaginable human suffering and death, but because contagious diseases used as weapons can spread readily and uncontrollably.[3] Nevertheless, BW are attractive weapons to many nations because they are the easiest and least costly weapon of mass destruction to manufacture, test, and deploy. A well-trained microbiologist could himself or herself make BW agents, although a more likely scenario – as in the case of Iraq – is that a few people will be involved. The raw materials, pathogens, are found in nature. The equipment and skills needed are exactly the same as those needed for medical or pharmaceutical research, and no highly specialized equipment or materials are required. Producing large quantities of deadly pathogens can require only a few hours or days. The facility can be nothing more than a room, and there may be no features that would distinguish it as being BW-related.

There are no current technologies that would enable one to find a clandestine facility, without accurate human-source intelligence. Even if one were to have such accurate intelligence and the suspect nation were to agree to an on-site inspection, it is unlikely that cheating would be detected with certainty. Inspectors may visit a facility and find only the capability to make BW agents – which is the same capability required for biological and pharmaceutical research. And, even if the presence of BW agents were detected, they could be represented as being for legitimate defensive work on vaccines, for example. Thus, there is no way at present of knowing how many countries have BW stockpiles or production facilities.

The BW problem is highlighted by Iraq, which began a BW programme in 1985 with a staff of about 10 people.[4] Five different sites were used to produce a variety of BW by 1990, including at least 19,000 litres of botulinum toxin and 8,500 litres of anthrax. Iraq also produced other agents such as diseases to attack plants and animals. Significantly, Iraq was able to successfully test and weaponize these agents into bombs, missile warheads, and spray tanks on aircraft – all without detection by foreign intelligence agencies.

Iraq's BW production and weaponization was not discovered by UN inspectors, although there were over 30 inspections between 1991 and 1995 designed specifically to try to find Iraq's BW production and storage sites. Iraq volunteered the information. Thus, despite anywhere–anytime inspections, UN teams were not able to uncover the location or extent of Iraq's BW efforts. There may still be hidden BW and Iraq's programme could be continuing clandestinely.

The treaty intended to outlaw BW production and use is the Biological and Toxin Weapons Convention (BTWC) of 1972. When the BTWC was drafted, it was widely recognized that verification was impossible, so no verification provisions were included. Although this technical assessment has not changed, there have been subsequent efforts by some arms control policymakers to 'strengthen' the BTWC by adding an inspections regime similar to that envisioned for the CWC. Technical experts continue to advise, however, that such measures will provide little, if any, confidence that cheating is not taking place. Arms control, unfortunately, will not solve the problem of BW proliferation.

In the future, the BW proliferation problem will be unavoidably exacerbated by advances in technologies for medicine and biotechnology, which will enable pathogens to be made more effective as weapons. For example, a virus may be made to circumvent any immunities to its 'conventional' strain, or a bacterium may be made resistant to antibiotics, as Russia has reportedly done.[5]

3   MILITARY UTILITY

A principal reason that nations throughout the world are acquiring chemical and biological warfare capability is the perceived military utility of such weapons. Even small arsenals of CW and/or BW can be very effective deterrents or tools in war-fighting. There are credible scenarios in which only tens of tons of CW agent might be used with highly significant effect, and BW are the most lethal weapon per unit of weight. Imagine that Iraq had fired chemical rounds at camps in Saudi Arabia during the Desert Shield build-up. It could have resulted in melting the resolve of the coalition, perhaps even breaking it up. Or, imagine Iraq had sporadically fired a few rounds containing chemical agent during the start of Desert Storm. Even if only one out of every several rounds had been chemical, it would likely have resulted in forcing troops to suit up and remain in their protective gear. Making the enemy don protective masks and clothing can be an end in itself; the objective need not be actual casualties. It is well known that chemical gear is hot, causes claustrophobia, inhibits communication, limits sight, and can make execution of tasks difficult.

The same sort of arguments can be made about BW. Their use could have tremendous psychological impact, and can force the donning of protective masks. Saddam Hussein – and other Third World leaders as well – probably learned from the experience of Desert Storm that, to defeat the United States, one cannot hope to succeed with conventional weapons alone. In any future confrontation involving US troops against a leader like Saddam, it should be expected that the leader will use chemical or biological weapons either to fulfil a military objective or to undermine US public support for intervention. Just because US leaders do not view CBW as usable does not mean that the leaders of other countries will view them similarly.

4 MISSILES

Ballistic missiles – missiles which are fired to a given height and then depend on gravity to complete their flight – were produced for decades only by advanced industrial countries because such missiles required sophisticated guidance systems and presented technological challenges that involve almost as much art as science. The Soviet-designed Scud missile, however, is relatively simple and has become the basis for some indigenous missile programmes, namely North Korea's and Iraq's. Because of the great inaccuracy of Scuds, however, they are not very useful with conventional warheads. Thus, it can be assumed that countries depending on Scuds probably intend to equip them with warheads of mass destruction.[6]

North Korea succeeded in modifying the Scud B to a missile often referred to as Scud C, which has a range of 600 km. This longer-range Scud has been marketed to Syria, Iran, and Libya. North Korea's 1,000 km Nodong missile has reportedly also been sold to Syria and Iran. Furthermore, North Korea is transferring technology for producing Scuds to Egypt and perhaps others.

China has also been an active supplier of ballistic missiles. It sold Saudi Arabia the 2,700 km CSS-2 missile, M-11 missiles and technology to Pakistan, and is reported to be supplying M-11s to Syria as well.[7] India, Iraq, and Israel also have ballistic missiles, as noted in Table 6.1.

Cruise missiles – missiles which use air-breathing engines and are powered the full distance to their targets – are of equal or greater utility as delivery vehicles for CBW warheads. Unlike ballistic missiles, cruise missiles can fly relatively slowly and close to the ground, making delivery easier and more sure. Also, the technology for cruise missiles is easier than ballistic missiles in many respects.

At least 40 non-Western countries possess or have the capability to make cruise missiles and they are likely to become increasingly widespread because the requisite technology has become less expensive and easier to acquire. In the past, guidance has served as a central obstacle to cruise missile proliferation because sophisticated, expensive technologies were needed to map terrain and guide the missile over obstacles to the target. Today, proliferants have a much easier time acquiring guidance technology. Inertial navigation systems for aircraft are commercially available and can be used in cruise missiles. Also, the advent of satellite positioning systems allow a missile to 'know' its position to an accuracy of 100 metres or better.[8]

Third World cruise missiles need not be sophisticated to be effective. They can be converted unmanned aerial vehicles or may be fashioned from small aircraft or 'airplane kits', the latter costing as little as $10,000. Iraq, for example, planned to deliver BW with a remotely piloted aircraft

Table 6.1   Selected Ballistic Missile Capabilities (≥ 300 km range)

Nation	Missile	Range (km)
Egypt	Scud B	300
	Scud C	600
India	Agni	2500
Iran	Scud B	300
	Scud C	600
Iraq	Al Hussein	650
	Al Abbas1	7502
Israel	Jericho (1)	480–650
	Jericho (2)	1500
	Shavit	2500–7500
North Korea	Scud B(3)	300
	Scud C	600
	Nodong	1000
Pakistan	M-11	300
Saudi Arabia	CSS-2	2700
Syria	Scud B	300
	Scud C	600
	M-9	600

Notes:
(1) The Al-Abbas is also referred to as the Al-Hijarah. (2) The range may be up to 900 km, with adjustment of payload-to-fuel ratio. (3) Scud B missiles have been provided to many countries, most of which are not listed in this table. The Scud B normally has a range of 280 km, but can be extended by reducing payload.

equipped with a spray tank. Also, cruise missiles do not need to be long-range to present a strategic threat. They can be launched from sea platforms off a nation's coast or from aircraft.

Countries capable of manufacturing aircraft are also technically capable of manufacturing cruise missiles. At least six Third World countries currently manufacture supersonic aircraft and a number of others produce light attack planes and trainers.[9] These countries do not need to use sophisticated engines; simple turbojet engines – like those built by Brazil for its remotely piloted vehicles in the early 1980s – will suffice for short-range cruise missiles. At least 15 countries in the Third World presently are capable of producing cruise missiles. Some may even be willing to sell or give them to others. Selected countries with cruise missiles having ranges greater than 200 km are listed in Table 6.2.

Table 6.2.   Selected Cruise Missile* Capabilities (≥ 200 km Range)

Nation	Missile	Range (km)
Argentina	Bigua MQ-2	900
Brazil	Aeromot K1	278
India	Lakshya	500
Iran	Silkworm (mod)	~450
Iraq	FAW 200	200
Israel	Delilah	400
	Harpy	500
North Korea	Silkworm (mod)	~450
South Africa	Eyrie 6A-60	1750
	Skua	800
Egypt	Scarab 324	≥ 1900
Libya	Mirach 100	400*

Note:
*Cruise missiles include drones and other aerial vehicles designed for such activities as reconnaissance, but which can readily be adapted for delivery of a small payload, including chemical or biological agents. Cruise missiles present a worldwide danger because they can be launched from simple sea platforms to reach any country near international waters. Also, the capabilities of cruise missiles to penetrate air defences are enhanced by the increasingly wide availability of radar absorbing materials which make missiles more stealthy, as well as the exceedingly slow flight of some cruise missiles, which limits their detectability.

5   EFFECTS OF AND ON NUCLEAR NON-PROLIFERATION

There are at least two key interrelationships between nuclear non-proliferation and the proliferation of chemical and biological weapons (CBW). One is causal. To the extent that the nuclear non-proliferation regime has been effective in making it difficult for countries to acquire nuclear weapons capability, it has driven nations that want weapons of mass destruction toward the easier options of CBW acquisition. It is not clear, however, whether these nations would not seek CW or BW anyway, regardless of the restrictions on their abilities to obtain nuclear weapons.

The more important relationship between CBW proliferation and the nuclear non-proliferation regime is likely to be the effect of the former on the willingness of some nations to disarm. This is particularly relevant in the case of the United States and any other country which has nuclear and conventional weapons, but has disavowed CW and BW. The reason is that conventional weapons capability may not be sufficient as a deterrent against CBW threats, and nuclear weapons will be increasingly relied upon to perform this role.

One problem with using conventional weapons to deter CBW use is that they are perceived as less terrible, and thus have less deterrent value. Another is that large-scale conventional retaliation may be stymied by logistical problems, time required, expense (in terms of lives lost as well as money), and use of effective countermeasures by the opponent. In fact, by threatening to use weapons of mass destruction against any US troops that may be sent to the region, proliferants can substantially reduce the likelihood that the United States will be willing to engage in conventional reprisal.

When the Bush administration was preparing to announce its unilateral renunciation of chemical weapons, it was recognized that conventional force might not be effective in deterring chemical weapons use by others. A view held by some top officials was that the US nuclear deterrent would be relied upon.

There are serious problems with the notion of nuclear deterrence as well. The question of proportionality must be considered carefully, as must the implications of using nuclear weapons to deter anything but nuclear weapons. And, current US policy is to not use nuclear weapons against any nation that is a member of a nuclear non-proliferation treaty and is not in alliance with a nuclear weapon state. In short, the issue of how the United States should effectively deter CBW has not been well addressed.

In the future, US policy, and the policies of other nuclear weapons states, may be changed to apply nuclear deterrence to CBW threats. This would directly affect the willingness of the nuclear weapons states to engage in further nuclear arms reductions.

6 CONCLUSION

Non-proliferation policies to limit the spread of missiles and warheads of mass destruction hamper nations pursuing such deadly weapons, but do not stop them. Proliferation continues and the world is likely to face increasingly severe threats from hostile nations in possession of CBW warheads and the missiles to deliver them.

Given that non-proliferation policies cannot stop a determined proliferator, it is in the security interests of nations which may become victims to prepare to counter the threats they may face. In the case of the United

States, these preparations could include: effective ballistic missile and air defences; capable detectors with rapid response to determine the presence or use of CBW; counterproliferation measures to destroy CBW stockpiles at their origin; and, better protective measures such as vaccines, antidotes, and prophylactics.

Additionally, the question of how best to deter the use of CBW must be addressed. The United States has forsworn in-kind retaliation against use of chemical or biological weapons, leaving only the options of conventional or nuclear retaliation. Yet, there may be cases in which a conventional response is impractical. Alternatively, today's nuclear capabilities, at least in the case of the US arsenal, may not be of the correct yield and design to respond appropriately and proportionally to a CBW attack.

NOTES

1. CW agents are of various types – choking, blood, blistering, and nerve. For a detailed description, see Satu M. Somani (ed.), *Chemical Warfare Agents* (New York: Academic Press, Inc., 1992). Also, it has been reported by dissidents working in the Russian CW programme that Russia has developed a new CW agent more deadly than the most potent classical nerve agent.

2. The US Defense Nuclear Agency sponsored a series of studies to determine the routes by which cheating might occur and to assess the prospects for US detection of CWC violations. The results were that there are a number of cheating scenarios which would be undetectable with current technical means. See Kathleen C. Bailey et al., 'Noncompliance Scenarios: Means by Which Parties to the Chemical Weapons Convention Might Cheat', US Defense Nuclear Agency Document DNA-TR-91-193, January 1992. This assessment was later 'red-teamed' by an independent group to determine if the cheating scenarios were truly as undetectable as presented. They were. See Manuel L. Sanches et al., 'Analysis of Signatures Associated with Noncompliance Scenarios', US Defense Nuclear Agency Document DNA-TR-92-74, January, 1993.

3. BW agents are living organisms (e.g. bacteria or fungi), viruses, or infective material derived from them that are used to harm or destroy enemy personnel, animals, or crops. For a detailed description, see John Cookson and Judith Nottingham, *A Survey of Chemical and Biological Warfare* (New York: Monthly Review Press, 1969).

4. UN Security Council Document S/1995/864, October 11, 1995.

5. Vladimir Pasechnik, a senior biologist who defected to Britain in 1989, appeared on the BBC's 'Newsnight' programme and stated that Russian scientists cultivated bacteria in containers of antibiotics to make them resistant to treatment. See Bill Gertz, 'Russia Has Biological Weapons, Defector Says', *The Washington Times,* January 22, 1993, p. A9.

6. Nuclear, radiological, or chemical weapons are most appropriate for ballistic missile delivery. Although ballistic missiles may also be able to deliver

biological warheads, the associated stresses may be lethal to BW agents. In some cases, these stresses may be overcome with technology, but more sophistication may be required.

7. The CSS-2 missile is highly inaccurate, with a circular error probably of 1 km at full range. China uses the CSS-2 with a nuclear warhead. Although there is no evidence that China supplied nuclear warheads with the CSS-2s sold to Saudi Arabia, it is possible. If so, it would help explain the tight operational control that Chinese personnel reportedly maintain over the CSS-2s deployed in Saudi Arabia.

8. A proliferant using differential GPS – GPS corrected for error introduced by selective availability – may achieve accuracy of 10 metres. See Irving Lachow, 'The Global Positioning System and Cruise Missile Proliferation: Assessing the Threat', CSIA Discussion Paper 94–04, Harvard University, June, 1994, p. 7.

9. India, Israel, North Korea, South Africa, South Korea, and Taiwan.

7 The NPT: Coping with the Best and Worst Cases[1]

Zachary S. Davis[2]

1 INTRODUCTION

The future of the Non-Proliferation Treaty (NPT) is still uncertain, despite the decision in May 1995 by 175 countries to extend the Treaty indefinitely. Uncertainty about the prospects for the NPT stem from the fact that we do not know if we are entering an era of peace and cooperation, or one of conflict and confrontation. In either case, the NPT will continue to be the corner-stone of the non-proliferation regime. The demise of the NPT would spell disaster for international non-proliferation policies. It would be fatal for the International Atomic Energy Agency (IAEA) and its safeguards system. It would unravel multilateral export control agreements, dash hopes for United Nations enforcement of non-proliferation, and cripple the non-proliferation norm. In short, a weakening of respect for the NPT by its parties would destroy the basis for cooperative international non-proliferation policies. The collapse of the non-proliferation regime could even undermine the norm of non-use which has prevailed since the last nuclear weapon was used in war on August 9, 1945.

The extension decision in 1995 was not the end-game for non-proliferation, because the world still faces many vexing proliferation problems. First, some proliferation will most likely continue. The emerging post-Cold War security order will do more than the NPT to determine whether nations perceive their security to depend on nuclear weapons. Second, indefinite extension does not resolve existing problems of non-compliance and non-membership. A few countries are bound to remain outside the Treaty or to challenge it from within. Third, the discrimination problem between the five nuclear weapon states and the non-weapon states will not be resolved in the short term. Such discrimination has a corrosive effect on the NPT's legitimacy. Without solving all of the world's proliferation problems, the NPT remains a necessary but not sufficient means of preserving world nuclear order. The decision to extend the NPT indefinitely perpetuates the 25-year struggle to assure the Treaty's effectiveness and its legitimacy. Anything short of indefinite extension would have increased the risk of creating a Hobbesian world of nuclear anarchy. But it would be short-sighted to assume that indefinite extension solves the proliferation problem.

This chapter describes several possible best and worst case scenarios for proliferation with and without the NPT. I begin with the most optimistic outlook of indefinite extension in a favourable security environment and then examine prospects for a weakened NPT in a chaotic world. I conclude with some observations on preferred outcomes and how they might be achieved.

2   ARMS CONTROL AND NON-PROLIFERATION WITH A PERMANENT NPT REGIME

On May 11, 1995, the members of the NPT agreed to extend the treaty indefinitely. In the short term, several trends that are already underway are likely to continue. However, the real test for the NPT will be to see how the Treaty holds up in face of long-term developments in world politics.

The Short-Term Outlook: Stay the Course

With the NPT status quo preserved, a number of incremental measures to strengthen the regime are likely to be implemented. These include improvements in safeguards,[3] continued coordination in export control policies among supplier states, and further reductions by the nuclear weapons states. With the NPT secured, the United States and Russia can be expected to continue to reduce their arsenals up to and perhaps beyond START-I and II levels. There is hope that further US–Russian reductions might encourage Britain, France and China to join the arms control process. Perhaps the most significant arms control consequence of indefinite extension is the likelihood that a comprehensive test ban treaty (CTBT) will be completed in the future. Weak endorsement of the NPT or a limited extension for a single fixed period would have dampened enthusiasm for a CTBT by the nuclear weapons states.

Indefinite extension of the NPT reinforces a general trend away from past levels of reliance on nuclear weapons. A world nuclear order defined by a robust non-proliferation regime maintains the existing barriers against horizontal proliferation and also encourages the nuclear weapons states to abide by their obligations under Article VI of the NPT to 'pursue negotiations in good faith on effective measures relating to cessation of the nuclear arms race at an early date and to nuclear disarmament...'. The strengthened review process for the NPT agreed to at the 1995 conference will closely monitor compliance with the Treaty.[4]

The Clinton administration has made unprecedented progress with respect to Article VI of the NPT. One result of the 1995 NPT Review and Extension conference was a new commitment by the nuclear weapons states to negative and positive security assurances.[5] In addition to its strong support for a CTB, the administration and Congress stepped up US efforts to assist the states of the former Soviet Union to secure and dismantle retired nuclear weapons. The Nunn-Lugar Cooperative Threat Reduction programmes have reduced dangers associated with the loss of control of nuclear weapons, materials, technology, and expertise in the former Soviet Union, although many problems remain. Ukraine's signing of the NPT and the removal of enough weapons-grade highly enriched uranium for about 20 bombs from an unsafeguarded facility in Kazakhstan in November 1994 both represent major successes for non-proliferation policy. The administration also began negotiations on a global cut-off of fissile material production for weapons and negotiated an agreement with North Korea to cap and roll back Pyongyang's nuclear weapons programme.

An argument can be made that very significant progress toward satisfying Article VI obligations has been made. Further reductions in US and Russian arsenals beyond START-I and II would continue the trend away from nuclear weapons.[6] The Clinton administration's 1994 review of US nuclear forces and strategy, known as the nuclear posture review (NPR), anticipated additional reductions in US and Russian arsenals, as did Russian President Boris Yeltsin in proposals made during his trip to the United States in September 1994.[7] Observers inside and outside of governments have outlined further steps to give substance to the disarmament obligations of the NPT. These include measures such as: verified dismantlement of retired nuclear weapons and disposal of nuclear weapons materials, a weapons materials production cut-off, no-first-use pledges, further downgrading of strategic alert status and detargeting by the weapons states, greater transparency in nuclear arsenals, and active support for nuclear weapons free zones.[8]

However, the future prospects for recent accomplishments were occasionally overshadowed by disappointment that the Clinton administration's 1994 nuclear posture review (NPR) did not go further in meeting expectations for rapid progress toward disarmament. The NPR confirmed the perceived deterrent value of nuclear weapons by the United States, and thus exacerbated longstanding objections among the non-nuclear weapons members of the NPT to the discriminatory aspect of the

Treaty. The administration's counterproliferation programmes also sent mixed messages to some non-weapons states about US intentions to hold open the option of pre-emptive military strikes.[9] Despite efforts by Pentagon officials to clarify the intent of the counterproliferation initiative and sooth fears of pre-emption, some observers still believe that it contradicts US non-proliferation diplomacy, and especially casts doubt on the credibility of US negative security assurances. Nevertheless, the Clinton administration provided leadership on a wide range of non-proliferation issues in the lead-up to the 1995 NPT Review Conference. That leadership made it possible to secure the future of the NPT. With indefinite extension in place, the outlook for arms control and non-proliferation for the short term is good.

A combination of strengthened enforcement and verification of non-proliferation obligations, on the one hand, and progress toward meeting Article VI obligations, on the other, is the surest way to secure the future of the NPT regime. Horizontal and vertical proliferation will not be reversed overnight, but a strong NPT provides the greatest impetus and best opportunity for progress on both fronts. Nor will the discriminatory aspect of the NPT disappear in the near term. Even the abolishment of nuclear weapons would not result in a more equal distribution of power among the nations of the world. Those who would view the NPT primarily as a symbol of the disparity of power between North and South, rich and poor, advanced and developing countries, overlook the shared benefits of non-proliferation for nearly all nations. In the end, there was a consensus among the members of the NPT that the security benefits of the Treaty should not be sacrificed to protest the inequities of world politics. They agreed that the surest way to narrow the gap between the nuclear 'haves' and 'have-nots' is through the continuation of the arms control process. That process is more likely to proceed with a permanent NPT than without it.

The Long-Term Outlook: Order or Chaos?

Unfortunately, indefinite extension of the NPT and progress in arms control are not enough to alleviate uncertainty about the evolving post-Cold War security order. While the NPT can help shape that order, global and regional security circumstances will weigh most heavily on the success or failure of non-proliferation efforts. Let us consider several possible directions for world security and their consequences for the non-proliferation regime.

First, some optimists remain hopeful that the end of the Cold War created new opportunities for peace. From this perspective, the removal of

US–Soviet rivalries from regional conflicts should enable warring groups and nations to resolve their problems without the burden of Cold War-inspired interventionism. Optimists see an expanded role for the United Nations in peacekeeping, peacemaking, humanitarian intervention, backed by a revival of Wilsonian notions of collective security. Some believe that the fruits of democracy and global interdependence are destined to cause peoples and nations to turn their backs on war. From this perspective, breakthroughs in peace negotiations in the Middle East and Northern Ireland, even Haiti, reflect the new realities of the post-Cold War world. Global problems of environment, resources, population, communication, and proliferation require global solutions which challenge the authority and viability of the nation-state.[10] Once the root cause of proliferation – insecurity – is eliminated, nuclear ambitions should fade away and allow nuclear disarmament to become a reality.[11]

A second possibility is that the post-Cold War security environment could degenerate into chronic instability, conflict, and unchecked nuclear proliferation. Instead of easing regional tensions, the retraction of super-power influence – including security guarantees – could unleash repressed animosities, creating insecurity and provoking many countries to 'keep their powder dry'. Even countries thought to have renounced nuclear weapons might reassess their nuclear options if the basic assumptions underlying their security are seriously undermined. For example, how would a build-up of Chinese power projection capabilities, growing uncertainty about North Korea, and the removal of US troops from Japan and South Korea affect security calculations in Asia?[12]

The best case would be one in which the NPT is extended indefinitely as the world enters an era of prolonged peace and stability. If the survival of all nations and peoples were guaranteed, nuclear weapons might become increasingly irrelevant as guarantors of security or symbols of prestige and power. In such a world, the NPT could become part of a new compact on the illegitimacy of weapons of mass destruction as tools of state power. The UN Security Council statement of January 1992 declaring weapons of mass destruction to be a threat to international peace and security, and the Security Council resolution on security assurances passed on April 11, 1995, could be interpreted as steps in this direction.[13] As the declared weapons states reduce their arsenals in the decades ahead, the three threshold nuclear states (India, Israel and Pakistan) would be expected to join the arms control process; the motivation for covert programmes would be eliminated and the proliferation problem would be solved.

In a somewhat less optimistic scenario, indefinite extension of the NPT might not be a prelude to perpetual peace. Instead of being a transitional period of uncertainty, the semi-chaotic post-Cold War order may simply endure indefinitely. If the status quo were to persist, the nuclear weapons states would probably retain some nuclear weapons as an insurance policy against further deterioration of the international security order. This rationale was evident in the Clinton administration's NPR, in French government statements and probably guides the thinking of British, Russian and Chinese strategists as well. If the status quo endures, the threshold states would probably not take major steps toward rolling back their undeclared arsenals, although they may agree to accept some limitations on them.

Under these circumstances, the NPT gives legitimacy to international efforts to preserve and strengthen the non-proliferation regime. Prolonging of the uncertainty that characterizes the post-Cold War status quo would not prevent a few nations from challenging the non-proliferation norm, nor would it encourage great strides in strategic arms control. But only the NPT could preserve the legal, moral, technical, and political barriers that constitute the non-proliferation regime. The regime would not prevent dedicated proliferators from acquiring nuclear weapons, but it raises the monetary and political costs to deter casual proliferation. In the absence of urgent new threats, the NPT can continue its historic role as a speed bump that slows down proliferation. Without the NPT regime, the status quo could easily slip into nuclear chaos.

At the other end of the spectrum of possibilities, shifts in the balance of power could threaten the security of nations and rekindle widespread interest in nuclear weapons.[14] The post-Cold War era could lead to a nuclear-armed 'Clash of Civilizations'.[15] In a world of confrontation and conflict, it might not take much to provoke a surge of proliferation in which worst case planning, such as that which drove the US–Soviet arms race for fifty years, drives other countries to overestimate threats. Once the action–reaction pattern has begun, arms race spirals gain momentum that may take decades to slow. The US–Soviet arms race demonstrated that deterrence can be an open-ended objective that has no finite conclusion. Perceptions of missile gaps and 'windows of vulnerability' could drive new nuclear states to duplicate the overkill arsenals of Washington and Moscow, and to reproduce the costs and risks of the US–Soviet deterrence model. South Asia may have already embarked on this path.[16]

There is little reason to believe that other countries will do a better job than Washington and Moscow of discerning between an adversary's declared intentions and its technical capabilities. Moreover, the current system of IAEA safeguards has not provided adequate verification to overcome distrust, and recent improvements in safeguards do not go far enough to dispel suspicions. Official denials are not sufficient to eliminate anxiety, as has been illustrated by ongoing concerns about the nuclear intentions of Japan, Iran, Algeria, and others. Assurances of peaceful intent can be clouded by circumstantial evidence of bomb-related activities. Whether or not such evidence provides conclusive proof of latent or 'virtual' nuclear weapons programmes, suspicious neighbours are likely to keep a watchful eye on developments.[17]

If the security situation in the former Soviet Union, South Asia, East Asia, or the Middle East were to degenerate into conflict, it is not hard to imagine proliferation spinning out of control. In the Middle East, what would be the result of Iran, Iraq, Libya, or Algeria acquiring fissile materials? In Asia, what are the prospects for proliferation when North Korea possesses a secret cache of plutonium and the ability to make more; Japan is producing tons of plutonium – albeit under safeguards; China continues its across-the-board military build-up, including nuclear testing in defiance of a global moratorium; and at least two other countries in the region – South Korea and Taiwan – have in the past taken steps towards developing a nuclear option. Even if South Korea does not revive its past interest in nuclear weapons, it is on track to inherit North Korea's nuclear legacy after reunification. How would the world respond to Mr. Zhirionvsky's bellicose threats and territorial claims if he were to take power in Russia? If the risk of future proliferation is not high, it is also not negligible.

Even a robust and perpetual NPT could not stem the tide of proliferation that could result from the disintegration of world security order. Nevertheless, even under these conditions the NPT would still represent the most effective instrument for preventing proliferation from spinning totally out of control. The value of the NPT actually increases as world security deteriorates and proliferation pressures rise. In a violence-prone world, the NPT represents humanity's hope that conflict can be controlled to exclude weapons of mass destruction.

3   IMAGINING A WORLD WITHOUT THE NPT

A group of countries associated with the non-aligned movement (NAM) opposed indefinite extension of the NPT. Some favoured a single extension for as short a time as two years. What would have been the result? If the NPT had ended five years ago, Argentina, Brazil, India, Pakistan, South Africa, Iraq, Iran, Ukraine, Kazakhstan and Belarus would probably be nuclear weapons states today. If the NPT were to end today, recent successes could be reversed and a few countries would probably join the nuclear club. A decision in 1995 to allow the NPT to lapse would have prompted defence planners around the world to begin preparing for the world without the NPT. Even a relatively long extension period such as 25 years would have set in motion events leading to the destruction of the non-proliferation regime. While the NPT is not the independent variable that shapes international security, it is a critical indicator of global trends. The demise of the NPT would not cause global anarchy, but it would indicate the dissolution of world nuclear order.

The Best Worst Case: No NPT in a Relatively Benign World

The best case one can imagine for a world without the NPT is that progress toward peaceful resolution of conflict could make war, nuclear weapons, and the NPT obsolete. The demise of safeguards, export controls, and multilateral cooperation would not matter if no one had nuclear ambitions.

A less optimistic outlook of a relatively stable but potentially volatile world would expect a few nations with particular motivations to initiate secret programmes to keep the nuclear option alive, but to do so within the constraints of the NPT while it remains in force. Barring a radical turn for the worse in the world security environment, one would not expect a massive surge of proliferation and breakout from the NPT. However, widespread hedging by weapons and non-weapons states against future contingencies would not be surprising. 'Virtual' weapons programmes might be a model for such a hedging strategy.[18] Decisions on nuclear options would be deferred. Cooperation in safeguards, export controls, and enforcement could continue, but on a gradually more bilateral and/or alliance basis as the collapse of the international NPT regime draws near.[19] Even after the official end of the NPT, vestiges of cooperation would remain, but the basis for global cooperation would be gone.

Another possibility for proliferation without the NPT would be that the spread of nuclear weapons continues at its current pace, but deterrence relationships mature without incident. Such an outcome would confirm the theories of those who have advocated proliferation as a remedy for insecurity.[20] The end of the NPT would allow countries with security problems to implement deterrence strategies that protect them from perceived threats. Deterrence might not rely exclusively on nuclear weapons, but might incorporate other weapons, such as chemical and biological weapons, defensive systems or exotic new technologies.

Contrary to conventional wisdom, such a hidden hand, or self-regulating, approach to proliferation might not lead to disaster and would have the advantage of being non-discriminatory. One variation on this theme would have the weapons states provide assistance to new nuclear states to make their arsenals safe and reliable. For proponents of this view, replacing the non-proliferation norm embodied by the NPT with a managed free market approach to proliferation would be the best antidote to regional or global instability.

The Worst Case: Uncontrolled Proliferation With No NPT in a Chaotic World

World nuclear anarchy might not lead to nuclear war, but the risk of nuclear war increases in a world of uncontrolled proliferation. Let us consider the prospects for proliferation if the world security situation degenerates significantly as described in a previous section. In this scenario, however, there is no permanent NPT and a debilitated non-proliferation regime.

The end of the NPT would mean the end of the non-proliferation regime and the end of the non-proliferation norm. The removal of the regime's barriers to proliferation would allow easy access to weapons materials and technology for motivated proliferators and casual proliferators alike. From a business perspective, there would be a huge surge in the manufacture and sale of weapons and weapons-related technology. While not all countries would exercise the option to acquire nuclear weapons, a few countries would probably join the nuclear club soon after the Treaty expired. The threshold states might no longer feel constrained against declaring their nuclear status and expanding their arsenals. Many countries concerned about the future could be expected to keep their nuclear options alive by instituting virtual programmes. New arms races would start, channelling enormous resources into weapons programmes. Without the NPT, nothing would prohibit transfers of nuclear weapons, materials, technology, and know-how among nuclear and non-nuclear states. Uncontrolled proliferation would prompt the five declared weapons states to forge ahead with improvements of their own weapons, delivery systems and counter-proliferation capabilities. Nuclear testing would probably resume. Some countries might acquire other weapons of mass destruction, dooming prospects for controlling chemical and biological weapons or missiles. The result would be more weapons of mass destruction in more countries.

Such developments may not have dire consequences in a relatively benign regional or global security environment. However, if the world has not seen the last of war and aggression – and nations have no recourse beyond self-help to ensure their survival – we cannot assume that in an age of proliferation nuclear weapons would never be used. The eclipse of the non-proliferation, or non-acquisition, norm would leave the norm of non-use as the last barrier to nuclear war. If international conflict is destined to be a part of a future world order which does not include the non-proliferation regime, what would be the prospects for nuclear war?

First, a complicated global network of deterrence relationships holds many opportunities for failure. The history of deterrence among the declared weapons states provides several lessons. While there is some validity to the argument that nuclear deterrence contributed to the absence of direct conflict between the United States and the Soviet Union throughout the 'Long Peace' of the Cold War,[21] the history of US–Soviet nuclear deterrence includes a number of disturbing episodes in which the risk of nuclear war escalated. Recent research on the Cuban Missile Crisis based on declassified documents and other materials, for example, suggests that officials in Washington and Moscow made decisions based on incorrect information and assumptions that could have had disastrous consequences.[22] Evolving deterrence dyads and triads are more likely than not to encounter similar crises on their way to maturity.

The nuclear relationship between India and Pakistan is a case in point. Strategic analysts from India and Pakistan (and a few in the United States) assert that the existence of undeclared, or 'opaque', nuclear capabilities in South Asia creates a stable nuclear deterrent relationship. These analysts think that an overt nuclear arms race between the two countries can be avoided, and that military conflicts such as those over the disputed territory of Kashmir do not pose unacceptable risks of nuclear escalation. To the contrary, in their view nuclear capabilities are believed to deter conventional as well as nuclear war. According to this view, nuclear deterrence in South Asia need not follow the US–Soviet model, but can evolve to fit the unique circumstances of the region. In a nutshell, low-level, or supposedly 'non-weaponized', nuclear deterrence between India and Pakistan is said to already exist without the need for nuclear testing, arms racing, or the necessity of having assured second strike capabilities to deter a disarming first strike. The Director of Central Intelligence, R. James Woolsey, expressed a different view when he said 'the arms race between India and Pakistan poses perhaps the most probable prospect for future use of weapons of mass destruction, including nuclear weapons.'[23] This perspective was supported by media reports that US intelligence officials concluded during the Kashmir crisis of spring 1990 that India and Pakistan were on the brink of a war that could have escalated to nuclear war. Military preparations in both countries reportedly supported this assessment. Consequently, many analysts take issue with the argument that nuclear weapons can contribute to peace and stability in South Asia. Instead, they argue that New Delhi and Islamabad are in the early stages of an arms race, which will eventually lead to their own versions of the Cuban Missile, Taiwan Straits, Korean, or Berlin Crises. Sooner or later, however, leaders may fail to avert disaster.[24]

A second source of instability stems from inherent risks of human miscalculation and accidents associated with very complex technical systems such as nuclear weapons and their associated command and control systems. Here too, the history of US and Soviet nuclear weapons programmes provides many examples of accidents involving nuclear weapons, demonstrating conclusively that nuclear weapons are not exempt from Clausewitz's 'fog of war'.[25] The mishandling, misfiring, and misplacement of nuclear weapons can have a wide range of severe consequences. Political instability in nuclear weapon states adds another disturbing variable to the equation. The former Soviet Union might not be the last country to lose control of its nuclear arsenal, raising the risk that criminal or terrorist groups might also join the nuclear club.

A third reason for concern about nuclear anarchy is that leaders may not be satisfied with passive deterrence, but may be tempted to seek political leverage from their weapons through veiled threats and not-so-veiled blackmail. After World War II, some US diplomats viewed the atomic bomb as a 'winning weapon' which could enable them to dictate terms to Russia. Other nations may make similar miscalculations regarding the political-military utility of nuclear diplomacy.[26] North Korea used nuclear blackmail to achieve many longstanding political and military objectives and extracted commitments for free nuclear reactors, free oil, and foreign investment to revive its moribund economy. Others may demand an even higher price. What would have been the effect on the UN-sanctioned Gulf War coalition if Saddam Hussein had announced during his invasion of Kuwait that he possessed nuclear weapons?[27] Uncontrolled proliferation would completely reshape alliances, erode collective security, and stifle power projection options.[28]

This leads to my last point, which is the possibility that some people may acquire nuclear weapons not for prestige and not as a deterrent, but to use them. It is not unthinkable that governments would attempt to advance territorial claims or hegemonic ambitions by wielding and using nuclear weapons. How would the world react to a nuclear attack, especially if it were limited, ended quickly and casualties were comparable to other human tragedies? It is possible that one or more small nuclear wars would not represent a dire threat to humanity. Would the 50-year-old consensus against the use of nuclear weapons endure? At the very least, any breech of the norm of non-use would call into question the most important constraint on the use of force in international politics. Accepting the legitimacy of offensive nuclear war fighting (as distinct from deterrence) would be tantamount to a repudiation of the just war tradition.[29] An unacceptable risk of nuclear chaos would result from a combination of widespread conflict and the demise of the non-proliferation regime.

4 FUNDAMENTAL NON-PROLIFERATION STRATEGY

Under any imaginable circumstances, preserving the NPT and the non-proliferation regime should remain a top priority for all countries. The NPT is not the main determinant of world order, but it is a key component of order. To the extent that man is capable of shaping human destiny through national and international policies, every effort should be made to preserve the non-proliferation norm as a central precept of any future world order. At a minimum, several prudent and timely steps would help to preserve the non-proliferation regime.

The consensus decision to make the NPT a permanent part of the international security architecture was a giant step towards preserving world nuclear order. Of course, the key to winning overwhelming support for indefinite extension was the commitments by the weapons states that there will be no backtracking on the timing and scope of a comprehensive test ban treaty. Other good faith efforts (such as those mentioned above) to satisfy Article VI and to a lesser extent Article IV regarding nuclear assistance to developing countries, add weight to the argument that the reciprocal obligations of the NPT are being respected. Finally, strengthened safeguards to deter and detect cheating, and rigorous international enforcement against violators would give all members of the NPT confidence in the effectiveness of the Treaty.

I would like to conclude by recalling the founding principles of the non-proliferation norm, which are embodied in the NPT. They were put forth by Ireland in four successive United Nations resolutions in 1958, 1959, 1960 and 1961. Recognizing that the risk of nuclear war would increase if nuclear weapons were allowed to spread, the Irish drafts sought to hold proliferation at bay while the world developed an equitable security order based on international law.[30] The logic of United Nations General Assembly resolution 1665 is no less valid in the post-Cold War era than it was when it was adopted unanimously on December 4, 1961. Recalling the previous Irish resolutions, the resolution warned:

> that an increase in the number of States possessing nuclear weapons is growing more imminent and threatens to extend and intensify the arms

race and to increase the difficulties of avoiding war and of establishing international peace and security based on rule of law...'[31]

The Irish resolution outlined the main tenets of non-proliferation and urged all countries to conclude an international treaty putting non-proliferation principles into practice. Twenty-five years after Hiroshima and Nagasaki, the NPT entered into force. The ensuing 25 years confirmed the wisdom of making non-proliferation a central precept of world order. The question in 1995 was whether to make non-proliferation a permanent norm of international behaviour, or to take our chances with nuclear anarchy. Prudence dictated the decision by the members of the NPT to make non-proliferation a centre-piece of the still-emerging world order. The next challenge is to promote a world order that will perpetuate non-proliferation norms and institutions for another 25 years and beyond.

NOTES

1. A version of this chapter appeared in *Irish Studies in International Affairs*, vol. 6, 1995.
2. Zachary S. Davis is a specialist in international nuclear policy at the Congressional Research Service, Library of Congress. The views expressed are his own, and do not necessarily reflect views or policies of the Library of Congress or the Congressional Research Service.
3. On recent plans to improve IAEA safeguards, see Bruno Pellaud, 'Safeguards in Transition: Status, Challenges, and Opportunities'; Lothar Wedekind and James Larrimore, 'International Symposium on Safeguards: Mirror of the Times'; and other articles in *IAEA Bulletin*, vol. 36, no. 3, September 1994. See also, 'IAEA Preparing New Safeguards System for Presentation to NPT Meeting', *Nuclear Fuel*, October 24, 1994; and Zachary Davis and Warren Donnelly, *International Atomic Energy Agency: Strengthen Verification Authority?* (Washington, DC: Congressional Research Service, September 1994).
4. 1995 Review and Extension Conference, 'Strengthening the Review Process for the Treaty', NPT/CONF.1995/I.4, May 10, 1995.
5. US Department of State, Statement by the Secretary of State Regarding a Declaration by the President on Security Assurances for Non-Nuclear-Weapon States Parties to the NPT, April 5, 1995; Barbara Crossette, 'UN Council Seeks Support for Nuclear Pact', *New York Times*, April 6, 1995.
6. For recent discussions of next steps in nuclear arms control see: McGeorge Bundy, William Crowe, and Sidney Drell, 'Reducing Nuclear Danger', *Foreign Affairs*, vol. 72, Spring 1993, p. 140; Jonathan Dean, 'The Final Stage of Nuclear Arms Control', *Washington Quarterly*, vol. 17, Autumn 1994, p. 31; Janne Nolan, 'The US Nuclear Arsenal: Its Past, Its Future', *Brookings Review*, Spring 1994, p. 30; Ivo Daalder, 'Stepping Down the Thermonuclear Ladder: How Low Can We Go?', University of Maryland,

Center for International Security Studies, Project on Rethinking Arms Control, Paper 5, June 1993.

7. Nuclear Posture Review, briefing slide number 18, 'Options Reviewed to Achieve Faster/Deeper Reductions'. On the Yeltsin proposal see Fred Hiatt, 'Yeltsin Arms Proposals Aimed at Russians, Historians', *Washington Post*, September 28, 1994; R.W. Apple, 'US and Russia to Speed Disarmament', *New York Times*, September 29, 1994; Campaign for the Non-Proliferation Treaty, 'Comparison of Presidents Clinton and Yeltsin's Arms Control Initiatives in Their Respective United Nations Speeches', September 28, 1994; Amy Woolf, *Nuclear Arms Control At the Washington Summit: Early Deactivation of Ballistic Missiles*, CRS Report for Congress, October 7, 1994.

8. Numerous recent publications have outlined arms control measures to satisfy Article VI obligations. These include: George Bunn, Roland Timerbaev and James Leonard, *Nuclear Disarmament: How Much Have the Five Nuclear Powers Promised in the Non-Proliferation Treaty?* (Washington, DC: Lawyers Alliance for World Security, Committee for National Security, Washington Council on Non-Proliferation, June 1994); William Epstein and Paul Szasz, 'Extension of the Nuclear Non-Proliferation Treaty: A Means of Strengthening the Treaty', *Virginia Journal of International Law*, vol. 33, no. 4, 1994, p. 736; 'Strengthening the NPT and the Nuclear Non-Proliferation Regime', a special issue of the journal *Disarmament*, vol. 16, no. 2, 1993; Frank Barnaby, ed., *Strengthening the Non-Proliferation Regime: 1995 and Beyond* (Oxford: Oxford Research Group, 1993).

9. See Mitchell Reiss and Harald Muller, eds, 'International Perspectives on Counterproliferation', Woodrow Wilson Center, Working Paper No. 99, January 1995; Zachary Davis and Mitchell Reiss, *US Counterproliferation Doctrine: Issues for Congress*, CRS Report for Congress, July 1994; Senator Pete Domenici, 'Countering Weapons of Mass Destruction', *Washington Quarterly*, vol. 18, no. 1, Winter 1995; and Pilat and Kirchner, 'Counterproliferation as a Technology Initiative', *Washington Quarterly*, *ibid*.

10. For a supra-national analysis of proliferation see Daniel Deudney, 'Dividing Realism: Structural Realism versus Security Materialism on Nuclear Security and Proliferation', in Zachary Davis and Benjamin Frankel, eds, *The Proliferation Puzzle: Why Nuclear Weapons Spread* (London: Frank Cass, 1993). Deudney argues that the nation-state can no longer serve its primary function of protecting citizens from external threats, and therefore should be replaced with a supra-national authority.

11. For a collection of visionary disarmament predictions and prescriptions see the special issue of *The Bulletin of the Atomic Scientists*, 'Agenda 2001', vol. 48, no. 4, May 1992. For an liberal optimist view of proliferation see Glen Chafetz, 'The End of the Cold War and the Future of Nuclear Proliferation: An Alternative to the Neorealist Perspective', in Davis and Frankel, *The Proliferation Puzzle*.

12. Barry Buzan and Gerald Segal, 'Rethinking East Asian Security', *Survival*, vol. 36, no. 2, Summer 1994.

13. United Nations Security Council Statement, January 31, 1992, Document S/23500; United Nations Security Council Resolution 984, S/RES/984, April 11, 1995.

14. Examples of worst-case predictions for future world order include Benjamin Frankel, 'The Brooding Shadow: Systemic Incentives and Nuclear Weapons Proliferation', in Davis and Frankel, *The Proliferation Puzzle*; and John Mearsheimer, 'Back to the Future: Instability in Europe After the Cold War', *International Security*, vol. 15, Summer 1990.

15. Samuel Huntington, 'The Clash of Civilizations?' *Foreign Affairs*, vol. 72, Summer 1993.

16. For alternative perspectives on the South Asian arms race, see Zachary S. Davis, *Nonproliferation Strategies for South Asia* (Washington: Congressional Research Service, May 1994); and George Perkovich 'A Nuclear Third Way in South Asia', *Foreign Policy*, Summer 1993.

17. The concept of virtual proliferation is developed by Roger Molander and Peter Wilson in *The Nuclear Asymptote: On Containing Nuclear Proliferation* (Santa Monica: RAND, 1993). Virtual proliferation creates the technical means to produce nuclear weapons following a political decision to do so, enabling countries to keep nuclear options open without violating non-proliferation commitments. Sweden and Japan are often cited as having such virtual capabilities.

18. A recent article described Sweden's nuclear programme as having virtual weapons capability. See Steve Coll, 'Neutral Sweden Quietly Keeps Nuclear Option Open', *Washington Post*, November 25, 1994, A1. Whether or not the charge is true, the article illustrates how evidence of nuclear capability can be interpreted to suggest intentions.

19. Lewis Dunn, 'The Collapse of the NPT – What If?' and David Fischer, 'What Happens to Safeguards if the NPT Goes?' in J. Pilat and R. Pendley, *Beyond 1995: The Future of the NPT Regime* (New York: Plenum Press, 1990), pp. 27–52.

20. The classic work is Kenneth W. Waltz, *The Spread of Nuclear Weapons: More May Be Better*, Adelphi Paper no. 171 (London: International Institute of Strategic Studies, 1981). John Mearsheimer also subscribes to this logic, albeit on a more selective basis, in his article, 'Back to the Future: Instability in Europe After the Cold War', *International Security*, vol. 15, Summer 1990.

21. John Lewis Gaddis, *The Long Peace: Inquiries Into the History of the Cold War* (New York: Oxford University Press, 1987).

22. On the 30th anniversary of the Cuban Missile Crisis in 1993, newly declassified documents confirmed that mutual misperceptions brought John F. Kennedy and Nikita Khrushchev close to nuclear war. Declassified documents and testimony of participants confirm that the missiles in Cuba were operational and were not equipped with permissive action links to prevent unauthorized launch by field commanders. Furthermore, Kennedy did not know that in addition to the medium range missiles, the Soviets had placed tactical nuclear weapons in Cuba which were to be used to protect the island during a US invasion. Unlike the missiles, which were to be launched only by a direct order from Moscow, tactical weapons were under the control of Soviet field commanders in Cuba. Against this backdrop, Fidel Castro apparently proposed to Khrushchev 'the immediate launching of a nuclear strike on the United States'. See Mary S. McAuliffe, ed., *CIA Documents on the Cuban Missile Crisis, 1962* (Washington: Central Intelligence Agency,

1992); Fedor Burlatsky, 'Castro Wanted a Nuclear Strike', *New York Times*, October 23, 1992; Tad Szulc, 'Cuba 62: A Brush With Armageddon', *Washington Post, Book World*, review of recent books on the Cuban Missile Crisis, November 15, 1992, 1. One participant in the Missile Crisis has warned of the parallels between the 1962 crisis and the 1994 standoff with North Korea. See McGeorge Bundy and Gordon Goldstein, 'A Lot Like the Cuban Missile Crisis', *Washington Post*, July 3, 1994. Also, in July 1994, secret White House tape recordings from the Crisis were declassified. The tapes confirm that Kennedy and his advisers were aware that miscalculation could result in an unintended nuclear war.

23.   R. James Woolsey, testimony before the Senate Governmental Affairs Committee, February 24, 1993, and before the House Foreign Affairs Committee, Subcommittee on International Security, International Organizations and Human Rights, July 28, 1993.

24.   Seymour Hersh, 'On the Nuclear Edge', *The New Yorker*, March 29, 1993, p. 56; William Burrows and Robert Windrem, *Critical Mass: The Dangerous Race for Superweapons in a Fragmenting World* (New York: Simon and Schuster, 1994); Mitchell Reiss, *Bridled Ambition: Why Countries Constrain Their Nuclear Capabilities* (Washington, DC: Woodrow Wilson Center/Johns Hopkins University Press, 1995). Debate continues over how close India and Pakistan were to nuclear war in 1990. Some analysts, particularly those from South Asia, remain sceptical about the interpretation that Delhi and Islamabad were on the brink.

25.   Scott Sagan, *The Limits of Safety* (Princeton: Princeton University Press, 1993); and Sagan, 'The Perils of Proliferation: Organization Theory, Deterrence Theory, and the Spread of Nuclear Weapons', *International Security*, vol. 18, Spring 1994.

26.   On early US nuclear diplomacy see Gregg Herken, *The Winning Weapon* (New York: Vintage, 1982). For a review of the debate about US intentions and nuclear diplomacy after Hiroshima see Barton Bernstein, ed., *The Atomic Bomb: The Critical Issues* (Boston: Little, Brown, 1976).

27.   This scenario is developed in Robert Blackwill and Albert Carnesale, eds, *The New Nuclear Nations* (New York: Council on Foreign Relations, 1993).

28.   See, for example, Remarks by Secretary of Defense Les Aspin, National Academy of Sciences, December 7, 1993.

29.   In some cases, war fighting capabilities may enhance deterrence. For purposes of analysis, one can distinguish between deterrent forces and offensive nuclear capabilities, although in practice this distinction may be blurred. On nuclear war and the just war tradition see Michael Waltzer, *Just and Unjust Wars* (New York: Basic Books, 1977); Michael Howard, ed., *Restraints in War: Studies in the Limitation of Armed Conflict* (London: Oxford University Press, 1979); and Joseph Nye, *Nuclear Ethics* (New York: Free Press, 1987).

30.   *The United Nations and Disarmament: 1945–1970* (New York: United Nations, 1970), p. 262.

31.   General Assembly resolution 1665 (XVI), December 4, 1961, reproduced in *The United Nations and Disarmament*, p. 263.

Part II
Regional Perspectives

8 Proliferation and Non-Proliferation in Ukraine: Implications for European and US Security
Stephen Blank

[The views expressed here do not represent those of the US Army, Defense Department, or the US Government.]

Ukraine inherited nuclear weapons when the USSR collapsed. It did not develop them. By 1993 Ukraine's public and élite were increasingly strongly inclined to keep control and ownership over these weapons, although Ukraine formally agreed to accept the START-I treaty, dismantle, and then transfer control over the weapons to Russia. Yet in January 1994 Ukrainian President Kravchuk signed a treaty with the United States and Russia to dismantle these weapons and return them to Russia in return for substantial economic and security guarantees. Therefore, we must explain why Kravchuk initially manœuvred to keep the weapons and then ultimately gave them up. Ukrainian 'nuclearization' was as much political as military. Today nuclear weapons are as much tools of political bargaining as they are of military threat and deterrence.[1] This insight helps clarify Ukraine's actions. William Overholt's 'checklist' of motives for states to go nuclear also comports well with Ukraine's motives.[2] The decision to forgo nuclear weapons can also be explained. Undoubtedly this issue also has profound implications and repercussions for European security and the future of the Non-Proliferation Treaty (NPT). Since the NPT came up for renewal and review in 1995, Ukraine's ultimate decision also had critical importance abroad.

1 UKRAINE'S OBJECTIVES

Ukraine's military doctrine stated its intention to be a non-nuclear state, renounced territorial claims against anyone, and claimed that Ukraine had no enemies. Indeed the doctrine urged nuclear free zones and regional security in Eastern Europe. But any state 'whose consistent policy constitutes a military danger for Ukraine, leads to the interference in internal matters, and encroaches on its territorial integrity or national interests' is viewed as an enemy.[3] Obviously that means Russia. Despite its disclaimers, Ukraine also was visibly moving to gain the weapons and positive control of them.[4]

While Ukraine's sense of threat is well founded, it exploited its potential nuclear status to extort political and economic guarantees and deter Russia, confirming that proliferators use their weapons for bargaining as much as for deterrence or warfighting. As compensation for removing the weapons Kiev demanded from Russia and NATO (and especially the United States) binding military, political, and economic guarantees.[5] To defray denuclearization's immense costs during an acute economic crisis Ukrainian officials spoke of billions of US dollars as compensation. While precise figures are unavailable, they apparently sought 2–5 billion dollars. Kiev also sought financial compensation for the highly enriched uranium (HEU) that Ukraine would forgo by dismantling, and which could bring desperately needed billions on the world market. The government sought guarantees that Ukraine would not suffer any outside economic pressure. This mainly refers to Russia's easy ability to strangle Ukraine's oil supply by charging world prices for energy sent to Ukraine. Hitherto that energy was shipped below cost, as a subsidy to Kiev. Both states know that Russia can ruin Ukraine's economy by its control over Ukrainian energy supplies.[6] Thus Russian energy subsidies was the second condition for denuclearization. Lastly, Ukraine sought from the West, again mainly the United States, a guarantee of political integrity and sovereignty against any Russian attack, conventional or nuclear.[7] Kiev wanted a guarantee going beyond those offered in the NPT, where any attack by a nuclear state upon a non-nuclear one would be taken to the UN.[8] Kiev demanded that the United States, and presumably the West, guarantee military action against any state attacking it, i.e. Russia, and that Russia guarantee its borders too. Nowhere was the form of this guarantee stated. Should the US act alone or should it act with and through NATO? Should the guarantee remain strictly limited to conventional counterattacks or escalate to the nuclear level?

Obviously these questions raise the most profound issues of allied and European security. But Ukraine has been unable to fashion a coherent security policy that could answer these questions. Indeed, Ukraine arguably sought the nuclear option because it cannot either afford economically or decide politically how to confront its various military-political-economic challenges by purely conventional military and political means. Nuclear weapons became a kind of magic talisman to ward off devils. And Ukraine renounced nuclear weapons partly because it told itself that the United States had somehow guaranteed Ukraine's borders and sovereignty and promised large sums. A crucial problem with Ukrainian policy is that diverse spokesmen advocated different security guarantees that are or could be incompatible, let alone unrealistic. They requested a document stipulating that any threat of force against Ukraine by a nuclear state would be regarded as unacceptable by other nuclear states. Or, as the nationalist Rukh Party chairman, Vyacheslav Chornovil stated, membership in NATO would be post-nuclear Ukraine's sole guarantee. Former Prime Minister, now President, Leonid Kuchma, even asked for US extended deterrence.[9] Deputy Foreign Minister Tarasiuk called for a document possessing the economic, territorial, and military guarantees listed above.[10] But Ukrainian Deputy and defence expert, Serhiy Holovatyy, told a conference devoted to the Partnership for Peace Programme that Ukraine opposed including any countries east of Germany in NATO. He even rejected an offer to consult with the North Atlantic Cooperation Council on threats to the states of Central and Eastern Europe because those situations could separate Ukraine from Western Europe and/or its neighbours in Central Europe, and even lead to renewed dependence on Russia.[11] He charged that Ukraine's security is determined by 'certain Russian tendencies and political forces'.[12]

These divergencies reflected the paralysis in Ukrainian political thinking and left Ukraine with only one option: unilateral isolated opposition to Russia, but now without nuclear weapons or potential allies. This belief that Russian trends are what determines security in Ukraine, or any other post-Soviet state, is common across the Confederation of Independent States (CIS). It also is a factor causing uncertainty and even paralysis in those states' policy because it concedes the initiative to Russia and throws the ball to the West's court, while the state in question shrinks from the hard job of devising and conducting a Russian policy.[13] At the same time leading officials like Kravchuk's adviser, Anton Buteyko, claimed that the US signature to the treaty made it more likely that it will be respected.[14] Or like ex-Foreign Minister Zlenko, they falsely claimed to now have a multilateral guarantee from the nuclear powers.[15]

Yet examination of the accord's published portions and statements by US Ambassador to Kiev, William Miller, and Defence Secretary Perry show that Kiev received much more tenuous guarantees than is claimed. Ambassador Miller observed that if any state either attacks Ukraine or makes territorial claims upon it the United States will appeal to the UN or similar international organizations as the NPT says.[16] Secretary

Perry publicly denied that the United States made any guarantees to Ukraine.[17] The text broadcast by Radio Ukraine World Service on January 15, 1994 confirms that US obligations do not transcend those in the NPT.

Once Ukraine ratifies START-I and signs the NPT, Russia and the United States will confirm to Kiev their obligations under the Conference on Security and Cooperation in Europe (CSCE) Final Act to respect member states' independence, integrity, and sovereignty. They will also recognize that border changes may be carried out only through peaceful means and by mutual accord. They will confirm their obligation to refrain from the threat or use of force against the territorial integrity and/or independence of any state. Additionally both states confirm that their weapons will only be used for defensive purposes, in accordance with the UN charter. Both states also assure Ukraine of their obligations under the CSCE Final Act to desist from economic pressure directed at subjecting Ukraine to their own interests and advantage. If a nuclear power attacks Ukraine they 'will confirm their obligations to demand immediate action on the part of the UN Security Council with the aim of giving assistance to Ukraine as a member of the Non-proliferation Treaty that does not possess nuclear weapons'. If Ukraine becomes a victim of an act of aggression or is threatened by an aggression involving nuclear weapons; they 'will confirm their obligations to Ukraine not to use nuclear weapons against it or any other non-nuclear signatory of the NPT unless they themselves, their allies or their territory is attacked by Ukraine or any state allied to it having nuclear weapons'.[18] Though these conditions seem to guarantee Ukraine against economic, territorial, and military-political threats, in reality the CSCE and UN have little value against economic pressure and/or support for Russian separatism involving the Crimea or Eastern Ukraine.

Second, the trend is away from extended US nuclear deterrence even as NATO's conventional forces are being decimated due to budget cuts. Third, this guarantee does not break the Russian military doctrine's threat to Ukraine in the event of adhesion to NATO, indeed it confirms Russia could use nuclear weapons against a Ukraine allied to NATO, even in a purely conventional war even if Ukraine was not an active belligerent. That clause aims to deter Ukraine from joining NATO in peacetime as it would automatically become a Russian target. This is another case of using nuclear weapons for political bargaining. Nor do US leaders believe they are committed in any way other than the NPT to protect Ukraine, though Kravchuk's government thought so. As Ambassador Miller and the treaty text indicate, Ukraine's guarantees are no better than those in the original NPT.

Since Russia can block action in the Security Council and the CSCE, while bringing other pressures to bear, these guarantees remain somewhat hypothetical. Therefore, many Rada (Parliament) members attacked the treaty. Some even called for compensation before adherence to the NPT which would have negated the treaty since the guarantees only come into effect after adherence to the NPT.[19] But raising this point showed the depth of the struggle between legislature and executive in Ukraine.[20] Given those conditions, internal threats to Ukraine due to mismanagement of reform and Russian unrest, it is doubtful that the Ukraine can either stabilize itself on this basis or put lasting credence in its guarantees. The challenges facing Ukraine are only now emerging in their full and daunting complexity. Equally noteworthy is the fact that Ukraine committed itself to denuclearize before it has proved able to devise an alternative security structure or programme. That lack of viable doctrine means that Ukraine cannot easily integrate into the Partnership for Peace and the hope of future membership in NATO or the EU. Rather it remains dependent on the vague superpowers' guarantee. Rada member and Environment Minister Yuri Kostenko argued for keeping nuclear weapons until it is clear that any aggression against Ukraine automatically threatens the interests of other European states. That option lets Ukraine play a key role in every Pan-European process and gradually exchange its deterrent for another system of effective structures and guarantees.[21]

Any analysis of these conditions, even one acknowledging Russia's real threat, must conclude that Ukraine's conditions were not only unrealizable, they bordered on the fantastic. Certainly there is no way Ukraine can receive a US commitment for nuclear strikes on an attacker, even a strictly conventional one, when neither the United States nor NATO will give similar guarantees to Poland, Hungary, and the Czech Republic. Nor is it likely that any such treaty clause could go through Congress unscathed. Ukraine cannot be secured by the superpowers' mutual suicide and the destruction of Western civilization. Nor can a rapidly demobilizing NATO adequately defend Ukraine against either nuclear or conventional attack though both scenarios are rather unlikely any time soon given the condition of the Russian army. Indeed, neither contingency is a likely foreseeable threat to Ukraine. Nor would Kostenko's scenario inspire Europe to welcome Ukraine, quite the opposite, since the weapons were targeted on the NATO allies and Ukraine is widely suspected of seeking positive control and retargeting capability over them. Certainly nobody in Europe would then trust Kiev. Indeed, loose talk in Ukrainian media of a nuclear umbrella over Poland, Slovakia, Czech Republic, and Hungary did not allay such fears until 1994.[22]

Further nuclearization in Europe instantly reopens the nuclearization agenda that we have largely overcome. States will then request to redeploy tactical or strategic US systems in Europe, create their own deterrents, and non-NATO states will seek US or Russian extended deterrence against Kiev.[23] One should be clear what this means. As Stephen Cimbala points out, extended deterrence means that one is ready to wage 'small wars' or threaten big ones to deter a nuclear power if need be.[24] It seems equally unimaginable that Ukraine can count on receiving billions from a Western world in the throes of the greatest recession since 1948 and at the same time demand to be immunized from the need to reform its economy. Though Washington and the EU provided significant financial assisance in 1994, the demand for immunization against economic pressure really meant a demand for immunity against reform. The 1994 assistance was clearly made contingent upon reform.

Finally we are urging Russia to decontrol energy prices to bring them to the world level for its own sake. We cannot then tell Moscow to exempt Kiev from this demand. Kiev's economic conditions were as unrealistic as its political-military ones. In the end the treaty subsidies will run out while Ukraine must keep to very strict denuclearization schedules to achieve them and immediately and comprehensively address its economic and military security problems. Though the financial terms of the treaty, including sale of the HEU with the proceeds going to Ukraine, a year's debt forgiveness by Russia of Ukrainian energy debts, compensation under Nunn–Lugar for the missiles, etc., do meet most if not all of Ukraine's demands, they extend over several years. Without reform the treaty's benefits will be squandered. Indeed Ukraine's prior economic conditions showed an unrealism and desire to escape from the real world of constant economic and political pressures into some never-never-land where Ukraine will have no problems and no need to take action since it will be guaranteed by foreign allies and immunized against any outside economic pressure. Essentially Ukraine told the West that Russia *per se* is an ontological threat whose policy defines Ukraine's whole policy, a common regional perception.[25]

In addition, without nuclear weapons Ukraine, on its own, cannot deal with the threat. Moreover it cannot take steps to strengthen itself domestically unless, third, the West categorically defends its sovereignty, integrity, and economic system while pouring in money to an unreformed Ukraine and guarantees it against the foreign economic pressure from policies that Russia must undertake for its own interests. This demand is not restricted to Kiev alone. But Ukraine's outlook, added to its political irresponsibility with nuclear weapons and internal political polarizations, was particularly unsettling. Even more unsettling is a decision to maintain Chernobyl and other atomic energy stations as main power sources. That policy could lead to a second Chernobyl catastrophe at a time when Ukraine's ability to manage its weapons and presumably nuclear stations is open to doubt in the West, Russia, and even at home. Equally, if not more, disquieting is the fact that analysts of Ukraine concede that Kiev had not the slightest understanding of the complexities of deterrence, second-strike capability, or the necessary architecture for nuclear systems.[26]

Ukraine was playing with fire. Kiev toyed with nuclearization and positive control over the weapons not only to deter Russia. It is widely believed that otherwise the United States and Europe would not have taken Ukraine seriously at all, and second, that these weapons reassured Ukraine about its importance. As Overholt suggests, prestige plays a big role as a motivator here, i.e. the nuclear weapons have an equally important psychological function for Ukraine.[27] Admittedly the Bush administration probably did not take the former Soviet republics seriously enough or devote sufficient attention to Ukraine. But the Clinton administration sought every avenue of negotiation with Ukraine and sent Secretary of State Christopher, Secretary of Defense Aspin, and then Undersecretary of State to Kiev, and even President Clinton personally called President Kravchuk to warn him against keeping nuclear weapons and only a conditional acceptance of the Lisbon Protocol. Ukraine's unwillingness to give up the weapons as pledged before 1994 had created the suspicion that we were being held up or blackmailed. That feeling could easily have poisoned Ukraine's relationship with the United States rather than helped it.[28]

Paradoxically the political bargain Ukraine wanted could have been undone precisely by its recalcitrance on the nuclear issue. With this in mind we can further employ Overholt's categories to explain Ukraine's motives. Russia's threat to Ukraine, for example, is a real, lasting, and deeply felt political-military phenomenon and perception.[29]

2   THE RUSSIAN THREAT TO UKRAINE

The Russian threat's gravity is large and existential. From the CIS' inception Russian leaders arrogated to Russia the leading role and formed the CIS in order to retain the greatest possible political union.[30] They also intended the CIS to preserve as much as possible of the military union inherited from the Soviet armed forces and carry it into the future under new political leadership.[31] Since then Russia has ever more overtly substituted itself for the CIS and reserves to itself the right to a Pax Russica or Monroe Doctrine throughout the former Soviet Union.[32] Ukraine's refusal to play along, its formation of its own army and its claims to the Black Sea Fleet and to nuclear weapons were major obstacles to the project to de-Sovietize the USSR but preserve a military-political union. There are also important figures who believe that the neighbouring CIS and Baltic states can only be satellites of Russia or of NATO, a mode of thought derived from Lenin and Stalin, and that Ukraine objectively bars Russia from Eastern Europe. Vladimir Razuvayev proclaims the main task of Russian foreign policy in the future to be to create conditions for a 'qualitative' change in the composition of Ukraine's ruling élite to include those who wish to cooperate with Russia before Ukraine's national identity is firmly consolidated.[33] When one adds to this resentment and frustration Russians' deep-rooted belief that a Ukrainian state is something between a bad joke and blackest treachery, the reasons for mutual suspicion grow.[34]

Since 1992–93 Russia's Parliaments have sought to detach Crimea from Ukraine and annex it to Russia. A growing Russian nationalist movement inside Crimea seeks the same goal.[35] Russia's ambassador to Ukraine stated that if enough Russian speakers (i.e. not just ethnic Russians) wanted to join Russia, Russia would act to support them.[36] So he added to the political doubts about Ukraine as a real state fears of a territorial fifth column and attempt to revise the borders, Indeed, careful examination of Russian security policy shows Russia increasingly combining or orchestrating all its economic, political, and military levers to have its way in the CIS. In the many local wars and crises on its periphery it has not hesitated to use or threaten direct military force to dismember insufficiently pro-Russian states as in Georgia, Azerbaidzhan, the Baltic states, Chechnya, and Ukraine or to play the cards of the Russian diaspora or of traditionally pro-Russian local minorities (as in Georgia).[37] In 1993 then Vice-Premier Shokhin asserted that the status of Russian minorities throughout the CIS would be present in 'all economic talks with CIS countries', including Ukraine.[38]

These remarks expressed the policy of the reform government that fell in December 1993 to a still more aggressively imperial-minded coalition. The recent defeat of the Russian reformers, who were less truculent on the territorial issue, and the switch to the right in Russia only alarmed Ukraine even more. Russian Foreign Minister Kozyrev has called Ukraine a mythical state. Russian diplomats have argued abroad that Ukraine will not be a state for long, attempted to isolate Ukraine from Poland in particular and frustrated its policy of creating a Baltic–Black Sea bloc in Eastern

Europe.[39] They also have worked to prevent Ukraine from joining any Western security system of which Russia is not a part. Russia thus seeks a veto over Ukraine's freely chosen entry into NATO or the European Union (EU).[40] Although Russia guaranteed Ukraine's borders, it did so only in the context of the CIS, not bilaterally, adding to Ukraine's fears. It also has been claimed in the West that the only Ukraine Moscow would accept outside of the CIS would be denuclearized, stripped of Crimea, Eastern Ukraine and the Black Sea Fleet, and economically impoverished.[41] Indeed, a uniform pattern of territorial and ethnic threats, and restored economic union based on highly exploitative relationships with the periphery where Moscow controls energy sources seems to char-. acterize overall Russian policy.[42]

Sadly, Ukraine's failure to reform gives Moscow too many chances to flash those trumps despite the treaty. The most visible threat appears in Russia's overall security doctrine of May 1993 and defence doctrine of November 1993. Russian policy since 1993 conforms to the objectives set forth in these documents. The consistency with which Russia pursues these policies strongly suggests a durable élite consensus on foreign and defence policies.[43] The security document asserted that Russia alone guarantees the entire CIS' security.[44] It implies a Brezhnev doctrine type approach to the security of those states and also a basis for a Russian version of the Monroe Doctrine. Since then Russia has argued for revising the Conventional Armed Forces in Europe (CFE) Treaty to put more troops on its southern frontier, ostensibly for defence against ethnic wars in the Caucasus. But these forces could easily threaten Ukraine as well. It is noteworthy that Ukraine too supports such revisions to redeploy its troops towards Russia. Russian officials are also pressing for Western recognition of the right to station Russian troops abroad in so called hot spots and enjoy a visibly hegemonial role in its neighbourhood as guarantors of their neighbours' security. They also often act or speak as if the West has assented to such a role.[45]

Of growing and particular significance are the sections in the 1992 draft and the 1993 doctrine that spell out Russia's self-proclaimed role of protector of Russian minorities abroad. Both documents state that Russia's armed forces and government regard threats to their civil rights, real or imagined, as potential causes for military action.[46] Russian leaders have conducted a 'tough' policy to defend those minorities' rights. At the CIS Ashgabat conference at the end of 1993 Russia unsuccessfully strove for special rights and agencies for that purpose, e.g. Russians' dual citizenship.[47] The danger facing a Ukraine with 11 million Russians is that any exacerbation of the fragile inter-ethnic truce there could cause an armed conflict. The most crucial current point is the Crimea where President Meshkov was overwhelmingly elected on a platform to return Crimea to military-political-economic union with Russia. If Crimea's situation cannot be resolved internally by peaceful political means, it could offer Russia an opportunity to validate the implicit threats in its doctrine and policy. Given Russia's present right-wing drift, its government would find it hard not to support the Russians in Crimea if they seek union with Russia under the right to self-determination. After all, its ambassador's words are already on record.[48] The Crimea could explode inside Ukraine. Here the ethnic consequences of Kiev's gross economic mismanagement are felt most acutely. There have already been attacks on nationalist Russians including newly elected President Meshkov. Any effort at Russian self-assertion there could also lead the indigenous Crimean Tatar population into a much more intense, even violent, affirmation of its historic rights (and by those terms they are Crimea's rightful heirs) against Moscow and/or Kiev.[49]

At the same time the impact of possible trouble in Crimea cuts both ways on the new treaty. Some, seeing Russia's threat to Ukraine's integrity, argued for nuclear weapons to deter any move by Russia or Russians in Crimea (and elsewhere in Ukraine) to organize for self-determination. This stance risks using the weapons as a political-military deterrent against a self-determination movement, an incongruity that is no less dangerous because such conflicts have a nasty habit of becoming protracted all or nothing affairs. An equally dangerous factor lies in the asymmetry of responses available to Kiev who showed no interest in or knowledge of what to do to alleviate the socioeconomic distress that provokes ethnic self-assertion. Lacking a viable or coherent reform policy other than a shrill effort to hold onto nuclear assets it does not control, Ukraine, confronting a nationalist movement under such circumstances, would have little means of devising an effective response to it.

On the other hand, treaty supporters see the Russo–US guarantees of Ukraine's integrity and sovereignty as limiting Russian support for Crimean self-determination even though a literal reading of the accord in no way precludes the Crimeans from rising or Russia from bringing pressure on Ukraine to let them go.[50] Russia's 1993 defence doctrine, like its earlier 1992 draft, also makes explicit threats to Ukraine. Though it claims to guarantee Ukraine (and all other members of the CIS) it does so within the context of the CIS, not in Ukraine's own right. This clumsy effort to satisfy Kiev's demands for a guarantee failed. Ukraine will resist any effort to guarantee Ukraine only in the CIS context. The defence doctrine seemed to offer Ukraine a concession by renouncing the use of nuclear weapons against any signatories of the NPT.

Arguably this should have provided the guarantee Ukraine sought. However, that guarantee was made in 1968 and Russia is already on record as adhering to this Soviet treaty, so it is nothing new. Moreover, the defence doctrine also states quite clearly that Russia will use nuclear weapons first against any attack, conventional or nuclear, by a power owning nuclear weapons or allied to nuclear states.[51] This provision threatens Ukraine even if it acts only conventionally and is a naked attempt to use nuclear weapons to gain a veto over Ukraine's security policy and preserve its isolation in Europe by preventing it from entering NATO or any other bloc. Russia here used atomic weapons as political bargaining chips as it tries to diminish the sovereignty of its neighbours. Since Russia uses nuclear threats in lieu of a robust conventional army, Ukraine lives under the threat of a power that does not accept its sovereignty or integrity and tries to extend deterrence to it against its will even as it threatens Ukraine with a nuclear first strike. These threats are compelling reasons for Kiev to go nuclear. As Overholt suggests, public demand for nuclear weapons, expressed in polls, legislators, or other forms of direct expression, could be a factor for proliferation. Ukraine confirms this. If one looks at Ukraine's political map one finds that the Russians are concentrated to the East and South while Ukrainian nationalism is strongest in the West and North. Throughout this century in Ukraine, ethnic and geographical stratifications marched together.

As Ukraine's economic condition approaches catastophe, it could come under mounting ethnic pressure as well. A 1993 US national intelligence estimate speculated that in two years Ukraine's fragmentation into clashing ethnic rivals is likely.[52] However, any such drastic action will probably rebound against the industrial Russian sector and aggravate latent ethnic tensions. The continuing tension between Moscow and Kiev on a host of military and political issues like nuclear weapons led to a more vocal Ukrainian nationalism, growing support for an independent Ukrainian arsenal, and sophisticated military rationales for it.[53] These rationales and support clearly influenced the Rada and forced Kravchuk to play a delaying and devious game with it, Moscow, and Washington, regarding passage of the START-I Treaty. When the Rada passed that treaty in November 1993, it added so many conditions to it as to negate the treaty. This action touched off a hail of attacks from NATO and Moscow, but it also showed the strength of public and élite support for nuclear weapons until and unless the security guarantees, financial considerations, and psychological recognition that the weapons' advocates demand are received.

The nationalist clamour for security and for overt use of nuclear weapons as bargaining counters narrowed Kravchuk's room for manœuvre *vis-à-vis* Moscow and the legislature. This public and political support for nuclear weapons corresponds to Overholt's categories of public demands for leaders to do something in response to tension or to a crisis as well as to the demand for international and national prestige. But it also partakes of his factor of national morale building inasmuch as it conveys the image of a Ukraine ready to stand up to Moscow and Washington for its rights.[54] Overholt also lists pressure from the military–industrial complex as a motive. There were charges in the Ukrainian press that this was the case and that military industries wanted nuclearization because it meant more contracts for them and a diminished risk of loss of workers, jobs, and funding.[55] This is plausible, but cannot be ascertained at a distance without direct confirmation. But what can be certified is that, in spite of the Chernobyl disaster, Ukraine, due to its lack of energy sources, has had to opt for an extensive and dangerous nuclear energy industry. Kiev knows that an independent energy base is a precondition of its freedom.[56] Non-Russian foreign suppliers, though important, cannot suffice. Therefore advocates for the nuclear power industry also argued for an ongoing weapons industry. Whether or not this is a rational ecological and military strategy (and local reactors' quality makes it seriously open to doubt); it quite clearly shows the military–industrial complex's role in nuclear military programmes and 'rationally' responds to the threat of economic dependency upon Russia.

3   UKRAINE'S MOTIVES FOR SIGNING THE TRIPARTITE TREATY

Yet finally in January 1994 Ukraine agreed with Moscow and Washington to dismantle its weapons, embark upon a complex process of denuclearization for which it will receive substantial American compensation and rely on Russian guarantees. Therefore we must assess why Kiev decided to renounce nuclear weapons. The Russian threat persists and could not have disappeared even if nuclear weapons never existed. Small nations next to big ones with a tradition of empire are existentially nervous about their safety. But it became clear to Ukraine that a nuclear system based on nuclear weapons reduced its security. NATO ministers said it was unthinkable that a nuclear Ukraine could join NATO and obtain the guarantees accruing thereby. Nor would NATO members, including Washington, guarantee nuclear action or financial assistance to defend a nuclear Ukraine whose missiles were targeted against it.[57]

Paradoxically possession of nuclear weapons reduced effective extended deterrence since no assured second strike or conventional riposte would be forthcoming from abroad. Ukraine had to admit that it could not manage its weapons or gain control of them, that its economy was in ruins and depended on Russia for energy. As Kravchuk told the Rada, the weapons, being under Russian control, offered Russia another pretext for intervention. Any effort by Ukraine to operationalize control over them spelt Ukraine's doom.[58] When Rada members combined those factors with the threat of intervention through a Crimean scenario and balanced it against the guarantees of both Moscow and Washington in this agreement, the latter looked like a better deal to safeguard Ukrainian integrity. They too realized that atom bombs were of little use against the Crimea.[59] Probably many also realized that any effort to achieve positive operational control of these systems would trigger Moscow's instant retaliation. Nobody would effectively contest that action because Ukraine's nuclear programme had isolated it abroad.

Equally important is the fact that without an adequate command and control system or second strike capability, had Kiev moved to gain control or gained control over the weapons, it would have created the ideal first strike target for a Russia committed to just such an action by its defence doctrine.[60] And by offering its C2 system as prime target it also increased chances that a pre-emptive strike would quickly lead to total war.[61] An unspoken factor may be related to Ukraine's deficiencies in command and control. Soon after the treaty was signed, members of the Strategic Rocket Forces of Ukraine who were guarding the weapons at Uzin indicated their desire to return to Russian service in the SRF. Since these men had only recently given loyalty oaths to Ukraine, it is clear that their loyalty to Kiev was tenuous. After signing the January accord, Ukraine made these troops reaffirm their loyalty oaths to Ukraine. While Russian media have charged that this means Ukraine seeks to evade the treaty and its military is procrastinating, it also denoted Kiev's effort to extract every last ounce of guarantees from Russia before relinquishing the weapons and signing the NPT.[62]

Because states with defective controls over nuclear systems tend to have volatile civil–military relations in the first place, as does Ukraine where nationalism in the armed forces is a bitterly contested issue, reliance on ethnic Russians to control these weapons may well have been a recipe for disaster. Furthermore, assuming the Ukrainian leadership sensed this dilemma it may have known that any effort to gain positive controls over the weapons could have precipitated the very intervention they feared from their own armed forces. Or even if the leadership had managed to weather that kind of crisis, it would know Ukraine faced a permanent threat of a preventive strike, and relied upon hair-trigger-C2 systems like launch-on-warning, especially if Kiev had no second-strike capability. These considerations highlight the importance of C2 features and structures among the new nuclear states.[63]

Another important factor leading to denuclearization was that Washington and Moscow had moved to satisfy Ukraine's economic concerns about the disposition and dismantling of the weapons and their components. If it failed to sign this accord Ukraine would lose the sizable economic and political benefits that flowed from Washington's serious effort to engage Kiev and its concerns. Presumably the US guarantee of Ukraine, and of Russia's affirmation of Ukraine's integrity in this context, evidently led many to believe that Ukraine's security was thereby strengthened. Perhaps Ukraine concluded that nuclearization derogated from security by heightening the risks of war, rather than deterring aggression and that even without formal guarantees Ukraine was existentially under the US nuclear umbrella due to this treaty. Or, in other words, Ukraine had reached the limit of what it could get by using the weapons as a bargaining chip and it was time to cash in.

However, it is by no means certain that Kiev calculated correctly about Washington, or that it matters in the end, given the crises it faces. In November 1994, after more domestic political struggle, Ukraine voted to accede to the NPT. In December 1994, Ukraine received the guarantees from the five nuclear states that it had sought and formally acceded to the NPT, closing the chapter on its nuclear flirtation. But given the rivalry between the executive and the Rada that is rooted in Ukraine's politics and the all-encompassing economic crisis, even the vote for the January 1994 accord and the NPT and the flowing of its benefits to Kiev may not prevent a crisis from tearing Ukraine apart because the economic crisis is the prime accelerator of nationalist unrest and politicization. In other words, this treaty closes the door only on one chapter of Russo–Ukrainian relations in the new Europe and abolishes the spectre of a nuclear Ukraine. But the task of ensuring a stable sovereign Ukraine within its current borders is a long-term one that is hardly finished.

4   THE IMPLICATIONS OF A NUCLEAR UKRAINE

The repercussions of Ukraine's nuclear flirtation have been felt in the Ukraine, the CIS, and Europe. First, despite US claims to the contrary and the secret nature of some of the agreement's clauses, it seems clear that Washington has incurred or is now seen to have incurred a moral, if not concrete political-military, obligation to Kiev.[64] Undoubtedly Ukrainian leaders believe so. Russian journalists, like Vitaly Portnikov, also have pointed out that the accord equalizes the US' and Russia's role as guarantors of regional security.[65] If an obligation or the perception of one exists, it raises the most serious questions about US policy in Europe. Washington still refuses to make such guarantees to all the former Soviet bloc states and instead created a Partnership for Peace programme that carries no guarantees whatsoever and includes both Russia and Ukraine as Moscow demanded. All the US is pledged to do is consult in the event of a crisis.

Meanwhile Central Europe looks at the Western paralysis and discord over Bosnia and cannot take even that guarantee too seriously. The logic of this treaty appears to be at odds with the seeming disengagement from Central European security issues that appears to dominate our policy and that of our allies because Washington apparently has formally guaranteed Ukraine's integrity, sovereignty and independence and Russia's affirmation of those principles. Thus it is committed to a much greater role in the regional security agenda than ever. Nor has there been any public debate over US replies if crises break out in Ukraine, e.g. a Crimean secession movement. In 1994 Tarasiuk made it clear that Russian intervention in the Crimea will cause Ukraine to stop denuclearizing.[66] Must the US then be obliged to resist that self-determination movement? This accord does not guarantee Ukraine against a self-determination movement in its own territory. The US and Kiev thereby would face a situation where a treaty guarantees Ukraine against a contingency which is highly unlikely to happen while the real threat to Ukraine is not covered and unanswerable from the United States. Alternatively is the US prepared to draw the European line at the German or Polish border and consign Ukraine (and thus Poland) not only to Russian extended deterrence but also to inclusion in a Russian security zone? That policy would seem to nullify any security guarantees given to Ukraine, but what practical remedies are available to Washington in the event of a Ukrainian crisis?

Ominously there has been no public discussion about these issues. After all, Russia strongly opposes any system that includes Ukraine but not Russia. Many Western analysts argue that should Ukraine formally move to any real system other than the CIS this will lead Moscow to renew its claims on Crimea and Eastern Ukraine.[67] After all one could argue that the CSCE's Final Act's clauses on the territorial integrity of the signatories has been irrevocably shattered by the decision to dismember Yugoslavia into several states in 1991–92. If that Helsinki treaty or CSCE's Final Act is effectively null and void (as would seem to be the case) or is superseded by the right of oppressed peoples to self-determination, Ukraine is vulnerable, even without Russian pressure, to a Crimean secessionist movement and the conditions under which its integrity is guaranteed in the 1994 treaty are also essentially nullified.

Analysts like Edward Luttwak also point out the decreasing utility and value of nuclear weapons for warfare in general and of US nuclear guarantees in particular.[68] This school of thought links proliferation to the existence of an ally who can extend deterrence, conventional or nuclear, to the would-be proliferator. In today's mulitpolar world the old bipolar alliance system that constrained proliferation is, they contend, breaking down. Thus threatened states like Ukraine will find it increasingly tempting to go nuclear.[69] Or states will seek their own defence to local nuclear threats due to uncertainty over US policy.[70] In addition, the temptation to use nuclear weapons to deter or threaten internal insurgencies that could receive foreign support could tie proliferation to states' internal instability, making nuclear systems hostage to ethnic wars.

Turning to Europe, we must remember that should Ukraine fall apart the repercussions will spread all over Europe and intensify pressures in multinational polities for fragmentation and further obstruct European integration. Can Ukraine continue to claim neutrality as it seeks to organize some sort of alternative security system in Central and Eastern Europe? We must remember that many Ukrainian figures advocated and tried to devise a security system from the Baltic to the Black Sea or an alternative system involving Ukraine's neighbours, especially Poland and Hungary, only to see these efforts fail due to Russian opposition, Ukraine's neighbours' wariness of involvement in Kiev's quarrels with Moscow, and the lure of NATO.[71] Or can Ukraine stay neutral in the face of Russian opposition and Western apathy? Nor can we consider Ukraine in isolation. It is the crucial variable as to whether Russia regains an empire or remains just a very important large state. The CIS' democratic future hinges on Ukraine's future because empire and democracy in Russia are antithetical. But could Russia refrain from intervening in a disintegrating Ukraine? After all, Russia faces a situation that has traditionally favoured its imperial prospects: strife-torn, ethnically polarized, and barely viable polities on its borders. Russian élites, even liberals, often define Ukraine as an objective impediment to Russia's interests. The Institute for the USA and Canada (ISKAN) charged that Ukraine blocks Russia's road to Southeast Europe.[72] Or else Russian élites see its nuclear policy as purely a cunning drive to nuclearization with no fault of Russia's.[73] Apart from this they see any nuclearization of the post-Soviet states as threatening nuclear encirclement within the CIS or from without, given Iranian and Chinese missile developments.[74]

Undoubtedly a nuclear Ukraine would have necessarily led Russia to crash programmes of missile defence, probably going beyond mere theatre missile defence (TMD), to encompass an entire system of air and space defence married to ground-based installations. That would have seriously strained, if not overturned, the ABM Treaty and threatened overall strategic stability with the United States while ruining Russia's economy. Anti-SDI advocates have repeatedly observed that any viable ABM system threatens the other side with a pre-emptive first strike since it could only respond with a second strike that the defences could then counter.[75] Since Russia had said that if Ukraine went nuclear it would renounce START-I and II, we would have then returned to intense vertical proliferation of thousands of warheads along with at least one side racing desperately to create an ABM system. A general strategic destabilization would occur along with heightened mutual pressures for pre-emptive first-strike capability *vis-à-vis* Kiev and Moscow.

Thus Russia had compelling and vital interests at stake in Ukraine's denuclearization. At the same time, it obviously also seeks to constrain Ukraine's autonomy in security policy and retain a nuclear monopoly in Central and Eastern Europe lest it find itself in a rivalry with a nuclear Ukraine for regional hegemony there. That is not an idle or purely speculative consideration. Some Ukrainians have already speculated in public on creating a Ukrainian centered system there apart from NATO or Russia, and on the virtues of a Ukrainian nuclear umbrella in Eastern Europe.[76] Thus we must devise solutions that preserve global and European strategic stability, deter Russian aggression against Ukraine, and safeguard regional balance and stability.

Similarly Ukraine's destiny is critical to Poland. A robust and healthy Ukraine is crucial to keeping a Russian threat away from Poland and Central Europe. But until now neither Poland nor Ukraine has been able to overcome their particular agendas and forge cooperation going beyond good neighbour relations.[77] Hence Poland looks west and south to co-operation with EU, NATO, and its partners in the Viségrad Four. Since Holovatyy accurately reflects Ukrainian policy, Poland would be wrong in looking to Kiev as too much of a bulwark against Russia. Indeed it would then be exposed to tremendous pressures from Russia.[78] All of this discussion suggests the complexities and numerous difficulties of the issues of local, regional, and European security that are involved in Ukraine's security agenda and that could be linked to or affected by its ultimate nuclearization or renunciation of that option.

Obviously it is clear to the United States and the West that Ukraine needs great assistance over a long period of time to climb out of the depths to which it has fallen. Only recently has it become apparent to the Clinton Administration that Russian policy declarations are menacing to all its neighbours and ultimately to Eurasian tranquillity. Therefore Partnerships for Peace took on a decidedly more anti-Russian hue.[79] But much more serious engagement with both Ukraine and Russia is needed. Indeed, if one examines the policy and professional analyses being published now it becomes clear that the task of engaging Russia and the other successor states who are deeply offended by the US insistence on Russia first is one of monumental depth, longevity, and investment of both time and resources in both the private and public sectors.[80]

To date, US performance, apart from actual legislation, has been quite insufficient in both Russia and Central Europe.[81] The challenges facing the US in Ukraine are no less daunting, extensive, and protracted. But from the examination here it also is clear that a truly viable and coherent US policy for Ukraine must also fully engage the United States' Russian policy and lead Washington into a truly comprehensive engagement with the complex, unresolved, and multiple problems of the other post-Communist states. Sadly there is only the slightest hint that the US grasps the full magnitude of its commitment by virtue of the treaty with Kiev and Moscow. By negotiating, imposing, and signing this treaty the US has also stated that it will not be content with playing a passive role in Russo-Ukrainian affairs. But the imminent crisis, whose solution can only involve a protracted social agony, ultimately makes the US to some degree hostage to subsequent developments in Ukraine. Those developments are bound up with many uncertainties. Ukraine's economic catastrophe, Crimea's unresolved strugles, both among Russian political forces there and between the local government and Kiev and, most of all, Russia's continuing belief that Ukrainian sovereignty is a horrible anomaly, if not worse, will not soon go away. But by getting rid of the nuclear spectre, Ukraine, at least, now has a chance, provided it has resolute and stable government, to move towards Europe and the West.

Although contradictory statements have emanated from the Clinton Administration concerning guarantees of Ukraine's security, there is also no doubt that Russia cannot for now afford to take on any burden of reintegrating Ukraine and has thus stayed out of the Crimean imbroglio. Nevertheless its military men still demand bases on the Black Sea and control of the Fleet there as a sign of their lack of reconciliation to the reality of Kiev's sovereignty.[82] Economically too, Russia is also driving a hard bargain over international aid to Ukraine that would encroach upon Ukraine's sovereignty.[83]

Finally, there is also the question of NATO expansion and its impact upon Ukraine's security. Should NATO expand to the East in the near future, Ukraine and the Baltic states will come under intense pressure from Russia which wants both a *droit de regard* over Central Europe and a sphere of influence over the CIS. Prominent analysts in the West and East believe that Russia would make a strong move to bring those states into a military-political union with Russia.[84] Indeed Grigory Yavlinsky told Finnish officials and analysts as much.[85] Obviously this represents a Russian élite consensus and is a cause for much concern in Kiev. And it is primarily for this reason that Ukraine opposes any NATO expansion as its new President Kuchma made clear both in private and publicly during his 1994 trip to Washington.[86]

Ukraine's continuing insecurity impels the greatest subtlety and caution among the statesmen responsible for addressing the questions bound up with it. Obviously nuclear weapons cannot substitute for a healthy economy and polity. In Ukraine they arguably distracted Kiev's attention from those issues which must now be addressed from a worse position. But Kuchma has promised reform and appears to be acting vigorously for it. In the final analysis it is those domestic factors of security which will make or break Ukraine's sovereignty. Russia's neighbouring example shows that its nuclear arsenal has not helped it stabilize its own poltiical order or integrity three years after the fall of Communism. While nuclear weapons are major elements of political bargaining, they cannot rescue states from the larger deficiencies of their overall security strategy.

In this regard, nuclear weapons are like the bayonets of which Talleyrand spoke to Napoleon, namely 'Sire, you can do anything in the world with bayonets except to sit on them.' Having relieved itself of the nuclear encumbrance Ukraine must now either step forward or else it and Eurasia will step backwards.

NOTES

1. For example, this view was uttered by Deputy Defence Minister for Russia, Andrei Kokoshin, just before he took up his post, '"New Defense Logic" Needs Consideration', *Foreign Broadcast Information Service: Central Eurasia* (Henceforth FBIS SOV), 92-043, March 4, 1992, p. 11.
2. William H. Overholt, *Incentives for Countries to Go Nuclear*, Hudson Institute Discussion Paper, HI-2129 DP, Mimeo, October 10, 1974.
3. 'Nuclear By Whim of History: Ukraine's New Military Doctrine', *International Defence Review*, No. 2, February 1994, p. 6.
4. Steve Coll and R. Jeffrey Sands, 'Is Ukraine Reaching for Control Over Nuclear Arms?', *Washington Post*, June 3, 1993, p. A1; Chrystia Freeland, 'Kiev Moves to Resolve Its Nuclear Limbo', *Financial Times*, August 17,

1993, p. 2; and for the most detailed account see Martin J. Dewing, 'Ukraine: Independent Nuclear Weapons' Capability Rising', Master's Thesis, US Naval Postgraduate School, Monterey, California, 1993, pp. 52–66.

5. Elaine Sciolino, 'US Offering to Mediate Russian–Ukrainian Disputes on Security', *New York Times*, December 4, 1993, p. A6.

6. Fiona Hill and Pamela Jewett, 'Back in the USSR: Russia's Intervention in the Internal Affairs of the Former Soviet Republics and the Implications for United States Policy Toward Russia', Harvard University, 'Strengthening Democratic Institutions' Project, Cambridge, Ma. January, 1994, pp. 66–7.

7. Sciolino, p. A6.

8. *Ibid.*, p. 32.

9. Dewing, pp. 105–6.

10. *Ibid.*; and 'Tarasyuk on START, Security Guarantees', *Foreign Broadcast Information Service: Central Eurasia*, FBIS Report (Henceforth FBIS USR), 993-029, March 12, 1993, p. 78.

11. 'Ukrainian Deputy Rejects Visegrad NATO Membership', *Foreign Broadcast Information Service: Western Europe* (Henceforth FBIS WEU), 94-017, January 26, 1994, pp. 11–12.

12. *Ibid.*

13. See for example the August 1993 Draft defence doctrine of Lithuania which also embodies this perspective, 'Draft National Security Concept' FBIS USR, 93-116, September 7, 1993, pp. 98–104.

14. 'Ukrainian Official Cited on Denuclearization', FBIS WEU, 94-014, January 21, 1994, pp. 1–2.

15. 'Zlenkor Shmarov, Radetskvy View Nuclear Accord', FBIS SOV, 94-011, January 18, 1994, p. 74.

16. 'US Envoy Explains Security Guarantees', FBIS SOV, 94-014, January 21, 1994, p. 39.

17. Karen Elliott House, 'The Second Cold War', *Wall Street Journal*, February 17, 1994, p. A16.

18. '"Text" of Tripartite Statement, Appendix', FBIS SOV, 94-012, January 19, 1994, pp. 49–50.

19. 'Ukraine Puts Off OK of Nuclear Treaty', *Washington Times*, February 2, 1994, p. 13; 'Pavlychko on Russian Relations, Elections', FBIS USR, 94-004, January 14, 1994, pp. 42–3. It is noteworthy that by February 1994 Pavlychko had supported the treaty, probably because of fears for the future of Crimea as discussed below. See also Dewing, pp. 123–30.

20. 'Deputy Claims START-I Resolution Falsified', *Radio Free Europe/Radio Liberty, Daily Report*, February 9, 1994.

21. As cited in Paula J. Dobriansky, 'Ukrainian Independence and National Security', *Demokratizatsiia*, II, No. 1, 1994, p. 81.

22. 'Ukrainian "Nuclear Umbrella" for Central Europe Urged', *Joint Publication Research Service: Arms Control* (Henceforth JPRS TAC) 92-035, December 5, 1992, p. 34.

23. Stephen J. Blank, 'Russia, Ukraine, and European Security', Strategic Studies Institute Monograph, US Army War College, Carlisle Barracks, Pennsylvania, 1993, pp. 6, 22.

24. Stephen J. Cimbala, 'Separating Nuclear War From Politics: Implications of Change in Soviet Perspective', *Arms Control*, XII, No. 1, May 1991, p. 51.

25. 'Draft National Security Concept Published', pp. 98–104.
26. Dewing, pp. 52–66. 'Kravchuk Views Ties With Russia Situation', FBIS SOV, 94-014, January 21, 1994, p. 45.
27. Overholt, pp. 3–5.
28. Dobriansky, pp. 80–81.
29. Zbigniew Brzezinski, 'A Plan for Europe', *Foreign Affairs*, LXXIV, No. 1, January-February 1995, pp. 38–9; Ilya Prizel, 'The Influence of Ethnicity on Foreign Policy: The Case of Ukraine', in Roman Szporluk, ed., *National Identity and Ethnicity in Russia and the New States of the CIS* (Armonk, New York: M.E. Sharpe & Co., 1994), pp. 105, 116–18.
30. Blank, pp. 10–15; Stephen J. Blank, 'Russia, the Ukraine and the Future of the CIS', *The World and I*, October 1992, pp. 588–608.
31. *Ibid.*
32. Hill and Jewett, *passim.*; Mark Smith, *Pax Russica: Russia's Monroe Doctrine*, Royal United Services Institute for Defence Studies: London, Whitehall Papers No. 21, 1993; 'Yeltsin Okays Russian Foreign Policy-Concept', *Current Digest of the Post-Soviet Press* (Henceforth CDPP), XLV, No. 17, May 26, 1993, pp. 13–15; 'Osnovnye Polozheniia Voennoi Doktriny Rossiiskoi Federatsii (Izlozhenie)', *Krasnaia Zvezda*, November 19, 1993, pp. 3–8.
33. *Ibid.*; 'Strategy for Foreign Policy Precepts Toward Ukraine', FBIS USR, 93-164, December 24, 1993, p.3; 'USA Institute Ponders Russian National Interests', FBIS USR, 94–005, January 26, 1994, p. 52; 'Expert Sees Hawks' Win on Military Doctrine', FBIS SOV, 93-221, November 18, 1993.
34. Roman Solchanyk, 'The Politics of State Building: Centre–Periphery Relations in Post-Soviet Ukraine', *Europe-Asia Studies*, XLVI, No. 1, 1994, pp. 47–50; and 'Ukraine, the Former USSR, and Russia', *Studies in Comparative Communism*, XXV, No. 1, March 1992, pp. 33–47.
35. For examples of the still derogatory attitude of Russian Duma members and advisers to Yeltsin concerning Ukraine's sovereignty over Crimea, see 'Kiev Protests Russian State Duma Stance', FBIS SOV, 94-227, November 25, 1994, p. 42; and 'Russia May Be Guarantor to Crimea–Ukraine Agreement', FBIS SOV, 94-167, August 29, 1994, p. 32.
36. Hill and Jewett, p. 76.
37. *Ibid., passim.*
38. *Ibid.*, p. 36. More recently high officials have moved to implement Shokhin's guidelines and openly speculate about a military force as well as a comprehensive policy to support Russians abroad. Suzanne Crow, 'Russia Asserts Its Strategic Agenda', RFE/RL Research Report, II, No. 50, December 17, 1993', pp. 1–8; 'Moscow Ready To Aid Ethnic Russians', RFE/RL Daily Report, February 9, 1994.
39. Hill and Jewett, p. 76; Lally Weymouth,'US Can Calm Ukrainian Fears', *Washington Post*, January 24, 1994, p. A17.
40. 'Daily Views Kinkel's Talks With Kozyrev', FBIS WEU, 93-244, December 22, 1993, p. 10.
41. Hill and Jewett, pp. 38–9.
42. *Ibid., passim.*
43. Crow, pp. 1–8.
44. Hill and Jewett, pp. 4–9.

45. Crow, pp. 1–5.
46. 'Osnovnye Polozheniia', pp. 3–8; *Joint Publications Research Service, Military Thought* (Voennaia Nysl), Special Edition, June 16, 1992 (Henceforth Draft Doctrine), p. 2.
47. 'Moscow Ready to Aid Ethnic Russians', RFE/RL, Daily Report, February 9, 1994; Steven Erlanger, 'Ex-Soviet Lands Rebuff Yeltsin On Protecting Russians Abroad', *New York Times*, December 25, 1993, pp. A1, 4.
48. Hill and Jewett, p. 76.
49. Robert Seely, 'Crimean Vote Result Could Spur Conflict', *Washington Post*, February 1, 1994, p. A16; Robert Seely, 'Russian Nationalist Winning in Crimea', *Washington Post*, January 31, 1994, p. 18; and report entitled 'Separatist Winning Crimean Presidency', *New York Times*, January 31, 1994, p. A8.
50. Robert Seely, 'Support for A-Arms Pact Seen Gaining in Ukraine', *Washington Post*, February 3, 1994, p. A21; 'Another Crimean War', *The Economist*, February 5, 1994, pp. 50–1.
51. 'Osnovnye Polozheniia', pp. 3–5.
52. Daniel Williams and R. Jeffrey Smith, 'The Conflict in Nuclear Ukraine', *Washington Post Weekly*, January 31–February 6, 1994, pp. 17–18.
53. 'SUPSOV Dep Gen Tolubko: N-Arms to Buy Time to Build Modern Defense', *Joint Publications Research Service, Military Affairs* (Henceforth JPRS UMA), 93-027, August 4, 1993, pp. 34–7; 'Ukrainian Deputy Argues Pro-Nuclear Weapons Position', JPRS TAC, 92-037, December 30, 1992, p. 25.
54. Overholt, pp. 3–7.
55. *Ibid.*, p. 1; Hill and Jewett, p. 82; 'Lobby Blamed for Decision on Chernobyl', FBIS SOV, 93-213, November 5, 1993, pp. 60–2.
56. *Ibid.*
57. 'NATO Threatens to Withhold Ukraine Aid Over Nuclear Issue', FBIS WEU, December 3, 1993, pp. 5–6; Frank Gaffney, 'NATO Allows Russians To Call Shots', *Defense News*, December 13–19, 1993, p. 23; John M. Goshko, 'US, Ukraine Fail To Resolve Nuclear Arms Dispute', *Washington Post*, December 4, 1993, p. A22.
58. 'Kravchuk Urges Supreme Council to Ratify START I', FBIS SOV, 94-024, February 4, 1994, pp. 41–4; 'Kravchuk Views Ties With Russia', pp. 42–3.
59. As many instances of post-1945 history show, possession of an atomic bomb does not exempt a state from having to fight low-intensity wars, if anything it makes it more likely that such will be the wars it ends up fighting. See Martin Van Creveld, *Nuclear Proliferation and the Future of Conflict* (New York: The Free Press, 1993), pp. 122–6.
60. Blank, 'Russia, Ukraine and European Security,' pp. 17–20.
61. *Ibid.*; 'Introduction', in Ashton Carter, John D. Steinbruner, Charles A. Zraket, eds., *Managing Nuclear Operations* (Washington, DC: Brookings Institution Press, 1987), p. 11; Walter A. Slocombe, 'Preplanned Operations', *ibid.*, p. 141.
62. '"Alarm" Over Status of Ukrainian Nuclear Arms', FBIS SOV, 94-020, January 31, 1994, pp. 20–1; 'Latest Ukrainian Moves Will Wreck Nuclear

Accord', *ibid.*, pp. 21–2; 'Servicemen in Ukraine Units Forced To Take Alliegance Oath', FBIS SOV, 94-023, February 3, 1994, p. 8.

63. Peter D. Feaver, 'Command and Control in Emerging Nuclear Nations', *International Security*, XVII, No. 3, Winter 1992–93, pp. 160–87; Janne E. Nolan, *Trappings of Power: Ballistic Missiles in the Third World* (Washington, DC: Brookings Institution Press), 1991, pp. 96–7.

64. Doug Bandow, 'Let 'Em Have Nukes', *New York Times Magazine*, November 13, 1994, pp. 56–7.

65. 'US–Moscow–Kiev Talks Seen Having No Losers', FBIS SOV, 94-009, January 13, 1994, p. 13.

66. Tarasiuk's remarks were reported on 'Morning Edition', National Public Radio , February 15, 1994.

67. Hill and Jewett, p. 85.

68. Edward N. Luttwak, 'An Emerging Postnuclear Era?', *Washington Quarterly*, XI, No. 1, Winter 1988, pp. 5–15.

69. Benjamin Frankel, 'An Anxious Decade: Nuclear Proliferation in the 1990s', *Journal of Strategic Studies*, XIII, No. 3, September 1990, pp. 1–13; Lawrence Freedman, 'The "Proliferation Problem" and the New World Order', in Efraim Karsh, Martin S. Navias, Philip Sabin, eds, *Non-Conventional Weapons Proliferation in the Middle East: Tackling the Spread of Nuclear, Chemical, and Biological Capabilities* (Oxford: Clarendon Press), 1993, pp. 163–75.

70. David Sanger, 'New Missile Defense in Japan Under Discussion With US', *New York Times*, September 18, 1993, p. 1; Andrew Pollack, 'Japan Lauches Rocket, Cutting Reliance on US', *New York Times*, February 4, 1994, p. A17; Selig S. Harrison, 'A Yen for the Bomb?', *Washington Post*, October 31, 1993, p. Cl.

71. Ian J. Brzezinski, 'Polish–Ukrainian Relations: Europe's Neglected Strategic Axis', *Survival*, XXXV, No. 3, Autumn 1993, p. 30; Arthur J. Rachwald, 'National Security Relations', in Richard F. Staar, ed., *Transition to Democracy in Poland* (New York: St. Martin's Press), 1993, p. 249.

72. 'USA Institute Ponders Russian National Interests', p. 52.

73. Sergei Rogov (director of the USA Institute), 'Russian–American Security Interaction', in Teresa Pelton Johnson and Steven E. Miller, eds, *Russian Security After the Cold War: Seven Views From Moscow*, CSIA Studies in International Security No. 3, Cambridge, Ma.: Center for Science and International Affairs, John F. Kennedy School of Government, Harvard University, 1993, pp. 113–17.

74. 'Ukraine's Security Fears Over START Viewed', JPRS TAC, 94–001, January 18, 1994, pp. 7–8. This article is also by Rogov.

75. *Ibid.*; Alexei G. Arbatov, 'Limited ABM: A Wrong Solution for the Real Problem', *Disarmamemnt*, XV, No. 1, 1992, pp. 5–6.

76. 'Ukrainian "Nuclear Umbrella" for Central Europe Urged', p. 34; Pavlychko on Russian Relations, Elections, pp. 42–4.

77   Ian Brzezinski, pp. 26–37; Rachwald, p. 249.

78. 'Strategic Points in East–West Relations Discussed', *Joint Publications Research Service, Eastern Europe*, Supplement (Henceforth JPRS EEU), 93-139-S, December 8, 1993, pp. 33–4.

79. Zbigniew Brzezinski, pp. 34–42; Thomas W. Lippman, 'Partnership for Peace's New Look: A Protective Shield Against Moscow', *Washington Post*, February 8, 1994, p. A11.
80. Fred Hiatt, 'Kazakh Leader Warns the West Not to Concentrate Aid on Russia', *Washington Post*, February 8, 1994, p. A11; Daniel Williams, 'US Shifts Policy Focus To Russian Border States', *Washington Post*, February 5, 1994, p. A1.
81. Devroy, p. A1; Thomas W. Lippman, 'US Aid to Ex-Soviet States "Insufficient" Group Says', *Washington Post*, January 11, 1994, p. A15.
82. RFE/RL Daily Report, December 6, 1994.
83. Charles Trueheart, 'Russia Tells International Lenders It Wants Share of Aid to Ukraine', *Washington Post*, October 28, 1994, p. A35.
84. Zbigniew Brzezinski, p. 37; Kathleen Mihalisko, 'Security Issues in Ukraine and Belarus', in Regina Cowen Karp, ed., *Central and Eastern Europe: The Challenge of Transition* (Oxford: Oxford University Press for SIPRI, 1994), pp. 255–6.
85. As told to the author by Finnish officials in December, 1994.
86. 'Kuchma Holds News Conference on US Visit', FBIS SOV 94-230, November 30, 1994, p. 47.

9 Japan's Nuclear Policy: Reflections on the Immediate Past, Prognosis for the 21st Century

Ambassador Ryukichi Imai

This assessment tries to present an overview of Japan's policy on nuclear weapons and on nuclear energy, although the two were not necessarily closely connected in the minds of Japanese policymakers. With the end of the Cold War and re-evaluation of nuclear energy as a modern technology, leaders are unsure of the role of nuclear energy in the 21st century. The prevailing thinking is to deny nuclear energy any role and nuclear non-proliferation is one of the most powerful voices in this regard. More realistic policy options for medium- to long-term strategies, such as reducing the stockpiles of warheads and cleaning up the radioactive contamination accumulated during the Cold War, are priority items requiring much effort and expenditure. As concerns about global environmental deterioration and depletion of natural resources take centre stage, Japan's nuclear policy also needs to shift from a Japan-centred, inward-looking, moral accusatory tone regarding nuclear weapons to a more global, problem management style. It is imperative to regain the proper balance between different policy, technology, security, scientific and other considerations that may be involved. Nuclear non-proliferation will also have to change in the post-START-II and post-CTBT world, where Japan should be more outward-looking.

1 PROBLEM AND CONTEXT

The 1995 Extension Conference of the Nuclear Non-Proliferation Treaty (NPT) in New York came to a predictable result. Terminating the NPT within a time limit was almost unthinkable. Extending it indefinitely without conditions was not acceptable to many non-nuclear weapons states (NNWS), especially because of the special privileges given to the five nuclear weapons states (NWS). The most feasible solution was to extend the effectiveness of the Treaty while placing conditions regarding the future status of NWS either under Article VI of the NPT or by other means. The fact that a freeze on nuclear testing gradually became an acceptable norm for major weapon states was an encouraging sign. The START-II Treaty between the two superpowers that produced a visible scheme for reducing their strategic warheads was also encouraging. Although definitive documentation of these reductions is not necessarily available, many countries – including non-members and long-term critics such as India – were willing to join in an ambiguously worded but firm commitment to extend the Treaty indefinitely.

Since then I have had opportunities to discuss the subject with my colleagues on the Canberra Commission on the Elimination of Nuclear Weapons (including those directly responsible for the NPT conference management). The Canberra Commission met four times in the first half of 1996 and issued a report in August.[1] The general consensus was that the outcome of the 1995 New York Conference may not be legally binding because of the irregularities in the conference decision processes, but must certainly be politically binding on all parties (including non-parties to the NPT).

The confusion around the Comprehensive Test Ban Treaty (CTBT) in the autumn of 1996 made things more complicated. No one so far has fully explained the effectiveness of a multilateral treaty adopted by majority, yet which still requires ratification by parties who are refusing to sign the document. The CTBT has been a subject of the Geneva Conference on Disarmament (CD) ever since I was the Japanese representative, some 15 years ago. (It is ironic to think that in those days the US was the most vehement opponent of even creating an *ad hoc* committee to consider the matter, while India spearheaded the movement with the Soviet Union's support). I recall an occasion when I was trying to promote the 'step by step approach' to the CTBT in some detail and Washington complained to Tokyo and suggested that its Geneva CD ambassador learn proper policy discipline.[2] It was the understanding even then that although a treaty based on majority (two-thirds or whatever) may be agreed upon at the General Assembly, the CTBT's importance as the final part of the process since the 1963 partial test ban agreement had to be confirmed by consensus of all parties in the Geneva process (i.e. all 40 members of the CD). Whether the CTBT can be technically and legally satisfying, given the level of sophistication in weapons test technology, is an arguable point. The original structure of the proposed treaty was to include India, Pakistan and Israel as essential elements in a worldwide seismic connection to detect underground explosions and thus to constitute an international verification network.[3] It was a very adroit move to avoid embarrassment while bringing the three threshold states into the test ban system. Without these countries, the effectiveness of the verification system should at least be technically re-examined.

The CTBT may someday join the family of multilateral arms control agreements, but even though the majority of states signed the treaty by the end of 1996, it is still not quite clear how. But there is a very important point regarding the treaty's handling. Even though it completed the link between nuclear arms control efforts by virtually everybody agreeing to freeze future nuclear testing, it (i) placed the role of the Geneva process – achieving consensus – in jeopardy and (ii) left the five NWS and three non-party threshold states (and for that matter everyone else) to retain future options regarding desirable levels of national nuclear weapons capabilities.

As we discussed in the Canberra Commission, even with the best of intentions, eliminating nuclear weapons from the five NWS, their dismantlement and safe disposal to a level of three hundred warheads each for example, would take approximately 20 years. By moving the CTBT from a Geneva Consensus forum to New York General Assembly voting, admittedly slow and tedious past efforts to achieve a nuclear-free world seem to have come to a very difficult impasse. It will be more difficult to achieve and ensure nuclear non-proliferation both horizontally – with nuclear weapon states between each other – and vertically – between those who have nuclear weapons and those who want them – especially if there is a twenty-year waiting period for the nuclear weapon states. But the Canberra Commission thought that the other extreme – a sweeping, multilateral zero-nuclear treaty proposal – would be unrealistic and unworkable.

Before further discussion of these recent subjects and before we begin to look into what Japan's nuclear policy might be in the next century, both in terms of energy supply and of nuclear non-proliferation, it is necessary to have a quick look at the past 50 years of the nuclear age. Until very recently, Japan's nuclear posture has been primarily inward-looking, defensive and concerned mostly about its own principles, energy requirements and technical and industrial issues. It is only since the end of the Cold War that Japan began to show interest in participating in more global policy concerns.[4]

2 NUCLEAR WEAPONS AND JAPAN

During World War II there was interest in Japan in creating atomic bombs, but this was considered to be too time consuming and beyond the resources available.[5] Japan's first encounters with nuclear weapons were at

Hiroshima and Nagasaki in 1945 and then at Bikini atoll with the dry-type hydrogen bomb tests in 1954. It is interesting to note that the initial reaction of the Japanese to the 1945 bombing was not like the violent anti-nuclear movements of later years. I mentioned this in a plenary speech at the August 1985 CD, quoting an inscription at the Hiroshima memorial that reads: 'Please sleep in peace for mistakes will never be repeated.' I argued that the inscription implied that the mistake was humanity's mistake in general for having used the fruits of advanced science and technology for the purpose of destruction.

The awakening of the Japanese people to the nuclear age was triggered more by an incident of radioactive contamination of the fishing boat *Lucky Dragon* near the Bikini test site with 13.5-megaton Castle Bravo in March 1954. The explosion eliminated a part of the Bikini atoll, sent radioactive ashes in the air and circulated contaminated sea water around the world. The *Lucky Dragon* crew was harmed by the radioactivity and for some time tuna fish, the Japanese favourite for sushi, was inedible. With major newspapers reporting, explaining and theorizing, all of Japan was caught in the panic over radioactive tuna.

December 1953 saw the now-famous Atoms for Peace speech by Eisenhower in the UN General Assembly. Post-war negotiations with the Soviet Union about international control of nuclear energy did not make any progress and with the behind-the-scenes revelations of what the two countries were doing then, one can well understand why.[6] Atoms for Peace was an effective counter-offensive to seize an initiative in the future use of nuclear energy and it became almost an instant hit. The Soviet Union decided to go along and agreed to the creation of the International Atomic Energy Agency (IAEA) and to the first UN-sponsored international conference on peaceful uses of atomic energy in Geneva, in 1955. Many new (sometimes wild) ideas, concepts and designs were revealed to the world for the first time at Geneva for making use of uranium fission energy for generating electricity, for ship propulsion – even designs of atomic trains and atomic aircraft were discussed. Radioactive isotopes for medical and other purposes were introduced. Plutonium was introduced as the future fuel for generating electricity. The only contribution Japan was able to make at this international festivity was an analysis of the Bikini contamination and complaints about adverse effects of being exposed to intense radioactivity.[7]

After the Atoms for Peace policy, Japan started to look into the great potential offered by atomic energy. But the way the Allied occupation forces controlled scientific and technical interests in Japan immediately after the war is shown by the fate of a small cyclotron which was dismantled and thrown into Tokyo Bay. Things changed very much after the Korean War and Japan became more confident that by having access to the fruits of the age of science and technology, the country could somehow at least recover the standard of living of the pre-war period and more if possible (which, by the way, was in express contradiction to the announced Allied occupation policy). Whether or not the occupation forces and former Allied powers tried to influence Japan's interest in nuclear weapons after the country regained sovereignty in 1952 is not clear; there are no documents or records available that indicate such an influence. Limiting nuclear activities to peaceful use seems to have emerged naturally from the Japanese. The early history of Japan's nuclear interests in the late 1950s to early 1960s seems to rule out any consideration of nuclear armaments.[8] The Atomic Energy Basic Law of 1955 states in Article 2 that research, development and use of nuclear energy is limited to peaceful purposes and should be conducted under democratic management, free from outside influences and results therefrom should be made public and also should work toward international cooperation. It is this provision and not Article 9 of the Japanese Constitution (prohibiting use of military forces for other than self-defence) that makes nuclear armament of Japan impossible. The very much talked about three non-nuclear principles, i.e. not manufacturing, not possessing and not admitting into Japan any nuclear weapons, is a much later development and is based on the administration's policy explanations at the Diet, which have no legal framework.

As much as people (both Japanese and foreign, including politicians, journalists and scholars) talk about possible nuclear armament of Japan, there is no administrative mechanism to make it possible. It would have to be by a government initiative and the government would have to break the Basic Law, submit budget requests and somehow convince the Diet (and the public) to approve nuclear weapons-related activities. Because of the legal arrangements described above, it may be possible to build and operate nuclear-powered submarines, and the administration at one point explained that when and if nuclear propulsion of commercial ships, including submarines, becomes a normal practice, Japan will also consider such a possibility. The nuclear ship *Mutsu* debacle (1974) and the recent fast-breeder reactor Monju trouble (1995) were examples of technical mishaps where public relations were poorly managed; they have nothing to do with legal issues or non-nuclear principles. By the time of NPT ratification in 1975, there were people who insisted on 'retaining the nuclear option', including conservative members of the national Diet. We shall return to these subjects later on. It is sufficient for now to note that there were no serious weapons-oriented interests in the 1950s and 1960s, when the country started to work with nuclear energy.

In fact, peaceful nuclear energy had become so fixed in the minds of many Japanese that they were not necessarily aware of the tensions over nuclear missiles that were developing between the East and West contemporaneous to the Sputnik in 1957, the missile gap in 1960, the Cuban Missile Crisis in 1962, the Partial Test Ban Treaty in 1963 and the enlargement of nuclear arsenals over many years. There was practically no information or discussion of the military uses of nuclear energy in the Japanese media. I wrote some articles in the early 1970s based on information from the Military Balance published by the then Institute for Strategic Studies (ISS – now the International Institute for Strategic Studies, or IISS). I found the discussion of different types of warheads, strategic missiles, tactical weapons and other materials very interesting and thought that the Japanese public should be more informed about the nuclear realities of the world and not simply wish these realities to go away. I particularly remember an occasion when the Asahi Shimbun devoted considerable space to introduce the 'strange and dangerous subjects' that I discussed. Some people thought that simply by examining these topics it meant the first step toward accepting their justification. Judging from these experiences and especially having been involved in NPT ratification debates in the early 1970s, I believe that both the Japanese leadership and public were not interested in the 'fine structures' of nuclear armament and even less interested in nuclear strategy debates. It should also be noted that until 1968, the year of NPT's drafting, Japan was not a party to international negotiations on control of nuclear energy. Even in 1983, when I arrived in Geneva as Japan's disarmament ambassador, I was surprised to find Japan a part of the Western group in a forum of multilateral disarmament negotiations and thus part of a military alliance and therefore not a member of the non-aligned group. I am afraid that such understanding about the status of the East/West confrontation was lacking in both Japan's public and private national assessment.

3 COMMERCIAL NUCLEAR POWER, INTERNATIONAL SAFEGUARDS

The Korean War revived interest in the reindustrialization of Japan and opened floodgates of modern advanced technologies, mostly from the United States. New coal- or oil-fired power stations were constructed, new steel mills were built, new chemical industries were brought in, all on a licence basis. The usual arrangements were first to import products, then along with purchase of licences and payment of royalties, to co-assemble, then to co-produce and finally to become an independent producer under licence. Often Japan further fine-tuned the production technology so that the Japanese products could compete well in the world market. Michael Armacost, former US ambassador and a long-term expert on Japan, gives a very vivid description of this process in his recent book with the FSX advanced fighter as an example.[9] It is clear as we look back that the Japanese have misunderstood commercial nuclear power as if it were an accomplished industrial technology ready for practical use and not a gigantic technology package still very much under development.

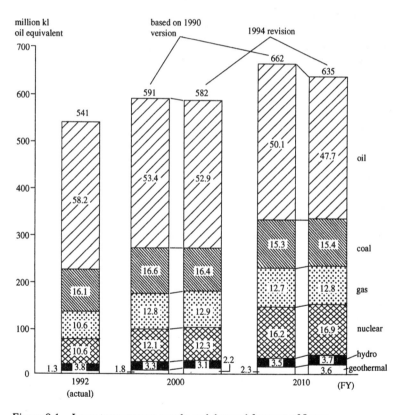

Figure 9.1   Long-term energy supply and demand forecast of Japan

Notes: These graphs indicate primary energy supply. Numbers in the graph are percentages. 1994 revision includes CO_2 considerations
Source: MITI as compiled by the Japan Atomic Industrial Forum

During my time as a science reporter for the Asahi Shimbun, a number of items stand out in my recollection regarding the early dawn of the nuclear age in Japan. Anything nuclear was very popular and as a young reporter with a natural science and political science background, I was lucky to be writing for a daily paper with a circulation of more than a million. Tokai-mura had just been chosen as the site for a new research institute, the Japan Atomic Energy Research Institute (JAERI), with the first nuclear fission in August of 1957 in a small US-made research reactor, and my report was the lead front-page story. In the city of Mito, near Tokai, many items were renamed 'atomic', including an 'atomic bean cake', a traditional Japanese sweet. There was a major disagreement between the scientific community, who wanted to build basic research capabilities and the industrialists, who wanted to import power reactors and immediately start nuclear power generation. There was also a complicated rivalry between the private electric companies and the newly created but powerful Ministry of International Trade and Industries (MITI) over who should have the upper hand in the nuclear industry.[10] After some compromise, it was decided that JAERI was to pursue research and MITI and the power companies compromised by creating a new entity called the Japan Atomic Power Co. (JAPCo), which was to import, build and operate the first nuclear power stations. Japan was also a good supporter of the newly born IAEA. Japan asked for IAEA's help in purchasing natural uranium for its first nationally designed research reactor. Japan also negotiated and transferred bilateral safeguards in US and UK nuclear cooperation agreements respectively to IAEA and placed its first nuclear power station, Tokai-I, under IAEA safeguards.

This early nuclear history is important in understanding Japan's subsequent nuclear policy. When NPT came on the scene, Japan had no quarrel with the Treaty's contents, although it had virtually no role to play other than as an interested bystander. Japan was pleased that the Treaty offered an opportunity to join the ENDC (Eighteen Nations Disarmament Committee), namely the Geneva disarmament process. Japan was, however, very much concerned that NPT's Article 3 obligations to abide by international safeguards might mean it would suffer commercial disadvantages in the future in an international market competing for advanced nuclear technology.

Japan was very active in the multilateral 1970 safeguards committee in Vienna that lasted more than a year and that wrote the 'model agreement' between NPT member states and IAEA. Another important consideration was that Japan should demand equal treatment and not be at a disadvantage compared to EURATOM with whom, it was then rumoured, had worked out a tacit understanding with the leading nuclear weapons states so the EURATOM safeguards would take the place of IAEA's safeguards.

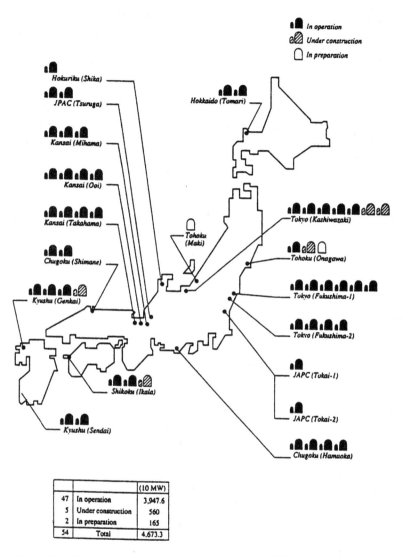

Figure 9.2   Nuclear power plants near Japan (August 1994)

Source: Data compiled by Japan Atomic Industrial Forum

Japan insisted on and obtained 'equal treatment' with EURATOM by creating its own national system of nuclear material control that could then be checked by the international agency, as would be the case with EURATOM's safeguards.[11]

4   NPT RATIFICATION, PLUTONIUM PRODUCTION

Japan and the Federal Republic of Germany (FRG) signed the NPT but delayed ratification, primarily using the excuse that the necessary technical arrangements for safeguard implementation had yet to be resolved. By 1975, the year of the first NPT review conference, ratification was overdue. FRG ratified it in 1975. Japan could not delay ratification much further and it became necessary to win over some hard liners within the Liberal Democratic Party (LDP). Mr. Yasuhiro Nakasone (who later became prime minister and who proposed the first nuclear research in the 1954 budget) led the way and I visited different Diet members to argue the case for NPT ratification. But 1975 happened to be a year when the LDP majority in the House of Councillors was small and if the LDP hard liners decided to vote with the opposition Japan Socialist Party (JSP), the Treaty would not be ratified.

I particularly remember having talked to Mr. Minoru Genda, a member of the House of Councilors and former fighter pilot who led the Pearl Harbor attack. His point was simple. He did not insist on nuclear armament of Japan immediately, but he thought that a country like Japan should not give up this important option. I presented the argument that nuclear energy would soon become a very important source of energy – 1973 was the year of the first oil shock – and without joining the NPT Japan could not obtain the necessary resources or technology from the US, the UK and France, on which we were depending. Moreover, if Japan were to have nuclear weapons, we would be capable of threatening both the Soviet Union and the United States. He agreed. Then, I argued, we would need a credible second strike, based on nuclear submarines and long-range missiles fired underwater. That was understandable to him. But the only way we could do that was to buy licences from the United States, hire US consultants, build a submarine reactor model on the ground, then repeatedly conduct tests because of the different operational modes used compared to electricity-generating reactors. 'Do you think, sir, that the US would grant us such licences?' I asked. 'Can we get funding for such a project? And after something like ten years of work, we would build a nuclear arsenal ten years obsolete. Is that what you want to do?' Mr. Genda accepted my points. On the day I was summoned as the LDP witness to the special hearing of the House of Representatives to approve NPT ratification, where I repeated practically the same argument, adding that the IAEA safeguards were being worked out in a satisfactory manner. There were some internal problems within the JSP at the time that delayed Japan's ratification of the NPT until 1976.

When President Carter announced a review of nuclear energy policy in 1977 and informed the Japanese government that the US would not agree to spent-fuel reprocessing in the newly finished Tokai reprocessing plant, he had unwittingly violated three points in my carefully reasoned argument mentioned above on why Japan should ratify the NPT. The new policy was a unilateral reinterpretation of NPT provisions that guaranteed 'the inalienable right of all the parties to develop research, production and use of nuclear energy for peaceful purposes without discrimination' (Article IV), which was the basis upon which freedom of access to nuclear technology and resources was predicated. The action also highlighted the basic inequality between EURATOM and Japan, for the US/EURATOM agreement did not include the provision requiring US prior consent for processing and/or reprocessing nuclear material of US origin. When I learned that a person in charge of this subject in the State Department was Professor Joseph Nye of Harvard, an acquaintance from an earlier discussion about nuclear non-proliferation, the Foreign Ministry and Japan Atomic Industrial Forum asked me to go to Washington, DC, and talk with Mr. Nye. I went and on my way I attended an annual conference of the US Atomic Industrial Forum in New York, where the President of the Forum also asked me to 'talk to Mr. Nye, because none of us can even see him'. All this happened because a year or so earlier, Joe Nye came to Tokyo as part of the Ford/Mitre Group nuclear review and could not find anybody to discuss non-proliferation meaningfully. The Foreign Ministry thought maybe I could say something meaningful and that was the first time we met. I found our discussion extremely interesting and serious and Joe also said that it was a very meaningful encounter.

In Washington, Joe Nye saw me practically every day, along with Professor Lawrence Scheinman of Cornell University, who was then his assistant. Mike Armacost, who was then in the National Security Council as an officer in charge of Japan, was very helpful. I visited Washington twice for a week each time in the spring of 1977, partly to prepare for the first discussion of Prime Minister Fukuda and President Carter, and had very serious but friendly discussions with Joe, Larry and Mike. We came to a basic understanding that later unfolded as an official US/Japan understanding to start operation of the Tokai reprocessing plant in a limited manner. Things were very complicated because the United States had applied political pressure to suspend similar reprocessing plant construction, also based on French technology, in Pakistan and the Republic of Korea. I was able to see many people in Washington, DC, including Senator Henry Jackson and his famous chief of staff, Richard Pertel, to promote the idea of 'energy security' and to argue that 'equal treatment' under an international treaty does not mean 'same treatment'. In other words, different countries under different conditions should be considered separately. Important allies like Japan and Germany, for example, should be treated differently and subject to different strategic evaluations than other countries. Coincidentally, Prime Minister Helmut Schmidt was visiting Washington, DC, at about the same time and part of the purpose of his visit was to discuss German/Brazilian nuclear arrangements.

There is an important outcome of the American 1977 nuclear policy. After the Nuclear Non-Proliferation Act of 1977 was adopted in the US, it became even more difficult to obtain prior consent to move plutonium-bearing spent reactor fuel. The Japanese government had concluded bulk arrangements by which Japanese utilities' long-term reprocessing contracts with COGEMA (France) and BNFL (UK) did not need approval for each movement and that could work according to a programme-based understanding. Spent reactor fuel was shipped from Japan according to an agreed general programme and extracted plutonium shipped back again according to an agreed programme. When the US/EURATOM nuclear agreement expired in 1995, the new agreement had to come under the Non-Proliferation Act. Since EURATOM did not have an obligation to obtain prior consent, this subject roused many bad feelings over the Atlantic Ocean and many were worried that a nuclear cooperation agreement might cease between the two parties. What has made the renewal of a EURATOM agreement possible was the example of the bulk arrangement which had been worked out between the US and Japan.

5   WEAPONS-GRADE MATERIAL ISSUES

A very complicated problem has been created because of the American insistence that so-called reactor-grade (R-G) plutonium (with fissionable plutonium 239 less than 80 per cent) could be usable as raw material for a nuclear bomb. At first glance, it means that whoever wants spent reactor fuel reprocessed – where the unused fissionable uranium and plutonium produced in the reactor are extracted – can go nuclear before anybody knows. This was why Washington tried to stop operation of the Tokai reprocessing plant. But in reality, although the R-G plutonium can make an explosion, it is not fit for making weapons. It took a very long time to reach a consensus on this. Power reactors, such as light-water reactors of a million kilowatts (KW), produce plutonium with about 60 per cent Pu-239 content, while even gas-graphite reactors of 160,000 KW, such as Tokai-I, produce Pu-239 content of less than 80 per cent. According to reliable information provided to me from US weapons laboratories, weapons-grade plutonium 239 of 93 per cent and above is used.

It is understood that one needs to develop weapons-grade (W-G) plutonium with a 93 per cent Pu-239 content (higher proportions of Pu-239 are possible but not practical because of reduced cost-effectiveness of production). W-G plutonium 239 is usually produced by special reactors built for the purpose, such as at Hanford Reservation and Savannah River in the US and Chelyabinsk 65, Krasnoyarsk 26 and Tomsk 7 in the former Soviet Union. North Korea's Nyungbyon reactor, a gas-graphite type with 5000 KW (electrical) output, produces spent fuel with 92 per cent Pu-239 content. This is the reason why arrangements have been worked out to replace Nyungbyon reactors with two 1 million KW Korean Energy Development Organization (KEDO) light-water reactors that presumably do not produce W-G plutonium.[12]

When I discussed with US experts in 1976 and 1995 the US allegation that R-G plutonium can be made to explode, I asked on both occasions if actual explosive devices have been built with R-G plutonium and the answer both times, using separate devices, was 'yes'. The devices exploded through an implosion mechanism. But it was explained that such a device's explosive power is unreliable and may deteriorate rather rapidly. As an English weapons expert once observed, anybody can build an aeroplane using iron and a powerful engine and might even make it fly. But when much lighter and stronger materials are available, you simply don't build an iron aeroplane. This is a classic example of the different treatment needed between industrially advanced and wealthy countries and less developed and aspiring countries, which was the basis of my argument in 1977 during the Tokai-mura negotiations, i.e. a small number of crude atomic bombs would only get us into deep trouble. This is also the same argument I presented to Mr. Genda regarding Japan's true chances of having a 'nuclear option'. It is well known that the problem of the would-be nuclear proliferator is first how to obtain a sufficient amount of weapons-grade material and second how to have available experts. An interesting point is shown in a recent study by the American Nuclear Society, chaired by Nobel Prize winner Dr. Glenn Seaborg, the discoverer of plutonium, and also in a report by the US National Academy of Sciences regarding disposal of the plutonium core recovered from dismantling nuclear weapons as required under the START-II Treaty, if it is ratified.[13] Both reports in effect say that since W-G plutonium isotopic composition cannot be altered either through chemical treatment or burial deep under-ground, the only way to make it unusable for weapons is to burn it – irradiate it with neutron beams – in nuclear reactors. The process of burning something means it is used as fuel and such actions would not be taken unless the process is sure to make dangerous material harmless. In other words, the US nuclear community is openly admitting that by turning W-G plutonium into R-G plutonium, it becomes unusable for nuclear weapons.

The important non-proliferation implication of this argument is that R-G plutonium in the hands of technically advanced, industrialized countries is no immediate threat, though the same material in the hands of desperate or unstable countries is a different matter. Even countries like North Korea look for ways to produce its own W-G plutonium. When one thinks about the technical problems of handling plutonium metal, fabricating it into the proper shape and making it implode with high-intensity explosives – and maintaining these stable conditions for a long time – the possibility that a terrorist group could make its own bomb from stolen R-G plutonium is highly unlikely. The level of expertise required is higher than novelist Frederick Forsyth would have us believe. It would have to be a national-level effort in a country or countries with technical capabilities less than that of North Korea but above the level of ordinary terrorist groups that would and could make crude nuclear explosives out of R-G plutonium.

Today the more worrisome case regarding nuclear proliferation is the process of dismantling and destroying excess nuclear warheads according to the START-II Treaty. The Center for Science and International Affairs at Harvard University has been concerned about the possible dislocation of such excess weapons or dismantled components falling into the wrong hands and becoming a threat to world security.[14] Because nuclear warheads are usually made of spherically shaped metallic plutonium of about 4.5 kg surrounded by high explosives, dismantling these warheads requires expert handling. Usually it is better to have them disassembled in the same plant where they were originally assembled by the people who assembled them. This means that the current disassembling capabilities in either the US or Russia are limited to two or three thousand warheads per year. A very carefully planned regimen would be required to make sure that warheads in storage or in transport prior to disassembly, or W-G plutonium spheres discharged from the disassembling process, do not fall into the wrong hands. Another serious problem is to make sure that unemployed nuclear weapons experts do not become enticed by high salaries from countries who want to make nuclear weapons.

South Africa has volunteered information that with its own uranium enrichment technology (usually referred to as 'nozzle process', originally developed in Germany) it has built six nuclear weapons. Highly enriched uranium is a very expensive product and the first nuclear weapon was designed as a gun-type, very bulky and heavy device. It is not clear what the shape or weight of the South African warheads was and what means they had of delivering them against what kind of target. Uranium enrichment technology was considered a military secret for a long time, but it has been compromised a number of times. Saddam Hussein was creating a magnetic uranium separation plant without anyone's knowledge, a process originally developed in Oak Ridge National Laboratory in the United States, but later declassified because it was believed to be such an expensive and bulky process that nobody would seriously try to make nuclear weapons using it. But Saddam Hussein did try.[15] There was also the Pakistani scientist who sneaked into Almero centrifuge plant, a FRG/UK/Dutch project, stole technology and started a government-backed enrichment plant of his own near Islamabad in Pakistan. No one seems to be sure if Pakistan has succeeded in making sufficient amounts of highly enriched uranium. Either Pakistan has succeeded in producing weapons-grade enriched uranium in sufficient quantities, or somebody else is supplying a plutonium core, if the Islamic bomb story is to be believed – a story, by the way, that is credible.

Another and more profound case took place in the 1970s, immediately following the first oil crisis of 1973. There was such great interest in nuclear power throughout the world that according to the US government tabulations (the ERDA, rather than the Atomic Energy Commission, took responsibility for this), there would be close to 3.5 billion kilowatts of nuclear power stations in operation throughout the world at the end of the 20th century. The numbers in 1996 are more like 350 to 400 million kilowatts, i.e. an order of magnitude less. The amount of uranium enrichment services required would exceed the available US capabilities in the early 1990s and the US government started to enlist advance financial commitments for privately financed uranium enrichment plants, even while the technology was still classified. At one point, certainly before the Carter administration, former AEC chairman Dixie Lee Ray led a mission to Iran to sell US reactors and also to obtain financing for a new uranium enrichment plant. There was even a requirement that any light-water reactor operator asking for a US uranium enrichment service contract had to make a prior commitment to use recycled plutonium as a part of their fuel cycle (the so-called mixed oxide scheme).

Countries like Japan and Germany were more interested in developing their own uranium enrichment technology that primarily relied on the ultra-centrifuge. Both Japan and Germany today have this technology, which is probably more advanced than that of the US, which discontinued commercial enrichment technology development. Fortunately, it seems that South Africa was the only country that went as far as actually producing enriched uranium-based nuclear weapons. Iraq did spend a lot of money, but the entire programme was very poorly managed. According to those in charge of UN supervision, it was comparable to purchasing large quantities of automobile parts in the hope that someday there would be a car.[16] It is easy to understand that loose weapons-grade material and unemployed, experienced weapons scientists are a more serious proliferation risk than a ton of R-G plutonium shipped from France to Japan in 1994, an event which Greenpeace used as an opportunity to attract worldwide attention to itself.

Additional comments concerning the status of weapons design sophistication are pertinent before we move into a discussion of nuclear power as an energy source. If the first atomic bombs weighed 4–5 tons and had 13–18 kilotons of explosive power (TNT equivalent to 13,000 tons and 18,000 tons, respectively), the first 'practical' hydrogen bomb or thermonuclear device was more than a megaton, or one million tons of TNT equivalent and weighed close to 20 tons, requiring an especially powerful new bomber called the B-36.[17] Advances in warhead design made them smaller and lighter so they could be mounted on top of long-range missiles. Whereas the accuracy of missile targeting has continued to improve, very high destructive power was neither necessary nor convenient. Safety and reliability when handling such weapons, as well as survivability in the radiation-filled atmosphere of a nuclear war, became important. The US Trident D-5 warhead is considered the most advanced in these aspects, while the Russian SS-N-23 is the most advanced sea-fired missile. France ignored public outcries and conducted underground tests until 1996 in order to develop the TN-75 warheads to mount on her new Triomphant-class submarines. China's stance in these modernization games and its intentions now that it has signed the CTBT remain unclear. It is quite certain that India lacks a sophisticated second strike capability. Israel has been concerned only in developing sufficient deterrence against assumed attacks from Arab countries. Any debutante to the world nuclear weapons game will not qualify as an equal because of the submarine-based deterrence capabilities by the major powers. That is an additional reason to think that nuclear proliferation can take place only in countries who have a different system of logic and values compared to most countries of the world.

6   ENERGY SUPPLY AND DEMAND IN THE 21st CENTURY

The Trilateral Commission is a non-governmental institution established in 1973 and comprised of US, West European and Japanese members. Every year the commission prepares reports on different subjects of interest and need and has recently asked three people, one each from the three regions, to conduct a comprehensive energy study and present a report. The report, 'Maintaining Energy Security in a Global Context', was released in September 1996.[18] The report looks at the trilateral countries (OECD members) up to 2010 and concludes that oil and gas can probably meet energy requirements, although increasing reliance on the Middle East, with its uncertain political stability, is a problem. New resource development in the Caspian Sea region of Central Asia also requires special attention. Although the US and Western Europe today do not need to increase reliance on nuclear power, Japan seems to need to do so, but the public relations problem with its prototype fast-breeder reactor Monju might make this difficult. If Japan's nuclear programme is to be delayed because of this, it will increase the country's reliance on the Persian Gulf and thus affect prices and import capabilities and thus energy security of other East Asian countries. The report noted that Russia and the former East European countries may want to increase reliance on nuclear power, but safety problems must be resolved before expanding. Although the report does not explicitly say so, nuclear power is probably one of the many energy problems, among others, of Russia and FSU countries.

What is more alarming is the predicted increase in energy demand in the developing world, especially in East Asia and China in particular. If Chinese energy demand expands as calculated, the currently available alternative is between increased use of coal and rapid expansion of nuclear power. Increases in coal burning in China are already producing a considerable level of acid rain in Japan, whereas the economics of coal burning in China are such that desulphurization investment is beyond its capabilities or interests. China is in the process of increasing nuclear power generation and indeed may be heading toward a very heavy build-up of nuclear power generation capabilities. It is not clear how China can finance such an expansion, nor is it clear that the country has sufficient social infrastructure to continue these activities. If there are multiple Chernobyl-style accidents, radioactive clouds will first hit Japan and then spread around the world. There is an increasing need in China to help develop cultural approaches to promote nuclear safety. It is not clear what Chinese intentions are regarding operation of a nuclear fuel cycle to support a very large-scale power programme. It is apparent, however, that currently available capabilities of uranium supply, uranium enrichment, fuel fabrication and fuel reprocessing have to be expanded greatly.

The fuel cycle is going to be an increasingly complicated problem, even if one only looks at South Korea and Taiwan. Their policies on spent reactor fuel are not yet clear and there are no excess processing facilities in Asia. Whether Japan can meet her own fuel cycle demands in time is also not very clear. There is a need to develop some kind of new regional arrangement to handle the nuclear fuel cycle in East Asia. It is apparent that after 2010, emphasis on the worldwide energy problem will be to find adequate and appropriate harmonization between increasing population,

Table 9.1   Primary Energy Requirements in China by 2010 (various sources) MTOE (million tons oil equivalent)

China Energy Research Institute (1993)	1392
IEA World Energy Outlook (1993)	1187
IEA World Energy Outlook (1994)	1423
IEA World Energy Outlook (1995)	1460
Institute for Science and Technology Policy (1993)	1450
EDMC (MITI contract study, 1994)	1740
EDMC (1995)	1549

Source: Professor Kenji Yamaji of Tokyo University

Table 9.2   Energy in China in 2010

Coal	1089 MTOE	78.2%
Oil	194 MTOE	13.9%
Gas	34 MTOE	2.4%
Hydro	37 MTOE	2.7%
Nuclear	39 MTOE	2.8%
Total	1392 MTOE	

Source: Professor Kenji Yamaji of Tokyo University (*forecast by the National Planning Committee, China according to the Japan–China Energy Exchange Assoc., 1993*)

Table 9.3   Nuclear Power (Proposed Installed Capacities, MWe)

Organization./Individual	1994	2000	2010	2020	2030	2040
China Electric Industry Corp.	2100	3000				
China Energy Institute	2100	2100	15 000			
CNNC (China Nuclear Corp.)	2100	3500	20 000– 25 000	64 000– 84 000	135 000– 170 000	300 000– 350 000
Hydro Electricity Institute	2100	2100	15 000– 20 000	35 000– 60 000		
IEA 1994	2100	2100	10 700– 15 000			
Yamaji	2100	2100– 2700	18,100– 25 700			

Global energy model calculations by Professor Yamaji show that with CO_2 stable emission restraints, China in 2050 will need 386.8 MTOE of nuclear, 419.6 MTOE of oil, 1995.0 MTOE of coal and 307.1 MTOE of commercial biomass.

Source: Professor Kenji Yamaji of Tokyo University

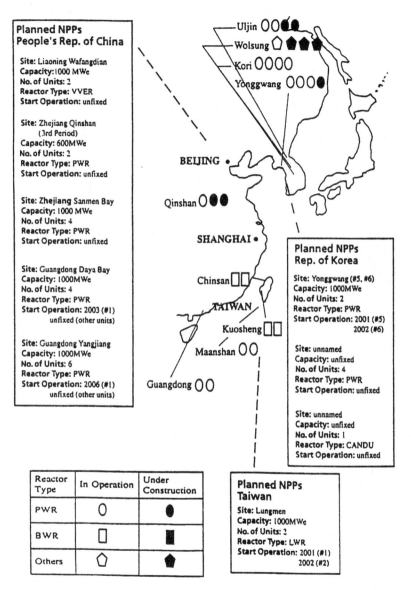

**Planned NPPs
People's Rep. of China**

Site: Liaoning Wafangdian
Capacity: 1000 MWe
No. of Units: 2
Reactor Type: VVER
Start Operation: unfixed

Site: Zhejiang Qinshan
(3rd Period)
Capacity: 600MWe
No. of Units: 2
Reactor Type: PWR
Start Operation: unfixed

Site: Zhejiang Sanmen Bay
Capacity: 1000 MWe
No. of Units: 4
Reactor Type: PWR
Start Operation: unfixed

Site: Guangdong Daya Bay
Capacity: 1000MWe
No. of Units: 4
Reactor Type: PWR
Start Operation: 2003 (#1)
          unfixed (other units)

Site: Guangdong Yangjiang
Capacity: 1000MWe
No. of Units: 6
Reactor Type: PWR
Start Operation: 2006 (#1)
          unfixed (other units)

Uljin
Wolsung
Kori
Yonggwang

BEIJING

Qinshan

SHANGHAI

Chinsan

TAIWAN

Kuosheng

Maanshan

Guangdong

**Planned NPPs
Rep. of Korea**

Site: Yonggwang (#5, #6)
Capacity: 1000MWe
No. of Units: 2
Reactor Type: PWR
Start Operation: 2001 (#5)
          2002 (#6)

Site: unnamed
Capacity: unfixed
No. of Units: 4
Reactor Type: PWR
Start Operation: unfixed

Site: unnamed
Capacity: unfixed
No. of Units: 1
Reactor Type: CANDU
Start Operation: unfixed

Reactor Type	In Operation	Under Construction
PWR	○	●
BWR	□	■
Others	⬠	⬟

**Planned NPPs
Taiwan**

Site: Lungmen
Capacity: 1000MWe
No. of Units: 2
Reactor Type: LWR
Start Operation: 2001 (#1)
          2002 (#2)

Figure 9.3   Nuclear power stations near Japan

Source: Interim Report by the Nuclear Subcommitee of the Advisory Commitee,
June 21, 1995

energy and resources depletion and environmental considerations, including acid rain and greenhouse gases. The Trilateral Commission report comments that only up to 2010 will the current knowledge of utilizing oil and gas be sufficient; after that something more than the market economy will be required in order to prepare for a long-term energy policy. Fission-based nuclear energy is certainly a very important option that has to be maintained worldwide. Development of clean coal technology and improved efficiency in energy consumption and generation will be very important. When we are able to use three-dimensional seismic analysis and use oil rigs to drill for oil horizontally as well as vertically to greatly increase recoverable oil reserves, one may be allowed to become optimistic about what technology may hold for us in the future. As one of the three authors of the commission report, I have to emphasize that our knowledge in these areas and therefore our capability to work out viable options for energy demand and supply, is very limited. The important uncertainty is the effect of carbon dioxide accumulation. One of the model calculations by the Japan Research Institute of Energy Economics indicates that if CO_2 emission levels are kept at or around the 1990 level, energy consumption of the world in the next century must be drastically reduced, mainly because burning coal has to be strictly limited. Even with known resources of uranium and whatever amount of plutonium that can be produced are added, nuclear power cannot make up the resulting energy supply shortage.

7   WHAT NUCLEAR POLICY CAN JAPAN PROPOSE?

In the post-Cold War world and especially considering the types of uncertainties I have discussed, it is much easier to analyse the difficulties than to propose viable solutions. With the Russian Duma delaying ratification of START-II and the five nuclear weapons states not taking joint steps toward further reducing nuclear weapons and failing to show a practical timetable for realizing a nuclear-free world, it is easy to be critical. The difficulty arises when one realizes that in spite of the criticism nothing happens. It appears that the US will keep seven thousand strategic warheads of START-I and Russia may be unwilling to manage their nuclear warheads. Since there is no immediately apparent value in highly-enriched uranium or weapons-grade plutonium and since safe-keeping, disposal and dismantlement of existing and ageing nuclear warheads merely means added expenditures, it is difficult to expect that somebody will pay the enormous costs for nuclear non-proliferation. The Nunn–Lugar annual fund of $400 million now seems like a fantasy. Japan's contribution of

$100 million is being spent mostly to clean the Sea of Japan and to maintain the Science and Technology Centre in the former Soviet Union in order to keep the weapons scientists from leaving the country. To ask for and receive more help from many other countries is easier said than done. Earlier in the 1990s, when the world economy was in better shape, joint efforts at increasing expenditures to quickly dismantle nuclear warheads was discussed more seriously by the OECD countries. This is not being discussed anymore. This retreat alone is as bad as – maybe even worse than – the threat of nuclear proliferation posed by North Korea or Iran.

There are two major directions Japan, or any industrially advanced nation, can begin to take as part of a long-term non-proliferation policy. One is toward the more careful use of modern technology, including dual-purpose technology. The London Guidelines and its 1992 Warsaw update are examples. The newly-emerging Wassenaar agreement may serve the same purpose. At the same time, with the rapid spread of modern communication technology and the increased ability of military satellites to observe the construction of nuclear facilities, it may be worthwhile for countries with the technical and financial capabilities to start a new international organization that can pool the 'national technical means' of each member and, with individual safeguard measures, provide a worldwide capability to monitor various signs and/or indications of 'unfriendly acts', including nuclear proliferation and environmental contamination. It requires a courageous leadership to handle sensitive technology, as was once demonstrated at the time of the Baruch Plan in 1946. The group should not open the door to the entire world immediately, but should start as a small group of like-minded countries that will build the required technical framework. With the CTBT, more than 20 years of quiet work by the Group of Scientific Experts in Geneva went into organizing detection of remote and distant seismic events.

Another important direction regards energy technology. It is easy to announce that plutonium as a fuel is not economic – which is true. But then again, the same holds for solar energy. When we worked on the Trilateral Commission's Energy Report that was mentioned earlier, one of our most important considerations was that time was running out. If we are looking only at the immediate future, oil and gas can handle the demand. But when the environmental factors are weighed, including the effects of greenhouse gases, things become complicated. Expected population increases, resource depletion and earth surface temperature changes that even the most powerful computers cannot calculate, are important factors that must also be considered over the long term.[19] When 'uncertainty' is the major element in forecasting the future, it is clear that we should keep all our technical options open. The difficult part, of course, is to determine what an adequate level is for each option. It is evident that higher efficiency in consumption and production of energy should have a high priority. These considerations also probably apply to solar energy, and nuclear fission is more realistic than nuclear fusion, at least for the first half of the 21st century. If many East Asian countries choose to utilize nuclear power as an important energy source, then Japan is in an excellent position to offer a feasible infrastructure for a non-proliferant fuel cycle and provide social and technical safety guidelines.

Unfortunately, my comments do not represent the Japanese view. Japanese leaders and the public are more concerned about immediate economic conditions and problems with the nation's financial system than long-term nuclear policies. The government and electric utilities are busy explaining that nuclear power is indeed safer than what some people claim. This may be true; but it is also true that there are some who would like to build Japan's national policy to deal with long-term, larger issues and to be more visionary.

NOTES

1. The Canberra Commission was created at the request of the Australian government and met in January, April, July and August. Its members were: Celso Amorim (Brazil), Lee Butler (US), Richard Butler (Australia), Michael Carver (UK), Jacques-Yves Cousteau (France), Jyantha Dhanapala (Sri Lanka), Rolf Ekeus (Sweden), Nabil Elarby (Egypt), Ryukichi Imai (Japan), Ronald McCoy (Malaysia), Robert McNamara (US), Robert O'Neil (Australia), Qian Jiadong (China), Michel Rocard (France), Joseph Rotblat (UK), Roland Sagdev (Russia), Maj. Britt Theorin (Sweden).

2. There was strong demand from the weapons laboratories in the United States that sample-based test explosions were necessary in order to maintain reliability of existing nuclear weapons, while new features in design had to be confirmed through explosion tests. The US became concerned when Japanese Foreign Minister Abe, in his CD speech, advocated a step-by-step approach with his disarmament ambassador ready to pursue it with detailed proposals. The relationship between weapons reliability and tests has never been fully clarified even with the recent US policy change to promote the comprehensive test ban regime.

3. Those interested in technical aspects will find partial answers in 'Budget '97'; *Science*, Vol. 270, 20 September 1996, which describes the budget for DoE weapons laboratories. Also 'New Missions for National Labs'; *Science*, 6 October 1995. These articles give some details of how to ascertain reliability of nuclear weapons without undergoing actual explosions.

4. During the Gulf War, Japan failed to reach a domestic consensus to give military and/or related support to the multinational forces. This was taken very seriously internationally, especially when a country relies on more than

forty per cent of its primary energy from the Gulf region. While Japan contributed some $13 billion, it has not been significantly appreciated. That was the first lesson to the Japanese people regarding the changing role of Japan in the very different post-Cold War world.

5. Professor Ryokichi Sagane of Tokyo University and Professor Kouji Fushimi of Osaka University are the two physicists directly involved and with whom I have discussed the subject. A group of scientists worked with the Army engineering study group, but failed to appreciate the importance of using plutonium fission with fast neutrons. The project was dropped as something beyond the scope of the 'on-going war efforts'.

6. See for example Richard Rhodes, *Dark Sun, the Making of the Hydrogen Bomb* (New York: Simon and Schuster, 1995), or David Holloway, *Stalin and the Bomb* (New Haven: Yale University Press, 1994), for accounts of fierce rivalry, spying, counter-spying, etc., in which the two countries were involved. It was as far as possible from a cooperative regime for international control of nuclear power.

7. A friend of mine, a scientist, was asked to join the UN secretariat for the preparation of the conference. Since Japan was not admitted into the UN itself until December 1956, he was the only Japanese in the UN system. I remember several discussions we had about Japan's interests in the nuclear era 'being out of phase' with the rest of the world. The world was, more or less, forward-looking in welcoming the advent of the nuclear age. Japan, it seemed, was least informed on the latest developments.

8. Among the different accounts of nuclear activities in Japan, the Japan Atomic Industrial Forum edited the early history in 1986. The forum also published an annual yearbook, which recorded various domestic activities in detail. I have often been involved in the process of these recordings, especially in the 1960s. I have not encountered anything indicating interests in nuclear weapons.

9. Michael Armacost, *Friends or Rivals, The Insider's Account of US–Japan Relations* (New York: Columbia University Press, 1996).

10. I shall not go into details of these debates and competitions. The situation had much to do with the wartime rivalry between various components of Japanese society. Nuclear research promised a large amount of spending and who took the initiative was of course very important. Rivalry regarding who controls the future of electricity generation was then considered to depend on who would build and operate the country's first nuclear power station. Not many documents are available on the subject, either in Japanese or in English. When I was trying to earn my PhD in political science, this was the subject I studied. Professor Everett E. Hagen of MIT and Professor Allan B. Cole of Fletcher School of Law and Diplomacy were kind enough to guide me in the early 1960s as I was working on the subject. Having moved to the newly created Japan Atomic Power Co. I was too busy to pursue such extra-curricular interests. Later on, I switched my PhD thesis to technology of nuclear material control, a subject I was very much involved in as a part of my job and interests.

11. I shall not try to claim my credentials by giving details. At the Japan Atomic Power Co. I was in charge of Tokai-I nuclear fuel and thus in dealing with IAEA safeguards (which was IAEA's first experience). With IAEA officials, we worked out practical details of conducting effective safeguards.

The Foreign Ministry, in the absence of people with technical background, found it convenient to appoint me (unofficial initially and official later) consultant. I was a regular attendant of the Vienna safeguards committee as Japan's alternate representative.

12.   It is not easy to understand the logic behind the KEDO deal. The cost on the KEDO side is enormous, two million kilowatt light-water (LWR) nuclear power stations do not come cheap. It is not clear what kind of social infrastructure (cargo unloading in port, transportation, vendors, sub-vendors, workers, reactor grade construction material, etc.) is needed and one has to add the price and cost of heavy oil until the first reactor goes into operation. More seriously, I have not met any electrical engineer who thinks that the North Korean (DPRK) power grid would be able to manage two million kW generation in Shinpo. In addition, the myth of a reactor-grade plutonium-based bomb has been destroyed without a word of explanation.

13.   American Nuclear Society, 'Protection and Management of Plutonium', Special Report, August 1995. National Academy of Sciences: Management and Disposition of Excess Weapons Plutonium, 1994.

14.   Graham T. Allison, Owen R. Cote, Jr., Richard A. Falkenrath, Steven E. Miller, *Avoiding Nuclear Anarchy, Containing the Threat of Loose Russian Nuclear Weapons and Fissile Material*, (Cambridge Mass.: MIT Press, 1996). It was preceded by Graham Allison, Ashton B. Carter, Steven E. Miller Philip Zelikow, *Cooperative Denuclearization*, Center for Science and International Affairs, 1993.

15.   For those interested in details, Kathleen C. Bailey, *The UN Inspections in Iraq, Lessons for On-Site Verification* (Boulder, Colo.: Westview, 1995), provides useful and interesting information.

16.   It is difficult to obtain objective information about Iraqi nuclear activities. David Albright has been writing often in the Bulletin of the Atomic Scientists. Some of the information I was able to obtain was through discussion with some of the members of the UN Special Commission (UNSCOM).

17.   Michael E. Brown, *Flying Blind, The Politics of the US Strategic Bomber Program* (Ithaca: Cornell University Press, 1992).

18.   William F. Martin, Ryukichi Imai, Helga Steeg, 'Maintaining Energy Security in a Global Context', A Report to the Trilateral Commission, 18 September 1996.

19.   'Redefining the Supercomputers', *Science*, Vol. 272, 20 September 1996.

10 Nuclear Imbalance of Terror: The American Surveillance Regime and North Korea's Nuclear Programme
Bruce Cumings

There is a real crisis brewing in a place the cameras don't go. [It is] the single most dangerous problem, the impending nuclearization of North Korea...None will sleep well with nukes in the hands of the most belligerent and paranoid regime on earth. The North Korean bomb would be controlled by either Kim Il Sung, the old and dying Great Leader, or his son and successor, Dear Leader Kim Jong Il...unpredictable, possibly psychotic, [he] would be the closest thing to Dr. Strangelove the nuclear age has seen.[1]

One of the world's most menacing powers [is now] bereft of its cold-war allies and on the defensive about a nuclear-weapons project that ranks among the biggest threats in Asia...'North Korea could explode or implode,' said General Robert Riscassi, the commander of the 40,000 US troops who remain here. As the Stalinist Government of Kim Il Sung is driven into a corner, its economy shrinking and its people running short of food, General Riscassi contends, 'it is a debateable matter' whether the country will change peacefully or lash out as it once did before...One senior Bush Administration official said last week that North Korea already had enough plutonium to build a crude nuclear weapon...this has helped fuel...fear that the country that has bombed airliners and tried to kill the South Korean cabinet would make one last lunge for survival.[2]

These two extracts from the two newspapers that come closest to being America's papers of record, were typical of the American commentary on North Korea in the early 1990s. A desperate regime run by a paranoid dictator now threatening the world with nuclear attack: these were the tropes, and they reappeared time and again from 1991 to 1994, until North Korea once more sank into the oblivion of media inattention. It is by definition impossible to predict the behaviour of a crazy person, and indeed American officials constantly harped on P'yôngyang's unpredictability. I want to argue, to the contrary, that North Korean behaviour was quite predictable and that an irresponsible and spineless American media, often (but by no means always) egged on by government officials, obscured the real nature of the US–Korean conflict. The media had the wrong tropes in the wrong place at the wrong time; the absurd result was that often one had to read North Korea's tightly controlled press to figure out what was going on between Washington and P'yôngyang.[3] Because of this severe and often state-induced media bias, it was exceedingly difficult to figure out the real stakes in this conflict.

Two logics clashed in this crisis: the first, a rationality of historically-informed, trial-and-error, theory-and-practice *learned* behaviour growing out of the Korean civil conflict going back to 1945, yielding intransigent bargaining strategies and extreme conceptions of national sovereignty; and the second, an instrumental reason of superordinate power keeping under surveillance and seeking to control the recalcitrant, the heterodox, the enemy, without any felt necessity to know that enemy, and yielding violations of national sovereignty. North Korea's stake in this confrontation, its position, was to use its nuclear programme to fashion a new relationship with the United States; its reserve card was the possibility that it might already possess one or two atomic bombs. In pursuing a shrewd diplomacy of survival, P'yôngyang used bluff, sham and brinkmanship to get what it wanted. The American goal was to stabilize an unruly post-Cold War world, one that had already produced a major war in the Gulf. Given an American public that often thought the world's problems were over with the end of the Cold War and the collapse of the Soviet Union, successive American administrations wanted multilateral support in policing intractable nations. The 1990s dealt North Korean leaders a very bad hand, but they played it with surprising skill; the 1990s dealt the US the best hand imaginable, and it very nearly plunged into another major war, three years after the Gulf War ended.

This experience, I would argue, meets the social science test of certain propositions yielding falsifiable hypotheses which, when tested empirically, prove to be reliable and valid. Both the American and North Korean logics were clear by 1991 if not earlier, providing testable propositions about the nuclear crisis that ensued for the next three years. The propositions are as follows:

1. The DPRK lives a civil war history, and acts according to civil war logic;
   a. The US denies this history and has dealt with P'yôngyang as a generic Soviet proxy or rogue enemy;
   b. This yields an advantage to the DPRK, and the disadvantage of inattention and inapplicable logic to the US;
2. The DPRK has been under American nuclear threat since 1950, and sought to use the non-proliferation regime to escape this threat after bipolarity collapsed;
   a. The way to do that was to trade its nuclear programme for a new relationship with the US;
   b. Most American analysts assumed the DPRK only wanted to develop nuclear weapons;
3. The US wanted to 'surveill' and discipline the DPRK, using the IAEA to fill out its surveillance regime;
   a. The DPRK responded with a shell game that, over time, allowed its own logic to be considered;
   b. US surveillance overreached itself by making the IAEA an adjunct of American intelligence;
4. The DPRK's self-reliant energy regime required domestic nuclear energy to compete with South Korea and Japan; the US knew this, but chose to ignore it until 1994, in the interest of maintaining the NPT regime and teaching rogue nations a lesson;
5. Hardliners in both countries drove the crisis to the brink of war in May–June 1994, whereupon the US relearned the Korean civil war logic and settled for a diplomatic solution.

Realpolitik conceptions of power, interest and rationality were of little help in figuring out a confrontation between a country of 22 million people spending about $2 billion per year on defence, which stood up to and stalemated the single superpower of our time, 260 million people spending $260 billion on defence; therefore it is predictable that realists have not praised the October 1994 Framework Agreement between the US and the DPRK, and have been waiting for (and predicting) it to fail ever since. As of this writing, however, North Korea is in full compliance with the terms of the agreement, notwithstanding various speedbumps and nettlesome problems that have made implementation difficult. Likewise a 'rational choice' logic on the part of those who favour game theory, prisoner's dilemmas, and the like, was never able to explain P'yôngyang's behaviour (some did try), because this was an abstract rationality devoid of context.

Max Weber taught that the conception of modern legal-rational authority really connotes a *belief* in that rationality. My belief is in a comprehensive rationality that comes with long immersion in a subject, such that the brain and the viscera connect, one shouts eureka!, and thereby creates a problem-solving logic. We find the same epistemology in the father of modern war doctrine, Clausewitz. For him, war is a fully *political* human activity in which a rational intelligence marries the means of warfare to the ends of policy. How this is done involves logic, strategy and cunning, but also an intuitive knowledge of the battlefield and the totality, the 'organic whole', of war and politics that can only come to one fully experienced in both. War is not for the generals; it is the province of the statesman or, in his time, the sovereign king or his executive minister of state.[4] I want to explore the 'organic whole' of the US–North Korean crisis in five parts.

1   MAD DOGS AND AMERICANS: WAR IS A STERN TEACHER

At a critical point in March 1994 when the US thought its diplomatic effort *vis-à-vis* North Korea was collapsing, *New York Times* reporter David Sanger began an article this way:

> Say this about North Korea's leaders: They may be Stalinist fanatics, they may be terrorists, they may be building nuclear bombs, but they are not without subtlety. They have mastered the art of dangling Washington on a string.

He went on to refer to North Korea as 'a country with a mad-dog reputation'.[5] Left unexplained was how mad dogs could simultaneously be subtle puppeteers. At a minimum, however, the mad dog had a memory of war, a presumably 'forgotten' war; meanwhile most Americans did not.

A first principle for understanding contemporary Korea is to know that a devastating civil war occured there in the recent past and that the war never ended: the warring sides agreed only to stop firing at each other – an armistice. Moreover, the conclusion of the hot phase of that war in 1953 left a split verdict in America. How could the US get stalemated by fourth-rate North Korea and third-rate China? Why was there 'a substitute for victory'? 'War', in Clausewitz's famous definition, 'is an act of violence intended to compel our opponent to fulfill our will' – a statement which leads logically to the idea that 'complete victory' is the goal of war, and thus 'moderation in war is an absurdity'.[6] This is the passage people cite most often from *On War* and it yields a logic that the powerful discharge all their power in war – and thus pundits like Harry Summers sprinkle their texts with quotations from Master Clausewitz and argue that the US failed in Korea and Vietnam because of politically-imposed limits on the use of its power.[7]

Summers, like so many others, misreads *On War*. For Clausewitz, the politics of war do *not* dictate the use of every means at one's disposal or the absolute obliteration of the enemy; like everything else about war, the conclusion of the victory is inevitably political. Here is Clausewitz's substitute for victory: 'The result in war is never absolute'; if war were mere force, 'the moment it is called forth by policy it would step into the place of policy'. But this idea is 'radically false', since war 'is not an extreme thing which expends itself at one single discharge; it is the operation of powers'.[8] War moves toward its goal, which is the surrender of the enemy. But that, too, is a politically-governed activity. 'Unconditional surrender' rarely occurs and 'is not a condition necessary to peace...the idea of a complete defeat of the enemy would be a mere imaginative flight...[9] The Korean War ended in a stalemate, with the restoration of the *status quo ante*, because American leaders could not pay the political price that victory would have required (e.g. taking the war to Chinese territory).

If the end of the Korean War is misunderstood in the US, likewise its origins and its nature are misconstrued. With handfuls of Soviet and Chinese documents spilling out in the 1990s, many analysts are once again sure that Stalin and Kim Il Sung 'started' the Korean War in June 1950, i.e. the original Truman administration position, and that it therefore constituted international aggression. But the civil conflict originated in the division of Korea just as World War II ended, proceeding from sharp political conflict in 1945 to peasant rebellion in 1946–47 to guerrilla war in 1948 and border wars in 1949, finally to general war in June 1950. Perhaps the most memorable line from Thucydides' *Peloponnesian War* – 'war is a stern teacher' – comes from the civil war in Corcyra, and the passage is almost a mnemonic for 'Korea'. Immediately after that famous phrase, Thucydides follows with this:

> So revolutions broke out in city after city...What used to be described as a thoughtless act of aggression was now regarded as the courage one would expect to find in a party member; to think of the future and wait was merely another way of saying one was a coward; any idea of moderation was just an attempt to disguise one's unmanly character; ability to understand a question from all sides meant that one was totally unfitted for action. Fanatical enthusiasm was the mark of a real man, and to plot against an enemy behind his back was perfectly legitimate self-defence. Anyone who held violent opinions could always be trusted, and anyone who objected to them became a suspect...[etc.][10]

This extended passage fits the Korean civil war with no necessity to dot 'i's' or cross 't's'; it explains the continuing blight on the Korean mind drawn by that war, just like a doctor drawing blood: to understand the Korean War 'from all sides' is still to go to jail in either North or South. But whatever else one may say about the North Koreans, they were sternly taught by this war.

The logic of this history means that the North Koreans understand how the Korean War began and ended, but Americans do not. The incessant intensity of the confrontation along the Korean demilitarized zone is something the P'yôngyang leadership deals with every day, as against the handful of witting Americans who know this quotidian conflict from the other side and the mass of Americans always surprised to learn that 40,000 American troops are still in Korea. P'yôngyang's media drum war stories into the brain so frequently that one might think the Korean War just ended; meanwhile that same war, never understood at the time and forgotten quickly after its conclusion, yields an American *tabula rasa*.[11]

It was therefore a simple matter to transfer all the media tropes by which Americans were led to understand the 1990–91 Gulf War onto North Korea: North Korea was not our daily enemy of 40 years' standing, but a new 'renegade state'. This began in the immediate aftermath of the four-day ground war that defeated Iraq: Leslie Gelb editorialized in the *New York Times* that North Korea was 'the next renegade state', a country 'run by a vicious dictator' with SCUD missiles, 'a million men under arms', and likely to possess nuclear weapons 'in a few years'. Another Iraq, in short.[12] I was amazed by Gelb's editorial when it appeared and the mimetic commentary that followed on its heels for three years; it made me understand that my professional knowledge was akin to palaeontology or some other arcane and remote discipline, and that the Korean War existed in the American mind under 'ancient history' – if not 'never happened'.

This ahistoricity went hand-in-hand with assertions that failed a freshman logic class. North Korea was the greatest security threat in the world, according to the leaders of our foreign policy, and simultaneously on the verge of collapse: how could it be ten feet tall and about to devour the South, with a basketcase economy? A huge military threat and a demolished economy, all led by a nutcase? On ABC's *Nightline*, correspondent Chris Bury described Kim Jong Il as 'a 51-year-old son about whom little is known other than his fondness for fast cars and state terrorism'. As for the country he runs, 'North Korea may be growing desperate. Its economy is in shambles...Yet North Korea maintains a huge army, more than a million soldiers on a permanent war footing, nearly 70 per cent of them within 60 miles of Seoul.'

Chris Bury, like all other mainstream reporters, did not say how many South Korean soldiers are between Seoul and the DMZ and thus 60 miles from P'yôngyang: probably 540,000, i.e. 90 per cent. Of course he did not say, because he would not know, that threats of a northern invasion began in March 1946 and have never ceased since. Take this quotation: 'There's signs of a big buildup....The [North Koreans] could be in Seoul in four hours if they threw in everything they have'. James Wade got this from an American engineer working for the US Army – in 1960.[13] South Korean sources are the authors of this one-sided chiaruscuro; they have succeeded for decades in getting Americans to stare blankly at one side of the Korean civil conflict, like a pigeon with nystagmus such that its head turns only toward the left.

Examining the history of the Korean conflict or the perpetual special pleadings of the two sides, or flashing some light into the shadows they hope one will not notice, takes time. Far easier is to take the word of an American official. On the same *Nightline* segment, Richard Solomon, Nixon/Bush China expert, said this: 'Not a bad way to look at it is to think of the Waco, Texas crisis, where you have a small ideological, highly armed and isolated community...'[14] Mad dog Kim Il Sung becomes David Koresh in this rendering, which was perfectly believable: if you are dealing with insanity, as I said at the beginning, anything is possible; Korea is an American *tabula rasa*, and any writing upon it has currency – so long as the words are negative. North Korea ended up thrice-cursed, a Rorschach inkblot absorbing anti-communist, Orientalist and rogue-state imagery. Since there is a virtually endless supply of similar quotations from the American media from 1991 to 1996, let me stop here and merely argue that history makes a difference and that only an historically-informed analysis can make sense of the relationship between North Korea and the US. Not just any history, however, but an appreciation of the actual conflict in Korea since 1945, examined dispassionately as if the two sides were blue and green rather than red and white.

2   AMERICAN NUCLEAR THREATS

Part of the problem in resolving the nuclear crisis was (1) the American desire to get P'yôngyang to submit to the inspection regime of the Nuclear Non-Proliferation Treaty (NPT) administered by the International Atomic Energy Agency in Vienna (IAEA), and (2) P'yôngyang's desire to get out from under a nuclear threat that had been palpable since the 1950s, and that gave it rights of self-defence under the NPT.[15] If we assume that

P'yôngyang's real goal was to build weapons, it had solid justifications for going nuclear: after all, it could argue that it is merely engaged in deterrence, that is, the classic argument that once both sides have nuclear weapons, the resulting Mexican standoff negates the possibility of use, and that a DPRK weapon returns the peninsula to the *status quo ante* 1991, before the USSR collapsed. Moreover, the DPRK was the target of periodic nuclear threats and extended nuclear deterrence from the US for decades, yet until now has possessed no such weapons itself. To my knowledge no mainstream reporter in the US examined this history during the crisis with North Korea.[16] But P'yôngyang would truly be crazy not to take this history with total seriousness.

After the Korean War ended the US introduced nuclear weapons into South Korea, in spite of the 1953 armistice agreement which prohibited the introduction of qualitatively new weaponry. How did this come about? The US took this drastic step primarily to stabilize the volatile civil war. In 1953 Syngman Rhee had opposed any armistice settlement, refused to sign the agreement when it was made and frequently threatened to reopen the war. In November 1953 Vice-President Nixon visited Korea 'and sought to extract written assurances from President Rhee "that he is not going to start the war up again on the gamble that he can get us involved in his effort to unite Korea by force"'. He got no such written assurance, but in the absence of it the American commander was directed, in a highly secret 'annex' circulated only to a few American leaders, to secure 'prompt warning of any decision by Rhee to order an attack' and to prevent its issuance or receipt by ROKA field commanders.[17]

In spite of being hamstrung in this way, Rhee well knew that there were Americans who supported his provocative behaviour and they were critically-placed people who advocated the use of nuclear weapons, should the war be reignited and the act clearly laid at the communist door. Among them was Chairman of the JCS Admiral Radford, who at a conference between the State and Defense Departments in September 1956 had 'bluntly stated the military intention to introduce atomic warheads into Korea'. On January 14, 1957 the NSC Planning Board, at the instruction of President Eisenhower, 'prepared an evaluation of four alternative military programs for Korea'. A key question was 'the kinds of nuclear-capable weapons to be introduced, and the question of storage of nuclear warheads in Korea'. In the ensuing six months of discussions, Secretary of State John Foster Dulles agreed with the Joint Chiefs of Staff that such weapons should be sent to Korea. There were two problems, however: the armistice agreement, and Syngman Rhee. A sub-paragraph in the agreement (section 13d) restricted both sides from introducing new types of weapons into the Korean theatre. Radford simply wanted unilaterally to suspend 13d, since in his view it could not be 'interpreted' to allow nuclear weapons. Dulles, ever the legalist, conditioned his support of the JCS proposal on the provision of 'publishable evidence confirming Communist violations of the armistice sufficient to justify such action to our Allies and before the UN'. The problem was that the 'publishable evidence' was not satisfactory, because the communist side had not seriously violated section 13d. It had introduced new jet aircraft, but so had the US, and neither innovation was considered a radical upgrading of capabilities. Nuclear weapons were quite a different matter. This bothered the British, but the US went ahead in spite of their worries and, in June 1957, relieved itself of its 13d obligations.[18]

There remained the problem of Syngman Rhee. Unverified intelligence reports in February 1955 'spoke of meetings in which Rhee told Korean military and civilian leaders to prepare for military actions against north Korea'. In October came reports that he had ordered plans for the retaking of Kaesông and the Ongjin Peninsula, firmly in North Korean territory since the armistice, and in 1956 came more alarms and diversions. Meanwhile, no doubt unbeknownst to Rhee, the Eisenhower administration in August 1957 had approved NSC 5702/2, a major revision of Korea policy that approved the stationing of nuclear weapons in Korea and, in what one official called 'a small change', allowed for the possibility of 'US support for a unilateral ROK military initiative in response to a mass uprising, Hungarian style, in north Korea'.[19] This is an amazing mouthful. It may have been a response to rumours around that time that a North Korean general had tried to defect across the DMZ with his whole division in tow, or it may merely have been a harbinger of the thinking that subsequently led to the Bay of Pigs fiasco in Cuba (a small provocation might touch off a general uprising against communism). It was, however, exactly what Rhee and his allies were looking for; who knows if they got wind of it, but John Foster Dulles certainly did.

Dulles was the man, it will be remembered, who famously eyeballed Kim Il Sung across the 38th parallel a week before the war started. He appears to have spent the rest of his life with unsettling whispers from that sudden Sunday, as if Banquo's ghost were shaking his gory locks. At an NSC meeting in 1954 he worried that the North might start the war up again – and in a rather creative fashion:

[Dulles] thought it quite possible that the Communists would launch their attack by infiltrating ROK units and staging an attack on the Communist lines in order to make it appear as though hostilities had been started on ROK initiative.[20]

At several other high-level meetings Dulles worried aloud that the US would not know how a new war might start in Korea, and that Rhee might well start it. At the 168th Meeting of the NSC in October 1953, Dulles had warned that 'all our efforts' must be to forestall a resumption of war by Rhee; in 1957 at the 332nd Meeting he still worried that Rhee might 'start a war'; two weeks later, 'If war were to start in Korea...it was going to be very hard indeed to determine which side had begun the war'.[21]

It is in this specific context that Dulles lent his agreement to the JCS desire to place nuclear weapons in Korea. Pursuing the civil war deterrent that Secretary of State Dean Acheson had applied to Korea before the war, he wanted to restrain both sides.[22] Hotheads like Rhee and Kim Il Sung would think twice before starting a war that would rain nuclear destruction on the peninsula. But Dulles' nukes would be kept under exclusive American control and would only be used in the event of a massive and uncontainable North Korean invasion.

In January 1958 the US positioned 280mm nuclear cannons and Honest John nuclear-tipped missiles in South Korea, and a year later the Air Force 'permanently stationed a squadron of nuclear-tipped Matador cruise missiles in Korea'. With a range of 1,100 kilometres, the Matadors were aimed at China and the USSR as well as North Korea.[23] By the mid-1960s Korean defence strategy was pinned on routine plans to use nuclear weapons very early in any new war. As a 1967 Pentagon war game script put it, 'the twelve ROKA and two US divisions in South Korea had...keyed their defence plans almost entirely to the early use of nuclear weapons'. In January 1968 the North Koreans seized the US spy ship Pueblo, capturing the crew and keeping it in prison for eleven months:

> ...the initial reaction of American decisionmakers was to drop a nuclear weapon on P'yŏngyang...the fact that all the US F-4 fighter planes held on constant alert on Korean airfields were loaded only with nuclear weapons did not help the leaders to think clearly.[24]

US atomic demolition mines (ADM) were defensive weapons designed to be used in South Korea, 'to contaminate an advance area and to stop an armored attack', as one ADM engineer put it; ADMs weighed only 60 pounds and yet had a 20 kiloton explosive force; 'you could get two weeks worth of contamination out of it so that an area was impassable'.[25] The ADMs were moved around in jeeps and placed by special teams who carried them in backpacks; meanwhile US helicopters routinely flew nuclear weapons near the DMZ. That one of them might stray across the DMZ during a training exercise (as a small reconnaissance helicopter did in December 1994) and give P'yŏngyang an atomic bomb was a constant possibility. Meanwhile forward deployment of nuclear weapons bred a mentality of 'use 'em or lose 'em'; even a small North Korean attack might be cause enough to use them, lest they fall into enemy hands.[26] These weapons would also deter either South Korea or Japan from going nuclear. In 1975 Richard 'Dixie' Walker, later the American ambassador to Korea during the Chun Doo Hwan regime, wrote this:

> The presence of American conventional and even tactical nuclear forces in Korea helps to confirm strategic guarantees for Tokyo and to discourage any Japanese thoughts about a French solution: a force de frappe of their own. This is a fact well understood by leaders of many political persuasions in Tokyo and also appreciated in Peking.[27]

In other words Korean lives were hostage to an American policy of dual containment: containing the communist enemy and constraining the Tokyo/Seoul ally.

The commander most enamoured of nuclear weapons for both defensive and offensive use was General Richard Stilwell, who originated the 'Team Spirit' war games that began in the late 1970s and continued into the 1990s. 'Team Spirit' exercises were the largest in the world, often including 200,000 troops of which about 70,000 would be Americans – those already in Korea – and others flown in for the games. In Stilwell's strategy, the games were 'a dry run for a retaliatory attack on the north and a precursor of the AirLand Battle doctrine' of the 1980s, emphasizing offensive strikes behind enemy lines.[28]

A famous August 1976 incident illustrated the extraordinary 'tripwire' nature of the DMZ confrontation, where a new war could occur on almost any day. Some American and Korean soldiers had entered a forbidden zone of the DMZ near P'anmunjôm to 'trim a poplar tree' which the US said was obstructing its vision northward. (The poplar stood alone by itself; anyone who has been to P'anmunjôm knows that the surroundings are largely denuded of trees, since the area took such a pounding in the war.) A North Korean team confronted the trimming team, and in the fight that ensued a North Korean grabbed an axe from one of the Americans and then killed two American soldiers with it. This was an unfortunate incident, but a completely predictable one given the ratcheted-up tension of this insanely militarized 'de-militarized zone'.

General Stilwell put US-ROK forces on high alert (for the first time since 1953) during this confrontation, and festooned the Korean theatre with American force – an aircraft carrier task force came to Korean waters and a phalanx of nuclear-capable B-52s lifted off from Guam and flew up the peninsula toward the DMZ, 'veering off at the last moment' – or as one analyst put it, 'we scared the living shit out of them'. According to another analyst, Stilwell asked permission from the Pentagon (and received it) to delegate to his subordinates the authority to initiate artillery and rocket fire, should they lose communications with him and be unable to consult, yielding the possibility that tactical nuclear weapons might be used without central command and control. Now a joint US-ROK task force entered the Joint Security Area, with seven helicopter gunships escorting another twenty helicopters carrying a full rifle company protecting them. They proceeded finally to chop down the offending limbs on the poplar tree.[29] Meanwhile another Washington informant, whom I cannot name, told me that it was actually Stilwell who exercised 'restraint' in this episode; he was fearful that back in Washington Henry Kissinger might want to start a war, thus to further lame-duck Gerald Ford's chances in the upcoming elections.

In 1991 I heard a high-level, retired official and former commander of US forces in Korea give an off-the-record presentation of US strategy as it had developed by the 1980s:

(1) The US planned to use tactical nuclear weapons in the very early stages of a new Korean conflict, at 'H + 1', or within one hour of the outbreak of war, if large masses of North Korean troops were attacking south of the DMZ. This he contrasted with the established strategy in Europe, which was to delay an invasion with conventional weapons, and then use nuclear weapons only if necessary to stop the assault. The logic was that we dared not use nuclear weapons in Europe because the other side had them, except in the greatest extremity, but we can use them in Korea because it doesn't. South Korean commanders, he said, had got used to the idea that the US would use nuclear weapons at an early point in a war with North Korea.

(2) The 'AirLand Battle' strategy developed in the mid-1970s called for early, quick, deep strikes into enemy territory, again with the likely use of nuclear weapons, especially against hardened underground facilities (of which there are many in North Korea). In other words the strategy itself implies 'rollback' rather than simple containment of a North Korean invasion.

(3) Neutron bombs – or so-called 'enhanced radiation' weapons – might well be used if North Korean forces occupied Seoul, thus to kill the enemy but save the buildings. (The neutron bomb was invented by Samuel Cohen, who first conceived of such a bomb while watching the battle to retake Seoul in 1951, and in the early 1980s news accounts spoke of its possible deployment to Korea.[30])

(4) North Korean forces both expanded and redeployed in the late 1970s as a response to the 'AirLand Battle' doctrine. The redeployment

led to the stationing of nearly 80 per cent of their ground forces near the DMZ. American and South Korean sources routinely cite this expansion and redeployment as evidence of North Korean aggressive intent, as we have seen; in fact it was done so that as many soldiers as possible could get into the South (regardless of how a war started), to mingle with ROK Army forces and civilians before nuclear weapons would be used, thus making their use less likely.[31]

This harrowing scenario became standard operating procedure in the 1980s, the kind written into military field manuals and the annual Team Spirit military exercises.[32] These implied an initial containment of a North Korean attack, followed by thrusts into the North, ultimately to seize and hold P'yôngyang and topple the regime. (In December 1993 the *New York Times* detailed such plans in a front-page article, erroneously stating that they had just been developed.) Such war games were also conducted in Korea because in the early 1980s NATO governments and strong peace movements would not allow similar exercises in Europe.

The Gulf War, however (again according to this source), caused a re-evaluation of the role of nuclear weapons. With 'smart' bombs that reliably reach their targets, high-yield conventional weapons are more useful than the messy and uncontrollable effects of using nuclear warheads. The Army, he said, wanted out of battlefield nuclear weapons as soon as possible. Thus American policy reached a point where its own interests dictated withdrawal of obsolescent nuclear weapons from Korea in the autumn of 1991. (The weapons removed included 40 203mm and 30 155mm nuclear artillery shells, plus large numbers of ADMs. Official spokesmen were silent, however, about some 60 nuclear gravity bombs for F-4 and F-16 bombers, reported in 1985 to be stored at an American air base at Kunsan.)[33]

From the Korean War onward, North Korea responded to this nuclear blackmail by building enormous facilities underground or in mountain redoubts, from troop and matériel depots to munitions factories, even to subterranean warplane hangars. American control of the air in that war illustrated a deterrence principle supposedly developed only with the advent of 'smart' weapons, namely that 'what can be seen is already lost'.[34] The North Koreans have long known this, and have acted upon the principle. In the mid-1970s P'yôngyang faced more threats as the Park Chung Hee government sought to develop nuclear capabilities, ceasing the activity only under enormous American pressure, while retaining formidable potentialities. The ROK went ahead with its clandestine programme to develop 'indigenous ability to build ballistic missiles' capable of carrying nuclear warheads. South Korea also garnered a reputation as a 'renegade' arms supplier toward pariah countries like South Africa, and Iran and Iraq during their war.[35] Much of this reads as if it were written about North Korea, not South Korea, and puts P'yôngyang's activity into perspective: much of it was responsive to US pressure and ROK initiatives. In any case, if we understand North Korea as 'team green' rather than TEAM RED, its behaviour has been consistent with the logic of the nuclear confrontation in Korea since 1958.

3   NORTH KOREA'S SELF-RELIANT ENERGY REGIME

Yôngbyôn is a relatively well known Korean town about 30 miles north of P'yôngyang. Its secluded geographic position led to its fortification at least by the early 15th century; later on it became a scenic spot and pleasure resort for the aristocracy. A silk producing town in the old days, Yôngbyôn a large synthetic textile (mainly rayon) industry, now has accounting for over 50 per cent of production in the region – and leading some American intelligence observers to think that alleged nuclear reprocessing facilities observed by satellites might just be textile mills. Here is the way a German geographer described it in 1942:

> Out of the way of the modern traffic routes the county seat of Yôngbyôn is concealed high above the meandering valley of the Kuryong River in a tremendous, well-preserved old Korean fortress sprawling out across the surrounding...dome-shaped granite mountains.[36]

By now any viewer of American television news will have seen a stock film clip of the Yôngbyôn nuclear facility, but never have they been told the meaning of the ubiquitous slogan affixed to the roof: *charyôk kaengsaeng*. This is a Maoist term meaning self-reliance (literally regeneration through one's own efforts). Here was the North Korean justification for Yôngbyôn from the beginning – to substitute nuclear power in an energy regime dependent on domestic coal and hydroelectricity and imported petroleum. In other words, P'yôngyang sought to do what Japan and South Korea have been doing for decades, with the difference that since the big powers refused to ship them any potentially processable nuclear fuel, they built a reactor that would utilize North Korea's substantial deposits of uranium. The problem was that such reactors produce plutonium from uranium, which, with a bit of refining, can become the high-grade fuel for nuclear weapons.

North Korea's per capita use of energy is still quite close to South Korea's, and for decades was much higher. Given that so much South Korean energy use goes to private automobiles and home consumption, the per capita energy use for industry and the military is much higher in the North. In an interview in 1978, Kim Il Sung told a Japan Socialist Party Delegation that in the late 1960s some Korean scientists wanted to start up a petrochemical industry for refining petroleum (probably because Park Chung Hee had similar plans). However, Kim said, 'our country does not produce oil', and the US influenced the world oil regime: ergo 'we are not yet in a position to depend on imports...[to do so] means allowing a stranglehold on our jugular'.[37]

Both Seoul and Washington agree that P'yôngyang is only 10 per cent dependent on imported petroleum for its energy use, a major achievement by any comparison. In 1992–93, the North Korean energy profile looked like this (in units of 10^{15} *joules*): 226 for petroleum, 1,047 for coal, 176 for hydroelectric and 38 for 'Other', yielding a total energy usage of 1,486 10^{15} *joules*. All petroleum was imported; 75.4 *joules* of coal was also imported (out of 1,047 total usage) – that is coking coal primarily, coming almost exclusively from China now that the USSR is gone. This data does not count fuelwood, which is also in heavy use, and minor exports to China of hydroelectricity from the huge dams along the Yalu River.[38] The 1990s have threatened even this self-reliant energy regime because of the demise of the USSR and the collapse of trade partners in East Europe.[39] All the more reason to go nuclear at home. To figure out this crisis, in short, you need to know P'yôngyang's energy regime. But you also have to know how to build an atomic bomb.

The DPRK obtained a small nuclear reactor for research purposes of perhaps four megawatts capacity from the USSR in 1962, which was placed under IAEA safeguards in 1977. It then built a 30-megawatt facility: construction probably began around 1979, and it went into operation in 1987 at Yôngbyôn. North Korea has lots of uranium 238, the radioactive element found in nature that has 92 protons and 146 neutrons. This atomic structure is intrinsically unstable; when bombarded with a neutron, the uranium atom will split, giving off two neutrons. Each of these can split an additional uranium atom, and thus a chain reaction is born – or was born in a crude graphite pile under Alonzo Stagg stadium at the University of Chicago in 1943. North Korea uses a magnox type reactor which is an improvement on Enrico Fermi's pile, but not by much: natural uranium is made into pellets and stuffed into hollow metal rods of a magnesium oxide alloy called magnox; these tubes are placed in a welded steel vessel, with a graphite pile or core inside, cooled by CO_2-gas. The chain reaction in the tubes generates heat, which is used to move turbines and generate electricity. As this heat is produced, so is plutonium: U-238 absorbs slow neutrons to become U-239, which then decays into fissile plutonium-239. All natural uranium reactors produce plutonium. When the process is finished, hot fuel rods are withdrawn and put in a cooling pond;

they are then immersed in nitric acid, which separates the plutonium from the uranium. A Nagasaki-type bomb can be made from as little as 5 kg of such plutonium.[40]

North Korea's reactor is very much like the British model 'Calder Hall' of the 1950s, which produced England's first atomic arsenal and which the Soviets and then the North Koreans copied. The Calder Hall generated electricity as a byproduct of plutonium production; generally rated at $50MWe$ in its second-generation 'Chapelcross' type, the size of the core was fourteen metres wide and eight metres high. Inside was a stack of six fuel elements, consisting of massive, solid rods of uranium metal. Each fuel element had about 1,691 fuel channels for a total of 10,146 fuel elements (or rods). The Magnox alloy is 0.8 aluminum, .002–.005 beryllium, .008 cadmium, and .006 per cent iron; when each ton of Magnix fuel is irradiated for 1,000 megawatt days, it contains 998 kg of unconverted uranium and 0.8 kg of plutonium, that is, about one-sixth of the fuel necessary for one atomic bomb. When used for making weapons instead of electricity, the British irradiated and removed the whole core about twice a year; when used for generating electricity, the rods are only removed every few years.[41] Although the North Korean version is similar to the Calder Hall, the Yôngbyôn reactor was clearly adapted to capture heat for making steam and generating electricity: the fuel load has only been removed twice, in 1989 and 1994.

Yôngbyôn, in short, began in pursuit of energy self-reliance, and ended as a bargaining chip to trade for a new relationship with the United States. No one paid much attention to it for several years, including an IAEA delegation that P'yôngyang asked to come have a look – only to be told that North Korea had missed that year's deadline and would have to reapply for IAEA inspections. Subsequently in 1989 American spy satellites monitored a 75- to 100-day shutdown of the reactor, while fuel rods were withdrawn and new fuel was added. The satellites also picked up apparent evidence of another reactor, of 50 to 200 megawatt capacity, which some thought would come onstream in the early 1990s; government experts also claimed to have spied a building nearby that looked like a reprocessing facility (but which others thought might be a textile mill).[42] But nothing much happened until the end of the Gulf War enabled prominent American officials to bathe North Korea in a new and threatening light.

4   'A MILL TO GRIND ROGUES HONEST': THE AMERICAN SURVEILLANCE REGIME

According to the United Nations Charter, Article 2.1, the Organization is based on the principle of the sovereign equality of all its Members.[43] In the

1990s the United States has stood for the worldwide extension of democracy and the market, i.e., liberalism; President Clinton's Wilsonian calls for self-determination of small nations have hearkened to the many new nations demanding recognition in the post-Cold War period. It is almost sacrilege to say that there is anything more to American policy than that: liberalism and self-determination. But the US has also become the world's singular policeman, seeking to contain and rein in unruly forces on both sides of the old bipolar divide; it has routinely violated other nations' sovereignty in so doing. But then liberalism has always had an underside of control and restraint.

Our understanding of international politics at the end of the 20th century remains deeply imbued with definitions of power inherited from the 16th and 17th centuries, namely, that to achieve social peace among highly imperfect human beings we need a state with an authoritative monopoly on coercion, that societies having such states and collected within (recognized) boundaries merit the name nation-state, that such nation-states (when properly recognized) have something called sovereignty, that no sovereignty exists above that of the nation-state (save what it may willingly delegate to an international body) and finally that the output of sovereign nation-states is called power. Power itself must also be 'recognized', however, for it to have much meaning: 'big' powers are the ones that count in international politics. The power of Chad may be relevant for Chadians and the rebels against that state, but it doesn't count for much else in the rest of the world. Still, Chad is a recognized 'sovereign state' and in that is no small thing; amid the contemporary chaos of micronationalisms, this is what hundreds of peoples in the world want right now: recognition as 'sovereign'. Sovereignty, once the weapon of the strong, became in the last century a weapon of the weak, a way for small or vulnerable peoples to claim independence and autonomy.

It was the British who did the most to propel this doctrine around the world, confounding and undermining their imperial practice with an abstract, idealist theory that transferred ideas about the free market to international politics: if every entrepreneur ought to be the equal of any other entering the marketplace, so every nation was equal and sovereign before the bar of international law. Or as Karl Polanyi put it, 'in the liberal theory, Great Britain was merely another atom in the universe...and ranked precisely on the same footing as Denmark and Guatemala'.[44]

Jeremy Bentham was a great exemplar of British liberalism and was the author of the modern era's definition of 'the Good': the-greatest-good-for-the-greatest-number, an idea which propelled the extension of democratic rights and equality and caught the aspirations of masses of people to rise into the middle class, just as it inspired ridicule from England's rivals.[45]

But Bentham was also a social engineer, indeed it was to this that he gave over 'his boundless imaginative faculties': decennial population censuses, 'frigidariums' for fruits and vegetables, poorhouses converted to armaments manufacture, convict-run textile factories, 'Chrestomathic Day Schools' for the upper middle class, contraceptives to keep the poor rate down, and so on.[46]

As Nietzsche noted, there was always 'a touch of Tartuffe' about Bentham's idea of 'the happiness of the greatest number';[47] far more representative of the modern positivist project were new power grids and techniques of surveillance and control by which the rational, 'modern' individual, understanding himself as the only important subject, held sway over the object: the irrational, the pre-modern, the colonized, the feminine, the heterodox. Heterodox human objects got defined, constituted and controlled by 'rational' human subjects, their interaction being purely instrumental rather than interactive and intersubjective. The *Panopticon* was the logical outcome of Bentham's brand of rationality; it combined the genius of a tinkerer with the moral disposition of Aunt Mathilda: techniques of 'inspectability' such that the top knows what the bottom is doing at all times.[48] Here Bentham defined not just the modern 'Good', but new conceptions of modern power.

Once called a 'mill to grind rogues honest, and idle men industrious',[49] the Panopticon was in fact a prison in which the individual cells surround a watch-tower, arrayed in circles that admit light and thereby silhouette every single inmate for the guard in the centre. The guard, however, cannot be seen by the inmates, creating 'an effect of constant, omniscient surveillance', and thus the prisoners police themselves.[50] Bentham's ingenious device became a metaphor for Michel Foucault, whose lasting contribution was to redefine power for our (modern or postmodern) time by looking not at its central fount (e.g. sovereign state power) but at its distant sources, in the rivulets and eddies where power affects daily life – 'those points where it becomes capillary'.[51] His empirical inquiries took him to mental hospitals, church parishes, prisons, and academic classrooms, with the goal of understanding power at what we might call its point of production. Ultimately you find power exercising itself even through the individual gesture or word, without the body necessarily knowing it. Such power becomes manifest through 'the production of effective instruments for the formation and accumulation of knowledge – methods of observation, techniques of registration, procedures for investigation and research, apparatuses of control'.[52]

Our understandings of power are deeply conditioned by where we expect to find it – looking for it at the central source, like the king, the parliament, or the state, discloses it. This is 'sovereign' power, from which most of our theories of sovereignty germinate, and a conception to which P'yôngyang clings with a passion. But who is the sovereign who takes my picture in the supermarket line? Who uses my social security number to get a record of my expenditures? Who manipulates the video cameras at the shopping mall or the parking garage? Why does the National Security Agency fear the Internet and wish to put a special chip in every American computer to monitor communications? Such power is exercised through continuous surveillance, and is indescribable in the traditional language of sovereignty or legal right, or in the daily American discourse of freedom and individualism. Instead it is a new kind of power founded and developed with modern society itself and advanced with every novel technology, for which we have little theory and often little awareness, and yet which ultimately deals in discipline and coercion just as does any courtroom – and often more effectively, as Bentham knew.[53]

The Gulf War was mediated and fought through nosecone cameras, laser-guided weapons, SLAM Walleyes, infra-red beams, terrain-mapping cruise missiles, AWACS surveillance aircraft, high-resolution spy satellites, Patriot anti-missile missiles and a Telestrator to explain it all on TV, thus appearing to realize 'ubiquitous orbital vision of enemy territory'.[54] The range of vision (or what I call Pentavision)[55] extended to the home front, where Pentagon briefers, compliant journalists, and advanced television technology brought into the living room the Gulf War as a kind of Pentagon hit series. The advance of American technology allowed people to sit home and watch missiles homing onto their Baghdad targets, relayed via nosecone cameras that had the good taste to cease transmitting just as they obliterated their quarry, thus vetting a cool, bloodless war through a cool medium. Here was 'a kind of video press release', said a pioneer of the use of images to manipulate pubic opinion:[56] a bomb that was simultaneously image, warfare, news, spectacle, and advertisement for the Pentagon.

The success of George Bush's 'television war' in the Gulf propelled utilitarian logic to a new conclusion: a war to end all (post-Cold War) wars inaugurates a 'new world order' in which the whole Third World must behave and police itself, or suffer the consequences from an omniscient, omnipresent, technologically-omnipotent America. It prepared a future in which the assumptions of positivism, the technology of smart weapons, and the unseeing but conforming eye of television combine to make a new form of war, simultaneously surveilling the homefront and an unruly world. In the 1990s the US replaced the Soviet bloc with new Third World enemies called renegade or rogue states, redeployed the immense intelligence apparatus for surveilling the Soviet bloc against these states, and utilized new technologies to keep rogue states weak. The Pentagon and the intelligence agencies gained from that a continuing (or marginally decreasing) hold on the national budget (worth $28 to $30 billion for the intelligence 'black budget', about $260 billion all told in 1996). The cunning of history, however, had provided fewer and fewer enemies to watch in the 1990s. Or as Colin Powell put it, 'I'm running out of demons. I'm running out of villains. I'm down to Castro and Kim Il Sung'.[57] In great measure, therefore, the Yôngbyôn facility fuelled much more than whatever P'yôngyang used it for: it fuelled the defence budget and the intelligence agencies for several more years, in a post-Cold War situation where hugely expensive facilities for surveilling the now-nonexistent Soviet bloc might otherwise seem obsolescent.[58]

Nayan Chanda has been one of the best reporters in Asia, writing for the *Far Eastern Economic Review*. In 1993 he prepared a major study of the nuclear crisis, which, for the first time in my reading, dwelled on the IAEA's use of American intelligence imaging to surveill North Korea.[59] On February 22, 1993, the IAEA unveiled for its board at their Vienna home office 'a series of amazingly detailed photographs taken by US spy satellites in 1989', which showed North Koreans 'working to hook up their plutonium reprocessing plant with a huge waste storage tank'. Spy satellite photos from 1992, also displayed at the time, showed that 'the entire area around the building had been filled with tonnes of earth gently sloping from the tank and had been landscaped with trees, a parking lot and a road. These extraordinary photographs suddenly threw a flood of light on the mystery of the missing nuclear waste'. The waste tanks were said to be eight metres underground, with a concrete slab on top and a building erected aboveground on the slab. Chanda's article contained an artist's rendering of this site in 1989 and how it was subsequently camouflaged.

As we have seen, the used fuel rods from a Calder Hall-style reactor are washed in nitric acid solutions to extract plutonium and the resultant hot chemical waste is stored in stainless steel tanks. Access to such tanks would enable specialists to determine how much plutonium was extracted in 1989. Chanda wrote that the IAEA had been told that the 'time signature' on the plutonium and waste samples that the North Koreans provided did not match: 'The isotopic content of reprocessed plutonium and its residue in the waste changes at a fixed rate. This allows scientists to determine the exact time when plutonium was processed'.[60] Who told them? Other evidence indicates that this determination also came from US intelligence, not the IAEA.[61] Chanda then drew the IAEA's conclusion: 'the

North Koreans had obviously processed more plutonium than they had admitted'.

The IAEA estimated that North Korea had reprocessed plutonium four times since 1989 (according to Chanda). Meanwhile the CIA said that the North pulled out 10–16 *kg* in 100 days in 1989, or 22–35 pounds; North Korea admitted to experimenting with reprocessing small amounts of plutonium from damaged fuel rods in 1990, telling the IAEA that it only separated 3.5 pounds (98 grams) of plutonium.[62] When the IAEA wanted a better sense of how much plutonium the Koreans had reprocessed in these episodes, 'the CIA then came up with the suggestion that the IAEA examine the waste sites'; this is why 'the CIA supplied the IAEA with satellite photographs'. *The Far Eastern Economic Review* quoted Hans Blix (Director of the IAEA) as saying he didn't worry about North Korean charges that he had compromised the IAEA's impartiality by using CIA information: 'Satellite imagery today belongs to the realm of conventional sources of information. I don't see any reason why anyone should object to that.'

What Mr. Blix did not say is that the resources of the US National Reconnaissance Office (NRO; even the name was classified until recently) are vastly superior to private-eye satellite imagery. In a 1994 letter from one of Japan's most experienced nuclear proliferation experts, addressed to a friend of mine who showed it to me on a not-for-attribution basis, we read this: 'There is a whole issue of the most delicate [nature, the] international problem of sharing of intelligence across national borders'. Delicate in any context, such intelligence sharing was incendiary in the Korean context.

North Korea has been the object of a kind of international proctology since 1950. Every day a variety of satellites keep its territory under surveillance, using equipment so sophisticated that it allegedly can record conversations in autos speeding through P'yôngyang; even the old U-2 retains a function in the Korean theatre, and P'yôngyang complains mightily whenever it tracks a U-2 or another spy plane above or near its territory – which is about once a week, judging from P'yôngyang's Central News Agency reports. Bereft of technologies to control its own air space (and 'space' space), over the decades North Korea built underground facilities and engaged in elaborate shell games to confound the eyes intruding from above. For example, much of the reevaluation of DPRK armed strength in 1978–79 that derailed Jimmy Carter's troop withdrawal strategy, was based on reinterpreting reconnaissance photos: tanks and other weapons originally thought to be wooden mockups were redefined as the real thing. So, what do we make of this regime unveiling a waste site in 1989 and then camouflaging it by 1992? Of course, it meant that they wanted the

NRO to witness these events; it wanted to show its ace in the hole, and then put it back in the deck.[63]

5   FROM NEAR-WAR TO RELAXATION: THE CRISIS UNFOLDS

The most dangerous crisis between Washington and P'yôngyang since the Korean War came in early 1993 and lasted for 18 months. It began for the American press on March 12, 1993, when North Korea announced that it would withdraw from the Nuclear Non-Proliferation Treaty. Once again Leslie Gelb (by then head of the Council on Foreign Relations) held forth, arguing that North Korea's nuclear activity will bring on 'the next crisis', where another 'bad guy' like Saddam may soon test the mettle of 'the sane nation[s]'.[64] For Congressman John Murtha (D-Pa.), chairman of the House Appropriations subcommittee on defence, North Korea had become 'America's greatest security threat'; if it did not let its nuclear facilities be inspected, he said in March, the US ought to knock them out with 'smart weapons'.[65] By this time it was routine for influential American analysts to argue that Kim Il Sung was evil or insane or both, that his regime ought to be overthrown, and that if necessary his nuclear facilities should be taken out by force.[66]

For North Korea, however, the crisis began on January 26, 1993, when newly-inaugurated President Bill Clinton announced that he would go ahead with Team Spirit war games, which George Bush had suspended a year earlier and then revived for 1993. In late February General Lee Butler, head of the new US 'Strategic Command', announced that the Pentagon was re-targeting strategic nuclear weapons (i.e. hydrogen bombs) meant for the old USSR, on North Korea (among other places). At the same time new CIA chief James Woolsey testified that North Korea was 'our most grave current concern'.[67] By mid-March 1993, tens of thousands of American soldiers were carrying out war games in Korea again, and in came the B1-B bomber, B-52s from Guam, several naval vessels carrying cruise missiles and the like: whereupon the North dropped another hole card on the table and pulled out of the NPT.

It is a basic principle of the non-proliferation regime that countries without nuclear weapons not be threatened by those that possess them,[68] and since the demise of the USSR, American war games in Korea aimed only at the North. By threatening to leave the NPT the DPRK played a strong card; implicitly it raised the spectre of other near-nuclear powers doing the same, when the current NPT was due for a global renegotiation in April 1995 and major countries like Japan and India were unhappy about it. But if North Korea merely wanted nuclear weapons it would have stayed outside the NPT regime. Once Team Spirit was over, however, the North agreed to high-level talks with the US and subsequently (on June 11, 1993) suspended its withdrawal from the NPT. That Team Spirit and other US nuclear threats were what motivated the North could not be clearer from reading the North Korean press, which warned against resuming the games since the autumn 1992 American elections. Yet amid the usual frothy bombast against American imperialism, all during this period P'yŏngyang continued to call for good relations with the US.

The other issue that energized P'yŏngyang in early 1993 was the IAEA's demand to carry out 'special inspections' of undeclared sites in North Korea, including the one that the IAEA said was a nuclear waste dump. The IAEA had never before demanded such an inspection for any other country, but it was under international pressure for not ferreting out several sites in Iraq, discovered after Baghdad was defeated. The North resisted these inspections on two grounds: first, that the IAEA utilized American intelligence to ferret out new sites to visit, and that since the US was a belligerent in Korea this violated the mandate of the IAEA; second, that the IAEA has passed the results of its inspections to the US, and should the DPRK allow this to continue, the US would eventually want to open up all DPRK military facilities to the IAEA.[69] (That is precisely what some high-level American officials advocated: unnamed officials travelling to Korea with George Bush in January 1992 told reporters that they would require 'a mandate to roam North Korea's heavily guarded military sites at will' before they could be sure of DPRK capabilities.)[70] Some Defense Department officials wanted to use the special inspections brouhaha as a springboard for finding ways to eliminate the DPRK's 'entire nuclear program'.[71]

The US became obsessed with getting the DPRK to comply with the IAEA, and the DPRK persisted in its perennial obsession with American threats to its existence as a state. So, here was the intricately-ravelled knot of the disagreement in 1993–94, with the IAEA demanding inspection of an alleged waste site and the North Koreans claiming that the waste site was a military installation and therefore off limits, while lambasting the IAEA for following the desiderata of the DPRK's sworn enemy, the US, and for not demanding equal time to see what the US might be doing at its many installations in South Korea. And as if someone had been trying to force-feed North Korean paranoia and tell them to summon even more of the blank recalcitrance for which they are justly famous, *The New York Times* featured an essay by a well-placed expert who referred darkly to 'faddish and misguided notions' in Washington's new strategic war plans

– such as 'forming a nuclear expeditionary force aimed at China and the third world'.[72] Little wonder that the DPRK worked assiduously on its medium-range (600 miles) missile, the Nodong 1, launching it well into the Japan Sea during a test in June 1993, banging the target precisely at a distance of 300 miles – and making no bones about its purpose this time.[73] (The Nodong 1 is a SCUD missile with additional engines wrapped around its waist, giving it medium-range thrust; foreign experts are not sure whether the precise targeting of the missile was an accident, or an indication of the North's technological prowess.)

When it took office in 1993 the Clinton administration was stuck with Bush's decision to renew Team Spirit and immediately faced a crisis over P'yôngyang's threat to withdraw from the NPT – one that President Clinton paid little attention to, however, because he had campaigned on the slogan 'it's the economy, stupid!', and did not want a foreign policy crisis to interrupt his domestic agenda. The North Koreans brought themselves insistently to Washington's attentions by hook or by crook, however, and after some months passed the Clinton administration took the road of negotiation (in spite of much provocation to do otherwise) and accomplished several things no previous administration has ever done: Clinton opened direct, high-level talks with North Korea not just on nuclear weapons, but also on a wide range of policy issues; the administration also proffered a number of potential concessions to the North, including an end to Team Spirit, a pledge that it would not use force against North Korea and an upgrading of diplomatic relations (including the opening of liaison offices in both capitals). And, of course, the administration mobilized various governments and the United Nations to warn North Korea of the dangers to the world as a whole, should it withdraw from the NPT, while offering to help North Korea with less threatening kinds of nuclear power generation. For once, in other words, the US used deft diplomacy to defuse a Korean crisis, instead of sending a hailstorm of B-52s, F-4 Phantoms, aircraft carriers, and troop alerts to face down Kim Il Sung, as all previous Presidents had done. The Clinton administration deserves much credit for this sober and artful effort.

This was not a one-way street of American concessions to P'yôngyang, as often reported. In recent years North Korea has also made many concessions, diplomatic and otherwise, that have gone generally unremarked in our press. It agreed to join the United Nations in 1991, in spite of extant resolutions branding it the aggressor in 1950. It allowed the International Atomic Energy Agency to conduct seven regular inspections of its nuclear facilities, a fact many American newspapers ignored, but also one that would have been unthinkable for P'yôngyang during the heyday of the

Cold War. It passed several unprecedented joint venture laws and tax-and-profit regulations and has numerous ongoing projects with foreign firms, including many from South Korea. (From 1993 to 1995 South Korean newspapers were filled with reports of business interest in the North, but relations between Seoul and P'yôngyang were still sufficiently bad in mid-1996 that much potential business activity between the two Koreas is still blocked.) P'yôngyang has also conducted normalization talks with Japan for several years. Above all it consistently called for better relations with the US throughout the nuclear crisis, and welcomed a wide range of Americans to visit.[74]

Agreement wasn't easy, and much mutual misunderstanding delayed a settlement. The North Koreans had 40 years of experience at P'anmunjôm with brinkmanship negotiations, but the American diplomatic team had to relearn some hard lessons. Clinton's chief negotiator, Robert Gallucci, first met DPRK Vice Foreign Minister Kang Sôk-ju on June 2, 1993:

> Gallucci didn't like the North Koreans and they knew it. When he talked to them, the body language was amazing. Then Kang would look at him like a Cheshire Cat about to claw you in the face, and we'd say 'Oh no, here it comes'. He'd light a cigarette, turn to his interpreter and say, 'What the hell kind of noise is this guy telling you?' Then our interpreter would say, 'Mr. Kang is puzzled by your remarks'.[75]

Despite what one participant called marathon haggling sessions, the route to an agreement began in June–July 1993, when the North Korean side proposed that their entire graphite reactor nuclear programme be replaced by American-supplied light-water reactors (LWRs), which are much less prone to weapons proliferation but which would also require that P'yôngyang become dependent on external supplies of fuel (mainly enriched uranium).[76] North Korea had often stated that it was forced to go with graphite reactors and its own uranium because no one would help it with nuclear energy. P'yôngyang instantly toned down its anti-American rhetoric, even as the anniversary of the beginning of the Korean War passed. Nothing came of the North Korean LWR proposal in the summer of 1993, however.

The two delegations met again in November 1993, and on November 11 North Korea tabled a 'package deal' to resolve the confrontation. It demanded an American statement assuring against the threat and use of force against the DPRK, but also included a plan for the general improvement of relations between the US and North Korea, suspension of Team Spirit, IAEA continuity-of-safeguards inspections (but no more than that), a termination of antagonism and especially American nuclear threats against the DPRK, and a fundamental resolution of the nuclear problem through the provision of LWRs. The DPRK declared its intention to renounce its entire graphite system in return.[77] Other sources say the still-unpublished November initiative went even further, toward a general resolution of all the difficulties remaining between P'yôngyang and Washington. Selig Harrison, who was the private analyst most aware of the significance of the November 11 proposal, listed ten items in the package deal, including liaison offices, a new peace treaty to replace the armistice, mutual force reductions, removal of trade restrictions and Trading with The Enemy Act items, a consortium to provide the LWRs, American support for Japanese and South Korean aid and investment in the DPRK, the admission of North Korea to APEC combined with American encouragement of private sector investment, and an American willingness to discuss ground force withdrawals from South Korea (timed to North Korean redeployments away from the DMZ).[78]

This was a diplomatic watershed in the history of US–North Korean relations, but it was all mostly secret. South Korea got wind of it, of course, and President Kim Young Sam went ballistic in a meeting with Clinton, fearing that somehow P'yôngyang might damage Seoul's relations with the US, or even isolate it.[79] Meanwhile, publicly P'yôngyang played the game it plays best: sabre-rattling. At the end of November 1993, P'yôngyang said: 'When we declared our decision to withdraw from the NPT, we had taken into account all possible consequences, and we are fully prepared to safeguard the sovereignty of the country even if the worst such as "sanctions" or war is imposed on us'.[80]

In a key statement on February 1, 1994, the Foreign Ministry in P'yôngyang stated:

> The United States has created a momentous crisis that is likely to develop into catastrophe, at this crucial juncture when prospects are in sight for saving the DPRK–USA talks from the current deadlock and striking a package solution to the nuclear issue.

P'yôngyang blamed the IAEA and 'hardline' forces in the US for creating the obstacles in the path to agreement, like the Pentagon's decision to deploy Patriot missiles in South Korea, rather than Clinton and his advisers. With the US pushing its allies and DPRK ally China toward supporting UN sanctions, P'yôngyang tabled its ultimate trump card: such sanctions would be taken as 'an act of war'.

The Pentagon had war-gamed a new Korean War many times over the years, but in late 1993 *Newsweek* leaked one outcome that showed the North Koreans winning; every outcome showed a death toll of at least

50,000 Americans and hundreds of thousands to millions of Koreans.[81] The North's Nodong–1 missile raised the spectre of Japan being drawn into a new war. Basically, Clinton's people looked down the barrel of this gun and blinked. They continued high-level talks trying to get a diplomatic settlement.

By mid-1994 there was still no agreement, however, so P'yôngyang forced Clinton's hand by shutting down its reactor (in May) for the first time since 1989, withdrawing some 8,000 fuel rods and placing them in cooling ponds. This called Washington's bluff and left administration officials with no apparent room for manoeuvre;[82] predictably this act also occasioned another irresponsible media blitz about a new Korean War. In this case, however, the alarms were warranted, unbeknownst to the media: the US and North Korea came much closer to war at this time than most people realize. On NBC's *Meet the Press* on April 3, 1994, Defense Secretary Perry said, 'we do not want war and will not provoke a war over this or any other issue in Korea'; but if US sanctions 'provoke the North Koreans into unleashing a war...that is a risk that we're taking'.[83] By mid-June the Clinton administration 'had devised a plan laying out the first steps the US should take to prepare for war', which included planning for the addition of 10,000 American troops in Korea, dispatching Apache attack helicopters, and moving in more Bradley Fighting Vehicles.[84] Furthermore,

> To make sure Clinton understood both the human and the monetary costs of a war, the Joint Chiefs had summoned all the regional commanders and four star generals in the service to Washington in late May [1994] to discuss Korea and brief the President. ...According to General Luck's estimates, as many as 80,000 to 100,000 American soldiers would die in a new Korean war, and Korean troop casualties could reach the hundreds of thousands. Moreover, if the North struck Seoul as expected, [Thomas] Flanagan notes, 'the number of civilian casualties would be staggering'. The cost of such a war, Luck predicted, could top $1 trillion, far higher than the almost $60 billion spent on Desert Storm, a sum largely borne by US allies.[85]

One way of expressing what happened in May and June 1994 is that Clinton and his advisers looked down the barrel of North Korean guns and blinked: well that they did, because P'yôngyang did not want war, either. But it seemingly had to rub American noses in the realities of the Korean conflict, however, before they would pay attention and settle the crisis through diplomacy (i.e. diplomacy in the sense that both sides give up something, not that one side imposes its will on the other). Former President Jimmy Carter had been invited to visit P'yôngyang some years before. Alarmed by what he had learned about the depth of the crisis from briefings by Clinton administration officials, he decided to fly off to P'yôngyang in mid-June 1994 and meet with Kim Il Sung (the first such meeting between Kim and a former US President). By a sleight-of-hand that depended on Cable News Network's simultaneous transmission of his discussions with Kim Il Sung on a yacht in the Taedong River (direct TV mediation that short-circuited the ongoing diplomacy), Carter broke the log-jam. He suggested that P'yôngyang freeze its Yôngbyôn facility in return for light-water reactors and a new relationship with the US, gaining Kim Il Sung's apparent assent with the TV cameras there to record it. President Clinton appeared in the White House press room within minutes and declared that if P'yôngyang were to freeze its programme (that is, leave the fuel rods in the cooling ponds and halt ongoing construction on new facilities), high-level talks would resume – which they did on July 8 in Geneva. That was what made possible the breakthrough that was consummated in October 1994.

The October Framework Agreement promised P'yôngyang that in return for freezing its graphite reactors and returning to full inspections under the Nuclear Non-Proliferation Treaty, a consortium of nations (including the US, Japan, South Korea and others) would supply light-water reactors to help solve the North's energy problems; the consortium also agreed to supply long-term loans and credits to enable P'yôngyang to purchase the new reactors, valued at about $4 billion. In the meantime the US would supply heating oil to tide over the DPRK's energy problems and would begin a step-by-step upgrading of diplomatic relations. In early 1995 the North balked at accepting South Korean light-water reactors because of fears of dependency on the South, but high-level negotiations in May solved that problem, essentially by re-labelling the reactors. As of this writing teams of diplomats have been in both capitals seeking appropriate facilities to set up liaison offices; still there are no official liaison offices. The framework agreement is predicated on mutual mistrust and therefore both sides must verify compliance at each step toward completion of the agreement, which will not come until the early part of the next century, since constructing the reactors and bringing them on line will take years. By that time, if all goes well, the US and the DPRK should finally have established full diplomatic relations and the North's nuclear energy programme should be in full compliance with the non-proliferation regime. Before the reactor construction is completed the North Koreans will finally have to open the famous 'waste site' to IAEA inspection, which will show us whether they ever reprocessed enough plutonium for an atomic bomb.

6 CONCLUSION

Here, in brief, are the principles I derive from this study: first, those who live a particular history know it in their bones, both because they have to, and because of the venerable argument that there is no theory without practice; thus the logic the weak derive can trump the logic of the powerful, which must be abstract by virtue of the number of abstractions it has to deal with. Robert Manning, a State Department official in the Bush and Clinton administrations, remarked that 'the North Koreans had a very weak hand, and they played it brilliantly'.[86] But then they had done so in 1950 as well, when they got Chinese troops to bail their chestnuts out of a very hot fire. This is the story of the Vietnam War, too. I do not think, however, that it is a story that Americans have yet learned, or want to learn.

A second point is that historically-informed analysis beats abstract 'rational choice' logic and the inveterate presentism of media analysis, but becoming 'historically-informed' is not easy. Third, knowing the 'rogue' enemy seems difficult, but is not so hard because their mind is concentrated by the power asymmetries. Fourth, knowing American foreign policy and the policy process seems easy, but it is extraordinarily difficult because of any number of false or misleading presuppositions placed before the analyst, especially by the American media. Last, in the absence of archival documents (i.e. to understand foreign policy crises in the present), multiple readings of the rogue and the American press constitute a useful empirical method, but only if one is schooled in principles 1–4.

Now that the nuclear crisis seems to have been resolved, North Korea (and Korea in general) has receded to the margins of American media attention, which now comes only when a department store collapses in Seoul or a Korean company takes over another American firm or psychotic playboy Kim Jong Il inherits another title from his deceased nutcase/father. I have no idea what the average American must think about a media that railed on for years about North Korea's evil intentions, only to have been proved completely wrong in its estimates, thence to sink into silence. Since I read the daily North Korean press and the country has been familiar to me for two decades, I cannot put myself into the shoes of Americans who read the yellow journalism of the 1990s, especially since the majority were born after the Korean War. But I do know that through this drumbeat of media disinformation, a few people who have long studied our problems with North Korea were proved right in arguing that P'yôngyang was sincere in saying it would give up its nuclear programme in return for better relations with the US. They include Anthony Namkung of the Rockefeller Foundation, Dae-sook Suh of the University of Hawaii, Steven Linton of Columbia University, and the author of this article – but above all Selig Harrison of the Carnegie Endowment, who was by far the most important private citizen involved in bringing Washington and P'yôngyang together.[87]

The point of this exercise is not to say that North Korea 'won' this recent political and diplomatic struggle, or that P'yôngyang has a better media policy: quite to the contrary, its policy for half a century has been to pile lie upon lie, exaggeration upon exaggeration, even when it would be more convenient and helpful to its cause to tell the truth. But that is what we have learned to expect from communist regimes. The DPRK is not a nice place, but it is an understandable place, an anti-colonial and anti-imperial state growing out of a half-century of Japanese imperialism and another half-century of continuous confrontation with a hegemonic United States and a more powerful South Korea, with all the predictable deformations (garrison state, total politics, utter recalcitrance to the outsider), and with extreme attention to infringements of its rights as a nation. What is the explanation for a lemming-like, mimetic and ultimately ignorant media in a raucous democracy like that in the United States, in spite of their (regrettably *post-facto*) protests about how the Pentagon herded the media like cattle during the Gulf War?

These conclusions deal only with the nuclear crisis as a kind of test case of post-Cold War conflict management. The deeper meaning of the North Korean case is the extension of post-Gulf War surveillance techniques to a small, independent Third World state threatening to do to others what has been done to it for decades, namely, to develop nuclear weapons and use them to influence political outcomes. Looming behind North Korea is another potential 'renegade state', the People's Republic of China, which the US also surveills continuously and which it would like to involve in non-proliferation and missile-control regimes in spite of China being a 'great power' as conventionally defined. Such surveillance violates not only China's conception of sovereignty, but the traditional conception as well – founded on equality, mutual non-interference in internal affairs, and expectations of reciprocity. After all, the rational and perfectly justifiable response to such American pressures would be Chinese and North Korean demands to inspect American nuclear facilities (to 'roam [American] heavily guarded military sites at will'), to monitor the dealings of American firms with countries like Iraq, Iran and Israel, and to make certain the US does not permit (or turn a blind eye toward) the export of materials that might be used to build weapons of mass destruction – such as the various American exports that helped build up Saddam Hussein in the 1980s.

Is this new pattern of high-tech frontier violation a source of strength or an admission of weakness? Do we respect those who watch us 24 hours a day, or vow to get even with them when we finally escape their prying eye? Are you powerful when you practise the equivalent of international proctology, or does it mean you cannot elicit compliance any other way? Does it serve the interests of international legality for a single superpower to use 'rogue' methods to go after those it unilaterally designates as 'rogue states'?

I don't have good answers to these questions, but the simplest answer is probably the one that worked all during the Cold War, namely, that when we raise the stakes of the game to a new level, the other side will find a way to do so as well. Surveillance will prompt counter-surveillance; violation of sovereignty in one place will lead to violation in another; rogue methods will yield rogue outcomes. Hanging in the balance will be an indispensable conception for the peace of the world, namely, Article 2.1 of the UN Charter: 'the principle of the sovereign equality of all its members'. Two scholars interpreted the meaning of that phrase in an era much more idealistic than ours, but what they said can bear repeating today: 'States are sovereign, and for that reason they have an equal capacity for rights as members of the international community. Every state, irrespective of origin, size or form of government, has an equal right to order its own internal affairs and and in general to direct its policy within the limits of international law'.[88]

NOTES

1. Charles Krauthammer, 'North Korea: The World's Real Time Bomb', *Washington Post,* November 6, 1993.
2. David E. Sanger, *New York Times*, December 16, 1992, p. A6.
3. I first presented this paper at the University of Chicago Workshop on East Asia, February 13, 1996. [Later also at the University of Arkansas, Marquette, UBC, etc.]
4. Carl von Clausewitz, *On War*, ed. Anatole Rapoport (New York: Penguin Books, 1968), pp. 199–200, 366–7, and especially 404–7.
5. David E. Sanger, 'News of the Week in Review', *New York Times*, March 20, 1994.
6. *On War*, pp. 101–2; and Rapoport, 'Editor's Introduction', p. 14.
7. Harry Summers, *On Strategy: A Critical Analysis of the Vietnam War* (Novato, California, 1982).

8. *On War*, pp. 108, 118–19, 121.
9. *On War*, pp. 124, 129.
10. Thucydides, *Peloponnesian War*, pp. 242–3.
11. My views are given in *The Origins of the Korean War, II: The Roaring of the Cataract, 1947–1950* (Princeton: Princeton University Press, 1990).
12. 'The Next Renegade State', Op-Ed Page, *New York Times* (April 10, 1991); see also *New York Times*, April 16, 1991. Gelb appeared to have based his article on Stanley Spector and Jacqueline Smith, 'North Korea: The Next Nuclear Nightmare', *Arms Control Today* (March 1991), pp. 8–13. Gelb's language is very similar to that in the Spector/Smith article, without identifying this source.
13. James Wade, *One Man's Korea* (Seoul: Hollym Publishers, 1967), p. 23.
14. *ABC Nightline*, Nov. 16, 1993, transcript no. 3257. Solomon was the first high official to highlight North Korea as 'the number one threat to Asian security', in a speech on October 11, 1990 that got wide media coverage.
15. Or under international law. On July 8, 1996, the International Court of Justice at the Hague stated that the use or threat of nuclear weapons should be outlawed as 'the ultimate evil'. It could not decide, however, whether the use of nuclear weapons for self-defence was justified: 'The Court cannot conclude definitively whether the threat or use of nuclear weapons would be lawful or unlawful in an extreme circumstance of self-defense, in which the very survival of a state would be at stake'(*New York Times*, July 9, 1996). By this standard, North Korea is far more justified in developing nuclear weapons than the US is in threatening P'yôngyang with nuclear annihilation.
16. I sought to do so in Cumings, 'Spring Thaw for Korea's Cold War?', *Bulletin of the Atomic Scientists*, 48/3 (April 1992), pp. 14–23, and 'It's Time to End the Forty-Year War', *The Nation*, 257/6 (August 23–30, 1993), pp. 206–8.
17. Donald Stone Macdonald, *US–Korean Relations from Liberation to Self-Reliance, The Twenty-Year Record: An Interpretive Summary of the Archives of the US Department of State for the Period 1945 to 1965* (Boulder, Colo.: Westview Press, 1992), pp. 18–20.
18. Macdonald (1992), pp. 23, 78–9.
19. Macdonald (1992), pp. 23–4, 80.
20. Eisenhower Library, Anne Whitman file, NSC, 179th Mtg, box 5, Jan. 8, l954.
21. *Ibid.*, boxes 4 and 9.
22. See Cumings, *Origins, II*, chap. 13.
23. Peter Hayes, *Pacific Powderkeg: American Nuclear Dilemmas in Korea* (Lexington, Mass.: Lexington Books, 1991), p. 35.
24. Hayes (1991), pp. 47–8.
25. Quoted in Hayes (1991), p. 49.
26. Hayes (1991), pp. 50, 58.
27. Quoted in Hayes (1991), p. 59.
28. Hayes (1991), p. 60.
29. Hayes (1991), pp. 59–62, 89.
30. Samuel Cohen was a childhood friend of Herman Kahn; see Fred Kaplan, *The Wizards of Armageddon* (New York: Simon and Schuster, 1983), p. 220.
31. Peter Hayes also makes this point in *Pacific Powderkeg*, pp. 148–9.
32. Hayes (1991), p. 91.

33. Hayes (1991), pp. 94–5. A Kennedy School case study asserts (without offering the evidence) that air-launched nuclear weapons were removed one month after the ground-launched weapons. See Susan Rosegrant in collaboration with Michael D. Watkins, 'Carrots, Sticks, and Question Marks: Negotiating the North Korean Nuclear Crisis', (Harvard University, John F. Kennedy School of Government, 1995), p. 7n.

34. See President Bill Clinton's Defense Secretary William Perry quoted to this effect in Paul Virilio, *War and Cinema: The Logistics of Perception*, trans. by Patrick Camiller (New York: Verso, 1989), p. 4.

35. Janne E. Nolan, *Trappings of Power: Ballistic Missiles in the Third World* (Washington: The Brookings Institution, 1991), pp. 48–52.

36. Hermann Lautensach, *Korea: A Geography Based on the Author's Travels and Literature*, trans. Katherine and Eckart Dege (Berlin: Springer-Verlag, 1945, 1988), p. 258.

37. Report on an interview with Kim Il Sung, December 22, 1978, in *Tokyo Shakaito* (March 1979), pp. 162–8 (US Joint Publications Research Service translation no. 073363).

38. Information from Energy Data Associates, cited in Economist Intelligence Unit, *China, North Korea Country Profile 1992–93* (London, 1993).

39. One source estimated that in 1993 China provided 72 per cent of NK food imports, 75 per cent of oil imports, and 88 per cent of its coking coal; the North's energy regime required 52 million metric tons of brown coal or anthracite, to provide 84 per cent of its energy needs at close to full capacity. In 1993 it produced only 29 million tons; North Korea has the capacity to refine 3.5 million metric tons of oil, but only imported 1.5 million tons in 1993. See Ed Paisley, 'Prepared for the Worst', *Far Eastern Economic Review*, February 10, 1994.

40. This information is culled mostly from Richard Rhodes' two books on the atomic and the hydrogen bombs: *The Making of the Atomic Bomb* (New York: Simon & Schuster, 1986), and Dark Sun: *The Making of the Hydrogen Bomb* (New York: Simon & Schuster, 1995).

41. This information is from Peter Hayes, Nautilus Research Center, 'Should the United States Supply Light Water Reactors to Pyongyang?' Carnegie Endowment, November 16, 1993.

42. *New York Times*, November 10, 1991.

43. Leland M. Goodrich and Edvard Hambro, *Charter of the United Nations: Commentary and Documents* (Boston; World Peace Foundation, 1946), p. 64.

44. Karl Polanyi, *The Great Transformation* (Boston; Beacon Press, 1944, 1957), p. 207.

45. Perhaps Nietzsche put 'the German view' best: 'ultimately [the utilitarians] all want *English* morality to be proved right – because this serves humanity best, or 'the general utility', or 'the happiness of the greatest number' – no, the happiness of England'. Friedrich Nietzsche, *Beyond Good and Evil*, trans. Walter Kaufmann (New York: Vintage, 1966), p. 157.

46. Karl Polanyi, *The Great Transformation* (Boston: Beacon Press, 1944), pp. 119–21.

47. Friedrich Nietzsche, *The Will to Power*, trans. Walter Kaufmann and R.J. Hollingdale (New York: Vintage, 1968), p. 267.

48. Polanyi, *The Great Transformation*, p. 140; see also Foucault's discussion in *Discipline and Punish* (London: Verso, 1977), pp. 192–206; also the excellent

discussion in Peter Dews, *Logics of Disintegration: Post-Structuralist Thought and the Claims of Critical Theory* (New York, 1987), pp. 148–56.

49. Sir L. Stephen, quoted in Polanyi, p. 121.
50. Dews, *Logics*, p. 149.
51. Michel Foucault, *Power/Knowledge*, ed. Colin Gordon (New York: Pantheon Books, 1980), p. 96.
52. *Ibid.*, pp. 97–8, 102.
53. *Ibid.*, pp. 104–6.
54. Virilio, *War and Cinema*, p. 2.
55. Cumings, *War and Television* (New York: Verso, 1992).
56. The phrase is David Gergen's, a former Reagan aide known for his deft use of images, who also had the job of sprucing up Bill Clinton's act. (*New York Times*, May 6, 1991.)
57. Quoted in *Newsweek*, April 22, 1991.
58. We saw at the beginning of this paper that General Riscassi, commander of US forces in Korea, warned many times that the DPRK might 'explode or implode'. This became an all-purpose trope for testimony before Congress when annual appropriations were being considered. Riscassi's replacement, General Gary Luck, told Congress in March 1996 that what concerned him most about a possible DPRK collapse was 'whether it will be an implosion or explosion'. The *Digital Chosun Ilbo*, March 18, 1996.
59. Nayan Chanda, 'Bomb and Bombast', *Far Eastern Economic Review*, February 10, 1994.
60. Chanda, *Far Eastern Economic Review*, ibid.
61. One source reported that a senior member of the IAEA had said that the IAEA shipped plutonium samples from North Korea to the US, 'where they were tested for their isotopic content'. See Kenneth R. Timmerman, 'Going Ballistic', *The New Republic* (January 24, 1994), p. 14. (Timmerman called the American tests on the waste samples – which allegedly showed three separate reprocessing runs according to him, whereas Chanda says four – 'a smoking gun' proving that North Korea was after a bomb.)
62. *Vantage Point*, vol. 17, no. 1 (Seoul. January 1994), p. 19.
63. Kent Wiedemann, the Clinton NSC's senior director for Asia, said in 1995 that 'We finally came to recognize that from the North Korean perspective, it's in their interest to maintain an ambiguity about this whole thing', i.e. the purpose of their Yŏngbyŏn programme. (Rosegrant and Watkins, 'Carrots, Sticks, and Question Marks', p. 29.) That recognition came about four years late by my reckoning.
64. *New York Times*, Op-Ed page, March 21, 1993.
65. *Chicago Tribune*, March 18, 1993.
66. See for example Fred C. Ikle, 'Response', *The National Interest*, vol. 34 (Winter 1993–94), p. 39.
67. *New York Times*, February 24, 25, 1993.
68. This was expressed in UN Security Council resolution no. 255, March 7, 1968. In order to obtain the requisite votes from non-nuclear states to get the NPT through the UN, the US, UK and USSR committed themselves to aid any 'victim of an act or an object of a threat of aggression in which nuclear weapons are used'. Quoted in Hayes (1991), p. 214.
69. Korean Central News Agency, P'yŏngyang, February 22, 1993. In fact as we have seen the IAEA had sent its plutonium samples to Washington for

examination, since its technology was not good enough to determine how much reprocessing the North might have done. I do not know if P'yôngyang was aware of this, but in my reading of their press, they never mentioned it.

70. Quoted in *the New York Times*, January 6, 1992. Such demands enter the realm of the unnegotiable, of course, since the North Koreans will not allow this, nor would any sovereign state. These officials were also quoted as saying 'what we don't know about the North is still terrifying...'.

71. Rosegrant and Watkins, 'Carrots, Sticks, and Question Marks', p. 13.

72. Bruce D. Blair (a senior fellow at the Brookings Institution), 'Russia's Doomsday Machine', *New York Times*, October 8, 1993. See another article on the front page of the *Times* on December 6, 1993, saying that American officials were retargeting strategic weapons onto 'rogue' Third World states, with Russian targets now relegated to 'secondary' status.

73. The Korean Central News Agency referred in September 1993 to a 'regular missile launching exercise in the DPRK', which Japanese authorities were 'making quite a noise about', wishing to add 'a "missile problem" to the "nuclear problem"', thus to block normalization of relations. It justified the missile test as a necessary measure of self-defence, given that Japan is dotted with American military bases of all kinds. See KCNA, DPRK Foreign Ministry statement issued September 24, 1993. (It is highly unusual for KCNA to report any DPRK military exercise.)

74. For example, at the height of US-DPRK tension Billy Graham toured North Korea for the first time, preaching before large audiences and meeting Kim Il Sung in a 'most memorable' visit. KCNA, February 1, February 2, 1994.

75. An anonymous American participant in the talks, quoted in Rosegrant and Watkins, 'Carrots, Sticks, and Question Marks', pp. 17–18.

76. The best source that I have found on the LWR issue is Peter Hayes, Nautilus Research Center, 'Should the United States Supply Light Water Reactors to Pyongyang?' Carnegie Endowment, November 16, 1993. North Korean negotiators raised the issue of LWRs at the second round of high-level talks in June 1993; the US at this time said North Korea should discuss LWRs with South Korea and Russia (the latter had already agreed to supply four such reactors when the North complied fully with its NPT obligations). LWRs again came up in high-level talks in Geneva in July 1993, when Kang Sôk-ju offered to give up the Yôngbyôn facility in return for US provision of LWRs; on July 16, the US agreed that LWRs would be a good idea, but said that LWRs could only work after the NPT safeguards were implemented fully. (Rosegrant and Watkins, 'Carrots, Sticks, and Question Marks', pp. 20–1.)

77. There was next to no information about this package deal in the American press in the winter of 1993–94. The Korean press in both Seoul and P'yôngyang was much bettter: see the summary in *Vantage Point*, vol. 17, no. 1 (Seoul, January 1994), pp. 16–17; on the DPRK's 'package solution', see also the pro-P'yôngyang *Korean Report*, no. 280 (Tokyo, November 1993), and KCNA, reporting a Foreign Ministry statement of February 1, 1994).

78. Selig Harrison, 'Breaking the Nuclear Impasse: the United States and North Korea', Subcommittee on Asian and Pacific Affairs, US House, November 3, 1993.

79. Rosegrant and Watkins, 'Carrots, Sticks, and Question Marks', p. 25.

80. Press Release, November 30, 1993, DPRK Mission to the UN, New York.

81. Rosegrant and Watkins, 'Carrots, Sticks, and Question Marks', pp. 1–2. Apparently this war game had been done in the Pentagon in the fall of 1991, and then shelved (*ibid.*, p. 27).

82. Thomas Flanagan, the JCS' representative on Clinton's interagency working group on Korea, believes this act was the key element that got everyone to focus on resolving the nuclear crisis. See *ibid.*, p. B-9.

83. Quoted in the *Chicago Tribune*, April 4, 1994. In a memorandum to the UN dated April 10, 1996, the DPRK stated that 'a second Korean War would have broken out had the United Nations chosen to repeat its past by unilaterally imposing "sanctions" against the DPRK'. Press Release, April 10, 1996, DPRK Mission to the UN, New York.

84. Rosegrant and Watkins, 'Carrots, Sticks, and Question Marks', pp. 2, 33–5.

85. *Ibid.*, pp. 34–5. Although this study discounts Pentagon desires to remove Yôngbyôn entirely with a 'surgical strike' (pp. 15, 32–4), State Department negotiators with North Korea told me they were constantly confronted with Pentagon and CIA officers who would say, 'Why negotiate with these people? We can handle the Yôngbyôn problem overnight'.

86. *Ibid.*, p. B-11.

87. It was Mr. Harrison who first got Kim Il Sung to think about freezing the Yôngbyôn facility, during a meeting in P'yôngyang in May 1994. I remember one appearance by Anthony Namkung on national television, where he said P'yôngyang would give up its nuclear programme for better relations with the US, and Lawrence Eagleberger of Kissinger Associates responded, 'If you believe that'.

88. Goodrich and Hambro, *Charter of the UN*, p. 65.

11 Is the Nuclear Option an Option for South Korea?
Tong Whan Park

1 NUCLEAR WEAPONS AND THE SECURITY OF THE KOREAN PENINSULA

While most of the world is busy trying to collect post-Cold War peace dividends, the two Koreas remain deadlocked in a half-century old system of confrontation. Under the unproven leadership of Kim Jong Il, the P'yôngyang government seems preoccupied with the task of survival – not only of the regime but also the nation. Undergoing a volatile transition to democracy, Seoul's foremost worry is about another armed conflict on the peninsula perpetrated by a desperate North. These are indeed genuine concerns given the memories of German and Vietnamese unification. In fact, each side may arguably be harbouring a scenario maximally favourable to itself. North Korea would welcome a socialist revolution in the South which would provide the opportunity for a military intervention. Likewise, should the North implode, the South will have no option but to absorb it.

Enter nuclear weapons to this security equation on the Korean peninsula and its solution becomes extremely challenging. On the one hand, nuclear weapons might have a simplifying effect. They could help P'yôngyang sustain its political system, whether it stays with its version of NCND (neither confirm nor deny) policy or smartly cashes in its 'nuclear chips' over an extended period of time. For Seoul, even the talk of reclaiming its nuclear option could help boost its deterrence capability in the form of added assurance from the US. On the other hand, nuclear weapons, or ambitions, could backfire and shake the precarious security balance on the Korean peninsula. Though costly and unrealistic, one cannot rule out an American air strike against the Yôngbyôn nuclear facilities in North Korea, which in turn will probably escalate to an all-out war. Should North Korea become a *de facto* nuclear weapon state, the US, South Korea and Japan will have to redesign their security strategy in Northeast Asia. It may prompt Japan to move from a nuclear-ready status to that of a nuclear power, while providing a strong incentive for Seoul to follow P'yôngyang's footsteps. In the eventuality of all regional players becoming nuclear weapon states, Northeast Asia will become a first test case of what Morton Kaplan had envisioned 40 years ago as a unit veto system.[1] It goes without saying that the international security arrangement in such a system would be difficult to forge and require an entirely new thinking.

Nuclear weapons have security impacts which go far beyond the Korean peninsula. Regionally, it will greatly complicate the emerging international order among the six powers – two Koreas plus the US, Japan, China and Russia. Globally, they are a threat to the non-proliferation regime which the US is keenly interested in upholding. P'yôngyang's nuclear weapons policy has apparently been crafted to maximize its gains in all three levels of interaction. The pattern to date has been one in which North Korea acts and other regional powers react. Especially, North Korea has made the US its primary partner in negotiation while treating South Korea as a non-player or at best a secondary player. By dealing directly with Washington, P'yôngyang's leaders must have calculated, their pay-off could be maximized across all three levels.

In this game of nuclear poker, what is the position of South Korea? What are the alternative courses of action available to it other than relying on the goodwill of the US and, to a lesser extent, Japan? Having given up its nuclear option, what would take Seoul to become a major player in the game? Can South Korea regain its nuclear option? Falling short of making an official proclamation to that effect, would it be possible to gain a *de facto* nuclear option? More importantly, would it want to and under what circumstances? These are indeed tough questions and it would be presumptuous to try to answer them all in this chapter. Instead, my effort will be to lay a first stepping stone to such an intellectual pursuit. As such, it begins with an overview of North Korea's nuclear weapons development and the concessions P'yôngyang has gained so far from the US-led consortium. Then it moves to the question of South Korea's nuclear dilemma. A discussion of its failed attempts in the past to develop nuclear weapons is followed by a sketch of current debate on nuclearization in Seoul. In particular, a view on why and how of reclaiming the nuclear option is introduced based on the argument of a growing body of South Korean experts who favour the adoption of the Japanese model of acquiring self-sufficiency in nuclear fuel cycle. Lastly, though hypothetical, the disposition of nuclear weapons programme in the unified Korea is examined.

2 NORTH KOREA'S NUCLEAR POKER GAME: THE RENEGADE WITH AN ABACUS

As to North Korea's nuclear threat, Joseph S. Nye, Jr., Assistant Secretary of State for International Security Affairs has observed:

> North Korea is a clear and present danger. Not only is it on the brink of a nuclear weapons capability, but it also has 1.1 million men under arms, with two-thirds of them deployed along the Korean demilitarized zone. Moreover, it is developing a new generation of ballistic missiles. The framework agreement negotiated by the Clinton administration last October has frozen North Korea's nuclear program and provides for its dismantlement. Over time it holds the promise of a peaceful resolution of tensions on the peninsula. But it will take a decade or more for the agreement to be fully implemented and there are many pitfalls along the way.[2]

Though somewhat optimistic, Nye's assessment accurately reflects the difficulty in dealing with a regime which regards the nuclear issue as the last straw. From the threat to withdraw from the Nuclear Non-proliferation Treaty (NPT) in March 1993 to the conclusion of the Agreed Framework with the US on October 21, 1994, the P'yôngyang regime has played its nuclear card rather skilfully by dangling the US, its primary negotiating partner, at the end of a fishing line. Simply put, it was North Korea's brinkmanship which worked. Had it not been for Washington's own brinkmanship in summer 1994 in which it demonstrated a resolve to go to war over the issue, P'yôngyang might not have agreed to the terms of the Agreed Framework while demanding even more concessions.

The Agreed Framework was the product of a compromise in which North Korea agreed to freeze its present and future nuclear activities while the US will take leadership in supplying two 1,000 megawatt light water reactors (LWR) and heavy oil until these reactors are completed. With regard to the establishment of *past* transparency in P'yôngyang's nuclear weapons programme, we would have to wait and see because there are many contingencies before North Korea would accept the special inspections of the International Atomic Energy Agency (IAEA). The earliest time for such inspections will be around 2003.[3] Hence the bottom line is that the Agreed Framework has allowed P'yôngyang to maintain the nuclear card hidden in the sleeve until such time it would no longer become necessary. In return, Washington was able to put a temporary cap on North Korea's nuclear weapons programme, a diplomatic coup which must have contributed in part to the indefinite extension of the NPT.

In order to implement the Geneva Agreed Framework, the Korean Peninsula Energy Development Organization (KEDO) was launched in March 1995 in New York with the US, Korea and Japan as 'original' members.[4] KEDO is charged with the task of securing the funds for and supplying the two LWRs along with the arrangement for the delivery of heavy oil to North Korea. It is also to negotiate with P'yôngyang the terms of repayment for the LWRs and to secure from it an assurance that all nuclear materials brought in from outside shall be used for peaceful purposes only. But the true significance of forming the KEDO is that it gave South Korea the pretext and opportunity to play a 'central role' in the LWR project. Whereas the Seoul government was not directly involved in the negotiation of the Agreed Framework, the KEDO has provided a mechanism in which South Korea can enter the process such that the interests of the all the players would be satisfied. By this two-tiered arrangement, North Korea can boast that it did not deal with the South but with the US. From the American perspective, it had the effect of killing two birds with one stone: meeting Seoul's demand to be part of the game while forcing it to shoulder the lion's share of the financial burden in the LWR project. By participating in KEDO, Japan can get the maximum mileage out of whatever contributions it may have to make, since its economic and political ties with North Korea cannot but increase at a rapid pace. Seoul's gain will also be substantial by assuming the central role in the KEDO. If South Korea is the only candidate to make a major financial contribution to the LWR project, it might as well do so in a manner which will make the Seoul government appear as if it were in charge. Such a posture may also provide South Korea with some leverage against other KEDO members.

The formation of the KEDO was followed by the bilateral meeting between the officials of the US and North Korea in Kuala Lumpur from May 19 to June 12, 1995, which produced the 'Joint US–DPRK Press Statement'. The sticking point in this meeting was the name of LWR model to be supplied to North Korea. It was over this issue that North Korea refused to sign the LWR supply agreement by the April 21, 1995, target date stipulated in the Agreed Framework. In the end, the two sides made a compromise, the result of which was a rather innocuous term of 'the advanced version of US-origin, design and technology currently under construction'.[5] It should be clear to everyone, including the North Koreans, that the name refers to the reactors of the Korean standard nuclear plant model with a capacity of approximately 1,000 MWe each. To further clarify this point, KEDO's Executive Board passed a resolution (No. 1995–12) which not only spelled out the Korean model but also listed Ulchin 3 and 4 as the reference plants. While acknowledging that it will get the Korean model LWRs, P'yôngyang tried to minimize Seoul's influence by insisting that the US 'serve as the principal point of contact' with the DPRK for the LWR project and that a US firm be a programme coordinator (PC). The Joint Press Statement also contained the provision that 'a DPRK firm will enter into implementing arrangements as necessary to facilitate the LWR project'. In essence, P'yôngyang's leaders have made it clear that they want to play as central a role as Seoul in the building of the two LWRs in North Korea.

Although a number of expert-level meetings had since taken place for the conclusion of the contract for the LWR project, it was not until the middle of December 1995 that the final agreement was reached between the KEDO and P'yôngyang. The main reason for the delay was P'yôngyang's attempt to squeeze more concessions from the KEDO including the construction of the infrastructure for the LWR project and the compensation for the sunken costs of the old graphite-moderated reactors which are to be scrapped. After many sessions of tough bargaining, P'yôngyang withdrew the demand for the latter while the KEDO agreed to provide the minimum for the former. Perhaps what sealed the December 15 contract was the extremely favourable terms of repayment of the principal only over a 20-year period including a three-year grace period.

Considering that the Agreed Framework will be implemented, what would happen to North Korea's nuclear weapons programme? If all goes well, the Agreed Framework could help uncover P'yôngyang's nuclear past and dismantle whatever remains of its nuclear weapons programme. But what is the probability of such an optimistic scenario? To probe this question, we need to trace the root of P'yôngyang's nuclear ambitions. Why did the North Koreans start the nuclear weapons programme and have they been successful in meeting their objectives?

Although there exist a number of conflicting speculations about what has driven P'yôngyang to the development of a nuclear weapons programme, the common wisdom among Korea watchers can be summarized as follows:

Domestically,

1. In order to complete the father–son succession and maintain the regime's viability in the rapidly changing international environment, North Korea needed a historic feat that can be attributed to Kim Jong Il who lacks the kind of charisma his father possessed;
2. Facing the economic hardship that is not likely to disappear in the foreseeable future and the rising sense of relative deprivation that its people may feel toward the South, P'yôngyang wanted not only a

diversionary instrument for domestic control but also an option that might eventually be traded, in part or whole, to the capitalist countries for economic and technological assistance;

3. As P'yôngyang has been able to spend barely half of what Seoul allocates to defence each year and yet its military burden amounts to a quarter of its gross national product (GNP), North Korean leaders chose nuclear weapons as a relatively inexpensive alternative to the conventional arms build-up;

Internationally,

4. Under the pretence of conducting the inter-Korean dialogue, P'yôngyang intended to improve its image in the international community and hence its chances of rapprochement with Washington and Tokyo – the two most important sources of political recognition and economic support. And it reasoned that the nuclear card would strengthen its hand against these capitalist giants;

5. Unlike the case of Iraq, P'yôngyang's strategists calculated that Washington will be extremely hesitant to utilize military sanctions, lest US troops in Korea be placed under a massive counterattack from the North;

6. As in the cases of China and India, P'yôngyang presumed that the international community might accept a *fait accompli* once it credibly demonstrates that it has developed nuclear weapons. Moreover, claiming that the NPT was an unequal treaty discriminating against the non-nuclear weapon states, it wanted to exercise leadership among the have-not countries when the NPT came up for renewal in 1995; and

7. Insofar as the nuclear card is played carefully, P'yôngyang saw that its utility would continue to remain very high in its external relations.[6]

The events of 1993–95 seem to support the claim that P'yôngyang's policymakers have made significant gains in all of these objectives. Encouraged by this initial achievement, they will become even more emboldened in their future dealings with the KEDO. They will try to exploit the many 'pitfalls' alluded to by Nye in the long and arduous process of implementing the Agreed Framework. The most critical of these pitfalls is, of course, the stipulation that the US and North Korea shall work together to promote 'peace and security' on the Korean peninsula. Because 'peace' and 'security' can be interpreted to mean many different things, they may be seen as an escape clause by P'yôngyang's leaders. At any time before the completion of the LWR project and especially thereafter, North Korea may renege some obligations of the Agreed

Framework by accusing the US of failing to work toward 'peace and security.' It is even possible for P'yôngyang to refuse the IAEA's special inspections. Their reasoning may be that if the US didn't, couldn't, exercise a military option before the Agreed Framework was signed, would it do so in the post-agreement phase? To go one step further, supposing that North Korea underwent special inspections, would it then establish that North Korea is free of nuclear weapons? Here the critical question is whether the LWR project is strong enough an incentive for P'yôngyang to kill the goose that lays golden eggs. Though it is premature for us to give any definitive answer to the question, one thing is certain. In the mind of many South Koreans, the answer would be a resounding NO. As long as the North Koreans keep their nuclear weapons and their fabrication facilities hidden in the tens of thousands of underground tunnels, there is no way the IAEA can detect them through challenge inspections. In light of such an uncertainty, what then are the alternative courses of action available to South Korea?

3   SOUTH KOREA'S NUCLEAR POLICY: ADOPT THE JAPANESE MODEL?

There have been no nuclear weapons in South Korea since 1991 when the US withdrew tactical nuclear weapons from the peninsula. Influenced in part by this withdrawal, the two Koreas signed the South–North Joint Declaration on the Denuclearization of the Korean Peninsula which went into effect on February 19, 1992. This agreement banned not only nuclear weapons but also uranium enrichment and plutonium reprocessing. Considering that North Korea would have completed the whole nuclear fuel cycle in the early 1990s[7] and the South Korean government must have known about it, why did South Korea sign such a grossly inequitable document? Setting aside the question of asymmetry between the two Koreas in nuclear fuel cycle, it made little sense for Seoul to give up the enrichment and reprocessing which are permissible as long as safeguarded.

As of November 1995 South Korea has ten nuclear power reactors in operation and seven under construction. Its dependence on nuclear-generated electricity is very high (about 28 per cent in capacity and 36 per cent in production) and expected to grow even further.[8] From the standpoint of energy security, it is thus critical for South Korea to become less dependent on foreign sources of reactor fuel. Because one way to reduce this dependence is through the acquisition of technologies for enrichment and reprocessing, the signing of the Joint Declaration which went beyond nuclear weapons was either a 'very dumb' decision or influenced by external pressures, especially that from the US. Circumstances surrounding the signing of the document strongly point to the latter.[9]

If indeed it was the US that insisted on the prohibition of uranium enrichment and plutonium reprocessing by the two Koreas, what was Washington's intention knowing that P'yôngyang has either already acquired the full nuclear cycle or was very close to it? The answer is twofold: one must have been to use the Joint Declaration as a lever against P'yôngyang in subsequent negotiations while the other to maintain control over South Korea's nuclear fuel market. Now that Japan has become an advanced industrial power in reactor fuel, it is reasonable to assume that the US must have felt edgy about South Korea, a potential nuclear power, becoming another Japan.

Furthermore, Seoul's failed attempts in the 1970s to acquire nuclear weapons technology from abroad should have contributed to Washington's decision to 'cut any nuclear bud that South Korea may nurture'. Shocked by the Nixon Doctrine of 1969 and Washington's decision to withdraw the Seventh Infantry Division from Korea, the late President Park Chung-hee started a programme of greater self-sufficiency in defence. For this purpose, Park's government established two organs: the Agency for Defence Development (ADD) to modernize South Korea's weapons system and the Weapons Exploitation Committee to obtain high-tech weaponry including nuclear devices. The fall of Vietnam in 1975 and the late North Korean President Kim Il Sung's visit to Beijing in the same year[10] had such a destabilizing effect on Korea's security environment that Park Chung-hee made a public statement about the possible development of nuclear weapons in the case of the withdrawal of America's nuclear umbrella in an interview with *Washington Post* (June 25, 1975). Until his assassination in 1979, Park is known to have pushed the nuclear weapons development programme with special emphasis on the acquisition of fissionable material. Because South Korea, unlike North, has insignificant deposits of natural uranium, it sought to purchase a reprocessing plant for spent nuclear fuel. In 1972 the Seoul government began negotiations with the French government about nuclear fuel fabrication and the supply of a reprocessing plant, which resulted in the 1974 Agreement for Technical Cooperation in Atomic Energy. In order to alleviate Washington's concern about 'the South Korean bomb', Seoul ratified the NPT in 1975 while the Seoul and Paris governments signed the Agreement for the Application of Safeguards under the IAEA. In late 1975, the French government notified South Korea of its readiness to supply nuclear reprocessing facilities worth $20 million, and Korea was about to acquire a reprocessing plant.

The US government had decided, however, that the French–Korean deal was not to materialize. Various forms of pressure were exerted on Seoul and, in January 1976, an acting Assistant Secretary of State for Oceans and International Environmental and Scientific Affairs named Myron B. Kratzer disclosed at a Senate Government Operations meeting that South Korea had cancelled its plans to purchase a French plutonium reprocessing plant. Though frustrated by American intervention, South Korea continued to show interest in obtaining the reprocessing technology. Under President Chun Doo-hwan, Park's successor, a proposal was allegedly made by the Canadian Atomic Energy Agency to recycle the spent fuel from a US-made LWR in South Korea into mixed oxide fuel (MOX), which would contain weapons-grade plutonium to be used in the Canadian heavy water reactor (HWR) at Wolsung. Again the proposal was reportedly blocked by the US government.[11]

After Roh Tae-woo succeeded Chun Doo-hwan in 1988, his primary foreign policy goal was to improve relations with the 'northern' countries including Eastern Europe, the former Soviet Union and China. Preoccupied with the Nordpolitik, Roh showed no interest in anything that might endanger his diplomatic initiative including the nuclear weapons development. President Kim Young-sam who took office in 1993 has been following Roh's foreign policy line as far as nuclear weapons are concerned. Though his administration was often accused of vacillating in its attitude toward P'yôngyang's nuclear weapons development, the foundation of his policy has been to establish nuclear transparency in both North and South Korea. Especially, Seoul's utmost priority is to uncover P'yôngyang's nuclear past and put a stop to any nuclear weapons programme it may have been undertaking to date.

Does it mean that South Korea will continue to refrain from nuclear weapons development in the foreseeable future? Unless there develops a radical change in the security environment of Northeast Asia, it is not likely to go nuclear. What then are the circumstances under which the South Koreans may think of developing their own nuclear weapons? It does not take a wild stretch of imagination to identify three contingencies which individually or in combination might encourage South Korea to start an indigenous nuclear weapons programme. They are the withdrawal of America's nuclear umbrella, the reduction of US troops stationed in Korea to a dangerously low level and Japan's joining of the nuclear club. Conspicuously missing in the list is the possible collapse of the nuclear deal between the KEDO and North Korea. The reason for this omission is that such a breakdown is not likely because P'yôngyang has too much to lose from it. If, contrary to a common belief, North Korea is nowhere near becoming a nuclear weapon state, then P'yôngyang's leaders will eventually abide by the terms of the Agreed Framework. If, however, North Korea has already fabricated a few nuclear devices and hidden them away, it has no reason to give up the pay-offs that will accrue from the LWR project. Simply put, P'yôngyang is in a 'no loss' situation as far as its dealings with the KEDO are concerned.

The three contingencies in which South Korea may go nuclear are indeed improbable. The sole military hegemon in the post-Cold War era, the US may reduce the number of nuclear warheads in its arsenal but will not weaken the capability to cover the globe with its nuclear umbrella. Since US troops in Korea are seen to be playing the role of 'dual deterrence' between the South and the North, their withdrawal or reduction to a token size is unthinkable. After all, their presence is welcomed in the region and they help protect America's political economic interest in the Pacific Asia. Lastly, the Japanese may be too clever to jump the nuclear threshold. As they enjoy all the benefits of a nuclear-ready status, they see no reason to irritate the other three major powers by becoming a nuclear weapon state. By staying just below the threshold, albeit able to cross it in a short period of time, militarily Tokyo can attract Washington's sustained attention while posing as an equal against Beijing and Moscow.

Even though these three contingencies are highly unlikely to occur, one cannot and should not, rule out the possibility of South Korea trying to go nuclear as it previously did. This argument becomes doubly compelling when one considers that Japan has become a nuclear-ready state even when there existed no such security threats as contained in these contingencies. Given the long lead time required in nuclear weapons development, it would be too late by the time any of these contingencies is about to materialize. Combine this with the fact that South Korea's energy industry would benefit immensely from the possession of a full nuclear fuel cycle and one can see why some South Koreans advocate the adoption of the Japanese model of 'asymptomatic nuclearization'.[12]

Asymptomatic nuclearization is for a country to climb the nuclear ladder without emitting the 'symptoms' normally associated with the production of nuclear weapons and, unless it becomes necessary, to stop just below the last rung. Those who claim that Seoul should follow Tokyo's example in this method of nuclearization base their argument on a very simple logic: if Japan could and did, why not South Korea? Even though I do not give blanket endorsement to this view, this is not the place to hold a debate on its merits and demerits. Instead, what follows is a summary of the scenario proposed by its proponents, which should shed light on the thinking of some intellectual leaders in South Korea on this critical matter of nuclear option. The scenario is based on the premise that there are moral, legal, political and economic imperatives for Seoul to reclaim its nuclear option. The only problem is hence one of practicality or how to do it facing the American opposition. The scenario has been designed to assure the best possible chance of solving this problem of practicality.

Acknowledging that South Korea cannot openly possess nuclear weapons, the advocates of asymptomatic nuclearization preach the inevitability of developing a nuclear option customized for the Korean setting. The Korean nuclear option would consist of three components: (1) the improvement of potential military capability through the modernization of peaceful nuclear power; (2) the acquisition of nuclear deterrence and the adoption of the NCND posture; and (3) the establishment of a system of nuclear mobilization for rapid response. Of these, the first component can be undertaken publicly, while the second and third should be carried out in extreme secrecy.

Modernization of nuclear technology for peaceful use is not prohibited in the international community as long as it is properly safeguarded. Especially for a country like Korea with heavy dependence on nuclear-generated electricity, the acquisition of nuclear fuel cycle, though not easy, should not pose a serious problem. Technically, the first step is to obtain technologies for uranium enrichment and plutonium reprocessing. South Koreans may cite as a supporting case the 1967 precedent in which Japan was allowed to do the reprocessing in return for a declaration to denuclearize. Along with the development of nuclear fuel cycle, it would be necessary to promote the related industries of electronics, material, chemical engineering and aerospace. At this stage, it would also be possible to invest in research and development for nuclear propulsion for use in nuclear-powered submarines, optics for military use, nuclear batteries, kinetic energy projectiles and radioactive sterilization techniques for the prolonged storage of battlefield rations. To make these technical advancements possible, however, Seoul's leaders should show a strong political will not only to persuade their domestic clientele about the high cost of investment but also to convince the international community that they will abide by the rules of the NPT.

The ultimate objective of this first component in asymptomatic nuclearization is to reach the point where South Korea would be able to obtain fissionable material. Since it is estimated that the process would take eight to ten years, it becomes important for South Korea to start this component of the programme as early as possible. Advocates of asymptomatic nuclearization claim that now may be the opportune moment to make such a beginning. Their reasoning is that the US may be less sensitive to South Korea's indigenous efforts to modernize nuclear industries for two reasons. One is that the NPT has been extended indefinitely in 1995 removing one big burden from the shoulders of the Clinton administration. The other is the conclusion of the contract for the LWR project between the KEDO and North Korea signifying a step-level improvement in the resolution of North Korea's nuclear weapons development. With the NPT regime in good shape and South Korea committed to the financing and construction of the LWR project in North Korea, Washington may arguably have become somewhat lenient about Seoul's attempt to build an industrial structure for the nuclear fuel cycle.

Toward the middle or end of the first stage, the second component of acquiring the capability for nuclear deterrence can be started. According to the scenario, the capacity to fabricate five 20 kiloton implosion-type plutonium bombs should be sufficient for deterrence against North Korea as well as other regional adversaries. Here the key word is the capacity and not the actual production of nuclear devices. As long as South Korea obtains the capacity to build nuclear bombs at short notice, it may be deemed to have achieved a nuclear deterrence. With such a capacity, a skilful manipulation of the NCND policy will give South Korea at least a nuclear-ready status. During this second stage, it is also necessary to modernize South Korea's missile technology to the range of at least 1,000 km. Combined with the preparation of the aircraft to carry nuclear bombs, this will give added credibility to South Korea's deterrence capability. At the same time, research and development need to be undertaken for the construction of nuclear-powered submarines, the third leg of the strategic triad.

While the second stage requires utmost secrecy, the third one may need more of it. This last component of asymptomatic nuclearization is a plan to prepare for the unthinkable before South Korea completes the second stage of acquiring a credible nuclear deterrence. Should P'yôngyang undertake a nuclear experiment or a conventional war break out on the Korean peninsula, it may be necessary for South Korea to accelerate the first two stages. The third component is to prepare for such an emergency by building and maintaining a contingency plan to mobilize human and physical resources for a South Korean version of the Manhattan project.

Nobody knows whether the current or future administration in Seoul would execute a plan for asymptomatic nuclearization. What is important is that there exists a community of experts in South Korea who believe that such a programme could be viable and may even be desirable. Regardless of whether it becomes a reality or is used as a lever against the US, one must keep an eye on the possibility of Seoul adopting the Japanese model of nuclear development.

4 NUCLEAR WEAPONS AND THE UNIFIED KOREA

The last question to pose about South Korea's nuclear option is what would happen if and when the two Koreas are united. The answer is not simple and straightforward since it can be affected by the type of unification – e.g. the German absorption, Vietnamese unification by force, or European-style integration. Insofar as we rule out the merger through an all-out war of destruction on the Korean peninsula, however, the types of unification may not matter too much regarding the nuclear question. Assuming that the military and scientific infrastructures of the two Koreas remain relatively intact after unification, so will their nuclear weapons capabilities. That is, North Korea would be in a virtually nuclear-ready, if not already nuclear, state while South Korea will have made significant advances in the peaceful use of nuclear technology. And the longer it takes for the two Koreas to merge, the more nuclear-capable South Korea would become. Should the Seoul government actively push a programme in the area of asymptomatic nuclearization, it may even be able to catch up with P'yôngyang in nuclear weapons development.

Given this picture of technological capabilities, what then would be the policies of nuclear option available to the leadership of the unified Korea and which one would they take? As reference, there are four different precedents that the Koreans may use: (1) the South African model of acknowledging the possession of nuclear weapons before dismantling them; (2) the Japanese model of staying ever-ready for nuclear armament; (3) the Israeli model of NCND but expressing its willingness to give up the nuclear option in exchange for regional denuclearization; and (4) the Chinese model of presenting the world with a *fait accompli*. Which one or combination of these four will be the choice of the unified Korea? Or would it come up with its own variant?

A prerequisite to answering this question is to ask whether the unified Korea would need its own nuclear weapons. A grand strategy which includes the acquisition of nuclear weapons would bring, at least from the perspective of the Korean leaders, additional security, prestige and leverage. But without nuclear weapons will the unified Korea face any mortal danger? As long as the four major powers play the game of balancing each other in Northeast Asia, one may argue that the security of a nuclear-free Korean peninsula is not likely to be threatened. If that is the case, is nuclear armament worth the cost, political and economic? Simply put, what is the marginal utility to be gained from the possession of nuclear weapons? This is the question that the political leadership of the unified Korea needs to examine very carefully.

An extremely critical component of such an assessment would be the possible responses of the major powers to Korea's attempt to nuclearize. Will they allow the unified Korea to become a nuclear weapon state? Will the prospect of the unified Korea becoming a nuclear power further reduce their enthusiasm for the unification of the Korean peninsula?

It is impossible and even unwise to prejudge what the leaders of the unified Korea would do with their nuclear option. It is also premature to suggest a specific course of action for them at this time. One general observation can be made, however, which should be of some help to them. And that is to leave the options open. During the last five years, South Koreans have been perhaps too quick to acquiesce to the demands of Washington on the nuclear issue. What have they gained from such a posture of compliance? Very little, one may say. On the other hand, what has P'yôngyang gained with defiance against the US in the partial resolution of the issue of its nuclear weapons development? Quite a bit, both politically and economically. The simple lesson that can be drawn from this experience is that power politics work *vis-à-vis* major powers, especially when the state of international relations is in flux as in today's Northeast Asia.

In sum, the unified Korea will most likely see little need for nuclear weapons, since even without them its security can be maintained. In addition, it may not want to possess them thanks to the power configuration in the new international system which is expected to be more cooperative than conflictual in nature. Technologically, however, it will be able to produce nuclear weapons. The challenge is then for the leadership of the unified Korea to balance this technical capability with the political and economic calculus. If, by any chance, the ledger favoured going nuclear, then it must give serious thought to nuclearization. If not, it should figure out how to trade its nuclear chip with maximum pay-offs from the major powers with interests in the Korean peninsula.

5 CONCLUSION

For now, it appears that the South Korean government is not in a position to take any public initiative about reclaiming its nuclear option. This is largely due to the issue of North Korea's nuclear weapons development, which is being resolved in a shaky and painstaking process. That all four surrounding powers have shown keen interest in its resolution leaves Seoul with very little room to manœuvre in the area of nuclearization. After all, it would make little sense for Seoul to seek a nuclear option while demanding that P'yŏngyang give up its. But it may be hasty to foretell that Seoul will remain without a nuclear option for a long time to come. The past record in Seoul's attempt to modernize the nuclear technology and acquire fissionable materials reveals that the external pressure, not the domestic sentiment, has been the main source of hindrance. In particular, it was Washington that has so far blocked Seoul's road to nuclear weapons development.

Then the keys to solving the puzzle of South Korea's nuclear option should boil down to two variables. One is how intensely the South Koreans would desire a nuclear option, while the other is how committed Washington will be in preventing Seoul from acquiring it. Compared to these two, concerns of the other regional players, albeit weighty, should be considered secondary.

As to the mood of the South Koreans, it may be safe to say that there would not emerge a nationwide anti-nuclear movement. Sandwiched between the maritime and continental powers, South Korea's survival has historically depended on the art of balancing dependence and autonomy. As such, South Koreans have developed an uncanny touch about playing one major power against another whenever possible. Possession of a nuclear option could be perceived by many as a means of enhancing the nation's autonomy in foreign policy and, therefore, would not face an overwhelming opposition. Put bluntly, there seems to be a base of support for nuclearization if it is done in a discreet manner.

Turning to the attitude of the US government, it will continue to favour non-proliferation. Especially of a country like South Korea which it considers lying in its sphere of influence, Washington may not tolerate any moves to develop nuclear weapons. But then how serious will the US become, should South Korea start a programme of asymptomatic nuclearization? Would it treat Seoul as it did Baghdad? Or would it turn its face the other way as it did to Tokyo and Tel Aviv? This is a tough question for which nobody can provide a convincing answer. It is doubtful too whether the policymakers in Washington have any. Given this uncertainty, some in Seoul may be tempted to test Washington's resolve. And this is what the international community will have to keep a watchful eye on. The case of South Korea's nuclear option is by no means closed.

NOTES

1. Kaplan, Morton. *System and Process in International Politics* (New York: Wiley, 1957).

2.   Nye, Joseph S., Jr., 'East Asian Security: The Case for Deep Engagement', *Foreign Affairs* (July/August 1995), p. 95.

3.   According to the Agreed Framework, the US and North Korea are to implement the following items. North Korea agreed to (1) the removal of the past nuclear suspicion prior to the delivery to North Korea of key parts of LWRs by fully implementing obligatory safeguard measures prescribed by the IAEA, including all such steps as special inspections deemed necessary by the IAEA; (2) overall freezing of the activities of the existing nuclear facilities and dismantling of all nuclear-related facilities concurrent with the stages of construction of LWRs, which includes the termination of plans to refuel its 5 MWe atomic reactor, suspension of the construction of 50 Mwe and 200 Mwe reactors and their dismantling later and immediate closure of the radio-chemical laboratory; (3) safe storage of spent fuel rods without reprocessing them during the period of the construction of LWRs and transfer thereof later to a third country; (4) complete return to NPT and acceptance of special and general inspections by the IAEA; and (5) show sincerity toward implementing South–North Korean relations through resumption of South–North dialogue and implementation of the Joint Declaration of the Denuclearization of the Korean Peninsula. The items to be implemented by the US include (1) the creation of an international consortium in charge of raising and supplying funds to finance 2,000 Mwe LWRs for North Korea and conclusion of a contract for the supply of LWRs to North Korea; (2) provision of heavy oil as alternative energy source in connection with the suspension of a 5 Mwe atomic reactor and of the construction of graphite-moderated atomic reactors (50 and 200 Mwe); (3) beginning with 50,000 tons in the initial phase, up to 500,000 tons of heavy oil to be provided per year until LWRs become operational; and (3) alleviation of trade and investment restrictions against North Korea and normalization of US–North Korea diplomatic relations by creating liaison offices in each other's capital cities following the resolution of consular and other technical problems through experts' talks, and elevating the bilateral relations to ambassadorial relationship as progress is registered in the resolution of matters of mutual concern (Office of the South–North Dialogue, *South–North Dialogue in Korea*, No. 62 (July 1995), pp. 46–7).

4.   The KEDO consists of 'original' members and 'members'. The original members are South Korea, the US and Japan, while members are to be those countries offering assistance to the KEDO with the approval of the KEDO's Executive Board. And participation in the Executive Board is limited to the three original member countries.

5.   In the version of this statement translated by North Korea, the word 'origin' has been omitted from 'US-origin'. Though the implication of this omission is not completely clear, presumably P'yôngyang may have wanted to convince its people that it is getting a US model not one that grew out of it.

6.   For more discussion on North Korea's motivations, see Park, Tong Whan, 'The Deadly Game of Survival: P'yôngyang's Nuclear Politics in the Changing Inter-Korean Relationship', *Korea Observer*, Vol. 24, No. 3 (Autumn 1993), pp. 395–415.

7.   The Ministry of National Defense, *Defense White Paper 1994–1995*. Seoul: The Ministry of National Defense, p. 67.

8. By the end of 1994, South Korea's total power generation capacity was 27,428 Mwe and that for atomic power amounted to 7,616 MWe or 27.8 per cent. Total electric power production was 164,993 GWh and the proportion for atomic power was 58,651 GWh or 35.5 per cent (Kim, Taewoo, 'Towards Constructive ROK–US Security Relations: Nuclear Pitfalls, Atomic Energy, Defense Industry, Peace Treaty, Ecology and Other Issues'. Paper presented at the 10th Annual Conference of the Council on US–Korean Security Studies', Arlington, VA, October 27–28, 1995.

9. According to the highly reliable sources involved in the preparation of the Joint Declaration, the initial draft included neither uranium enrichment nor plutonium reprocessing. After this draft had gone through the inter-agency coordination, however, these two items, which have no direct relevance to denuclearization, were inserted. There was strong opposition to this insertion, mostly from the agencies in charge of science and national defence. The resulting compromise was to include these two elements with the proviso that as long as the threat of war existed on the Korean peninsula. But when the final version was released by the Blue House (presidential office), that proviso had been dropped. To date, it is conjectured in Seoul that Washington must have had a strong hand in influencing the Ministry of Foreign Affairs to include enrichment and reprocessing as part of the denuclearization package.

10. With the fall of South Vietnam, South Koreans believed that P'yŏngyang was seeking Beijing's permission and support for an armed invasion of the South.

11. For a more detailed discussion of South Korea's previous attempts to acquire the reprocessing technology, see Park, Tong Whan, 'South Korea', in Thomas, Raju G.C. and Bennett Ramberg, eds, *Energy and Security in the Industrializing World* (Lexington: The University Press of Kentucky, 1990), pp. 35–53.

12. The idea of and action agenda for asymptomatic nuclearization are from my conversation with Dr.Taewoo Kim, a noted specialist in nuclear affairs. I am indebted to Dr. Kim for an in-depth interview in which he succinctly summarized the views of those Korean experts who advocate the importance of 'nuclear sovereignty'.

12 South Asia's Nuclear Revolution: Has it Occurred Yet?

Peter R. Lavoy

Does mutual deterrence occur naturally when international rivals acquire nuclear weapons? Some observers argue that nuclear deterrence is nearly automatic: the mere presence of nuclear forces in a conflict-prone region creates a situation of such obvious danger that neither side to a dispute would dare threaten the vital interests of the other.[1] Others believe that nuclear deterrence is a delicate condition, the achievement of which requires thoughtful defence planning, clear communication of interests, adroit handling of crises, and a little luck.[2] These analysts doubt that the conditions in which new and emerging nuclear weapon states find themselves, and the skills and resources these countries possess, would suffice to sustain a robust deterrence relationship along the lines of the superpower competition during the Cold War.

The strategic impact of nuclear proliferation is more than a theoretical concern when considered in the context of South Asia. Nuclear deterrence presently exists between India and Pakistan. At least, most regional defence experts and many Western observers believe in its existence and its capacity to support a durable peace in the region. Although neither India nor Pakistan are known to have deployed or even assembled nuclear weapons, the presumed ease with which these forces could be manufactured and delivered, combined with the mutual view that each country is prepared to use them in war, leads to the peculiar condition of 'non-weaponized deterrence'.[3]

The primary objectives of this chapter are to: (1) identify the basic features of non-weaponized deterrence in South Asia; (2) explore whether this novel strategic situation can serve as the centre-piece for a robust regional security regime in the region; and (3) regardless whether non-weaponized deterrence can foster peace in South Asia, identify what steps must be taken to ensure that this political-military situation remains stable indefinitely or until a different security structure emerges to take its place.

The chief argument of the chapter is that the stability of any relationship of nuclear deterrence – weaponized or non-weaponized, global or regional – rests on the willingness and ability of the concerned states to understand the responsibilities of nuclear ownership. Deterrence is not new to South Asia; nuclear weapon and ballistic missile capabilities are. The threat of war, explicit or implied, has long been an instrument of diplomacy by which India and Pakistan have deterred each other from conducting provocative political or military actions. Islamabad and New Delhi have no short supply of disputes serious enough to fight over; but they have not fought since 1971. If mutual deterrence has prevented the outbreak of war for over two decades, why is there reason to be concerned about its failure in the future? The answer to this question becomes apparent when we understand how the advent of missiles and nuclear weapons can alter the political-military landscape in South Asia.

1   THE NUCLEAR REVOLUTION IN SOUTH ASIA

What is new and most significant about a nuclear-armed subcontinent is the predicament of *mutual vulnerability*. Waging the past three Indo-Pakistani wars proved very costly, even to the side that won. In a future war, however, the side that is 'losing' the conflict will be able to inflict as much destruction on the side that is 'winning' as the winner can on the loser. Furthermore, the possible level of destruction in a fourth round would far surpass that of the previous wars. Indian and Pakistani leaders clearly realize the seriousness of the situation in which they find themselves, but do they understand, and are they prepared to act on, the implications of this condition for the conduct of political and military affairs.

The chief implication of South Asia's nuclear revolution – of regional mutual vulnerability – is that the security of India and Pakistan now requires some level of cooperation *between* India and Pakistan. Based on the theory of the nuclear revolution and on the historical conduct of nuclear relations between the superpowers, we can deduce three areas in which Indo-Pakistani cooperation has become necessary: each state must accept that military victory over the other is impossible; neither side must attempt to use the fear of nuclear war as a lever to change the territorial and political status quo; and both countries should avoid initiating or escalating bilateral crises, especially those that could escalate to military and potentially nuclear conflict.[4]

These three points are accepted by nearly all nuclear experts. Somewhat more controversial is a fourth implication of the nuclear revolution – the need for arms control to stabilize deterrence, to provide reassurance that each side grasps the need to cooperate to avoid nuclear war. Bernard Brodie viewed this imperative as 'the need to limit or control the unsettling effects of our deterrent posture'.[5] Brodie explains the relationship between deterrence and this form of arms control:

> Deterrence...depends on a subjective feeling which we are trying to create in the opponent's mind, a feeling compounded of respect and fear, and we have to ask ourselves whether it is not possible to overshoot the mark. It is possible to make him fear us too much, especially if what we make him fear is our over-readiness to react, whether or not he translates it into clear evidence of our aggressive intent. The effective operation of deterrence over the long term requires that the other party be willing to live with our possession of the capability upon which it rests.[6]

Although Brodie's sage advice was to be disregarded by US and Soviet leaders many times during the Cold War – notably during the 1962 Cuban and 1973 Arab–Israeli crises – we should not underestimate the importance of arms control, or 'reassurance', for the achievement of deterrence and the avoidance of war, especially in the shadow of nuclear weapons and ballistic missiles. Arms control was essential for preserving the 'long peace' between the superpowers; and it is essential for India and Pakistan today.

This said, it must be acknowledged that not all arms control is equally effective or equally necessary. It is possible that much of the superpowers' arms control diplomacy played little or no role in preserving the long peace. What kind of arms control measures then are required to sustain nuclear deterrence and what kind of arms control schemes are nonessential (to use a term that has taken on a new meaning for US government employees)? Is it possible that some arms control schemes, which are designed to increase transparency for the nuclear, missile and conventional military capabilities held by India and Pakistan, might actually erode strategic stability?

2   NUCLEAR ARMS CONTROL: WHAT IS NECESSARY AND WHAT IS NOT

If it can be agreed that the new priority for enhancing South Asian security is to prevent two nuclear-armed states from going to war – rather than preventing two war-prone states from going nuclear – then it follows that the most useful arms control measures will be those that assist in war avoidance. As Thomas Schelling and Morton Halperin explained in 1961, effective arms control can have three general goals. It can seek to lower the likelihood of war's occurrence, lower the destruction of war should it occur, or lower costs of preparing for war.[7] Defined in this manner, arms control hardly has been practised in South Asia.

India and Pakistan have brokered a few cease-fire arrangements, negotiated away several pestering disputes, and arranged a handful of confidence-building measures (CBMs) on marginal military matters, but they have been reluctant to pursue meaningful arms control. And *nuclear* arms control in the region is non-existent. India and Pakistan each have advanced numerous proposals for curbing the nuclear danger, but all of these schemes have had as their stated objective the removal of an entire class of armaments – nuclear weapons. Thus they ought to be seen as proposals for disarmament rather than arms control. Moreover, the government officials responsible for making these disarmament proposals appear to have been more concerned with scoring political advantages over the adversary than with making any real progress toward the proclaimed objective of minimizing the dangers of regional nuclear war.

Although fashioned first to stabilize the nuclear competition between the superpowers, nuclear arms control is now suitable for South Asia. Arms control and CBMs can help India and Pakistan avoid a war that neither side wants, minimize the costs and risks of their arms competition, and curtail the scope and violence of conflict should it reoccur in South Asia. Regional arms control is important because each side engages in coercive strategic behaviour – provocative troop movements and military exercises near tense borders, alleged support for militant groups in unstable regions of the other country and cross-border firing along the line of control in Kashmir – and yet both governments know they can not afford escalation to full-scale combat, much less nuclear conflict.

Several confidence-enhancing measures have been proposed for India and Pakistan: a regional cut-off of fissile material production, a regional nuclear test ban, safeguards on new and existing nuclear facilities, extension of the nuclear no-attack pledge to cover population centres, enhanced international security assurances, regional risk reduction centres, upgraded hotlines between military and political officials, regular exchanges of military personnel, elimination of certain classes of missiles in the region, and a general protocol to the NPT requiring a wide range of security commitments from the world's nuclear-capable states.[8] However, even the best ideas cannot succeed in the absence of a stable arms control culture.

Effective and durable arms control requires India, Pakistan, and the United States – the only outside power capable of facilitating regional arms control – to develop the institutions and attitudes required for nuclear stability. Elsewhere, Raja Mohan and I identify several obstacles which have impeded efforts to foster nuclear arms control in South Asia. Briefly, these are (1) the diplomatic preoccupation with nuclear disarmament to the detriment of modest but feasible nuclear restraint measures; (2) reluctance to acknowledge the military purposes of Indian and Pakistani nuclear programmes in order to permit a realistic debate about reasonable limits on nuclear forces and strategies; (3) an unwillingness of either state to pursue arms control as a vital source of national security; (4) an inability to transform the India–Pakistan strategic dialogue from tacit to explicit bargaining; and (5) the persistence of resentment and defiance among the three powers.

These factors raise doubts about the ability of India and Pakistan to agree on meaningful ways to cooperate for the purpose of avoiding nuclear war. But it must be understood that not all arms control requires politically difficult negotiations and agreements. Sometimes effective arms control simply entails 'self-control'. The mutual reluctance of the superpowers to issue direct nuclear threats during the Cold War, for example, reflected a kind of self-restraint that may have had more beneficial consequences than any of the formal US–Soviet arms control texts. Formally negotiated treaties are desirable for documenting mutual understandings and compromises and they make later policy reversals more costly, but they are not requirements for living with nuclear weapons. In the present political climate of South Asia, it might be more sensible to explore the utility of unilateral, possibly reciprocated, forms of military and political self-restraint.

Indian and Pakistani observers frequently claim that non-weaponized deterrence is a reflection of mutual self-restraint. I am dubious. To be sure, both sides practise tremendous restraint in their nuclear activities – neither state conducts nuclear tests, deploys nuclear weapons, or issues direct nuclear threats. But what are the reasons for this restraint? I suspect that they have more to do with Indian and Pakistani concerns about the adverse reaction of the United States and other members of the non-proliferation community than to concerns about enhanced deterrence stability in the subcontinent. Therefore, non-weaponized deterrence might be viewed most accurately as a rationalization for decisions which have no coherent strategic rationale.

3 NON-WEAPONIZED DETERRENCE: CONDITION OR DOCTRINE?

Scholarly consideration of deterrence in South Asia – or in any other region for that matter – often conflates two distinct empirical questions. The first question is whether India and Pakistan currently exist in a situation of mutual deterrence. That is, does the *condition* of nuclear deterrence presently obtain in South Asia? The second question is whether India and Pakistan currently pursue *doctrines* of nuclear deterrence. In other words, does the leadership of each country fashion its nuclear capabilities and its strategic policies in such a manner as to maximize the likelihood that the other side will refrain from aggressive conduct owing to the fear of nuclear retaliation? And do the region's nuclear doctrines reflect the imperatives of the nuclear revolution?

Most analysts focus their attention on the first of these issues – whether the condition of deterrence now exists or is likely to emerge in the region.[9] Perhaps they presume that deterrence would be the obvious doctrinal choice for India and Pakistan, or possibly for any other state coming into possession of a nuclear arsenal. But is this assumption prudent? It is by no means clear that all of the political and military leaders of each of the nuclear weapon states will embrace the theory of the nuclear revolution (which posits, among other things, that military victory is impossible in the shadow of nuclear weapons).[10] Why would a state not be tempted to use its military forces, possibly even its nuclear forces, for defensive, offensive, or compellent ends, rather than for the presumed purpose of deterrence? Regardless of the actual military doctrine a nuclear weapon state adopts, moreover, it is by no means certain that mutual deterrence will result from the strategic interaction between this state and any of its nuclear-armed adversaries. Deterrence doctrines do not guarantee deterrence outcomes; and deterrence outcomes do not require deterrence doctrines.

Table 12.1 summarizes four possible scenarios for different combinations of nuclear doctrines and strategic conditions in South Asia (or, for that matter, in any other nuclear region of the world). The first possibility, mutual assured destruction, occurs if two nuclear powers pursue deterrence strategies and the condition of mutual deterrence ensues. By most accounts, this was the scenario that occurred during the Cold War between the superpowers.[11] Many South Asian authors expect that India and Pakistan now enjoy – or are in the process of developing – such a condition.[12] Several American authors also subscribe to this view.[13]

If both parties pursue deterrence strategies, but fail to achieve a stable deterrence relationship – that is, if they fail to act on the other imperatives of the nuclear revolution – then the outcome is likely to be a dangerous arms spiral, a situation where the search for security by one state produces military behaviour which is so menacing to other states that it drives them to increase their own armaments.[14] This situation can be very unstable and possibly result in war either through preventive or pre-emptive military attacks or through the escalation of a political crisis to higher and higher levels of violence.[15] A common fear in the West is that the deployment of

Table 12.1   Four Possible Scenarios for the Nuclear Competition in South Asia

| | | Condition | |
		Deterrence	*No Deterrence*
Nuclear Doctrine	Deterrence	Mutual Assured Destruction *US–Soviet Model*	Dangerous Arms Spiral
	No Deterrence (Defence, Offence, or Compellence)	'Non-weaponized' or Existential Deterrence	Cooperative Relations, Strategic Asymmetry, or Dangerous Arms Spiral

nuclear weapons and sophisticated missiles will plunge India and Pakistan into a destabilizing arms race, and possibly into war.[16]

If a nuclear-armed state opts to pursue a military doctrine of defence, offence, or compellence, rather than deterrence, then many strategic outcomes are possible, including cooperation, strategic asymmetry, arms spirals, or deterrence. The form of deterrence produced by 'unintentional' deterrence strategies, however, is not likely to resemble the type of deterrence generated by 'intentional' deterrence strategies. I believe that the current condition in South Asia can be seen as a form of deterrence, but not a common one. I doubt that either India or Pakistan have developed specific nuclear deterrence doctrines; yet some level of strategic stability prevails between them. Whether this condition is best viewed as 'existential deterrence' or 'non-weaponized deterrence', the meaning is similar: the possession of nuclear weapon capabilities by India and Pakistan creates a situation where serious political crises, heated religious and ethnic tensions, and frequent border clashes do not escalate to full-scale warfare.[17] The question is whether this happy outcome can be sustained in the future.

This chapter cannot examine these various strategic possibilities in detail. But it is instructive to focus on the selection of military doctrines by new nuclear states – in this case, India and Pakistan. Will these countries pursue deterrence strategies, and if so, how will they formulate them? As suggested above, different observers have different opinions about what ought to happen when international rivals possess nuclear weapons; what we need to understand is how these countries actually behave and how they are likely to behave in the future. Because the Indian and the

Pakistani governments have not disclosed their nuclear weapons-use doctrines (and because they might not have even formulated them yet), we are forced to make inferences about the enigmatic doctrines using the facts we do know.

4 POLITICAL CONDUCT IN A NUCLEAR SOUTH ASIA

Indian defence analyst P. R. Chari asserts that 'nuclear weapons impose a logic of their own', a logic that 'is equally applicable to the existing nuclear weapons states and the near-nuclear countries'.[18] Although Chari does not elaborate, his point is clear: all states are compelled to accept certain constraints on their political and military behaviour owing to the enormous destructive power of nuclear arms and to the possibility that nuclear weapons could be used in a conflict. At one level, Chari's comment is unobjectionable: nuclear forces universally are viewed differently than conventional arms. But precisely how are nuclear forces perceived by their owners? It is likely that different countries will make different calculations about the various constraints and opportunities occasioned by the acquisition of nuclear arms.

India and Pakistan obviously desire modern military forces (including nuclear weapons and missiles) for security purposes. In fact, recent statements by a wide variety of officials in each country suggest that neither country is prepared to live without these military capabilities. This said, it is not altogether clear that the nuclear weapon and missile capabilities in the region are designed to counter any *specific military threats*. On the contrary, the decisions to undertake nuclear weapons development programmes in each country were taken by political leaders in response to troubling political conditions created by the country's military defeat by a more powerful neighbour.

In the case of India, Prime Minister Jawaharlal Nehru initiated a broad-based nuclear research and development programme chiefly to spur industrialization and economic development and to enhance Indian power and prestige throughout the world. After China's nuclear test in October 1964, Nehru's successor, Lal Bahadur Shastri, authorized scientific preparations for a nuclear weapon option, but refused to plan for the development, deployment, or military use of nuclear forces. Although Indira Gandhi instructed Indian scientists to conduct a nuclear explosive test in 1974, she too resisted efforts to manufacture nuclear weapons, much less to undertake serious planning for their military employment. Even today it is not clear that Indian officials have formulated specific military plans for the use of nuclear weapons. Therefore, the Indian bomb is best seen as a weapon only in the country's political and symbolic arsenal.

Nuclear weapons are mainly political instruments for Pakistan as well. Although Zulfikar Ali Bhutto evidently initiated Pakistan's bomb programme in January 1972 – immediately after Pakistan's surrender to India in the Bangladesh war – the close connection between Bhutto's decision and Pakistan's military defeat can be misleading. From statements Bhutto had made throughout his early political career (as Foreign Minister, Atomic Energy Minister and Ambassador to the United Nations), it is clear that he was interested in a Pakistani bomb long before the war of 1971. While Bhutto may have viewed nuclear weaponry as the best available means to offset India's conventional military (and after 1974, nuclear) superiority, he might have been more interested in the bomb as a way to enhance his personal power and prestige throughout the world, especially among non-aligned and Islamic nations. Subsequent Pakistani officials may have taken steps to formulate plans for using the country's nuclear capabilities for specific military purposes, but public information on this issue is scarce.

5 CONCLUSION

There is no reason to doubt that Indian and Pakistani officials understand the very serious security predicament which they have created for themselves through the acquisition of nuclear weapon and missile capabilities. But it is not evident that they are prepared to act on the time-tested implications of the nuclear revolution. Perhaps because the nuclear weapons programmes of each country were initiated and sustained for political rather than specific military reasons, or perhaps because the leadership of each country appears to be concerned more with deflecting non-proliferation pressures than with avoiding a dangerous nuclear and missile arms race, we must be sceptical about the future of the nuclear peace in South Asia. Owing to the lack of progress in regional arms control, we must hope that the serious implications of the nuclear revolution will be reflected in sensible and restrained Indian and Pakistani nuclear doctrines.

NOTES

1. For a prominent example, see Kenneth N. Waltz, 'More May Be Better', in *The Spread of Nuclear Weapons: A Debate* (New York: Norton, 1995), pp. 1–45.

2. For one recent example, see Scott D. Sagan, 'More Will Be Worse' and 'Sagan Responds to Waltz', both in *The Spread of Nuclear Weapons,* pp. 47–91, 115–36. For a review of the Waltz–Sagan debate, see Peter R. Lavoy, 'Strategic Consequences of Nuclear Proliferation', *Security Studies* 4, no. 4 (Summer 1995): pp. 695–753.

3. The term 'non-weaponized deterrence' was used first by George Perkovich in 'A Nuclear Third Way in South Asia', *Foreign Policy,* no 91 (Summer 1993).

4. The logic and historical evidence supporting the validity of these three imperatives is not discussed here. For background on these points, see Robert Jervis, *The Meaning of the Nuclear Revolution* (Ithaca: Cornell University Press, 1989), especially chapter one.

5. Bernard Brodie, *Strategy in the Missile Age* (Princeton: Princeton University Press, 1959, 1965), p. 397.

6. Ibid.

7. Thomas C. Schelling and Morton H. Halperin, *Strategy and Arms Control* (New York: Twentieth Century Fund, 1961), p. 1.

8. For detailed discussions of these and other arms control proposals, see the many fine chapters in Michael Krepon and Amit Sevak, eds., *Crisis Prevention, Confidence-Building, and Reconciliation in South Asia* (New York: St. Martin's, 1995). See also Pervaiz Iqbal Cheema and Zafar Iqbal Cheema, 'Nuclear Arms Control in the Indian Ocean', *Defence Journal* 20, nos. 5–6 (June–July 1994): pp. 13–29; Zafar Iqbal Cheema, 'Nuclear Arms Control in South Asia', *USI Journal* (July–September 1993): pp. 354–75; and Abdul Sattar, 'Reducing Nuclear Dangers in South Asia: A Pakistani Perspective', *Nonproliferation Review* 2, no. 2 (Winter 1995): pp. 40–54.

9. For one example, see Devin T. Hagerty, 'The Power of Suggestion: Opaque Proliferation, Existential Deterrence, and the South Asian Nuclear Arms Competition', in *The Proliferation Puzzle: Why Nuclear Weapons Spread and What Results,* ed. Zachary S. Davis and Benjamin Frankel (London: Frank Cass, 1993).

10. Bernard Brodie introduced the 'theory' of the nuclear revolution with the following sentences: 'The writer...is not for the moment concerned about who will *win* the next war in which atomic bombs are used. Thus far the chief purpose of our military establishment has been to win wars. From now on its chief purpose must be to avert them. It can have almost no other useful purpose'. Bernard Brodie, et al., *The Absolute Weapon* (New York: Harcourt, Brace, 1946), p. 76.

11. Some authors challenge this conventional wisdom. For example, Lebow and Stein argue that 'the strategy of deterrence was self-defeating' for the superpowers; 'it provoked the kind of behavior it was designed to prevent'. Although Lebow and Stein contend that the United States and the Soviet Union practised 'too much deterrence', even they agree that the existence of nuclear weapons on both sides of the iron curtain created a politically stabilizing *condition* of deterrence. See Richard Ned Lebow and Janice Gross Stein, 'Deterrence and the Cold War', *Political Science Quarterly* 110, no. 2 (1995), pp. 180, 181; and Lebow and Stein, *We All Lost the Cold War* (Princeton: Princeton University Press, 1994).

12. The Indian and Pakistani proponents of this argument are all advocates of their country's efforts to go nuclear. For instance, see General K. Sundarji, *Blind Men of Hindoostan: Indo-Pak Nuclear War* (New Delhi: UBS

Publishers, 1993); Sundarji, 'Proliferation of Weapons of Mass Destruction and the Security Dimensions in South Asia: An Indian View', in *Weapons of Mass Destruction: New Perspectives on Counterproliferation*, ed. William H. Lewis and Stuart E. Johnson (Washington, DC: National Defense University Press, 1995), pp. 55–70; General Mirza Aslam Beg, *Development and Security: Thoughts and Reflections* (Rawalpindi: Foundation for Research on National Development and Security, 1994), esp. pp. 137–62; General K.M. Arif, 'Retaining the Nuclear Option', in *Pakistan's Security and the Nuclear Option* (Islamabad: Institute of Policy Studies, 1995), pp. 121–9; and Krishnaswami Subrahmanyam, 'The Emerging Environment: Regional Views on WMD Proliferation', in Lewis and Johnson, *Weapons of Mass Destruction*, pp. 41–54; Subrahmanyam, ed., *India and the Nuclear Challenge* (New Delhi: Lancer International, 1986).

13. See Peter R. Lavoy, 'Nuclear Arms Control in South Asia', in *Arms Control Toward the Twenty-First Century*, ed. Jeffrey A. Larsen and Gregory J. Rattray (Boulder: Lynne Rienner, 1996); C. Raja Mohan and Peter R. Lavoy, 'Avoiding Nuclear War', in *Crisis Prevention, Confidence-Building, and Reconciliation in South Asia*, pp. 25–52; Peter R. Lavoy, 'Civil-Military Relations, Strategic Conduct, and the Stability of Nuclear Deterrence in South Asia', in *Civil-Military Relations and Nuclear Weapons*, ed. Scott Sagan (Stanford, Calif.: Stanford Center for International Security and Arms Control, June 1994), pp. 79–109; George Perkovich, 'A Nuclear Third Way in South Asia', *Foreign Policy*, no. 91 (Summer 1993): pp. 85–104; and Devin Hagerty, 'The Power of Suggestion'. In addition to the individual analysts cited, several prominent think tanks have come to embrace the nuclear status quo in South Asia, provided that India and Pakistan do not increase the size or sophistication of their current nuclear capabilities. See, for example, *Preventing Nuclear Proliferation in South Asia* (New York: Asia Society Study Report, 1995); and Selig S. Harrison and Geoffrey Kemp, *India and America after the Cold War*, report of the Carnegie Endowment Study Group on US–India Relations in a Changing International Environment (Washington, DC: Carnegie Endowment for International Peace, 1993).

14. For discussion of the dynamics of arms spirals, see Robert Jervis, *Perception and Misperception in International Politics* (Princeton: Princeton University Press, 1976), chapter three.

15. For a detailed discussion of 12 possible pathways to war involving new nuclear states, see Lavoy, 'Strategic Consequences of Nuclear Proliferation'.

16. For example, Mitchell Reiss calls the deployment of ballistic missiles 'the single greatest near-term threat to strategic stability in South Asia'. See his statement to the Senate Foreign Relations Subcommittee on Near Eastern and South Asian Affairs, 9 March 1995. See also Reiss, *Bridled Ambition: Why Countries Constrain Their Nuclear Capabilities* (Baltimore: Johns Hopkins University Press, 1995), pp. 194–7. A similar concern is expressed by Jed C. Snyder in 'South Asian Security', Institute for National Strategic Studies *Strategic Forum*, no. 43 (August 1995): p. 3.

17. 'Existential deterrence' refers to a situation where the presence of nuclear weapons induces caution in national leaders irrespective of the geographic location, the system of governance, or the political culture of the countries in question. McGeorge Bundy described this idea in 'The Bishops and the Bomb', *New York Review of Books*, 16 June 1983; see also Lawrence Freedman, 'I Exist; Therefore I Deter', *International Security* 13, no. 1 (Summer 1988): pp. 177–95. 'Non-weaponized deterrence' is a better term to describe the condition that emerges when rivals possess the capabilities to manufacture nuclear weapons, but not the weapons themselves.

18. P.R. Chari, 'The International Nuclear Regime and the Near-Nuclear Countries', in *Interpreting World Politics*, ed. Kanti P. Bajpai and Harish C. Shukul (New Delhi: Sage, 1995), p. 142.

13 The Indian and Pakistani Nuclear Programmes: a Race to Oblivion?

Sumit Ganguly

1 THE ORIGINS OF THE INDIAN PROGRAMME

The Indian and Pakistani programmes arose quite differently.[1] The Indian nuclear programme can be traced to the pre-independence era, to an enterprising Indian physicist, Homi Bhaba, who had worked under Lord Ernest Rutherford at Cambridge University. Upon his return to India in 1944, Bhaba sought the assistance of a prominent industrial family, the Tatas, to promote research in the uses of nuclear energy. The Tatas viewed Bhaba's proposal sympathetically and, in 1945, Bhaba became the first director of the Tata Institute of Fundamental Research in Bombay. After India's independence Bhaba also persuaded Prime Minister Jawaharlal Nehru to create a Department of Atomic Energy (DAE) in 1948. Bhaba had little difficulty in convincing Nehru of the peaceful uses of atomic energy. Nehru firmly believed that India had to harness its scientific knowledge to overcome the country's economic backwardness.

In the 1950s, under Bhaba's guidance, the DAE set up a three-stage nuclear energy programme. This programme used natural uranium reactors and Indian uranium to produce both electricity and plutonium. The plutonium was used in fast breeder reactors to generate more plutonium and uranium 233 from thorium; the resulting uranium 233 was used to sustain breeders converting thorium to uranium 233.[2] India chose to rely extensively on thorium because of the existence of vast deposits of natural thorium in the state of Kerala.

Despite this commitment to master all the elements of the nuclear fuel cycle, the Indian nuclear programme was initially focused solely on nuclear power as a source of energy, not of weaponry. The reasons are not difficult to adduce. Prime Minister Nehru was passionately committed to the notion of a nuclear-weapons-free world. Even as early as 1954, he had called for a cessation of all nuclear tests.[3] Furthermore, he was acutely concerned about the opportunity costs of defence spending and firmly opposed to the militarization of Indian society.[4]

It should be noted, however, that Homi Bhaba did not entirely share Nehru's views. As early as 1958, according to a reliable account, Bhaba had told the British physicist Lord P.M.S. Blackett of his interest in India acquiring a nuclear weapons capability.[5]

2   THE SINO-INDIAN WAR AND ITS AFTERMATH

The first public shift in the Indian position on nuclear weapons occurred shortly after the 1962 border war with China. This war was a complete disaster for the Indian Army. In virtually every sector of the Sino-Indian border, the Chinese People's Liberation Army (PLA) had routed the Indian Army. In addition to significant losses of men and material, India lost some 14,000 square miles of territory.[6]

The consequences of the 1962 war led to important changes in both Indian foreign and defence policies. Nehru, although weakened politically (as well as physically), refused to abandon India's commitment to non-alignment. However, he did seek limited military cooperation with the United States. Among other matters, he permitted American reconnaissance aircraft to use Indian Air Force markings and to conduct reconnaissance missions along the Sino-Indian border from military bases in Orissa.

The reorientation in Indian military strategy and spending was more dramatic.[7] Despite his resistance to defence spending, Nehru recognized India's military vulnerability. To address these shortcomings, the Indian Army was authorized to create ten new mountain divisions designed for high-altitude warfare. The manpower ceiling of the Indian Army was also raised to 825,000. Plans were also set in motion for the development of a 45-squadron air force equipped with supersonic aircraft and for the upgrading of the Indian Navy.[8]

India had barely recovered from the shock of the 1962 military débâcle when the Chinese exploded their first nuclear device at Lop Nor in October 1964. The Chinese nuclear explosion set off a firestorm of political debate in India.[9] Right-wing politicians called for the abandonment of non-alignment and the pursuit of an Indian nuclear weapons option. Nehru's successor, Lal Bahadur Shastri, ably fended off both demands. He did, however, take two other important steps. First, in a significant departure from previous policy, Shastri publicly conceded that India might consider nuclear explosions for peaceful purposes.[10]

Second, he directed the chiefs of staff of the Indian armed forces to assess the newly emerged threat from China. Their study, which was completed after Shastri's death in January 1966, concluded that the principal threat to India's security remained at the conventional level. The nuclear threat, it concluded, would have to be dealt with through diplomacy.[11]

To this end, it is believed, India embarked on an effort to secure a nuclear guarantee from the United States, the Soviet Union, and the United Kingdom. India's efforts, as well as the precise terms under which India was prepared to accept such a guarantee, remain shrouded in secrecy.[12] The United States and the United Kingdom initially showed lukewarm interest in providing such a guarantee. In the end, none of these countries provided India with a nuclear guarantee. It is reasonable to surmise that India's unwillingness to compromise on the question of non-alignment handicapped its efforts to secure a nuclear guarantee.

The precise timing of the Indian decision to obtain a nuclear weapons capability remains a matter of conjecture. Clearly, in the late 1960s, the pressures within India's 'attentive public' – to borrow Gabriel Almond's term – to obtain a nuclear deterrent had begun to intensify. These pressures grew as the Chinese not only continued their nuclear testing but also acquired thermonuclear weapons.[13]

It is important and pertinent to note that, during the late 1960s, India's position at the Eighteen Nation Disarmament Committee meetings in Geneva underwent a perceptible shift. Previously, India's delegates had unequivocally called for nuclear disarmament. From 1966, however, the Indian delegate, Vishnu Trivedi, argued that India would join the emergent NPT regime only if the nuclear weapons states would undertake reciprocal measures toward nuclear disarmament. Furthermore, India for the first time publicly reserved the right to conduct nuclear explosions for peaceful purposes.[14]

3   TOWARD THE PNE

The decision to acquire a nuclear weapons capability was most likely made shortly after the 1971 war with Pakistan. Several underlying and proximate factors were significant.

The underlying factors were the Chinese threat, India's growing nuclear capability, and its desire to affirm its status as the regional hegemon in the wake of the 1971 war. The first two factors have already been discussed. In the aftermath of the 1971 conflict, which saw the creation of Bangladesh, India had emerged as the pre-eminent power on the subcontinent. The acquisition of a nuclear weapons capability would only strengthen India's claim as the regional hegemon. These underlying factors explain the drive to acquire a nuclear capability.

The timing of the decision, however, is explained by two more proximate factors. After the immediate flush of victory over its principal adversary, India faced a series of domestic and external problems. Domestically, despite a massive electoral victory in 1972, Indira Gandhi's ability to govern the nation came under increasing challenge. Congress governments were being voted out at the state levels, economic growth was sluggish and a country-wide movement against corruption (which was rampant in Mrs. Gandhi's administration) had begun.[15]

External events compounded these domestic difficulties. In 1974, in the wake of the third Arab–Israeli conflict, the Organization of Petroleum Exporting Countries (OPEC) quadrupled international oil prices. The impact of this price hike was particularly harsh for a resource-poor country like India. It caused significant economic dislocation, particularly in India's colossal agricultural sector, which was acutely dependent on petrochemical fertilizers and diesel-fuelled pumps.

The demonstration of a nuclear capability could not and did not address India's myriad social and political problems. But it did briefly bolster the sagging political fortunes of the regime in New Delhi. The development of a nuclear weapons capability was (and still is) enormously popular among large sections of India's populace. For many educated Indians, it was and remains a powerful symbol of India's growing technological and scientific prowess. The public demonstration of India's mastery of nuclear technology bolstered national self-esteem and, for a time, renewed the country's regard for its political leaders.

The long-term gains from the nuclear explosion, however, were limited. For one thing, it greatly complicated India's relations with Canada, the United States, and many other industrialized states in the West. Immediately after the nuclear explosion, the Canadian government cut off all nuclear cooperation with India on the grounds that India had illegally diverted nuclear fuel from a Canadian-supplied reactor to conduct the nuclear test. The United States began to press India to accept full-scope IAEA safeguards on its nuclear reactors and expressed its reluctance to supply nuclear fuel for the General Electric-built reactor at Tarapur. Finally, the major Western powers, under American leadership, created the Nuclear Suppliers Group, which sought to sharply restrict nuclear commerce to nations that had not signed the NPT or accepted full-scope IAEA safeguards.

These strategies of technology denial appear to have had two important consequences for the Indian nuclear programme. On the one hand, they have driven India to pursue a strategy of technological autarky in the nuclear arena. On the other hand, they have inhibited India from conducting a second nuclear test.

4   PAKISTAN'S NUCLEAR DEVELOPMENT

Unlike in India, Pakistan's national leaders showed scant interest in the development of nuclear energy in the early years of the nation's independent history. This lack of interest in the development of nuclear infrastructure is easily explained: the Pakistani leadership was faced with far more compelling and immediate tasks of nation-building and consolidation.

The very structure and organization of the Pakistani nationalist movement hobbled efforts at national consolidation. Unlike its Indian counterpart, which was a broad-based, internally democratic movement, Pakistani nationalism was woven largely around the charismatic leadership of Mohammed Ali Jinnah, whose Muslim League, the principal nationalist organization, had made little or no effort to expand its narrow social base. Consequently, upon the attainment of independence, the League found itself ill-equipped for the extraordinarily demanding work of national consolidation in polyethnic society.[16] Under these exacting circumstances, the preoccupation of the national government was the maintenance of public order. Thus it is hardly surprising that the development of nuclear energy was not one of the new government's highest priorities.

It was the Eisenhower administration's 'Atoms for Peace' programme, launched in December 1953, that first stimulated the Pakistani interest in nuclear research. In October 1954, the Pakistani government declared its interest in the development of nuclear energy. Two years later, the Pakistan Atomic Energy Commission (PAEC) was set up under the chairmanship of Dr. Nazir Ahmad, a Cambridge-trained physicist who had previously worked as the head of the Cotton Committee of Pakistan. It was during Ahmad's tenure in office that the PAEC decided to create the Pakistan Institute of Nuclear Science and Technology (PINSTECH). This facility, located near Islamabad, which has a 5-megawatt research reactor, was completed between 1960 and 1961.

Dr. I. H. Usmani, another British-trained physicist, took over as the chair of the PAEC in 1959 and is credited with laying the foundations of Pakistan's nuclear infrastructure. As chair, Usmani formulated the plans and initiated the implementation of Pakistan's power reactor programme.[17]

5 DEVELOPING THE BOMB

The real impetus toward acquiring a nuclear weapons option did not materialize until after 1971. Unlike India, Pakistan's international nuclear diplomacy had been far more limited. In the discussions leading up to the NPT, Pakistan's diplomacy, though formally couched in universalistic terms, was primarily concerned with matching India's nuclear policies. When India eventually chose not to sign the NPT, objecting to its discriminatory features, Pakistan followed suit.

In 1971, the third Indo-Pakistani War broke out.[18] This war caused the breakup of the Pakistani state and the creation of Bangladesh, and had deep psychological consequences for Pakistan's decisionmakers. Not only was Pakistan truncated, now it faced an acute security dilemma.[19] Its principal adversary had been shown to possess overwhelming conventional superiority and also strategic depth. Furthermore, with the loss of its eastern section, Pakistan had lost its ability to tie India down on a second front. In any future conflict, unless it could dramatically raise the cost of an Indian attack, Pakistan's very existence as a state could be in question.

The perceived unreliability of Pakistan's allies during the 1971 war enhanced its sense of vulnerability. Neither the United States nor the People's Republic of China (PRC) had, in Pakistan's eyes, done much to aid Pakistan during the crisis. Finally, the Soviet–Indian treaty of 'peace, friendship, and cooperation' of 1971 had heightened Pakistan's sense of isolation.

States customarily rely on two strategies to augment their security. The first, of course, involves enhancing their domestic military capabilities. The second involves building alliances with larger, more powerful states. After 1971, Pakistan saw itself as bereft of both options. The war had left the country's economy in shambles, which only made a significant conventional military build-up more difficult. And, as argued earlier, it saw few allies waiting in the wings. Under these trying circumstances, Pakistan had to find an easy solution to its strategic problems. The acquisition of nuclear weapons seemed to provide a possible answer. Even an incipient nuclear capability would deter India's overwhelming conventional superiority.

Accordingly, in 1972, President Zulfiquar Ali Bhutto committed his country to the pursuit of a nuclear weapons option.[20] The Indian PNE of 1974 gave a tremendous boost to this initial decision to acquire nuclear weapons. New Delhi's professions that the nuclear explosion did not alter the nation's aversion to nuclear weapons provided little comfort to Pakistan's leadership. As far as they were concerned, India could now combine its conventional advantage with a nuclear deterrent. As Pakistan's Foreign Secretary, Agha Shahi stated,

A qualitatively new situation has thus arisen, a situation full of menace to the security of India's immediate neighbours. The barrier to nuclear proliferation interposed by the NPT has been demolished. A precedent has been set.[21]

Pakistan's efforts to obtain a nuclear weapons capability were only enhanced by India's nuclear test. In fact, over the remainder of the 1970s, Pakistan made systematic efforts to obtain uranium enrichment facilities through every possible means, including clandestine efforts.

6   THE US STEPS IN

The United States has taken the lead in thwarting the further development of nuclear weapons in South Asia. Its ability to put pressure on India has been limited, largely because India's programme is primarily indigenous. Since, the US has prohibited the transfer of any technology that could possibly benefit the Indian nuclear weapons programme. US sanctions in 1993 halted the transfer of Russian cryogenic rocket engine technology to the Indian space programme. The US has also refused to provide fuel for the Tarapur reactor and has pressured other countries to do the same, leading India to rely on China for the necessary nuclear fuel. Aside from these efforts, however, there has been little direct pressure that the United States could use against India.

The Pakistani nuclear programme, however, because of its lack of sophistication and its dependence on foreign components, was more susceptible to American pressure. The US Congress passed an array of legislation that directly affected the Pakistani nuclear programme. In 1976 the Symington Amendment prohibited American aid to any country that imported uranium-enrichment technology without accepting IAEA safeguards. The Glenn Amendment barred assistance to countries that imported plutonium-reprocessing technology without accepting full-scope safeguards. In 1978 the Carter administration successfully stopped French plans to sell reprocessing technology to Pakistan.

The Soviet invasion of Afghanistan in 1979 put a temporary halt to these American non-proliferation pressures. The Reagan administration wanted to raise dramatically the cost to the Soviets of their occupation of Afghanistan. To pursue this goal, the United States had to use Pakistan as a staging ground for support to the Afghan *mujahideen*. Consequently, and in a marked departure from previous policy, Washington decided to downgrade its non-proliferation goals in the subcontinent. The waiver provisions of the Symington and Glenn amendments were invoked to permit American assistance to Pakistan.

The US Congress nevertheless maintained an interest in non-proliferation and made fitful attempts to pursue an agenda. The 1985 Solarz Amendment barred aid to non-nuclear weapons states that illegally exported nuclear commodities from the United States for use in nuclear weapons. Then, later that year, a compromise was worked out between the Reagan administration and Congress, resulting in the Pressler Amendment. The very precise legal language of the Pressler Amendment required the president of the United States to certify that Pakistan 'did not possess a nuclear explosive device'. Only after receiving that certification would Pakistan be eligible for American assistance. Unlike the previous amendments, the Pressler Amendment did not have any waiver provisions. Thus Reagan and his successor, George Bush, certified to Congress that Pakistan met the Pressler standard. In 1990 the Bush administration failed to provide the certification and all assistance to Pakistan drew to a close.

During much of the 1980s, General Zia-ul-Haq, the Pakistani military dictator, continued the enterprise that his deposed predecessor, Zulfiquar Ali Bhutto, had started. Even after Zia's death in 1988, the nuclear weapons programme, which was carefully ensconced in the hands of the Pakistan Army, continued uninterrupted.

The withdrawal of the Soviet forces from Afghanistan and the later collapse of the Soviet regime dramatically reduced Pakistan's importance to the United States. Both Congress and the new Clinton administration attached renewed significance to the control of the spread of weapons of mass destruction. Consequently, both India and Pakistan came under greater scrutiny and pressure to constrain and eventually abandon their nuclear weapons programmes.[22] The United States has taken a number of steps toward this end. It has strongly urged both states to accept full-scope safeguards and to sign the NPT, and it has supported a Pakistani proposal to convene a five-power conference (involving India, Pakistan, China, Russia and the United States) to discuss nuclear issues in South Asia. India has rejected all the American proposals, including the five-power talks. The reasons for the Indian hostility toward these proposals are well worn: none of them entail reciprocal obligations for the nuclear weapons states. India also rejected the five-power talks once the Chinese made clear that their own nuclear status would not be discussed at such a conference.

In 1994 the US launched yet another abortive initiative, offering to release the 40 F-16 aircraft that had been denied to Pakistan after the Pressler Amendment was invoked in 1990. In return, Pakistan would have to accept a verifiable cap on its nuclear weapons programme. Predictably,

Pakistan refused to comply. In May 1995 the Clinton administration introduced legislation that would modify the Pressler Amendment and permit non-military assistance to Pakistan.[23]

A number of complex calculations influenced the US decision to modify the Pressler Amendment. Some analysts in the Pentagon argue that, despite the end of the Cold War and of the policy of containment, Pakistan remains important to the United States. In their view, Pakistan is a 'moderate' Islamic state and can be useful to the United States in its dealings with the Islamic world. Furthermore, some also contend that attempts to isolate Pakistan through a strategy of technology denial have failed. Consequently, they argue, it is necessary to engage Pakistan once again.

A second, unstated, factor also influences this strategic calculus. India's closeness with the Soviet Union during much of the Cold War still rankles many influential decisionmakers. Consequently, overtures to Pakistan are seen as providing a useful point of leverage over India on a variety of bilateral issues.

7   THE PROSPECTS FOR REGIONAL STABILITY

The US will continue to press both India and Pakistan to abandon their nuclear weapons programmes. India, and consequently Pakistan, will remain equally determined to stave off American pressures. Will the incipient nuclearization of South Asia make the region more unstable? Or will the acquisition of nuclear capabilities by both subcontinental adversaries produce a degree of stability?

The answer is not nearly as clear-cut as the principal debate on regional security and nuclear weapons seems to suggest.[24] The dangers of war as a consequence of organizational biases and institutional errors are not as great as some fear. The 1971 military débâcle made the Pakistani military far more circumspect in its war plans against India.[25] Yet one cannot be sanguine about the likelihood of regional stability. The poor command, control, communications and intelligence (C3I) in the region could well contribute to a spiral of misperception and inadvertent escalation.

The consequences of nuclear proliferation in the region are complex and varied. The acquisition of nuclear weapons capabilities in the region may well have produced a variant of Glenn Snyder's 'stability/instability paradox'.[26] Despite the exchange of bitter words over the insurgency in Kashmir and two crises in 1987 and 1990, neither India nor Pakistan has resorted to war.[27] It appears that decision makers in New Delhi and Islamabad have recognized the dangers of inadvertent escalation stemming from a conventional conflict.[28] On the other hand, both sides continue to support insurgent movements in their respective countries, although official statements deny such meddling. Pakistan has long been involved in supporting both the Kashmiri and Sikh insurgencies; India has been implicated in the Sindhi–*Muhajir* conflict in Sindh. Both sides see the risks associated with domestic subversion and support for insurgencies as controllable and calculable. Thus far, the evidence seems to support this sanguine conclusion.

Would the introduction of ballistic missiles in the region significantly alter the prospects for strategic stability? Even the deployment of short-range ballistic missiles – the Chinese-built M-11 by Pakistan and the indigenously-manufactured Prithvi by India – in South Asia probably would not further destabilize the crude nuclear balance. As long as neither side has complete confidence in its ability to seek out and destroy the entire nuclear arsenal of the other in a preemptive first strike, the acquisition of ballistic missiles is unlikely to destabilize the nuclear balance. The introduction of ballistic missiles may contribute to a conventional arms race in the region, however, which would impose severe opportunity costs on both states. Furthermore, the deployment of such missiles could also invite American sanctions.

8 CONCLUSIONS

Along with Israel, India and Pakistan are the only two major states that remain outside the NPT framework. The historic ties that bind Israel to the United States, its conventional inferiority *vis-à-vis* several of its hostile Arab neighbours, and its recent efforts to settle the Palestinian question will, in all likelihood, enable it to easily fend off American pressure to sign the NPT. India and Pakistan cannot make similar claims on the United States, however. Consequently, at least for the foreseeable future, they will be subjected to American and other international blandishments.

Yet there are limits to American influence on India, unarguably the principal power in the region. Non-proliferation is increasingly competing with other American priorities in South Asia. Furthermore, as the Indian economy continues to expand and foreign investment grows, India will acquire a degree of reverse leverage on the United States.

At a regional level, India remains concerned about the continuing Chinese threat, despite a significant improvement in relations with China in recent years.[29] Finally, the strength of Indian public opinion, and particularly élite opinion, on nuclear weapons remains strongly pro-nuclear.[30] Few governments are secure enough to counter such a tide of popular sentiment.

Under these circumstances, the most strategically desirable vision for South Asia is a regime of institutionalized arms control and confidence-building measures. Such a regime would enhance transparency, limit the pursuit of dangerous military activities and promote crisis stability. Despite significant and deep-seated differences over the Kashmir issue, it behoves decision makers in New Delhi and Islamabad to pursue these measures with renewed vigour.

NOTES

1. There are few dispassionate accounts of either the Indian or the Pakistani nuclear programmes. An important exception is Ziba Moshaver, *Nuclear Weapons Proliferation in the Indian Subcontinent* (New York: St. Martin's, 1991). A detailed but tendentious account of the Indian nuclear programme can be found in David Hart, *Nuclear Power in India: A Comparative Analysis* (Winchester: Allen and Unwin, 1983). Ashok Kapur, *Pakistan's Nuclear Development* (London: Croom Helm, 1987), despite its scholarly façade, is a hostile analysis. A Pakistani perspective is offered in Akhtar Ali, *Pakistan's Nuclear Dilemma* (Karachi: Economist Research Unit, 1984).
2. Hart, *Nuclear Power in India,* p. 35.
3. Moshaver, *Nuclear Weapons Proliferation in the Indian Subcontinent*, p. 110.
4. On this point see Sumit Ganguly, 'From the Defense of the Nation to Aid to the Civil: The Army in Contemporary India', *Journal of Asian and African Studies*, 26, nos. 1–2 (1991).
5. Shyam Bhatia, *India's Nuclear Bomb* (Ghaziabad: Vikas Publishing House, 1979), p. 114.
6. Steven Hoffman, *India and the China Crisis* (Berkeley: University of California Press, 1990).
7. Ganguly, 'From the Defence of the Nation to Aid to the Civil: The Army in Contemporary India'.
8. Lorne J. Kavic, *India's Quest For Security: Defence Policies, 1947–1962* (Berkeley: University of California Press, 1967).
9. The debate is nicely summarized in G.G. Mirchandani, *India's Nuclear Dilemma* (New Delhi: Popular Book Services, 1968).
10. Bhatia, *India's Nuclear Bomb,* pp. 120–2.
11. The study remains classified. Excerpts from it are cited in Mirchandani, *India's Nuclear Dilemma.*
12. For a discussion of India's efforts to obtain a nuclear guarantee, see A.G. Noorani, 'India's Quest for a Nuclear Guarantee', *Asian Survey*, 7, no. 7 (July 1967), pp. 490–502.
13. See for example, 'Options For India', *Institute for Defence Studies and Analyses Journal*, 3, no.1 (July 1970), pp. 102–18.
14. Bhatia, *India's Nuclear Bomb,* pp. 134–6.
15. See Paul Brass, *The Politics of India since Independence,* 2nd ed. (Cambridge: Cambridge University Press, 1994).

16. Peter Hardy, *The Muslims of British India* (Cambridge: Cambridge University Press, 1972) and Khalid Bin Sayeed, *The Political System of Pakistan* (Lahore: Oxford University Press, 1967).

17. Ziba Moshaver, *Nuclear Weapons Proliferation in the Indian Subcontinent*, p. 101.

18. Sumit Ganguly, *The Origins of War in South Asia*, 2nd ed. (Boulder, Colo.: Westview Press, 1994).

19. For a discussion of the concept of the 'security dilemma' see John Herz, 'Idealist Internationalism and the Security Dilemma', *World Politics*, January 1950, no. 2.

20. Steven Weissman and Herbert Krosney, *The Islamic Bomb* (New York: Times Books, 1981).

21. Agha Shahi, as cited in Moshaver, *Nuclear Weapons in the Indian Subcontinent*, p. 130.

22. The US non-proliferation goals are spelled out in *The President's Report to Congress on Progress towards Regional Non-Proliferation in South Asia* (Washington, DC: US Government Printing Office, 1993), p. 2.

23. 'Senators Act to Ease Pakistan Sanctions', *New York Times*, May 24, 1995, p. A3.

24. The most sophisticated version of this debate can be found in Scott D. Sagan and Kenneth N. Waltz, *The Spread of Nuclear Weapons: A Debate* (New York: W.W. Norton, 1995).

25. On this point see Stephen P. Cohen, *The Pakistan Army* (Berkeley: University of California Press, 1984).

26. This phenomenon arose during the Cold War, when the central nuclear balance between the United States and the Soviet Union produced a degree of stability. Both sides, cognizant of the dangers of nuclear escalation, carefully avoided direct conflict. However, both the superpowers supported client states in the Third World and fought proxy wars. In effect, stability at one level produced instability at another. See Glenn Snyder, 'The Balance of Power and the Balance of Terror', in Paul Seabury, ed., *The Balance of Power* (San Francisco: Chandler, 1965)

27. See Sumit Ganguly, 'Avoiding War in Kashmir', *Foreign Affairs*, Winter 1990/91, and Sumit Ganguly, 'Indo-Pakistani Relations and the Stability/Instability Paradox', *Studies in Conflict and Terrorism*, October 1995.

28. On this point see Devin Hagerty, 'The Power of Suggestion: Opaque Proliferation, Existential Deterrence and the South Asian Nuclear Competition', *Security Studies*, 2, nos.3/4 (Spring/Summer 1993).

29. David Shambaugh, 'Growing Strong: China's Challenge to Asian Security', *Survival*, 36, no. 2 (Summer 1994), pp. 43 –59.

30. David Cortright and Amitabh Mattoo, eds, *India's Nuclear Choices* (Notre Dame: Notre Dame University Press, 1995).

14 Should India Sign the NPT/CTBT?[1]
Raju G.C. Thomas

1 INDIA'S NUCLEAR QUANDARY

First the NPT, and then the CTBT. While India had always opposed the Non-Proliferation Treaty since its inception in 1968, does it make sense for India to oppose the Comprehensive Test Ban Treaty finalized in 1996? India had always supported such a treaty ever since it was first considered in the 1950s and 1960s. Indeed, India was one of the earliest advocates of this Treaty back when Jawaharlal Nehru was its prime minister.

Like the widespread opposition to the NPT that spanned ideology and party affiliation, whether politician, bureaucrat, journalist, academic, or other profession, the opposition to the CTBT in 1996 was overwhelming. The Indian Foreign Minister, I.K. Gujral, stated that 'India remains committed to elimination of all nuclear weapons and bringing forth a genuine and comprehensive nuclear test ban treaty'.[2] Gujral demanded that the pact should 'outlaw not only nuclear weapons testing but also non-explosive techniques for refinement of nuclear weapons', a reference to the fact that the CTBT would outlaw all nuclear weapons testing but allow for simulated tests in the laboratory. This official Indian opposition to the CTBT was greeted in nearly all Indian circles of the attentive public as a 'principled stand'. A leading Indian news daily called the Indian position on the CTBT one of 'Splendid Isolation'.[3]

The Indian refusal to sign the CTBT brought about an even greater emotional response in Pakistan. During the summer of 1996, 15 opposition groups in Pakistan warned Prime Minister Benazir Bhutto's government that 'there should be no unilateral signature by Pakistan on the Comprehensive Test Ban Treaty and any rollback of the [Pakistani] nuclear programme would be unacceptable'.[4] Munawwar Hasan, the secretary-general of the right wing Jamaat-i-Islami Party declared that if Pakistan signed the CTBT, 'the people would come out on the streets to oppose it. ...We think that the nuclear issue is a life-and-death matter for Pakistan.'[5] Similar warnings had been issued earlier against the NPT by the leader of the Jamaat-i-Islami, Qazi Hussain Ahmed, who warned that any Pakistani leader who signed the NPT would be 'lynched'.[6]

India's opposition to the CTBT in 1996 rides on two considerations. First, India's idea of a CTBT was really a Comprehensive Nuclear Disarmament Treaty (a CNDT), or at least the first part of a two-stage process whereby nuclear testing would be banned followed by complete universal nuclear disarmament. A CTBT and CNDT was to be inextricably linked. The finalized CTBT in 1996 provides for no time table for the next stage, a CNDT. The NPT at least had Article VI which called for comprehensive nuclear disarmament even if Article VI was ignored by the nuclear 'haves' throughout the Cold War because they found it incovenient. Only towards the end of the Cold War did the Strategic Arms Limitation Talks become the Strategic Arms Reduction Talks. And it was only following the collapse of the Soviet Union and the near economic collapse of Russia, that the US was willing to push for considerable nuclear disarmament but short of comprehensive nuclear disarmament. Russia is now virtually subservient to the West because it is dependent on the West for economic loans, grants and investments. India can no longer play the Soviet/Russian card.

As far as India was concerned, the end of the Cold War had not changed its strategic environment and threat perceptions substantially. On the one hand, the Chinese nuclear threat remains. And on the other hand, there continues to exist three 'White' nuclear weapons states as part of the Western alliance to which in all likelihood a fourth one, Russia, may be added when its 'Partnership for Peace' merges into NATO. It may be recalled that following the Indian atomic test of 1974, President Zulfikar Ali Bhutto of Pakistan had reportedly said that there was a Christian bomb (US, Britain and France), a Marxist bomb (Soviet Union and China), a Jewish bomb (Israel's bombs-in-the-basement) and now a Hindu bomb (India), but no Muslim bomb. Likewise, India could possibly complain now that there were four White bombs, one Yellow or Beige bomb, but no Brown or Black bombs, an unfair and unacceptable situation. While China may continue to show some defiance against the policies of the West on occasion, the nuclear distribution indicated the continuing domination of the traditional White imperialists in an overwhelmingly non-White world.

Second, there is a simple explanation for India's strong opposition to the CTBT. If India were to sign the CTBT, it would amount to signing the NPT which India has hitherto opposed because it wishes to retain the nuclear weapons option. After all, India's opposition to the NPT was because of its discriminatory nature between 'haves' and 'have-nots', and the failure of the nuclear 'haves' to fulfil Article VI of the NPT calling for comprehensive nuclear disarmament. The willingness of the US to push the CTBT in 1996 was also presumed to arise from technological advancements which would allow it to conduct simulated nuclear tests in the laboratory thus rendering nuclear testing obsolete. The nuclear condition in the world had not changed substantially. The NPT's renewal in 1995 without any change illustrated the Indian perception that no real progress had been made regarding nuclear disarmament and the discriminatory nature of the nuclear non-proliferation regime. India's resistance continues to revolve around the unacceptability of the NPT. This chapter will, therefore, focus on the arguments that may be made for or against the NPT within and outside India, and the implications of this debate for the CTBT.

Background to the NPT Debate in India

The question of whether India was more secure within or outside the 1968 NPT took on particular significance at the beginning of 1989 when news reports in India alleged that Pakistan had acquired and stockpiled nuclear weapons or was about to acquire such weapons. Such Indian allegations were made periodically since the late 1970s and continue to be made some two decades later. But the problem had taken on greater urgency and credibility in 1989 since Indian reports of the Pakistani nuclear programme were also being derived from American sources.[7] Under the 1984 Pressler Amendment, the administration of President George Bush would have to discontinue its economic and military aid to Pakistan, unless it could certify that Pakistan was not making the bomb, a certification that would be difficult to issue based on the evidence available in 1989 with the US government.[8] Given the evidence, US military and economic aid to Pakistan was cut off in 1990.

Other Indian reports in 1989 claimed that China was arranging a nuclear test for Pakistan at its Lop Nor testing ground.[9] This speculation was based on the visit to China in November 1988 of Abdul Qadir Khan, Pakistan's chief nuclear scientist and head of the Kahuta nuclear enrichment plant. Pakistan and China had signed a nuclear cooperation agreement in 1986, and Indian news sources have claimed that China had assisted the Pakistani nuclear weapons programme at Kahuta by providing the designs of a tested fusion bomb. Not even the return of civilian democracy in 1988 under Prime Minister Benazir Bhutto served to alleviate these fears in India. Such allegations and fears continued into the mid 1990s.

Initial Indian suspicions and fears of Pakistan's motives had arisen from its earlier unsuccessful efforts in the 1970s to acquire from France waste fuel reprocessing capabilities to be located at Chasma under the leadership of Munir Khan of the Pakistan Atomic Energy Commission. Later, in the 1980s, Pakistan's successful acquisition of uranium enrichment capabilities located at Kahuta under the leadership of Abdul Qadir Khan – before it had set up a serious nuclear energy programme – raised serious doubts about Pakistan's ultimate nuclear intentions.[10] While such plants may be considered legitimate needs for acquiring control of the nuclear fuel cycle and self-sufficiency in nuclear energy, they also provide a country with weapons grade plutonium and uranium.

Perhaps Pakistan, and Dr. Abdul Qadir Khan in particular, may be deliberately feeding the Indian belief about its weapons capability in order to provoke India into taking the first step towards acquiring nuclear weapons so as to justify a Pakistani decision to go nuclear. On the other hand, Pakistan has pointed out repeatedly that India had already tested an atomic device in 1974 and had stockpiled weapons grade plutonium. Meanwhile, both sides continued to claim that they do not possess nuclear weapons but were merely pursuing a peaceful nuclear energy programme. Neither side believes the other.

There is, however, a fundamental difference in the propensity to go nuclear by India and Pakistan. In India, it has always been an 'energy-to-security' situation. India had rationalized and justified the need for nuclear power-generated electricity to meet shortfalls between rising industrial and consumer demands for electricity and total electricity output provided by coal-fired thermal power plants and hydroelectric plants. Accordingly it had planned a major build-up of nuclear power plants to provide about 10 per cent of electricity needs by the turn of the century. But this nuclear energy programme also gave India the technological ability to produce nuclear weapons from its waste fuel reprocessing facilities at what India calculates to be an affordable incremental cost over the nuclear energy programme. On the other hand, for Pakistan it has always been a 'security-to-energy' situation. In the 1970s, Pakistan first sought to buy a reprocessing plant from France to be located at Chasma and, when that failed, it managed to assemble a uranium enrichment plant at Kahuta. These objectives were not part of a planned nuclear energy programme which for the greater part was confined to 125 MW Karachi atomic power plant, but to generate plutonium or highly enriched uranium to build nuclear bombs. Subsequently, however, Pakistan has argued for nuclear energy to meeting rising electricity demands given its lack of coal resources and technical problems of siltation in harnessing the Indus River in order to generate hydroelectric power.

While India was always concerned about both the Chinese nuclear threat and the potential Pakistani nuclear threat from about the late 1960s onwards, the nature of threat perceptions before and after the Indian atomic test of 1974 were significantly different. Before 1974, India focused primarily on the Chinese nuclear threat and in determining whether it should respond to this threat, it had to assess the secondary consequences of a Pakistani nuclear response to an Indian nuclear weapons programme. After 1974, India has focused primarily on the clandestine Pakistani nuclear weapons programme and, in determining whether it should respond with nuclear weapons, had to assess the secondary nuclear threat consequences arising from a Chinese reaction. Perceptions of primary and secondary nuclear threats appear to have been reversed since. At one time, India could determine and dictate whether South Asia would become nuclearized by choosing to counter China's nuclear arms build-up with one of its own. Pakistan could choose to respond in due course of time while it developed its own capability. Ever since Pakistan acquired the capacity to build nuclear weapons, it is Pakistan that controls the decision whether South Asia would become nuclearized, while India can only respond.

Herein lies the problem. If successive Indian governments believe that Pakistan has acquired the bomb, they will find it difficult not to follow suit. Through such a cycle of fears and pre-emptive policy responses, the seeds of horizontal nuclear proliferation have been sown on the subcontinent. The relationship between India and Pakistan at present is probably best described as a case of 'Mutual Nuclear Brinksmanship' where each side is seeking or threatening to become a nuclear weapons power to preempt the other side's ability to obtain such capability but without actually carrying out that threat. The ability to sustain indefinitely such a precarious strategy of 'brinksmanship' would call for considerable political dexterity on both sides. More likely, with both sides believing that the other side has covertly stockpiled nuclear weapons – a situation of suspected mutual 'bombs in the basement' – they may be compelled eventually into an overt and fully-fledged nuclear arms race with all its attendant adverse consequences for the international non-proliferation regime.

US non-proliferation policy in South Asia has not succeeded except to contain an overt Indo-Pakistani nuclear arms race. In the late 1970s, President Carter had attempted to use the stick. During the 1980s, President Reagan had attempted to use the carrot. Neither approaches worked. Just before and during the Carter administration, a series of internal legislation was passed to stem the proliferation tide in South Asia. In 1976 and 1977 the Symington and Glenn amendments were passed to the Foreign Assistance Act which prohibited American economic and military aid to countries attempting to acquire reprocessing and enrichment capabilities for weapons purposes. Both amendments were essentially directed at Pakistan.[11] In 1978, Congress passed the Nuclear Non-Proliferation Act (NNPA) that called on the US government to withold cooperation on peaceful nuclear programmes with countries that would not allow the IAEA inspection of its nuclear facilities. This Act was expected to be enforced retroactively, the target clearly being the 30-year Indo-American agreement of 1963 that had assured the supply of enriched uranium to the two General Electric light-water nuclear power reactors set up at Tarapur near Bombay. In accordance with the NNPA, the supply of enriched uranium was witheld by by the Carter administration. India claimed that the US had violated an international agreement. The US claimed violation of the peaceful nuclear uses clause because American heavy water was allegedly used in the Canadian-supplied *Cirus* research reactor from where India had obtained the plutonium for the 1974 atomic test. Subsequently, to circumvent the NNPA and Congressional pressures, and to fulfil the contractual obligations arising from the 1963 agreement, the Carter administration allowed India to obtain the enriched uranium from France and later Germany.

The Reagan administration ignored the proliferation issue in order to maintain Pakistani cooperation and goodwill in the US policy of assisting the Afghan *mujahideen* in its war against Soviet occupation forces in Afghanistan. The reward for such Pakistani cooperation was large-scale economic and military aid to Pakistan, the third largest US aid to any country after Israel and Egypt, and a US policy of minimizing Pakistan's clandestine nuclear weapons programme. The Reagan policy succeeded on the Afghan front in bringing about the eventual defeat and withdrawal of Soviet forces from Afghanistan, but reduced to shambles the non-proliferation regime in South Asia. Whereas India ended its efforts to acquire nuclear weapons after its 1974 test, Pakistan accelerated its nuclear weapons programme leading to the present nuclear brinksman-ship. The 1984 Pressler Amendment, had failed to stop Pakistan's nuclear advanced, and in 1996 was revoked by the Brown Amendment.

A central question here is whether the nuclear dilemmas of South Asia may be resolved by an Indian decision to sign the NPT along with Pakistan. After all, Pakistan has declared on several occasions that it was prepared to sign the NPT, or establish South Asia as a nuclear-free zone, if India would accept the same terms or arrangement. India has constantly rejected such offers on the grounds that the nuclear prolifera-tion issue is a global problem that include the spread and growth of nuclear weapons among 'have-nots' and 'haves', and that the NPT and the nuclear-free zone proposals do not resolve the problem of a Chinese nuclear threat to India, a nuclear weapons power and rival of India that has not signed the NPT.

India's Nuclear Choices

The question of *whether India should become a nuclear weapons power* initially became a burning issue in response to the first Chinese atomic test in October 1964. That test was conducted just two years after the sudden Sino-Indian war of October–December 1962 when the Indian army was crushed by Chinese forces along their Himalayan frontiers. Thereafter, India participated in the negotiations that led up to the formulation of the 1968 Non-Proliferation Treaty but then refused to sign because of the discriminatory clauses between the nuclear 'haves' and 'have-nots'. Subsequently, a second question emerged as to *whether India should sign the NPT* along with several other states of the East, West and Third World blocs who have acceded to the Treaty at various times over the last 20 years. With the exception of the 1974 atomic test, the Government of India's policy has been not to build bombs in response to the first question, and not to sign the NPT in response to the second question in order to keep open its policy option on the first question.

The NPT, of course, is not the only international legal arrangement that could be adopted to curb proliferation in South Asia. In lieu of the NPT, a regional treaty could be reached that would establish South Asia as a nuclear weapons free zone, along the lines of the 1967 Treaty of Tlatelolco that has sought to make Latin America a nuclear weapons free zone. With the exception of Cuba who has refused to sign the Treaty until the United States vacates the Guantanamo naval base, all the states of Latin America and the five nuclear weapons powers have signed the Treaty. Such a regional alternative would serve an almost equal purpose as adherence to the NPT, and may be considered a significant step by India and Pakistan towards the global arrangement represented by the NPT. Opposition to a regional arrangement establishing South Asia as nuclear weapons free zone appears to be less intense than against the NPT but sufficient at present to make the prospects here seem just as hopeless. Such a zone without China does not resolve some of India's basic arguments against the NPT, nor does it resolve the problem of discrimination between nuclear 'haves' and 'have-nots'. For these reasons, arguments for or against the NPT will be assumed to cover a regional nuclear-free zone as well and proposed NPT substitutes so long as these are formal agreements that bar the acquisition of nuclear weapons by non-nuclear states.

In the present circumstances where Pakistan is on the brink of a nuclear weapons capability or may have already acquired it, there are then three basic options that India needs to consider. The first option would be the continuation of India's present policy of neither the bomb nor the NPT and involves resisting both the internal pro-bomb and external pro-NPT lobbies. The second option of going for the bomb would involve the future management by the Government of India of a three-way nuclear arms race between India and its traditional rivals, China and Pakistan. The third option of signing the NPT or an NPT substitute would call for a significant amount of political will-power on the part of the Indian government to reverse its present policy, and to accept a calculated risk that adherence to the NPT may not curb the covert stockpiling of nuclear weapons on the Pakistani side.

A similar set of choices appears to have arisen in 1996 with regards to the CTBT. Since adoption in the Committee on Disarmament in Geneva required unanimity, India first prevented the adoption of the CTBT within this 44-member Committee by voting against it. Then at the General Assembly, India, Bhutan and Libya were the only states who cast votes opposing the resolution on adopting the CTBT. Subsequently, Pakistan stated that it would not accept the Treaty unless India did. As in the case of the NPT, the three-part choice for India would be to proceed with nuclear testing, or sign the CTBT, or do neither. As in the case of the NPT, India's response was essentially to stick to its three 'No's' – no signing, no obstruction of the Treaty, no testing.

At least in the public debate in India, and with occasional exceptions, alternative policy choices do not appear to have been fully explored both within and outside parliament. (There may have been more extensive discussions that looked at the full range of possibilities within the Indian foreign and defence policy-making bureaucracies although little is known about their deliberations.) To begin with, over the years, there has grown a monolithic and unified resistance to the NPT as a worthless, if not a harmful, international treaty.[12] This negative attitude towards the NPT and the new resistance to the CTBT, tend to span the political spectrum from left to right: among the Congress and the Janata parties in its various split factions and political reincarnations; within the Janata Dal and the United Front coalition; and among the various socialist, communist and, especially Hindu, religious parties such as the old Jan Sangh and its successor, the Bharatiya Janata Party. If there is any support for the NPT or the CTBT, it may lie in a few pockets of intellectual institutions in some of the major cities of India.[13]

There is a more rigid polarization between those who advocate that India stay with the policy of strategic ambiguity by maintaining the nuclear weapons option, and those who advocate the bold step forward of becoming a nuclear weapons power. In India, the first group may be labelled the 'doves', and the second group, the 'hawks'. This may seem surprising to overseas observers who perceive the Government of India's resistance to the NPT and periodic threats to go nuclear as a hawkish posture. But in a situation where the pro-Treaty advocates are virtually invisible, all that the Indian government can do for the time being is resist the pressure from those who advocate the bomb. One leading Indian strategist, who has persistently advocated the bomb for India, declared at a conference in New Delhi in January 1989 that the Government of India was the greatest lobby against the bomb in India.[14] Others have contended that the Indian government is doing what it does best: inaction where bold action is needed, where bold means going nuclear, not signing the NPT. In fact, there appears to be little or no cross-over between the 'pro-bomb' and 'pro-option' lobbies in India, each perceiving the other's position to carry inconclusive merits.[15] There is no such thing as a pro-NPT lobby.

The positions appear to have crystallized on either side, each advocating the same persistent and perennial arguments under changing strategic circumstances over time. On the other hand, even those Indian strategic analysts who strongly disagree with the pro-bomb hawks prefer to distance themselves from the NPT either out of conviction that it is a seriously flawed Treaty, or because they feel that their credibility to argue against the bomb may be lost in a domestic political environment that is overwhelmingly hostile to the NPT. This attitude is reminiscent of 'the effectiveness trap' during the middle part of the Vietnam War when some US decision-makers who disagreed with the policy of military intervention and escalation chose to remain silent in the hope of proving more effective at a more opportune time in the future.[16] Thus the poor NPT, signed by virtually all the non-nuclear nations of the world, appears to have no support in India.

Nuclear Weapons and Regional Stability

My position here is that India should either become a nuclear weapons state and withstand the economic consequences of likely sanctions imposed by the Western powers and international agencies controlled by the US; or, India should sign the NPT (and CTBT). It should make this choice between the bomb and the Treaty and settle the issue. India's 'middle ground', viz., neither the bomb nor the Treaty, provides no security dividends. In advocating that one choice is a nuclear India and therefore also a nuclear Pakistan, I will argue first that this does not necessarily imply regional strategic instability although there may be severe economic costs arising from a three-way nuclear arms race with China and Pakistan and from likely economic sanctions imposed by the West.

In principle, the argument could be advanced that if a three-way strategic nuclear relationship among the United States, the Soviet Union and China could be maintained on a stable basis during the Cold War, then it should be possible to maintain a similar three-way stable relationship among China, India and Pakistan. China would occupy the same position as the United States in the global Cold War strategic triangle, India that of the Soviet Union, and Pakistan that of China. A situation of 'mutual assured destruction' would exist between China and India similar to that which existed between the United States and the Soviet Union; and one of strategic nuclear superiority between India and Pakistan similar to that between the Soviet Union and China. Any imbalance in the India – Pakistan relationship would be offset by the intrusion of China on the Pakistani side. This would be similar to America's closer relationship with China after Nixon's visit to Beijing in February 1972, a relationship that may have tacitly offset any threatened Soviet nuclear strike against China's nascent nuclear capabilities.

Although the traditional rules of deterrent relationships in the old Cold War may apply and exist in South Asia, the actual behaviour of the states may prove to be quite different. Perhaps four arguments may be advanced as to why the China–India–Pakistan nuclear relationship may be more unstable than the old Cold War US–USSR–China relationship. (I will argue here against all four arguments.) First, there is a difference in the emotional intensity of the relationship among the US, the the USSR and China, even at the height of the Cold War, compared to that between India and Pakistan. The argument may be advanced, for instance, that ideological differences do not generate as much fear and irrationality between two states as antagonism based on religion. Therefore, under conditions of acute crisis between India and Pakistan, there may be a greater temptation to launch pre-emptive attacks than between the United States and the Soviet Union during the Cold War.

However, Western fears of potential Indian and Pakistani irrationality or irresponsibility may be exaggerated or misconceived. Whereas Hindu–Muslim rioting and killing have been spontaneous, savage and endemic before and after partition, the decisionmakers in India and Pakistan have generally remained quite rational and responsible during crises. Indo-Pakistani wars have been essentially 'gentlemanly' wars compared to other wars in the Middle East, Central and Southeast Asia and Southeastern Europe. Civilian targets, or even targets where civilian casualties could occur, were never attacked; prisoners of war were treated humanely and returned after the cessation of hostilities. Nuclear responsibility between the two sides was demonstrated also in a formal treaty signed by India and Pakistan in 1991 not to attack each other's nuclear energy installations in case of war. This behaviour has been quite unlike the American war in Vietnam, the Soviet war in Afghanistan, and the allied assault on Iraq where large numbers of civilian casualties were inflicted in search and destroy missions or bombing raids on cities. The allied forces, for instance, also bombed Iraq's nuclear reactors twice during the Gulf War, which India and Pakistan refrained from doing during the 1971 war.

Second, the geographical proximity of the two countries would generate greater paranoia about a nuclear attack by the other side since there will be virtually no warning time. The proximity of the location of weapons of mass destruction in India and Pakistan – virtually in each other's backyards – may cause a certain amount of political apprehension and nervousness on either side increasing the probability of its use. Mutual rules of 'No First Use' may be introduced in principle, but may not work out in practice. This argument too may be countered. Geographical proximity and the inter-related nature of societies on either side may in themselves constitute a deterrent. An attack by India on Pakistan may cause radioactive fallout in India, and vice versa. Even if Pakistan were to attack distant targets in India with intermediate range ballistic missiles (which Pakistan does not possess at present), death and destruction would also be inflicted on millions of Indian Muslims whom Pakistan (at least in its original ideological conception at the time of its creation) is supposed to protect. After all, it was the Muslims of areas that are still part of India that were mainly responsible for creating Pakistan.

Third, the movement from a non-nuclear condition in South Asia to a nuclear condition will constitute a sudden and dramatic change so as to produce a great deal of uncertainty and paranoia. The virtual overnight transition from conventional to nuclear capabilities would imply that the antagonists have not had sufficient time to understand the nature of nuclear deterrent relationships – quite unlike the evolution of nuclear thought and doctrine among the nuclear powers during the Cold War. At least in the short run, and especially under conditions of crisis such as the one in Kashmir at present, a conventional war could quickly escalate to a nuclear war in South Asia. Again, an opposing argument may be advanced to counter this belief. A sudden change does not necessarily imply that Indian and Pakistani decision-makers have not learnt the nature and operation of deterrent relationships from the experience of the Cold War nuclear antagonists. Indeed, both India and Pakistan have been on the brink of nuclear weapons capabilities for a sufficient length of time so as to have already taken into account the probable consequences of nuclearization in South Asia.

Fourth, inter-state wars have been more frequent in South Asia than in any other region except the Middle East. Unlike the existing five nuclear powers, India and Pakistan have fought three major wars with each other since their independence in 1947, and have been on the brink of a fourth war over Kashmir since 1990. Therefore, it may be argued, that nuclearization of the subcontinent is more likely to lead to nuclear wars. But this argument may be countered as well by pointing out that no wars between India and Pakistan have occurred since 1971.

Arguments claiming that a nuclear South Asia may be stable would suggest that even conventional wars may be avoided by India and Pakistan in the future for fear that such wars may escalate to nuclear levels.[17] Such behaviour would duplicate that of the nuclear powers during the Cold War when no direct conventional wars occurred. However, wars of proxy, as in Vietnam and Afghanistan are likely to take place in South Asia as well. Such a war has been taking place in Kashmir where Indian forces are engaged in combatting Pakistani-armed Kashmiri guerrillas. On the other hand, the often predicted fourth Indo-Pakistani war has not yet taken place over Kashmir, and this may be attributed perhaps to the fact that India and Pakistan are on the brink of a nuclear weapons capability, or may already possess such capability, thus deterring both sides from taking any conventional military risks as well.

All of this is not to suggest that a nuclear South Asia may be preferable to a non-nuclear one in the 1990s. Although the China–India–Pakistan strategic nuclear triangle may display the same stable characterstics of the old US–USSR–China Cold War strategic nuclear triangle, the inevitable failure to confine proliferation to South Asia would undermine the stability of this region as well. The spread of the bomb to the Middle East and Central Asia followed by an overt Israeli nuclear arms build-up could complicate both Indian and Pakistani nuclear deterrent strategies. An Iranian bomb with appropriate delivery systems (and for the time being we will assume that Iraq is no longer a nuclear weapons threat) would make India less secure. Similarly, if the development of a Pakistani bomb is perceived as an 'Islamic bomb', then this would not only face east towards India, but west towards Israel thus possibly inviting an Israeli pre-emptive attack. There were indications in the late 1980s that India may provide launching facilities to Israel for such an attack, causing much apprehension in Pakistan. In October 1991, Vice President of Iran, Ayatollah Mohajerani, stated that 'Some time ago they [Israel and India] wanted to use a Sri Lankan air base to destroy the nuclear centres in Pakistan. This implies that Israel has already felt the threats, and that it wants to have the upper hand in its dealings with the Muslim states'.[18]

No doubt, weapons in other Muslim countries may not be directed at India and, in any case, India with its IRBM capability could deter potential threats from this direction together with those stemming from Pakistan and China. But maintaining such a multiple deterrent posture could prove to be both tenuous and costly for India. In general, efforts to establish deterrent relationships among several states involved with different or cross-cutting conflict issues can prove to be unstable and dangerous for South Asia and the world.

2   THE NPT DEBATE

In order to demonstrate my present position – that it is in India's interests to sign this flawed and discriminatory NPT if it is not prepared to risk becoming a nuclear weapons state – I will attempt to make a strong case without prejudice for each of the policy options under consideration.

Policy 1: No Treaty, No Weapons, No Testing

The Indian policy of maintaining the nuclear weapons option was perceived to be a middle strategic ground between the extremes of inaction and action. The formal renunciation of nuclear weapons by signing the NPT was considered unacceptable since the potential threat from a nuclear China during times of crisis on the subcontinent may call for a change of policy in the future.[19] Following the 1962 Sino-Indian war and the Chinese atomic test in 1964, arguments for countering the growth of Chinese nuclear weapons capability were strong. China's ultimatum to India during the 1965 Indo-Pakistani War strengthened the claims of the pro-bomb lobby in India at the time, mainly led by the right-wing pro-Hindu party, the Jan Sangh. But as the Chinese threat receded in the late 1960s and the dual hostility of both the Soviet Union and the United States was perceived against China, the need for embarking on a nuclear weapons programme was considered unnecessary. At that stage an Indian nuclear weapons programme may have aggravated the Chinese threat without providing India with a credible nuclear deterrent. While China was capable of hitting the major Indian cities from New Delhi to Calcutta with its aircraft taking off from Tibetan bases, India was a long way off from possessing a delivery system capable of reaching China's major cities of Beijing and Shanghai or its industrial bases in southeast China.

Although the bomb was rejected, there were also serious problems seen in the text of the NPT. Thus, while India took part in the negotiations that drew up the draft of the NPT, it subsequently refused to sign the Treaty.[20] From the Indian standpoint, the Treaty was not only discriminatory, but formalized the two existing groups of nuclear 'haves' and 'have-nots' indefinitely. Article III calling for supervision and inspection of all nuclear and ancillary facilities by the International Atomic Energy Agency was seen further as a violation of the sovereignties of nations, a condition that the existing nuclear powers until recently were unwilling to accept. [The mutual on-site inspection and verification clauses agreed to in the 1988 INF treaty by the superpowers was the first departure from this attitude.] Article VI that called on the five nuclear powers to negotiate 'complete [nuclear] disarmament' in 'good faith' appeared to be a dead letter since the nuclear arms race continued unabated during the Cold War as newer and more sophisticated weapons of mass destruction were periodically introduced. Meanwhile, there was little progress being made in reaching an agreement for a Comprehensive Test Ban Treaty during this time.

India had argued repeatedly that the growth and complexity of newer forms of nuclear weapons among the 'haves' (vertical proliferation) pose as much, if not greater danger to international security as the potential spread of nuclear weapons among the 'have-nots' (horizontal proliferation.) Yet there was insufficient attention being paid to this problem. And surely, if more and complex nuclear weapons are perceived to be the only antidote to perceptions of nuclear threats by the nuclear states, then the same argument must apply to the non-nuclear weapons states who may face nuclear threats from across their borders in the future. Such was the case of the nuclear threat to India from China, a state that had not signed the NPT or the Limited Test Ban Treaty of 1963, and with whom India fought an unexpected war in 1962. The best that India could do under the circumstances was to refrain voluntarily from acquiring nuclear weapons, but also keep its option to acquire them if the situation became intolerable in the future.

The problem of proliferation, according to India, may be resolved only globally. India could not give up its nuclear weapons option unless China got rid of its nuclear stockpile. However, during the intensity of the Cold War, China would not give up its nuclear weapons unless the Soviet Union did; and the Soviet Union would not do so unless the three Western nuclear powers did. Thus, nuclear proliferation did not begin with the Indian atomic test of 1974, but much earlier when the Soviet Union responded with its first atomic test in 1949 to counter American atomic weapons capability which, in turn, had begun with the first US test at Alamo Gordo in 1945.[21] Stemming the forward advance of the nuclear proliferation chain – real or potential – called for unravelling the chain backwards all the way to the Soviet Union and the United States. The problem called for comprehensive nuclear disarmament.

The NPT was an unsatisfactory document for other legal and technical reasons. Articles I and II, on the one hand, and IV and V, on the other, are perceived to be in contradiction of each other. According to the first two articles, nuclear weapons states should not provide assistance or encouragement to non-nuclear weapons states to acquire nuclear weapons, while the non-nuclear weapons states should make no efforts, domestic or international, to acquire such weapons. On the other hand, the fourth and fifth articles encourage the sharing and transfer of peaceful nuclear technology between the 'haves' and 'have-nots', including the 'peaceful applications of nuclear explosions'. A basic problem with the aims of these provisions is the difficulty of distinguishing nuclear programmes that are intended for civilian purposes from those which are intended for, or which may be diverted to, military purposes.

Such problems are further compounded by Article X which allows any signatory to the NPT to withdraw giving only three months' notice if it perceives that 'extraordinary events... have jeopardized the supreme interests' of that country. Theoretically, a signatory state may embark upon an IAEA-supervised nuclear energy programme, allowing it to acquire enrichment and reprocessing facilities more readily, and subsequently may withdraw on the grounds of 'extraordinary' changes in its strategic environment. Indeed, North Korea sought to do this in 1993 but was prevented from doing so by the US. With such inherent flaws and contradictions within the NPT, it seemed to make little difference whether a state remained within or outside the treaty.

Hence, the Government of India followed a policy of strategic ambiguity by maintaining its nuclear weapons option. Under this policy, India would not make nuclear weapons, but would constantly threaten to do so and, indeed, carried out the threat once in 1974. Such a posture carried a dual purpose, first, by serving notice to the nuclear powers that it needed adequate security guarantees against regional nuclear threats to itself; and, second, by pressuring the nuclear powers into eliminating their stockpiles thereby reducing the dangers of a global nuclear holocaust in which non-nuclear states would also be engulfed.

Policy 2: A Nuclear India

Arguments that India should acquire nuclear weapons have been made periodically since the Chinese atomic test of October 1964. These pressures intensified during the East Pakistani revolt against West Pakistan and the ensuing civil war that began in March 1971. That crisis ended with the Indo-

Pakistani war of December 1971 and the creation of the new state of Bangladesh. During this prolonged crisis that kept India and Pakistan on the brink of war, efforts by President Richard Nixon and Secretary of State Henry Kissinger, to seek the normalization of US relations with China, suddenly raised doubts about the credibility of external nuclear guarantees against China. The signing of the Indo-Soviet Treaty of Peace and Friendship in August 1971 may be interpreted as the immediate Indian reaction to these global realignments among the major powers.[22] The Treaty was intended to paralyse Chinese threats to intervene in the looming Indo-Pakistani conflict by formalizing Indo-Soviet ties, thereby increasing the risk of of Soviet military intervention against China on behalf of India.

However, in spite of the Treaty, doubts remained about the long-term effects of the new Sino-American relationship on India's nuclear security. The nuclear insurance provided by the hostility of both superpowers against China before 1971 now seemed to have been reduced to a more dubious Soviet nuclear guarantee alone. Because the United States and the Soviet Union were perceived to neutralize each other with their retaliatory strike capabilities, potential Chinese nuclear threats in the future were feared to become more credible.

The intrusion of the American nuclear-powered carrier, the *USS Enterprise,* into the Bay of Bengal in a show of force against India during the Indo-Pakistani war of December 1971, further strengthened the case for nuclear weapons. An Indian decision was therefore made in 1972 to go for the bomb, and the 1974 atomic test may be seen as the delayed response by Prime Minister Indira Gandhi to the evolving global realignments. Note also, however, the decision to detonate in May 1974 was probably (and primarily) directed at a domestic Indian audience to shore up the Prime Minister's sagging prestige.

Pakistani military defeat and its dismemberment produced a similar decision in 1972 on the part of Prime Minister, Zulfikar Ali Bhutto, to acquire nuclear weapons. This policy was accelerated following the Indian atomic test in 1974. While the Western outcry against India's 'peaceful nuclear explosion' immediately reduced the Indian stockpile from one to zero and appeared to have ended the prospect of an Indian nuclear weapons programme, Pakistan proceeded headlong into various avenues for acquiring a nuclear weapons capability. It first sought to acquire a waste-fuel reprocessing plant from France to generate plutonium but was frustrated by pressures from President Carter to prevent the sale; it then sought more successfully to put together a uranium enrichment plant through the clandestine transfer of various sensitive machines and parts from Western Europe, the United States and Canada.[23] Other Indian reports in the late 1970s and early 1980s indicated that the Pakistani nuclear bomb was being developed with uranium supplies from Niger and with indirect Libyan and Saudi financing.[24] These developments climaxed in 1988 and 1989 when Indian reports claimed that Pakistan had produced a few bombs based on the uranium enrichment process or, at least, had acquired the capability to assemble the bomb at short notice.

Herein lies the case for the bomb in India.[25] While it was one thing to accept the risk of a Chinese nuclear threat all these years without an Indian counter-response, it was quite another to expect India to ignore a nuclear China as well as a Pakistan with 'bombs-in-the-basement', Israeli-style. With further allegations that India's two traditional adversaries had colluded in the design and development of the Pakistani nuclear weapons programme, the situation appeared intolerable.

Considerations of international and domestic prestige may also have played a part in earlier arguments for the bomb in India, although they were not as important as it was in the case of Brazil. If they were, then in combination with security arguments, India would have gone nuclear long ago. Much of the arguments for the bomb at this level arises from anger at the United States for its treatment of India on par with Pakistan instead of, and more appropriately, with China. While the United States has shown a great deal of sensitivity about providing arms to Taiwan in order not to alienate China, India has constantly alleged that various US administrations had attempted to maintain a military balance between India and Pakistan, a nation once a quarter of India's size, and now only an eighth. Compared to China, India has never received much respect from the West although in population, size and economic potential, India and China are comparable.

To be sure, going nuclear would provoke a similar decision in Pakistan. But as with the present trend in the conventional military balance, India's superior economic resources and technological manpower would simply overwhelm Pakistan's nuclear capability and match that of China whose nuclear technology is considered to be less sophisticated than that of India. On the other hand, the nuclearization of the subcontinent, at least in the perception of some advocates of the bomb, would bring greater international attention that would benefit all the states of the region.[26]

Policy 3: Adherence to the Treaty

Despite the arguments that may be advanced in support of maintaining the nuclear weapons option or becoming a nuclear weapons power, on balance, India is best served by adhering to the NPT (and therefore also the CTBT). There are a variety of arguments for signing the NPT. First, unlike going for the bomb which may lock India into a permanent three-way nuclear arms race with Pakistan and China, signing the NPT is a reversible step. If the policy proves to be unsatisfactory (i.e. it does not halt and reverse a covert Pakistani nuclear weapons programme), India could withdraw from the NPT in the future as permitted under Article X. But the value and effectiveness of the NPT ought to be tested before the apparent irreversible step forward (i.e. going nuclear) is taken. Such a step backward would not constitute a radical change from the earlier policy since India had not embarked on a nuclear weapons programme. On the other hand, in the present circumstances of an ambiguous Pakistani nuclear posture, India does not obtain the advantages of being a nuclear weapons power nor of being a signatory to the NPT.

With the exception of the 1974 atomic test, India has behaved as though it had already signed the NPT. No doubt, India has not allowed inspection of its indigenously-built nuclear power plants by the International Atomic Energy Agency. There were occasional allegations that weapons-grade plutonium derived from the Kalapakam Atomic Power Plant at Madras was being stored ready for weapons use if necessary.[27] Unlike the Canadian-assisted Rajasthan Atomic Power Plants and the American-supplied Tarapur Atomic Power Plants, KAPP is not under IAEA safeguards. And there is the exception in India's behaviour when the Canadian-supplied Cirus research reactor was alleged to have been used to obtain the plutonium for the 1974 atomic test. For the rest, India has voluntarily adhered to most of the terms of the NPT especially those pertaining to the construction of bombs and transfer of sensitive technology to other potential proliferators (e.g. the Indian rejection of Libya's request in 1974). If India plans to go on doing this, then it might as well sign the NPT and avoid the periodic pressures and harrassment from some members of the international community, especially the Western powers.

Second, signing the NPT and relying on a large conventional military force may be a more cost-effective way of dealing with the Sino-Pakistani threat than going for the bomb. The argument advanced by General De Gaulle at one time that the acquisition of nuclear weapons by France would reduce the overall military cost by allowing for heavy reductions in conventional forces, has not become apparent among any of the existing nuclear powers including France. No doubt, the relative cost of strategic nuclear forces are much less than the maintenance of large-scale conventional forces, but the former has not usually displaced the latter. Again, it is possible to argue that the size and cost of conventional forces might have been even larger if it were not for nuclear forces. However, the lesson of China is particularly significant for India where its conventional forces remained the same or even increased as China continued to build up its nuclear forces. Nuclear forces have been rarely treated as a substitute for conventional forces, but more often as a supplement.

One basic criteria in India for the allocation of resources to the armed services and their military programmes is the degree to which their claims tend to be labour-intensive or capital-intensive.[28] Thus, the Indian Army has always been able to muster the bulk of the resource allocations for defence because it emphasizes the employment of manpower on a larger scale, and relatively smaller and cheaper weapons systems produced in bulk, than the Indian Air Force or the Indian Navy. In a country with an abundance of cheap labour, it makes more economic sense to emphasize army programmes even if this may sometimes distort the essential military strategy that needs to be adopted to deal with the external strategic environment. Thus, in 1995, the Army employed 1 million armed personnel, the Air Force, 110,000 and the Navy, 55,000.[29] Moreover, for every uniformed member of personnel employed by the Army, two more civilians have to be employed for administration, accounts, provisions, stores and other work, compared to one for the other two services. Air Force and Navy allocations were more heavily utilized for the procurement of sophisticated and costly weapons systems.

In this context, a nuclear weapons and delivery systems programme in India would be highly capital-intensive even if the total cost of such a programme is relatively smaller than the total cost of the conventional military programme. And as suggested above, a nuclear weapons programme in India is not likely to reduce the size and cost of conventional forces.[30] Going nuclear would be an additional cost, a cost that may constantly accelerate as both Pakistan and China respond in the familiar action-reaction arms spiralling process. Eventually this could lead to less Indian security at a much higher price.

Third, offering to sign the NPT would be a means of testing Pakistan's sincerity. Pakistan has repeatedly indicated its willingness to sign the Treaty or establish South Asia as a nuclear-weapons-free zone if India reciprocated. Pakistani diplomatic strategy has been to blame India for increasing the threat of proliferation in South Asia. However, Pakistan may have stronger reasons for not signing the NPT since nuclear weapons may be perceived as the ultimate option to negate the growing Indian conventional military superiority on the subcontinent. By offering to sign the NPT, India would shift the burden of demonstrating good faith on to Pakistan. Failure on the part of Pakistan to reciprocate would give India a form of diplomatic victory since the blame, unlike in the past, would fall on Pakistan.

Much of the Indian fears of a covert Pakistani nuclear weapons programme may be deliberately fed by Islamabad in order to provoke India into jumping the gun towards the bomb, thus generating the preferred Pakistani position of a nuclear military balance on the subcontinent based on mutual retaliatory strike capabilities. Under these conditions, India's conventional military superiority will have been rendered less relevant, while (say) 10 Pakistani bombs would sufficiently deter 100 Indian bombs as well as its much greater conventional military capabilities from being used. In contrast, the mutual signing of the NPT by India and Pakistan, as one State Department official informed me in 1989, would leave India as the 'winner of the conventional arms race' in South Asia and the dominant power in the region.

Fourth, signing the Treaty will allow India to obtain peaceful technological know-how more readily, both for its nuclear energy as well as space programmes. There would be a greater willingness on the part of international suppliers to provide spares, parts and new technologies for the Indian nuclear energy programme without the constant tensions and delays that India had to cope with in the past. Japan, South Korea and Taiwan are all signatories to the NPT and they have relatively larger nuclear energy programmes than India. Membership of the NPT has given them more easy and ready access to the best and most advanced peaceful technologies available in the field. On the other hand, maintaining the nuclear option merely gives India the worst of all possible technological worlds, military and civilian.

Ultimately the question boils down to whether a nuclear India facing both a nuclear China and nuclear Pakistan is the preferred security postion to a non-nuclear India having to live in the shadow of a nuclear China with whom India's relations have been improving in recent years. If India could live with the Chinese nuclear threat for more than 30 years under worse circumstances, then it may be worth continuing with this risk indefinitely especially if the potential Pakistani nuclear threat could be checkmated through mutual adherence to the NPT.

CONCLUSIONS AND PROSPECTS

Each of the three policy options discussed above are viable and minimally reasonable for a country such as India to pursue, but each option also carries potential risks. In the case of maintaining the option (the continuation of the present Indian policy), there is some danger that the existing posture of mutual nuclear brinkmanship between India and Pakistan could irretrievably slide into a covert and unstable nuclear arms race that may tempt one or both sides to pre-empt the other under conditions of paranoia. Nuclear secrecy and uncertainty are unlikely to contribute to political confidence on the subcontinent, a problem that is already evident in the case of the clandestine Pakistani nuclear weapons programme.

It seems unlikely also that the Indo-Pakistani agreement of December 1988 (formalized in a treaty in 1991) not to attack each other's nuclear installations will prevent such attacks on such targets if war did occur, or lessen the probability of a nuclear war if nuclear weapons have been stockpiled covertly by both sides. This may appear to be a worst-case scenario but surely contingency plans based on such fears and eventualities must exist in both countries. After all, nuclear installations on either side – the source of much fear and mistrust – are the most logical targets for pre-emptive strikes under conditions of paranoia and subsequent war as already demonstrated by the Israeli attack on Iraq's Osirak nuclear reactor in 1980. Chasma and Kahuta on the Pakistani side, and Kota and Trombay on the Indian side may not be spared in an intense crisis leading to armed hostilities.

In the case of signing the NPT (along with Pakistan), the Chinese nuclear threat, as well as Pakistani bombs that may have already been stockpiled secretly (as some Indian observers claim), will remain unaccounted. The risk from China has been tested for more than 30 years under far more adverse security conditions than those which prevail today and have proven relatively safe. Indeed, if India is threatened in the future by China or any other nuclear power, that would be sufficient reason for India to withdraw from the NPT, and subsequently to go for the bomb. Although such a post crisis decision will not resolve the immediate problem arising from that particular nuclear threat, neither will the strategy of merely maintaining the nuclear weapons option. As regards the second risk, Pakistan has denied that it has produced and stockpiled nuclear weapons, and for the time being this declaration will have to be accepted until further evidence surfaces. Besides, Pakistan may have similar fears of India as well.

In determining which of the three policy options optimizes India's security needs, there are certain pitfalls that India should avoid. The first pitfall is that of attempting to teach the vertical proliferators a lesson. India has repeatedly questioned the moral right of the nuclear 'haves' to lay down the restrictive guidelines for the nuclear 'have-nots'. And, indeed, it makes no sense for the real nuclear proliferators to ask those states on the brink of nuclear weapons capability, but who have voluntarily shown restraint, not to proliferate. Part of India's resistance to the NPT arises from this attitude of indignation. However, the relevant question for India is the more simple one: 'Under what policy option is India most secure?' Threatening to imitate the five nuclear states when no other state has chosen to do so will not maximize India's security, double standards or no double standards.

The second pitfall may be found in making demands that essentially defeat those very demands. India's demand that the proliferation issue should, and can only, be resolved globally, is a self-defeating objective. If India's ultimate objective is to eliminate all nuclear weapons, then however remote the success of this objective at present, the demand makes India's objective even more difficult to achieve. With several nations on the brink of nuclear weapons capability as well as with the motivation to acquire that capability, and with the existing nuclear powers nowhere near the goal of complete nuclear disarmament, the actual result of the Indian demand would be to push even more nations into nuclear arms races and to eliminate the prospect of global nuclear disarmament for all time to come. Horizontal proliferation will not resolve vertical proliferation.

The other perplexing aspect of India's demand for the global resolution of the proliferation issue is that in the past India has usually sought regional solutions to the problems of the subcontinent. Then why the exception in this particular case when a regional solution within the sub-continent has a greater chance of success than a global solution? Indeed, achieving a regional solution to the proliferation issue on the subcontinent through the NPT will increase the pressure on Israel to do the same. That, in turn, will put greater pressure on the nuclear 'haves' to carry out in good faith Article VI of the NPT calling for global nuclear disarmament.

The third pitfall is one of political and bureaucratic inertia under changing strategic conditions. There have been several landmark events that mark a significant change in India's nuclear strategic environment: the 1964 Chinese atomic test; the introduction of the NPT in 1968; the seeds of Sino-American rapprochement in 1971–72; Pakistan's nuclear responses to its defeat in the 1971 Indo-Pakistani War and the Indian atomic test of 1974; the first major reports of clandestine Pakistani acqui-sitions of uranium enrichment capabilities in 1980–81; reports in 1989 that the US government could not certify that Pakistan had not already acquired a nuclear weapons capability; and the end of the Cold War and substantial reductions in US and Russian nuclear arsenals. Throughout these changes the nuclear weapons option has been maintained by the Government of India.

The fourth pitfall is the tendency to treat the NPT as an issue unrelated or separate from India's broader strategic nuclear interests, and then to

resist the NPT for its own sake.[31] For India, questions on whether to sign
the NPT or to go for the bomb are seemingly posed separately. The fact
that signing the NPT may partially resolve India's nuclear dilemma in
South Asia does not appear to be taken seriously. India's resistance to the
NPT makes even less sense when one considers that nearly all the other
non-nuclear states have signed the NPT. While their strategic concerns are
probably less critical than that of India, their overriding concern and goal
is that global security cannot possibly be enhanced if more states become
nuclear weapons powers. Thus, while regional security goals may provide
compelling reasons for India to become a nuclear weapons power, global
security concerns provide compelling reasons for India to sign the NPT.

The reason that India has not exercised its nuclear weapons option is
because it has calculated that a nuclear arms build-up in a three-way
nuclear arms race with Pakistan and China may provide India with less
security at a higher economic price. It is also aware that it may face severe
economic sanctions from the Western industrialized states making the economic cost of going nuclear even higher and perhaps quite crippling. The
nuclear option would appear not to be an option at all. Not having exercised the option after more than 30 years of sitting on the fence is evidence
regarding the meaningless nature of India's nuclear option. Then why not
sign the NPT and use the threat of withdrawal allowed under Article X of
the NPT as a diplomatic instrument? Since the real choice is between
going nuclear and signing the NPT, it would appear that the NPT may be
on balance – from the security, economic and political standpoints – the
better choice.

Given all the weaknesses of the NPT, it may be the best possible document under the worst of circumstances. No doubt, serious problems with
the NPT will remain. So long as a technological 'fix' between nuclear
energy programmes and nuclear weapons development cannot be found,
the contradiction between clauses that attempt to prevent nuclear weapons
transfer, and those which attempt to encourage peaceful nuclear cooperation among the 'haves' and 'have-nots', will continue to pose problems.
India will need to live with such weaknesses in the NPT.

If nothing else, India should open the domestic debate once again on its
nuclear policy. When doing this, India should remember that in the 21st
century the international prestige of nations is going to be determined by
the economic prosperity race and not by the nuclear arms race. It is going
to be countries such as Japan, South Korea and Taiwan that will be recognized as national success stories, and not a nuclear Pakistan, Israel or
Libya. Under such circumstances, it may be in India's interest to get the

nuclear issue behind it by signing the NPT, and to concentrate on the more important business of rapid economic advancement.

NOTES

1. This chapter is reproduced with some adaptation and updating from my chapter of the title in Joseph F. Pilat and Robert E. Pendley, eds, *Beyond 1995: The Future of the NPT Regime* (New York: Plenum Press, 1990), pp. 133–50. In reading through that chapter again, I felt that my views had not changed much since I first wrote it in 1989.
2. Bill Tarrant, 'India Resists Pressure Over Nuclear Test Ban Pact', *Reuter's News Service*, July 24, 1996.
3. See Sanjeev Miglani, 'India's Nuclear Stance Spells Economic Doom', *Asia Times* (New Delhi), July 11, 1996.
4. *Reuter's News Agency*, July 24, 1996.
5. *Ibid.*
6. See report by Kesava Menon, 'Pro-Bomb Lobby Align in Pakistan', *The Hindu* (Madras), January 13, 1992.
7. Two earlier studies in India of Pakistan's efforts to acquire the bomb may be found in P.K.S. Namboodiri, 'Pakistan's Nuclear Future', in K. Subrahmanyam, ed., *Nuclear Myths and Realities: India's Dilemma* (New Delhi: ABC Publishing House, 1981), pp. 139–94; and in P.B. Sinha and R. R. Sinha, *Nuclear Pakistan: Atomic Threat to South Asia* (New Delhi: Vision Books, 1980).
8. *Hindustan Times*, January 29, 1989; and *Times of India*, January 29, 1989. See also Leonard S. Spector, *The Undeclared Bomb*, (Cambridge, Mass., Ballinger Publishing Company, 1988), pp. 128–43.
9. *Times of India*, January 13, 1989.
10. Two detailed studies have been undertaken by an Indian analyst demonstrating Pakistan's path toward nuclear weapons. See S. R. Sreedhar, *Pakistan's Bomb: A Documentary Study* (New Delhi: ABC Publishers, 1987); and his *Dr. A.Q.Khan on Pakistan Bomb* (New Delhi: ABC Publishers, 1987).
11. A detailed description and evaluation of US non-proliferation policy in India and Pakistan may be found in Spector, *The Undeclared Bomb*, pp. 80–148.
12. See T.T.Poulose, 'Nuclear Proliferation and the Second NPT Review Conference', in K. Subrahmanyam, ed., *Nuclear Myths and Realities*, pp. 21–37.
13. Arguments against the bomb may be seen in a study by the Centre for Policy Research put together by one of the leading opponents of the bomb in India, Bhabani Sen Gupta, *Nuclear Weapons: Policy Options for India* (New Delhi: Sage Publications, 1983).
14. K. Subrahmanyam made this remark in response to a comment by me deploring the lack of diverse positions on the issue at a conference on Indo-American relations at the India International Centre in New Delhi, January 31, 1989.
15. See S.P.Seth, 'The Indo-Pak Nuclear Duet and the United States', *Asian Survey*, vol. 28, no. 7, July 1988, 719–22; and Shrikant Paranjpe, *US*

Nonproliferation Policy in Action: South Asia (New York: Envoy Press, 1987), pp. 89–90.

16. This and other problems with Vietnam decision-making was brought out by James C. Thompson, Jr., 'How Could Vietnam Happen? An Autopsy', *Atlantic Monthly*, April 1968, 47–53.

17. Air Commodore Aliuddin writes: 'The relationship between India and Pakistan remains so volatile that there has been virtually no reduction in traditional antagonism and little progress towards a comprehensive peace. No balance in conventional forces, no war pacts or alliances have to date afforded a modicum of security to either of the two. The introduction of a nuclear deterrence on both sides of the equation appears to be the only hope for restraint, stability and enduring peace. The reservation that a nuclear weapons status might tempt India or Pakistan to opt for a pre-emptive strike on the other's installations is valid only as long as one of the two remains nonnuclear.' Air Commodore Aliuddin, 'Pakistan's Nuclear Dilemma', *Seaford House Papers, 1990*, London: Royal College of Defence Studies, p. 10.

18. See *The Nation*, October 24, 1991. See also *Pakistan Times Overseas Weekly*, November 22, 1991.

19. For a more detailed discussion of this policy, see Raju G.C. Thomas, *Indian Security Policy* (Princeton, NJ: Princeton University Press, 1986), pp. 28–30, and 44–50.

20. This observation was made by Ratakonda Dayakar, the Press Counsellor of the Embassy of India, Washington DC, in a letter to the editor entitled, 'India Believes in Global Path to NonProliferation', *New York Times*, February 8, 1989.

21. See Raju G.C. Thomas, 'India's Nuclear Programs and the Nuclear Non-Proliferation Treaty', *Wisconsin International Law Journal*, 1986, 111–17.

22. See Raju G.C. Thomas, *Indian Security Policy*, p. 45.

23. Reported in the *Statesman*, June 23 and 24, 1984. See also earlier reports in the *New York Times*, April 28 and 30, 1981.

24. See *Hindustan Times*, December 21, 1980.

25. The strongest case for an Indian bomb may be found in the collection of articles in K. Subrahmanyam, ed., *India and the Nuclear Challenge* (New Delhi: Lancer International, 1987). Here K. Subrahmanyam Jasjit Singh, P.K.S. Namboodiri, C. Raja Mohan, R. R. Subramaniam, and Rikhi Jaipal point out the several problems underlying threats from the nuclear superpowers, China and Pakistan, failures of perceptions and deterrence theories, fears of nuclear terrorism, and the failings of nuclear-free zones and verification proposals, as justifications for India to abandon the non-proliferation regime and to embark on a nuclear weapons programme. Subrahmanyam concludes by arguing that the only way for India to avoid going nuclear would be the total elimination of nuclear weapons everywhere.

26. See footnote 25 above.

27. See Leonard Spector, *The Undeclared Bomb*, pp. 84–93.

28. See Raju G.C. Thomas, 'The Armed Services and the Indian Defense Budget', *Asian Survey*, vol. 20, no. 3, March 1980, 280–97.

29. From *The Military Balance, 1996–97* (London: Oxford University Press for the International Institute for Strategic Studies, 1996), pp. 159–61.

30. K. Subrahmanyam has argued, in the particular case of Pakistan, that going nuclear would please the generals on one of their pet objectives and enable Prime Minister Benazir Bhutto to cut down on Pakistan's conventional military spending. See K. Subrahmanyam, 'Dialogue With Benazir-I', *Hindustan Times*, January 12, 1989.

31. This point was made by Ravi Shastri, a doctoral candidate at Jawaharlal Nehru University, during my presentation on the NPT at the Institute for Defence Studies and Analyses in New Delhi, January 12, 1989. Although the observation was from only one member of the audience, it has since occurred to me that the point indeed reflected the Indian approach to the NPT and nuclear weapons issues.

15 Iran's Nuclear Quest: Motivations and Consequences

Haleh Vaziri

Since the 1991 defeat of Iraq in Operation Desert Storm, members of the international community, led by the Bush and Clinton administrations, have turned their attention to the threat of nuclear proliferation in the Middle East and elsewhere in the Developing World. The discovery of a relatively advanced Iraqi nuclear weapons programme has fuelled speculation and concern about the existence of similar covert programmes in other so-called outlaw states. In the Middle East, Washington has worried most about Iran's conventional military build-up and development of a nuclear infrastructure.

Persistent American charges that Iran's clerical leadership seeks to violate the non-proliferation regime[1] should inspire observers to raise the following questions about the Islamic Republic's nuclear development policy: (1) What is the status of Iran's nuclear weapons capability? (2) What are Iran's motivations for acquiring this capability? (3) If Iran attains this capability, what declaratory posture will the clerics adopt? In other words, will Iranian officials choose an opaque posture similar to that of Israel during the late 1970s and early 1980s; or will they declare publicly their possession of this capability, as India did in 1974?

To answer these questions, I shall review the Shah's nuclear legacy to the Islamic Republic, examine the clerics' motivations for acquiring a nuclear weapons capability, and venture predictions about their declaratory posture. My analysis suggests that the clerics' military build-up and especially their development of a nuclear infrastructure are motivated by the perceived need to deter threats from their two principal enemies, Iraq and the United States, and by their aspiration to project Iran's hegemony over the Middle East. Furthermore, the clerics' choice of declaratory posture – should they acquire a nuclear weapons capability – is likely to reflect ideological divisions within their ranks over how to achieve these defensive and offensive objectives.

1 THE SHAH'S NUCLEAR LEGACY

When revolutionaries toppled the Shah Mohammad Reza Pahlavi in 1979, he inadvertently bequeathed to his clerical successors the most ambitious nuclear development programme in the Middle East, other than Israel's.

During much of his rule, the Shah professed to be an opponent of proliferation who, nevertheless, understood the value of nuclear energy in a country where oil and natural gas are plentiful but finite resources. In 1957, Tehran and Washington agreed to cooperate on the peaceful uses of nuclear energy and, in 1970, Iran signed the Nuclear Non-Proliferation Treaty (NPT). In 1974, the Shah supported the idea that the Middle East should be a zone free of weapons of mass destruction.

That same year, the Shah established the Atomic Energy Organization of Iran (AEOI) with the aim of executing a grand plan to construct 23 nuclear power plants within two decades. Although Iran's nuclear infrastructure consisted of only one US-supplied reactor at the Tehran Nuclear Research Centre, within months of the AEOI's establishment, the Shah began negotiating with France, West Germany, and the United States for the purchase of more than a dozen nuclear power plants. Moreover, the AEOI negotiated extendable, ten-year fuel contracts with Washington, Bonn and Paris in 1974, 1976 and 1977, respectively – thus ensuring long-term supplies of low-enriched uranium fuel. And in 1975, Iran purchased a 10 per cent share in an enrichment plant built in France by the EURODIF consortium of Belgium, France, Italy and Spain. By 1978, two West German-designed power plants were well under construction in Bushehr, on Iran's south-western Persian Gulf coastline, and site preparation work had begun for two more French-supplied plants in Darkhovin, near the southern tip of the border with Iraq.

Besides developing this overt nuclear infrastructure, evidence suggests that the Shah was pursuing a covert nuclear weapons programme. Although a signatory of the NPT, the Shah had negative and positive incentives to proliferate. He feared the nuclearization of the Arab–Israeli conflict and the Indo-Pakistani rivalry. While the monarch worried most that his archrival Ba'athist Iraq may attain the atomic bomb, India's explosion of a 'peaceful nuclear device' in 1974 was also disconcerting. Furthermore, a secret nuclear weapons programme was consistent with the king's ambitions; he sought to transform Iran into an industrial power and to project Iran's hegemony[2] over the Persian Gulf and Indian Ocean regions. As the Shah explained to Egyptian journalist Mohamed Hasanein Heikal, 'I tell you quite frankly, that Iran will have to acquire atomic bombs if some upstart in the region gets them'.[3]

Apparently, the Shah pursued four clandestine avenues of research and development: First, during 1976–77, the Tehran Nuclear Research Centre negotiated with American scientist Dr. Jeffrey Eerkens, who had designed a laser device to enrich uranium. Iran purchased four of the devices with the approval of the US Department of Energy.[4] Eerkens lied to the Department, claiming that the lasers would be used for plasma research. Department of Energy officials, for their part, must have either believed Eerkens' lie, ignored critics of the Iranian purchase, or remained sceptical that the lasers could actually enrich uranium.[5] The lasers were shipped to Iran in October 1978, just months before the Shah's downfall.

Second, the monarch negotiated a secret contract to buy $700 million worth of natural uranium concentrate, known as 'yellowcake', from South Africa. This material probably would have been sent to France, West Germany, or the United States for enrichment to turn it into fuel for Iran's nuclear power plants. Washington knew about the Iranian deal with South Africa which was documented in a confidential 1976 US Department of State cable.[6]

Third, the Tehran Nuclear Research Center was quietly working on reprocessing technology to obtain plutonium as an alternative to highly enriched uranium. Fourth, shortly before his downfall, the Shah had organized a secret research group to work on the nuclear weapons themselves.[7] It is unclear whether members of the scientific community knew of each other's research. Given the Shah's penchant for compartmentalizing information, it is quite possible that he had scientists working unaware of each other's projects.

When the Islamic revolution erupted in 1978–79, the Shah had not only built the most extensive, overt nuclear infrastructure in the Middle East, but had also pursued substantial, covert efforts to attain atomic weapons with at least the tacit knowledge of the United States.[8] Although Tehran was a decade or more away from producing nuclear weapons, the revolution and subsequent establishment of the virulently anti-Western Islamic Republic created a dilemma for the United States and its European allies. Washington, Paris, and Bonn would have preferred to remove their nuclear assets from Iran but could not have done so without signalling their lack of confidence in the Shah.

2   THE CLERICS' NUCLEAR DEVELOPMENT POLICY: LESSONS LEARNED OVER TIME

The clerics inherited the Shah's overt and covert nuclear development programmes. Yet, during their 15-year rule, they have been elusive or made contradictory statements on the subject of nuclear weapons. Consequently, I will sometimes infer the clerics' evolving attitudes towards these weapons by examining their broader defence and foreign policies. Despite their initial disdain for modern military technology, the clerics, much like the Shah, have acquired negative and positive incentives to proliferate. More than any other event, the Iran–Iraq war convinced the clergy that modern military technology – and perhaps even the atomic bomb – would most effectively deter threats to the Islamic Republic's political and territorial integrity. Besides seeking to alleviate the intense security dilemma posed by Ba'athist Iraq, the clerics have probably come to realize that possession of a nuclear weapons capability will enhance their efforts to project Iran's hegemony over the Middle East. While the Shah tried to assert Iran's influence over the Persian Gulf and Indian Ocean regions in the name of Persian nationalism with Washington's approval, the clerics have sought to export the Islamic revolution to other Middle Eastern state-society complexes and, thus, to vindicate their ideology, which I have called 'Islamic universalism'.[9] Significantly, the Reagan, Bush and Clinton administrations have opposed the Islamic Republic's hegemonic aspirations – another motivating factor in the clerics' quest to develop a nuclear infrastructure.

For the sake of simplicity, I shall divide the Islamic Republic's evolving policy toward the acquisition of a nuclear infrastructure into three phases: (1) the anti-modernization phase, February 1979–September 1980; (2) the learning-the-hard-way phase, 22 September 1980–1984/1985; and (3) the active pursuit phase, 1984/1985 – the present.

Arguably, the ideology of Islamic universalism has informed the clerics' defence and foreign policies and, thus, their attitudes towards nuclear weapons. While a comprehensive analysis of the formulation and subtleties of Islamic universalism is beyond the scope of this discussion of Iran's nuclear development policy,[10] a summary of the ideology's five core tenets is instructive: (1) Islam offers prescriptions for the believer's personal and political life that transcend spatio-temporal boundaries; (2) The clerics, or *'ulema* [those of religious learning], have the responsibility and right to implement the *Shari'a* [divinely revealed law] and create the just government of God on earth; (3) Muslims must shirk national and sectarian divisions to unite around Iran's leadership in the struggle against imperialism; (4) Iran must export the Islamic revolution which is a relevant political model for the Muslim community and for the rest of the Developing World; (5) The Islamic Republic must liberate Iranians and the rest of the earth's oppressed from economic and political dependence on the great powers; the clerics have summed up this last tenet with the slogan 'Neither East, nor West, only the Islamic Republic!' [*'Na sharq, na gharb, faqat jumhuri-ye islami!'*]

The last three of these tenets have been most relevant to the formulation and implementation of Iran's foreign policy. Yet Islamic universalism is not an irrational impulse which has driven the clerics' behaviour. Rather, this ideology has reflected a process of dialogue between the clerics themselves and with their domestic constituents. As such, Islamic universalism is more than a prism through which the clerics' view the world. This ideology has been integral to the clerics' definition and pursuit of policy goals since their rise to power.[11]

Ayatollah Khomeini's return from exile to Tehran on February 1, 1979 ushered in a brief but intense *anti-modernization* phase in Iran's domestic and foreign policies. The clerics rejected the Shah's plans to finance the rapid modernization of the civilian and military infrastructures with Iran's oil revenues. In fact, they reduced oil exports, allowed much of the American military hardware purchased by the Shah to fall into disrepair, purged the armed forces of suspected opponents and did not impede the flight of many scientists who had worked on Iran's nuclear development projects. As the clergy focused on the task of Islamizing Iran's political and socio-economic institutions and norms during the 'Cultural Revolution' of Spring 1980, the nascent nuclear infrastructure constructed under the Shah languished. Work on the Bushehr nuclear reactors and the Darkhovin reactor site ground to a halt in 1979.[12]

However, some evidence suggests that even during the anti-modernization phase, the clerics examined the possibility of acquiring a nuclear weapons capability. A March 1980 internal report of the US Defense Intelligence Agency cites a source in Iran who surmised that the revolutionary government was planning to use reactors smaller than those at Bushehr because of its interest in attaining nuclear weapons.[13] Yet Iran apparently never pursued the smaller reactor option.

In May 1979, Ayatollah Mohammad Beheshti, one of Khomeini's closest advisers, met with Dr. Fereidun Fesharaki – an energy adviser to the Shah who had led a group of specialists in preparing a proposal for the clandestine development of nuclear weapons. Beheshti explained to Fesharaki that he had a 'duty' to build nuclear weapons for the Islamic Republic because '[o]ur civilization is in danger and we have to have it'.[14] When Fesharaki responded that developing nuclear weapons would be costly, Beheshti was not dissuaded.[15] The Ayatollah was assassinated in June 1980.

Although some Iranian leaders may have tentatively explored the nuclear weapons option, anti-modernization attitudes persisted among the clerics at least until Iraq initiated hostilities against the Islamic Republic on 22 September 1980. Iraq's armed forces launched massive air strikes on Iran's southwestern ports and oil refineries and six mechanized divisions invaded the province of Khuzistan in a *blitzkrieg* of rapid and deep advances.[16] The initial trauma of Iraq's attack and subsequent brutality of combat led the clerics *to learn the hard way* that modern military technology and especially weapons of mass destruction can make a decisive difference in war.

The Islamic Republic responded to the Iraqi invasion with alacrity. Blending nationalist and religious themes, the clerics mobilized Iranians for hostilities that included trench warfare, hand-to-hand combat, and extensive civilian casualties. Unlike the Iraqi Ba'ath, which purchased over half of its military hardware from France and the Soviet Union, the clerics lacked a major reliable arms supplier.[17] Consequently, the clerics transformed the necessity of international isolation – largely a result of the American hostage crisis (4 November 1979–20 January 1981) – into the ideological virtue of self-sufficiency. Exalting the power of faith and the cult of martyrdom, the clerics often sent lightly armed youths to confront Iraqi hardware.

Just a week after the Iraqi invasion, Ayatollah Khomeini proclaimed:

> ...when war breaks out – even an imposed war [*jang-e tahmili*, a reference to Iraq's aggression] – it brings one out of the feeling of fatigue and slackness...Man's potential which should never lie dormant, will manifest itself...when a war breaks out and a situation of epic proportions has emerged, when the nights are blacked out and the days are lit up, when shelling takes place...man reveals his inner capacity, which is active and moving.[18]

Khomeini went on to recall the Prophet Muhammad's courage, imploring Iranians to remain steadfast during wartime:

> The difference between us and them [the Iraqi Ba'ath] is that our motivation is Islam. Those who from the early days...have served Islam and...showed self-sacrifice are recorded in history. The Holy Prophet faced more hardships than we have...Nevertheless he resisted and had to resist; and the Iranian nation will resist and has to resist.[19]

To their credit, the Islamic Republic's regular armed forces and Revolutionary Guardsmen managed to evict Iraqi troops from Iranian soil and to turn the tide of battle during Spring–Summer 1982. This hard-won success seemed to vindicate the clerics' belief that Iranians could overcome Iraq's superior manpower-to-hardware ratio by embracing faith and self-sacrifice. Khomeini summarized this belief in a March 1982 speech, proclaiming: 'Victory is not achieved by swords, it can only be achieved by blood. Victory is not achieved by large populations, it is achieved by strength of faith'.[20]

However, while Khomeini extolled the military's revolutionary virtues, the Islamic Republic made the mistake of taking the war into Iraq. As the Iranians became bogged down in the marshes of southern Iraq, the Ba'ath escalated the hostilities horizontally and vertically. In so doing, the Ba'ath showed no compunction about violating the international laws of war conduct. After 1983–84, Iraq waged air strikes against commercial shipping travelling to and from Iran, used chemical weapons against Iranian forces (and Iraqi Kurds suspected of pro-Iranian sympathies) and launched anti-ballistic missiles against Iran's cities.[21] Vigorous Iranian protests about Iraq's conduct of the war provoked little response from the United Nations and other international organizations. Eventually, the Islamic Republic retaliated in kind for attacks on shipping as well as the use of chemical weapons and anti-ballistic missiles.[22]

Equally ominous from the Islamic Republic's perspective was the existence of Iraq's nuclear development programme, revealed to the world when the Israeli Air Force bombed the Osiraq reactor on 7 June 1981. While the clerics could not publicly condone an attack by the 'Zionist entity' against another Muslim country, they must have privately breathed a sigh of relief that their archenemy's nascent nuclear weapons capability had been destroyed.[23]

The first four or five years of the Iran–Iraq War shocked the clerics into realizing the value of modern military technology. The use of such technology – and perhaps even a nuclear weapons capability – would have deterred Iraq's initial aggression against the Islamic Republic and resort to violations of the international laws of war conduct. Confrontations between the Iranian and American militaries during the reflagging of Kuwaiti oil tankers reinforced this lesson. During 1987–88, Iranian and US forces engaged each other four times with the result that most of the Islamic Republic's small navy was destroyed.[24] From the clerics' perspective, the Reagan administration not only had opposed their hegemonic aspirations but also had allied with the Iraqi Ba'ath in the effort to defeat Iran.[25] Had the Islamic Republic possessed a nuclear weapons capability, the United States may have thought twice about interjecting its navy into the Persian Gulf and about engaging the Iranians.

In October 1988, shortly after the ceasefire with Iraq, commander-in-chief of Iran's armed forces Ali Akbar Hashemi Rafsanjani acknowledged the value of weapons of mass destruction. Addressing a group of

Revolutionary Guardsmen, Rafsanjani declared that their ethos of self-sacrifice, while praiseworthy, would not suffice to deter and defend against attacks by the Islamic Republic's enemies:

> With regard to chemical, bacteriological, and radiological weapons training, it was made very clear during the [Iran–Iraq] war that these weapons are very decisive. It was also made clear that the moral teachings of the world are not very effective when war reaches a serious stage and the world does not respect its own resolutions and closes its eyes to the violations and all the aggressions which are committed in the battle field.
>
> We should fully equip ourselves both in the offensive and defensive use of chemical, bacteriological, and radiological weapons. From now on, you should make use of this opportunity and perform this task.
>
> ...if we are to rely on the IRGC [Iranian Revolutionary Guard Corp] as an armed force, if the regime is to survive to God, the IRGC must not think that when it is attacked it can fight with Molotov cocktails. An armed force must be so prepared that others will not dare to attack. It is the guardian of borders and territory.[26]

In 1984, four years before Rafsanjani and other Iranian officials would publicly admit the value of modern military technology, the Islamic Republic shifted toward a policy of *actively pursuing* a nuclear infrastructure. While this infrastructure would enable the clerics to produce nuclear energy – thus, alleviating chronic electricity shortages throughout the country – it could also become the technological foundation for the eventual production of nuclear weapons. In fact, the clerics wanted to restart work on the Bushehr plants, but West Germany would not resume construction until hostilities with Iraq had ceased. In March 1987, Iranian officials sought to negotiate with a consortium of West German, Spanish, and Argentinian companies in the hope of resuming work on the Bushehr project; during the fall of that year, the Islamic Republic did preparatory work on the site. Yet, more than a year after the Iran–Iraq ceasefire of 20 August, 1988, work had not begun on the Bushehr plants which Iraq had bombed repeatedly during the hostilities. Iran's participation in the EURODIF enrichment consortium as well as its fuel supply relationship with the United States, France, and Germany have remained unresolved since the Islamic revolution.[27]

In light of Western reluctance to deal with the clerics, they have pursued other paths to the development of a nuclear infrastructure, stressing South–South cooperation as consistent with their revolutionary motto 'Neither East, nor West!' In 1984, the Islamic Republic opened a new nuclear research centre in Isfahan with possible Chinese assistance, demonstrating its commitment to continued nuclear research even during a costly war of attrition. In 1987, Tehran signed an agreement with Pakistan for cooperation in the nuclear field which included the training of 39 Iranian scientists at Pakistani installations. That same year, Iran signed a $5.5 million agreement with Argentina for the supply of uranium enriched to 20 per cent and the training of Iranian scientists at an Argentinian nuclear research centre.[28] During 1988–89, the clerics also reportedly obtained significant quantities of yellowcake from South Africa, probably for enrichment in Iran or Pakistan.[29]

The Islamic Republic has accelerated its development of a nuclear infrastructure since the Persian Gulf crisis of 1990–91. Iraq's invasion of Kuwait on August 2, 1990 and the US-led coalition response proved to the clerics that President Saddam Hussein and the Ba'ath would zealously pursue their regional ambitions despite seemingly intolerable costs, and that the United States would use its overwhelming military superiority to prevent any local actor from dominating the Persian Gulf region.[30]

Since 1990 the Islamic Republic has consolidated relationships with China and Russia in the area of nuclear development. That year, Tehran signed a ten-year agreement for scientific cooperation with China and President Rafsanjani met with an official from the Chinese Council of Science and Technology which supervises that country's nuclear programme. The clerics' purchase of an electromagnetic isotope separator, or calutron, from China has alarmed the United States and other states worried about Iran's nuclear ambitions. The discovery of Iraq's calutron-based uranium enrichment facilities at Tarmiya has aggravated concerns about Iranian intentions.

Yet it is doubtful that the Islamic Republic will use the calutron method of uranium enrichment in the short to medium term. Iran lacks the scientific and technical know-how as well as the electrical power necessary to pursue this method.[31] Moreover, the Chinese-supplied calutron is 'desk-top sized' and thus only useful for medical and research purposes.[32] Nevertheless, it is plausible that the clerics could eventually use the small calutron to develop larger machines as the Iraqi Ba'ath had done.[33]

In 1992, Tehran and Beijing signed a 'preliminary agreement' for the sale of nuclear reactors and other related technologies, but disagreements over the design and site of the reactors have delayed the deal. Despite these disagreements and the Clinton administration's objections, China has not abandoned cooperation with the Islamic Republic in the area of nuclear development. Responding to Washington's concerns that the Islamic Republic seeks to attain an atomic weapons capability, Chinese officials have insisted that the Islamic Republic has consistently abided by the terms of the NPT and has passed inspections by the International Atomic Energy Agency (IAEA).[34]

Russia has also defied Washington by helping the clerics to develop Iran's nuclear infrastructure. Since the Soviet Union's break-up during 1990–91, the clerics courted Russian nuclear scientists to work in Iran. In 1992, Tehran and Moscow negotiated a 'framework agreement' on the peaceful uses of nuclear energy.[35] In light of Germany's refusal to complete the Bushehr project, Russian technicians – some 200, according to Reza Amrollahi, the head of the Atomic Energy Organization – have helped the Iranians to finish one of two power plants.[36] Moscow has also been negotiating the $800 million sale of a nuclear reactor and related technologies to the clerics but has denied plans to sell them a gas centrifuge, which would be useful in enriching uranium to weapons grade.[37]

Like China, Russia has rebuffed the Clinton administration's protests about the clerics' nuclear ambitions, noting Iran's compliance with the NPT and clean record with IAEA inspectors.[38] Moreover, Russian officials have claimed that they would not sell nuclear technology to the clerics if they had the intention and technological base to build atomic weapons. As Russia's Ambassador to Tehran Sergei Tretyakov explained:

>...Iran's military capability is of no less concern to Russia than it is to the United States – because we are much closer to Iran...We are convinced that Iran has no ambitions in the nuclear field. You know, when someone wants to develop a nuclear bomb, they must have the political will and the technological base. The Iranians don't have such aspirations – but even if they had, I think it would take them 50 years.[39]

Even as the Clinton administration and members of Congress have threatened to reconsider US economic aid to Russia, Moscow has continued its dealings with the clerics.[40]

While repudiating the Clinton administration's charges that the Islamic Republic has nuclear ambitions, Iranian officials have maintained the Islamic Republic's right as an NPT signatory to develop its nuclear infrastructure for peaceful use.[41] As President Rafsanjani stated during his April 1995 visit to New Delhi, 'We know that the Americans will exert their pressure. But Iran is determined to have the construction of the nuclear power reactor for peaceful purposes.'[42]

The clerics have interpreted China's and Russia's disagreement with the United States over the transfer of nuclear technology as part of the ongoing struggle between the *mostazafin*, or earth's oppressed peoples, and the world's leading imperialist. Remarks by the Secretary of the Supreme National Council Hassan Ruhani epitomized this point of view:

> So what is the United States trying to do? A country in the Third World, because it is independent, because it does not surrender to the United States, because of its rightful stances, and because of certain empty allegations and the suspicions that are raised against it...They [the Americans] are trying to deprive this country [Iran] of a modern form of technology which it wants to use for peaceful purposes.
>
> What the United States is doing is illegal and illogical...They are trying impose their wish. I believe the issue is one of honour for the Chinese and the Russians...if they surrender to the United States, they will lose face internationally and their own people will think they have suffered a great defeat.
>
> ...the days when the United States used to say something to another country and it would accept what the United States said unconditionally are, more or less, over.
>
> I don't believe the Chinese will surrender. The Russians too, although their country is not as stable as it could be, I don't think they will sacrifice their political honour for the sake of the United States.[43]

Arguably, the clerics' appeal to 'honour' has resonated in Beijing and Moscow, where officials appreciate American economic assistance but are anxious to assert their independence from the United States.

In short, despite the clerics' initial anti-modernization attitudes, 15 years after their rise to power they seem quite determined to acquire a nuclear infrastructure, insisting that it will be used solely for the peaceful production of energy. Their determination in the face of growing, American-led, international pressure suggests that they are more than aware that a nuclear infrastructure, once achieved, may be modified for the production of atomic weapons. The clerics' shift in attitudes toward nuclear technology has resulted from a painful learning process. In light of the Islamic Republic's costly war of attrition with Iraq and Washington's vehement opposition to Iran's hegemonic aspirations, the clerics probably wish to keep open the option of building nuclear weapons when they do finally achieve the necessary technological base. From the Iranian leadership's perspective, possession of a nuclear weapons capability may be the only way to deter local or extra-regional threats against the Islamic Republic. Of equal importance, possession of this capability would enhance the Islamic Republic's efforts to assert regional hegemony.

3   THE CLERICS' DECLARATORY POSTURE: PREDICTIONS VENTURED

Without access to classified documentation, it is difficult to know exactly how far away the clerics are from securing a nuclear weapons capability. Although the Iranian leadership expressed reservations about loopholes within the NPT and the existence of an international double standard on the issue of proliferation,[44] the Islamic Republic did agree to the Treaty's extension in April 1995.

Given their decision to continue legal participation in the non-proliferation regime, it is also difficult to predict what declaratory posture the clerics will adopt should they acquire a nuclear weapons capability. Nevertheless, I shall predict that the clerics' choice of declaratory posture will reflect divisions within their ranks over the implications of Islamic universalism for the formulation and implementation of defence and foreign policy.

A brief discussion of the decision-making process and, specifically, of factionalism in Iran is the necessary empirical foundation for my predictions. Since Ayatollah Khomeini's death in 1989, the Islamic Republic's decision-making process has changed substantially. As the linchpin of this process, Khomeini adopted a deliberative and sometimes distant approach to policy making, encouraging officials to debate the issues in order that the proper solution to a problem would emerge. Khomeini was the final arbiter of all disagreements. Foreign policy debates have generally pitted two relatively fluid factions against each other – the pragmatists and the *maktabis*. While agreeing on the core tenets of Islamic universalism, these factions have diverged over the methods by which to export the Iranian revolution and the extent to which Iran should confront the great powers, particularly the United States.

The pragmatists – incorrectly known as the 'moderates' in the West – have included Rafsanjani and Foreign Minister Velayati and much of his staff, particularly Iran's former and current UN Ambassadors Mohammad Jaafar Mahallati and Kamal Kharrazi. Seeking to maximize Iran's limited economic resources, this faction has sought to deter threats by Iran's arch-enemy, Ba'athist Iraq; worked to improve ties with the Gulf monarchies while assisting Muslim militant movements in the Middle East where chances for successfully exporting the revolution are better; cultivated commercial ties with Eastern and Western Europe; and left open the possibility of normalizing relations with Washington under the right conditions.

The *maktabis* – which may be translated as those who are 'doctrinaire' – have included former Interior Minister Ali Akbar Mohtashemi, the late Ahmad Khomeini, former Speaker of the Parliament Mehdi Karrubi and the current Speaker Nateq Nouri, as well as the Islamic Republic's Supreme Guide Ali Akbar Khamene'i. This faction has understood the export of revolution to the rest of the Muslim world as inextricably linked to the defence of the Islamic Republic's political and territorial integrity. Moreover, the *maktabis* have preferred economic and military cooperation with the former East Bloc over ties with the West and rejected the possibility of restoring relations with the United States.

Because Ayatollah Khomeini sided at times with the pragmatists and at times with the *maktabis*, the Islamic Republic's behaviour appeared erratic to the rest of the world. Yet Khomeini accomplished his goals of maintaining a balance of power between these factions and preserving the clergy's supremacy inside Iran. Since the Ayatollah's death, élite factionalism has intensified; neither President Rafsanjani nor Supreme Guide Khamene'i has the charisma or religious stature necessary to mediate ideological disagreements over defence and foreign policy. Consequently, the Islamic Republic sometimes speaks to the world with more than voice.[45]

Arguably, factionalism will affect the clerics' choice of declaratory posture in the event that Iran attains a nuclear weapons capability. The pragmatists would be most likely to adopt an opaque posture. Although total opacity may not be feasible given advances in satellite technology, this posture would keep the Islamic Republic's enemies and friends guessing. As such, adopting this posture would not only deter enemies from threatening the Islamic Republic's political and territorial integrity, but would also enhance its hegemonic aspirations. Furthermore, the pragmatists would adopt this posture to avoid intimidating the Gulf Cooperation Council states outright, to avert an Israeli air strike on Iran's nuclear reactors and to minimize conflict with Washington over the issue of proliferation. While President Rafsanjani's credibility has waned particularly on the inter-related issues of socio-economic reconstruction and improved ties with the West, the pragmatists have maintained control, albeit tenuously, over defence policy. Should this be the case when Iran achieves a nuclear weapons capability, the Islamic Republic would adopt a relatively opaque declaratory posture.

After Iran was compelled to accept a ceasefire in its war with Iraq on 20 August, 1988, the *maktabis* lost control over foreign and defence policy. The pragmatists and much of the Iranian public blamed the *maktabis* for the prolongation of a futile war of attrition and for Iran's status as a global pariah. However, as Rafsanjani's credibility has waned, the *maktabis* have tried to reassert themselves under the leadership of Ayatollah Khamene'i, who succeeded Khomeini as the Islamic Republic's Supreme Guide in 1989. Should the *maktabis* be in control of defence policy when Iran attains a nuclear weapons capability, they would probably favour a transparent declaratory posture.

The *maktabis* would be less likely than the pragmatists to worry about provoking an Israeli air strike and offending American sensibilities over the issue of proliferation. In fact, they may relish irritating Washington and depicting the 'zionist entity', itself a possessor of nuclear weapons, as the aggressor against a once long-standing signatory of the NPT. The faction would declare the Islamic Republic's achievement of a nuclear weapons capability in order to reap domestic and international prestige. In the domestic arena, the *maktabis* seek to restore their reputation particularly among their constituency – the peasantry, small merchants of the bazaars, urban slum-dwellers and members of the lower middle class, who made the greatest economic and human sacrifices during the war with Iraq. Of equal importance, declaring the achievement of a nuclear weapons capability would compel the international community to take seriously the Islamic Republic's claim to protect the world's downtrodden masses, be they Lebanon's Shi'as, Palestinians living under Israeli occupation, or Bosnian Muslims.

In sum, the clerics' motivations to attain a nuclear weapons capability are external in nature – namely, the security dilemma posed by the Iraqi Ba'ath, and the Islamic Republic's hegemonic aspirations as opposed by the United States. Yet the clerics' choice of declaratory posture – like other key defence and foreign policy decisions – will be largely a function of the domestic political process which has become more unruly since Ayatollah Khomeini's death.

4   IRAN AS A PIVOTAL CASE FOR THE NON-PROLIFERATION REGIME

The Islamic Republic's quest for a nuclear infrastructure should be instructive to those decision makers and scholars seeking to preserve the integrity and vigour of the non-proliferation regime. Tehran's shifting attitudes towards military technology and particularly nuclear weapons suggests that states are tempted to proliferate, first and foremost, because they feel threatened. The clerics have sought to balance against the Iraqi Ba'ath's threats and capabilities with their recent conventional build-up and acquisition of nuclear technology. The fact that the international community did not unequivocally condemn Iraq's 1980 invasion of Iran nor its subsequent violations of the laws of war conduct taught the clerics a rather sobering lesson about the potential deterrent value of weapons of mass destruction in a self-help system.

The Islamic Republic's acquisition of nuclear technology also signals that the clerics will not abandon their aspirations to project regional hegemony in the face of American-led opposition. The reflagging of Kuwaiti tankers in 1987–88 and Operations Desert Shield/Storm in 1990–91 convinced the clerics that the United States will not allow a local power – whether Iran or Iraq – to dominate the Persian Gulf region. Despite the Clinton administration's accusation that the clerics' nuclear ambitions threaten the region, Tehran has reaffirmed its right as a signatory of the NPT to acquire nuclear technology for peaceful usage and continues to denounce '[d]estructive and anti-human nuclear weapons [which] are against the culture, ideology, and political viewpoint of this honorable system [the Islamic Republic].'[46]

In fact, it is most unlikely that states aspiring to project regional hegemony – such as Iran in the Middle East, Algeria in North Africa, Argentina or Brazil in South America, or North Korea in Asia – will forfeit their right to acquire nuclear technology, whether for peaceful or military purposes, even in the face of intense international disapprobation. Confronting the United States over the issue of nuclear technology may even enhance such a state's regional and domestic prestige. Thus, the NPT's extension in April 1995 may pose a barrier to states that wish to keep open the option of acquiring a nuclear weapons capability. Yet this barrier is not insurmountable, nor will it diminish the motivation of the Islamic Republic and other states living in a dangerous neighbourhood where the race for the acquisition of conventional and nuclear weapons technology has been underway for more than a decade.

NOTES

1. For examples of official and unofficial American charges, see Testimony of Rear Admiral Thomas A. Brooks (Director, Office of Naval Intelligence) before the Subcommittee on Seapower, Strategic, and Critical Materials of the Committee on Armed Service, US House of Representatives, February 22, 1989; George L. Church, 'Who Else Will Have the Bomb?', *Time*, December 16, 1991, 47–8 – claims that Ayatollah Khomeini personally authorized the renewal of the nuclear weapons programme started under the Shah; Lynn E. Davis, Under Secretary for Arms Control and International Security, 'Non-proliferation Priorities for 1995', *US Department of State Dispatch*, Vol.6, No.11 (issued, February 28, 1995), 192–3; Thomas W. Lippman, 'For Christopher, Iran is Public Enemy No. 1', *The Washington*

Post, May 8, 1995, A4; David Segal 'Atomic Ayatollahs', *The Washington Post*, April 12, 1987, D1-D2; Kenneth R. Timmerman, 'Iran's Nuclear Menace,' *The New Republic*, April 24, 1995, 17–19; and Ray Wilkinson, 'Springtime in Teheran', *Newsweek*, April 27, 1992, 38 – cites unnamed sources in Tehran.

2. As I use the term, 'hegemony' refers to the condition in which an actor, typically a state, possesses the military capability, economic and human resources, and coherent ideology that enable it to assert power at the regional level and to aspire to global influence. This definition lacks any pejorative connotations and contrasts with conceptualizations that owe their intellectual debt to realism. These conceptualizations tend to minimize the ideological dimension of power, stress the hegemon's global influence and benevolence, and generalize from the British and American hegemonic experiences. Conceptualizations of hegemony that draw from the realist tradition include: Charles F. Doran, *The Politics of Assimilation–Hegemony and Its Aftermath* (Baltimore: Johns Hopkins University Press, 1971); Robert Gilpin, *War and Change in World Politics* (Cambridge: Cambridge University Press, 1981); and Robert O. Keohane, *After Hegemony: Cooperation and Discord in the World Political Economy* (Princeton, NJ: Princeton University Press, 1984).

3. *Kayhan International*, September 16, 1975, as cited in K.R. Singh, *Iran: Quest for Security* (New Delhi: Vikas Publishing House Pvt., Ltd), pp. 329–30.

4. For a detailed account of Eerkens' negotiations with the Tehran Nuclear Research Centre, see Leonard S. Spector, *Going Nuclear* (Cambridge, MA: Ballinger Publishing Company, 1987), pp. 47–9.

5. See *Circumstances Surrounding the Government's Approval of Nuclear-related Exports to Iran* (Washington, DC: General Accounting Office, March 17, 1980), pp. 4–7.

6. See 'The Atomic Energy Organization of Iran', Airgram P-750-060-1115, from US Embassy, Tehran, to US Department of State, April 15, 1976.

7. Leonard S. Spector with Jacqueline R. Smith, *Nuclear Ambitions: The Spread of Nuclear Weapons 1989–1990* (Boulder, San Francisco, Oxford: Westview Press, 1990), pp. 205–6. See also Akbar Etemad, 'Iran', in Harald Muller, ed., *European Non-Proliferation Policy* (Oxford: Oxford University Press, 1987); Etemad was the chairman of the Atomic Energy Organization of Iran during its most vibrant days under the Shah.

8. For a thorough but little known analysis of Pahlavi Iran's capabilities and motivations to acquire nuclear weapons, see Anne Hessin Cahn, 'Determinants of the Nuclear Option: The Case of Iran', in Onkar Marwah and Ann Schulz, eds, *Nuclear Proliferation and Near Nuclear Countries* (Cambridge, MA: Ballinger Publishing Company, 1975), pp. 185–204.

9. See Haleh Vaziri, *The Islamic Republic and Its Neighbors: Ideology and the National Interest in Iran's Foreign Policy during the Khomeini Decade* (PhD Dissertation, Georgetown University, Washington, DC, 1995).

10. For a detailed exposition of Islamic universalism, see *ibid.*, pp. 173–204 in Chapter 3.

11. For a thorough discussion of the impact of ideology on the Islamic Republic's foreign policy, see *ibid.*, pp. 779–828.

12. Spector with Smith, *Nuclear Ambitions*, p. 204.
13. Defense Intelligence Agency document IRI-517-0007-80, from 7602 AINTELG Fort Belvoir, VA, to INER, DIA, Washington, DC, March 13, 1980; as quoted in Spector with Smith, *Nuclear Ambitions*, p. 208.
14. As quoted in Segal, D1. Fesharaki's account of his meeting with Beheshti should be treated with some caution, for he was summoned before the Ayatollah upon being arrested. Fesharaki tricked Iranian officials into believing that he would assemble a team of scientists to pursue the development of nuclear weapons. He volunteered to travel abroad to persuade colleagues who had left Iran to return. Yet when Fesharaki obtained an exit visa from Beheshti, he fled to the United States. Fesharaki has since visited Iran at the clerics' invitation.
15. *Ibid.*
16. Works that examine the causes of the Iran–Iraq war include: John Bulloch and Harvey Morris, *The Gulf War: Its Origins, History, and Consequences* (London: Methuen London Ltd, 1989); Shahram Chubin and Charles Tripp, *Iran and Iraq at War* (London: I.B. Tauris & Co Ltd, 1988); Dilip Hiro, *The Longest War: The Iran–Iraq Military Conflict* (New York: Routledge Chapman and Hall, Inc., 1991); and Eric Hoogland, 'Strategic and Political Objectives in the Gulf War: Iran's View', and Phebe Marr, 'The Iran–Iraq War: The View from Iraq', both in Christopher C. Joyner, ed., *The Persian Gulf War: Lessons for Strategy, Law, and Diplomacy* (New York; Greenwood, CT: London: Greenwood Press, 1990), pp. 39–58, 59–74.
17. A list of those states from which the clerics bought arms reveals the impact of the shortage of American spare parts on the Iranian armed forces. During 1981–85, the Islamic Republic imported $6.4 billion worth of arms from:

People's Republic of China	9.9 %
Soviet Union	5.7 %
United Kingdom	1.6 %
Czechoslovakia	0.5 %
Poland	0.3 %
Other	83.0 %

These other suppliers included Argentina, Brazil, Chile, Ethiopia, India, Israel, Italy, Japan, Libya, the Netherlands, North Korea, Pakistan, Portugal, South Africa, South Korea, Spain, Sweden, Syria, Taiwan, the United States (1985–86) and Vietnam. See Anthony Cordesman, 'Arms to Iran: The Impact of US and Other Arms Sales on the Iran–Iraq War', *American-Arab Affairs*, No.2 (Spring 1987), 13–29; and Martha Wenger and Dick Anderson, 'The Gulf War', *MERIP: Middle East Report*, Vol.17, No.5 (September–October 1987), 25–26.
18. Ayatollah Rouhollah Khomeini, Tehran Domestic Service in Persian, 30 September 1980 – 'Khomeyni Addresses Nation on Threat from Iraq', *Foreign Broadcast Information Service, Daily Report – South Asia* (*FBIS–SA*), 1 October 1980, 11.
19. *Ibid.*, 12.
20. Ayatollah Rouhollah Khomeini, Tehran Domestic Service in Persian, 9 March 1982 – 'Khomeyni Addresses Combatants, Guards 9 Mar', *FBIS–SA*, 10 March 1980, 12.

21. For a discussion of the phases of the Iran–Iraq missile battle, see W. Seth Carus, 'Missiles in the Middle East: A New Threat to Stability', *Policy Focus* (Washington, DC: Washington Institute for Near East Policy, Research Memorandum, June 1988), pp. 5–6. During 1980–85, Iraq alone possessed surface-to-surface missiles, launching some 150–200 against Iranian cities. In May 1985, Iran fired 14 Scud-B missiles acquired from Libya against Iraq, which retaliated with some 80 missiles. During 1986–88, the Ba'ath continued to launch sporadic missile attacks against Iran. On February 29, 1988, Iraq initiated the 52-day 'War of the Cities'; the Ba'ath fired 190 'Al-Hussein' at Iran, and the clerics launched 80 Scud-Bs and some 250 domestically produced Oghab missiles at Iraq.

22. For a balanced discussion of the United Nations' stance in the Iran–Iraq war, see Anthony Clark Arend, 'The Role of the United Nations in the Iran-Iraq War', in Joyner ed., *The Persian Gulf War*, pp. 191–208.

23. The clerics actually worried that Iranians and other Muslims might believe the Iraqi Ba'ath's charges that the Islamic Republic had collaborated with Israel in the attack on the Osiraq reactor. For the clerics' rebuttal of the Ba'ath's accusations and denunciations of Israel's attack, see Ali Akbar Khamene'i, Tehran Domestic Service in Persian, 19 June 1981–'Khamene'i Interviewed on Defense Council, War, Israel', *FBIS–SA*, 22 June 1981, I19; Speaker of the Parliament Ali Akbar Hashemi Rafsanjani, Tehran Domestic Service in Persian, 9 June 1981 – 'Reaction to Israeli Raid on Iraqi Nuclear Reactor: Rafsanjani on Attack', *FBIS–SA*, 10 June 1981, I1–I2; and Tehran Domestic Service in Persian, 12 June 1981 – 'Joint Staff Communique on Israeli Raid on Reactor', *FBIS–SA*, 15 June 1981, I16.

24. For insightful analyses of the causes and consequences of the American reflagging of Kuwaiti tankers, see David D. Caron, 'Choice and Duty in Foreign Affairs: The Reflagging of Kuwaiti Tankers', in Joyner ed., *The Persian Gulf War*, pp. 153–72; Elizabeth Gamlen, *US Military Intervention in the Iran–Iraq War, 1987–8* (Peace Research Report Number 21, School of Peace Studies: University of Bradford, March 1989); and R.K. Ramazani, 'Iran's Resistance to the US Intervention in the Persian Gulf', and Gary Sick, 'Slouching toward Settlement: The Internationalization of the Iran–Iraq War, 1987–1988', both in Nikki R. Keddie and Mark J. Gasiorowski, *Neither East Nor West: Iran, The Soviet Union, and The United States* (New Haven and London: Yale University Press, 1990), pp. 36–60, 219–45.

25. For the Iranian leadership's initial reactions to the American reflagging of Kuwaiti tankers, see President Ali Akbar Khamene'i, Tehran Domestic Service in Persian, 21 July 1987 – 'Khamene'i Discusses UN Gulf Resolution, France', *Foreign Broadcast Information Service, Daily Report – Near East & South Asia (FBIS–NES)*, 22 July 1987, S1-S3; Kamal Kharrazi (Office of War Information), Hamburg *Der Spiegel* in German, 17 August 1987 – 'Kamal Kharrazi Interviewed by DER SPIEGEL', *FBIS–NES*, 19 August 1987, S2-S6; Prime Minister Mir Hussein Musavi, Tehran Domestic Service in Persian, 20 September 1987 – 'Musavi Interviewed on UN Resolution on War', *FBIS–NES*, 21 September 1987, 34; Speaker of the Parliament Ali Akbar Hashemi Rafsanjani, Tehran IRNA [Islamic Republic News Agency] in English, 22 September 1987 – 'US Attacks "Cargo Ship" Carrying Food: Hashemi–Rafsanjani Vows "Decisive

Blow" to US,' *FBIS–NES* (22 September 1987), 42–3; and Minister of Foreign Affairs Ali Akbar Velayati, Tehran Domestic Service in Persian, 1 October 1987 – 'Velayati Message to ICO [Islamic Conference Organization] on US Aggression', *FBIS–NES*, 1 October 1987, 36.

26. Rafsanjani, Tehran Domestic Service in Persian, 6 October 1988 – 'Hashemi–Rafsanjani Speaks on the Future of the IRGC', *FBIS–NES*, 7 October 1988, 52–3.

27. David Albright and Mark Hibbs, 'Nuclear Proliferation: Spotlight Shifts to Iran', *The Bulletin of Atomic Scientists* (March 1992), 10; Kai Bird and Max Holland, 'Iran: Khomeini's Nuclear Program', *The Nation*, Vol. 239 (December 8, 1984), 608; and Spector with Smith, *Nuclear Ambitions*, pp. 204–5. The Islamic Republic has pressed EURODIF officials to resume supplies of enriched uranium. While Iran retains an indirect share in the consortium, EURODIF officials have insisted that they were no longer obliged by a supply contract that expired in 1990.

28. Ahmed Hashim, 'Iran's Military Situation', in Patrick Clawson, ed., *Iran's Strategic Intentions and Capabilities* (Washington, DC: National Defense University, Institute for National Strategic Studies, McNair Paper 29, April 1994), p. 203; and Leonard S. Spector, 'Nuclear Proliferation in the Middle East', *Orbis*, Vol. 36, No. 2 (Spring 1992), 186.

29. Mark Hibbs, 'Bonn Will Decline Teheran Bid to Resuscitate Bushehr Project', *Nucleonics Week*, May 2, 1991, 17.

30. For a thorough discussion of the Islamic Republic's position *vis-à-vis* Iraq and the United States during the Persian Gulf crisis, see Haleh Vaziri, 'Iran's Response to the Iraqi Invasion of Kuwait – The Vindicated Free Rider?', in Andrew Bennett, Joseph Lepgold Danny Unger, eds, *Friends in Need: Burden Sharing in the Persian Gulf War* (New York: St. Martin's Press, 1996).

31. Hashim, p. 206.

32. Albright and Hibbs, pp. 10.

33. *Ibid.*, pp. 10–11.

34. See Steven Mufson, 'Chinese Nuclear Officials See No Reason To Change Plans to Sell Reactor to Iran', *The Washington Post*, May 18, 1995, A22; and R. Jeffrey Smith, 'China in Rebuff to US, Defends Its Nuclear Dealings With Iran', *The Washington Post*, April 18, 1995, A13.

35. Russian Ambassador to the Islamic Republic Sergei Tretyakov, as quoted in Robert Fisk, 'Envoy Ridicules Iran's Nuclear Ambitions', *Independent*, 30 May 1995, 10.

36. Amrollahi, Tehran IRNA in English, 12 March 1995 – 'Bushehr Power Plant Director Interviewed', *FBIS–NES*, 16 March 1995, 55. See also Tehran *Ettela'at* in Persian, 3 April 1995, 2 – 'Nuclear Cooperation With Russia Viewed', *FBIS–NES*, 19 April 1995, 62–5. Moscow's ambassador to Iran Sergei Tretyakov puts the number of Russians working on the Bushehr project at 150. See Fisk, p. 10.

37. Fred Hiatt, 'Russian Agency Disputes US on Iranian A-Arms', *The Washington Post*, March 24, 1995, A28; and Hiatt, 'Russia Denies Plan to Sell Gas Centrifuge to Iran', *The Washington Post*, May 5, 1995, A29.

38. Fred Hiatt, 'US Efforts to Block Iran Reactor Sale Cause Anger in Moscow', *The Washington Post*, March 3, 1995, A32.

39. Tretyakov, as quoted in Fisk, p. 10.

40. John F. Harris, 'GOP Urges Tough Stand With Russia', *The Washington Post*, May 19, 1995, A1, A4; Fred Hiatt, 'Perry Hints at Iran Compromise', *The Washington Post*, April 4, 1995, A19; and Jonathon S. Landay, 'US Puts Pressure On Russia to Halt Iran Reactor Deal', *The Christian Science Monitor*, April 5, 1995, 1, 7.

41. See IAEA Representative Sadeq Ayatollahi, Munich *Focus* in German, 15 May 1995, 273 – 'IAEA Representative: We Are Not Building Atomic Bomb', *FBIS–NES*, 16 May 1995, 53; Ayatollahi, Tehran IRNA in English, 25 September 1993 – 'Official Denies Tehran Seeking Nuclear Weapons', *FBIS–NES*, 29 September 1993, 39–40; Senior Deputy Minister of Foreign Affairs Ali Mohammad Besharati, Tehran Voice of the Islamic Republic of Iran First Programme Network in Persian, 27 November 1992 – 'Besharati Denies Nation Seeking Nuclear Weapons', *FBIS–NES*, 30 November 1992, 73; President Ali Akbar Hashemi Rafsanjani, Tehran Voice of the Islamic Republic of Iran in English, 14 April 1995 – 'Rafsanjani Issues Statement on US Threats', *FBIS–NES*, 19 April 1995, 59; IRGC Mohsen Reza'i, Tehran IRNA in English, 23 February 1994 – 'IRGC General Says Country Not for Nuclear Weapons', *FBIS–NES*, 24 February 1995, 43; Secretary of the Supreme National Security Council Hassan Ruhani, Tehran IRIB [Islamic Republic of Iran Broadcast] Television Second Programme Network in Persian, 20 April 1995 – 'Ruhani: No Russian, PRC "Surrender" on Nuclear Issues', *FBIS–NES*, 21 April 1995, 53–4; and Deputy Minister of Foreign Affairs Mahmud Va'ezi, Paris AFP [*Agence France Presse*] in English, 11 May 1995 – 'Views on US–Russian Talks on Ties to Iran – Va'ezi: Clinton Achieved No Success', *FBIS–NES*, 11 May 1995, 34.

42. Rafsanjani, as quoted in Molly Moore, 'Iran's President Vows to Pursue Nuclear Program', *The Washington Post*, April 20, 1995, A29.

43. Ruhani, Tehran IRIB Television Second Programme Network in Persian, 20 April 1995 – 'Ruhani: No Russian, PRC "Surrender" on Nuclear Issues', *FBIS–NES*, 21 April 1995, 53–4.

44. See Iranian Ambassador to Pakistan Mehdi Akhundzadeh, Tehran IRNA in English, 5 April 1995 – 'Diplomat Assails West's "Hostile" Attitude on NPT', *FBIS–NES*, 6 April 1995, 59–60; Tehran Voice of the Islamic Republic of Iran in English, 2 April 1995 – 'Commentary Views Mubarak's US Visit, NPT Position', *FBIS–NES*, 3 April 1995, 53; Tehran Voice of the Islamic Republic of Iran in English, 7 April 1995 – 'NPT, Israel's Nuclear Weapons Viewed', *FBIS–NES*, 11 April 1995, 54–5; Tehran Voice of the Islamic Republic of Iran First Programme Network in Persian, 17 April 1995 – 'Radio on NPT Revision, US "Double Standards"', *FBIS–NES*, 17 April 1995, 55; Minister of Foreign Affairs Ali Akbar Velayati, Milan *Panorama* in Italian, 7 March 1995, 96–8 – 'Velayati Eager to Sign NPT if Israel Does', *FBIS–NES*, 14 March 1995, 64–5; and Velayati, Tehran IRNA in English, 21 April 1995 – 'Velayati Arrives in New York for NPT Session: Outlines "Major Obstacles" to NPT', *FBIS–NES*, 24 April 1995, 48.

45. I have more thoroughly explained the impact of ideological factionalism on the Islamic Republic's decision making in *The Islamic Republic and Its Neighbors*, Chapter 3, pp. 172–260.

46. President Rafsanjani, Tehran Voice of the Islamic Republic of Iran First Network in Persian, 9 February 1995 – 'Rafsanjani on Nuclear Weapons, Other Issues', *FBIS–NES*, 10 February 1995, 55.

Part III
Retrospect

16 The Realities of Nuclear War: Memories of Hiroshima and Nagasaki

James N. Yamazaki, MD

1 MY EXPERIENCE IN WORLD WAR II

My memory is selective in attempting to recall the impact of the news of the atomic bombing of Hiroshima and Nagasaki that ended the wrenching years of World War II five decades ago. As a Japanese-American, my involvement in this great war began as an army doctor in Europe where I was assigned by the United States Army.

In August of 1945, former POWs of the 106th Infantry Division, including myself, who were captured in the 'Battle of the Bulge', were assembled at a sumptuous 'Rest and Rehabilitation Inn' in the foothills of the tranquil Appalachian Mountains.[1] We still grieved for our comrades who were left behind and buried in the snow-covered Ardennes Forest. Most of them were youths barely out of their adolescence. The recollection of the carnage of dismembered bodies remains deeply etched within me. I was a fledgling physician assigned to care for them in battle. A few days after our capture we were locked inside a boxcar. The train halted in the marshalling yards of Hanover as the Allied bombers unleashed their bombs. They narrowly missed us. Several months later, early one April morning, as I joined a long procession departing from a POW camp in Nuremberg, a massive Allied air armada darkened the sky overhead until mid-afternoon. The tail end of the long columns of POW marchers still on the outskirts of the city were felled by their bombs, among them were slain many of our soldiers of the 106th Division.

It is understandable then, that no one complained when a celebration did not take place at the Inn when Japan surrendered a few days after the atomic bombing of Hiroshima and Nagasaki. All the killing had finally ended and I was left pondering what to do with the life that had been spared.

When I returned from the European battlefield, I was relieved to find that our families of Japanese descent who were imprisoned in internment camps during the war were intact and well, especially when I learned of the terrible toll of life that was inflicted on the Jews during the holocaust in Germany, a fate that could have happened to our family even in America, and not without historical precedent.[2] Because we are of the same human family, we must recognize that within us all, beneath our veneer of civility, there is this propensity of man to commit such savage aggressions – all the acts of war – in the name of defence and survival, but also sometimes fuelled by ethnocentric beliefs.[3]

My remaining service in the army was spent at an Army General Hospital caring for the returning veterans before resuming my medical training. Meanwhile the lot of Hiroshima and Nagasaki disappeared from my consciousness, only to return at the beginning of the year 1948, when I was made aware of the studies just getting underway in Japan to study the delayed effects of the atomic bombings.

2   THE DEAD AND LIVING AFTER HIROSHIMA AND NAGASAKI

Returning from a meeting at the National Academy of Sciences – National Research Council (NAS/NRC), Dr. Ashley Weech, the Director of the Children's Hospital in Cincinnati where I was a resident, informed me that based on the initial report of the unprecedented medical affects of the atomic bomb by the Joint Commission composed of the physicians of the United States Armed Forces and Japanese government, President Truman authorized the continuation of the medical study of the survivors, with the formation of the Atomic Bomb Casualty Commission (ABCC) under the supervision of the NAS/NRC.[4]

Because little information was then available about the effect of whole body radiation on humans, NAS encouraged us to submit a proposal for investigation. It had been observed that following pelvic radiation therapy in pregnant women, profound injury to the conceptus resulted, especially to the developing brain.[5] Following a discussion of this matter with the Committee on Atomic Casualties, I was informed that one of my responsibilities would be to evaluate the outcome of pregnancies following exposure to the atomic bomb. Dr. Josef Warkany, the distinguished teratologist, guided me in the design of this study.[6]

In the aftermath of the atomic bombings of Hiroshima and Nagasaki, the genetic effect of the radiation exposure was a compelling concern to both scientists and the general public. In every plant and animal species adequately studied, radiation resulted in deleterious mutations. It would be untenable to consider that the human gene was an exception. Clearly the threat to the well being of the children of the atomic bomb survivors, that perhaps may extend to children of generations far into the future, provoked universal concern. Indeed, the first study that was initiated by the ABCC was the genetic study proposed by Dr. James Neel, medical geneticist of the University of Michigan. At Ann Arbor, he explained to me that the pediatricians would be involved in the examination of the survivors' children to assess untoward pregnancy outcome: congenital malformation, stillbirth, neonatal death, growth and development of the live born.

On arrival in Hiroshima in the Fall of 1949, we faced situations that were not discussed in Washington at NAS/NRC. Because of my Japanese descent, housing and transportation were not available to my family under the policy of the British Commonwealth Occupation Forces (BCOF) in the Hiroshima region, a policy reminiscent of the centuries-old British colonial rule in Asia.[7] My protests were to no avail. A short period after my arrival I was dispatched to Nagasaki as the Physician-in-Charge, the sole American physician, to develop the ABCC operation in that city.[8]

Meanwhile, we were still not briefed on the initial survey of the medical effects of the atomic bomb under the aegis of the Supreme Commander of the Allied Forces (SCAP) with the collaboration of the Japanese physicians, shortly after the occupation of Japan began. This aura of secrecy was pervasive during this period so that the official public report of the human toll of the bombing was delayed until 1956 with the publication of the *Medical Effects of the Atomic Bomb in Japan*, authored by Drs Ashley Oughterson and Shields Warren as part of the declassified portion of the National Nuclear Energy Series – Manhattan Project Technical Section, Atomic Energy Commission.[9] Furthermore, in Japan, a censorship was invoked by SCAP soon after the occupation of Japan began, in a press code that prohibited the publication of all accounts of damage and injury from the A-bomb. This also had the effect of prohibiting investigations of the casualties by the Japanese themselves.[10] The report of the initial investigation by the Japanese physicians, under the auspices of the National Research Council of Japan, which began immediately after the bombing prior to the Allied occupation, has not appeared in the English literature.[11] Thus, except for John Hersey's article, 'Hiroshima' in the *New Yorker*, in 1946 (censored in Japan), the public in Japan and elsewhere remained virtually unaware of the poignant reality of an atomic attack to man.[12]

3   THE MEDICAL INVESTIGATION IN THE BOMBING OF NAGASAKI

It was four years after the bombing when I arrived in Nagasaki in 1949. I was 33 years old. I barely spoke the language and was undoubtedly a foreigner in my father's homeland, wearing the hat of the US Atomic Bomb Medical Team and the lead Physician. I would have to develop a relationship with the people if we were to conduct a long-term study, perhaps more than 50 years, if we were to observe the life-time atomic bomb effect of the youngest survivors.

My assignment in Nagasaki was to lay the groundwork for conducting a study paralleling the burgeoning programme of Hiroshima, where a full complement of administrative and medical personnel was already in place. With the recent acquisition of one of the few remaining office buildings in the city, remodelling the building was intended to conform to the clinical and laboratory needs of the programme to be undertaken. The genetic programme that was started in the prior year was possible because the newborn infant was examined in the home, and the administrative data compilation was conducted in temporary quarters; and I inherited the oversight of this programme.

Through the grapevine we soon learned of misgivings about the Atomic Bomb Casualty Commission among the citizenry of Nagasaki. Many survivors thought we had come to use them simply as guinea pigs and that our sole interest was to gain information to protect Americans in the United States in the event of an atomic attack.[13] They were sceptical about our real concern for them. I felt it was imperative to explain the Commission's medical mission to the medical community and to government officials. Furthermore, because I was not briefed about the consequences of atomic bombing, it was incumbent upon me to learn about the experiences of the people of Nagasaki and to gradually become acquainted with the people and their environs.

More than in other parts of Japan, Nagasaki had contact with visitors from afar: Portugese traders and Jesuit priests preceded me 400 years earlier leaving lasting impressions; later the Dutch, although sequestered on a small, man-made island connected to the city by a footbridge, remained and introduced western medicine to Japan, in Nagasaki;[14] and prior to the onset of the Russo-Japanese War in 1904, the Russian Asiatic fleet spent every winter in Nagasaki Harbour.[15]

Nagasaki, a city of approximately 260,000 people, lies on the south-western tip of the Island of Kyushu, the southernmost of the main Japanese islands. The city encircles the head of the beautiful long and narrow bay cradled by verdant mountainous terrain that beckoned seafaring voyageurs from distant shores for centuries. A mountain ridge extends to the head of the bay in either side of which are the two main valleys of the city. On the western shore of the bay are the large shipbuilding industries. The valley to the north-east is the Urakami Valley through which the Urakami River winds for four miles through the valley. On its bank were the massive Mitsubishi steel and armament industries and torpedo assembly plant surrounded by residential areas. It was in the middle of the Urakami Valley that the atomic bomb burst. The mountain ridge on the east rim of the valley had acted as a shield preventing the total destruction of the city that Hiroshima encountered because it was built on a flat delta.

4   THE NATURE OF ATOMIC BOMBING

During a courtesy visit to the Chief of Police Deguchi, I learned he was the assistant chief of the air raid warning unit when the atomic bomb exploded. His story, described in considerable detail, provided my first insights into the events of August 9, 1945 viewed from his vantage point at Katsuyama school which was shielded by the mountain ridge from the explosion in the Urakami Valley. The men he had sent to Urakami Valley to investigate the explosion soon returned as the massive conflagration already blocked any entry into Urakami Valley and signs of massive destruction and death were widespread. A few hours later those who were able to walk crossed the mountain path and found their way into the city and straggled by his office. No part of the city had been spared. Deaths of key members of families resulted in family dissolutions. Despair and demoralization were pervasive. The injured were so numerous that rescue efforts did not reach some for two weeks and cremation and burial efforts lasted for a similar period. A large segment of the population fled from the city.

His story prompted me to visit Urakami Valley where the only remnants of the once thriving industrial valley were the skeletal remains of a few concrete buildings on the valley floor and the mountain side. On the eastern slope of the valley, I inspected the badly damaged and deserted university medical school hospital buildings. Close by atop a hill where once stood a magnificent cathedral, only fragments of the wall remained. On the hillside nearby were many shanties, dwellings of the survivors, built from scavanged material. One of these was the home of Dr. Takashi Nagai, the hospital radiologist whom I later visited. There was just enough sleeping space for himself and his two children; the mother was killed at the time of the bombing. A little window allowed the air and light to enter the room. A small cooking area occupied the remaining space of the small abode.

I rode down the hill to the mid-valley to a clearing. On a berm was an obelisk marking the hypocentre, the point on the ground 500 metres above which the atomic bomb exploded. On the adjacent placard was a brief summary of the destruction in Japanese and English. Seventy thousand people were killed by one atomic bomb on August 9, 1945. The enormity of the instant destructive power of a single atomic bomb can be understood better in perspective when one considers, for example, that in the Korean War which lasted three years, from 1950 to 1953, among the Armed Forces of South Korea, the United Nations, and the United States, 118,000 men were killed. The number of deaths following the Hiroshima attack from an explosion that lasted but a few microseconds was about the same, and the consequences were more complex and foreboding for the victims that survived.

I would have to learn more about the atomic holocaust from the doctors at the Nagasaki University Medical School, the oldest medical school in Japan and one of the most respected. At the first meeting with Dean Kaguera, he designated the Director of the Hospital and Professor of Surgery, Dr Raisuke Shiradbe, to be the liason with ABCC, as he was in the hospital that day and had cared for the victims of the aftermath. The genial Dr. Shirabe guided me through the ruins of his hospital and pointed out through a window, that 800 metres toward the mid-valley below was the hypocentre. He then pointed to a medical school and laboratories of wooden framed buildings that were instantly ignited and crushed, killing all of the students and faculty inside, among them his son.

Initially there was a sound of a diving plane followed by a bright light like a magnesium flare, followed by a thunderous roar as the building shuddered and the ceiling and walls crashed around me and then a blast shook the room, the walls and ceiling buried me and then complete darkness prevailed, later to learn it was caused by the dense dust cloud, stirred by the blast that covered the city and eclipsed the sun when the explosive force stirred the earth's surface.[16]

Shirabe related that some of the deaths were caused by falling beams. Those outside were burned and died instantly on the spot. As the thermal radiation and the penetrating nuclear radiation travel at the same speed as light, these individuals also received a large dose of radiation. Many died of radiation illness without any signs of trauma or thermal radiation burns. Thus those who survived (60%) at the Medical School hospital, protected by the concrete walls of the buildings, were as close as you can be to the atomic bomb detonation and still be alive.

In the subsequent weeks and months, meetings and symposia were arranged for us with other survivors of the hospital staff under Dr. Shirabe's direction.[17]

The thermal radiation consisting of ultraviolet rays, infra-red and light rays follows a nuclear explosion which creates a tremendous amount of heat, comparable to the interior of the sun in a volume of space a few inches in diameter. Because the reaction is completed in microseconds a violent explosion results. Near the hypocentre the temperature of 6,000 degrees centigrade incinerates the body, blisters tile surfaces and instantly ignites flammable objects. At distances of about three kilometres the skin is charred, but at distances closer to the hypocentre, internal tissues are injured as if they are roasted and death occurs immediately. As thermal radiation and the penetrating nuclear radiation of gamma rays and neutrons act upon the body simultaneously, the combined effects were lethal for those out in the open within 1,500 metres of the hypocentre, even for those who were not injured by the trauma. Most of these receiving care in the immediate aftermath were treated for burns (90%). Maggots quickly appeared in burns and wounds in the fly-infested environs. Recollection of the pervasive stench of the burnt skin made it impossible for some to ever partake of barbecued meats again.

The blast waves caused injury not only because of their tremendous force that buckled concrete walls like the force of an earthquake at close distances from the hypocentre, but in addition they created a blast wind of hurricane speed that flung bodies off the ground several metres, that turned loose objects into flying missiles and the shattered glass fragments of varying size into flying blades cutting or penetrating the body. Furthermore, the skin that just seconds before was scorched by the thermal radiation was ripped off leaving strips of skin hanging from the body and exposing bleeding skin surfaces. The blast wind left clothing in tatters while others were completely naked. Most of the homes in Urakami Valley were reduced to ashes. All homes in the city were damaged to some extent.

At the Medical School hospital it was often noted that individuals without burns or trauma injury died, some instantly, slumping at their workplace, while others died in the next day or two after the bombing and solely from what was later determined to be radiation effect on the brain, 'brain death'. In common they soon experienced extreme malaise, extreme thirst, vomiting and diarrhoea. With a longer survival period epilation developed followed by bleeding from the skin and other parts of the body and painful ulceration in the throat and gums, often accompanied by sustained high temperature and emaciation prior to death. Those who developed infections required a long period before healing ensued. Otherwise localized infections often spread into a generalized fatal sepsis. Victims in whom radiation sickness was delayed for several weeks after the exposure were more likely to survive.

When Dr. Shirabe recovered from his radiation sickness, he undertook a survey of the records of the 7,000 casualties from records where victims were treated and from a canvas of the survivors of the neighbourhood blocks in Urakami Valley. Although he had discussed much of the information with us earlier, he brought this data to ABCC for our perusal, whereas data on casualties and the physical destruction gathered by the Joint Commission was classified until the end of 1954.[18]

During this initial period *fallout* was mentioned for the first time when an investigative team sent by the Atomic Energy Commission came to Nagasaki to conduct an interval reassessment of radioactivity that still remained in Nishiyama Valley just over the mountain ridge behind the University Hospital. They explained how the plutonium fragmented into highly radiocative particles at the instant of the explosion. These were swept upward by the incredible heat with the mushroom cloud. With condensation of the superheated cloud, the radioactive particles were incorporated in rain droplets and returned to the earth as an oily 'black rain'. Protected by the mountain ridge from the atomic explosion, the residents of Nishiyama Valley in this region did not present any serious direct radiation effects.[19]

One of the primary purposes of the investigating group immediately dispatched to Japan after the surrender by the Manhattan Engineering Group was to ensure the safety of troops that would occupy these atomic-bombed cities from exposure to any significant quantities of radioactivity on the ground and, if it was present, to record the amounts. The group was led by Dr. Stafford Warren, who was responsible for the radiation safety of the Manhattan Project that developed the atomic bomb. No harmful amount of persistent radioactivity was present with careful measurements of radioactivity over a wide area surrounding Nagasaki and the induced radioactivity in materials from neutrons and gamma rays near the hypocentre. Thus clearance safety was given so that a special US Marine landing brigade was permitted to disembark on the docks of Nagasaki on September 25, 1945.[20]

Warren had been vexed with the hazards of radioactivity in the vast undertaking in the production and handling of enriched uranium and plutonium. Discussing his concern at Los Alamos, prior to the first atomic test blast at Alamogordo, New Mexico, physicists had explained to him that on detonation of the atomic bomb radioactive particles equivalent to a ton of radium would be released in the air which would then settle to the earth which would present potential, yet unknown, radiation hazards. The magnitude of this amount of environmental contamination was keenly felt, for Warren, a radiologist, had successfully treated patients with cancer by killing malignant growths, 'I had 10mg needles of radium for this purpose and it was quite dangerous to handle'. Concerned for the safety of the residents living around the test site, he monitored the radioactivity in the sparsely populated areas near the test site, but fortunately the radiation levels detected presented no health problems.[21]

War came back to East Asia on June 25, 1950, six months after our arrival in Nagasaki. North Korea had invaded South Korea and the military force of the United States, with allied nations, was being deployed under the banner of the United Nations. The impact of the Korean War on Nagasaki, only 150 miles from Korea, was enormous. Nearby Sasebo served as the major staging area and debarkation port for American troops. Units stationed in the Nagasaki/Sasebo area were sent immediately to the front and suffered very high casualties.[22]

My most direct contact with that war came in the form of a three day meeting with the admiral commanding the American amphibious forces. I had been instructed to arrange a thorough briefing for him on the bombing of Nagasaki. The admiral came to Nagasaki aboard his command ship, with escorting navy combat vessels. My colleagues and I presented a full picture of what the atomic bomb had done. There was still physical evidence for them to see. We provided graphic examples of the human cost. I can only guess at the reasons why that briefing was requested.

5   EFFECTS OF ATOMIC BOMBING ON PREGNANCY AND CHILDREN

Despite that war affecting funds and personnel for our programme the remodelling of the office building continued so that by October the ABCC clinic was opened. Furthermore, with the arrival of two fine pediatricians from the University of Rochester, our American professional staff increased to three, allowing us to begin our investigation. The insight provided by Dr. Shirabe and his colleagues and the collaboration being developed with them were invaluable in conducting the studies at ABCC.

Still at the forefront of my thoughts was the study of adverse influence of radiation on foetal development, the very work that I had plotted out at Children's Hospital Research Foundation in Cincinnati with Dr. Warkany before I left for Japan. Two other programmes were already moving ahead. The genetic study, under Dr. Schull's supervision from Hiroshima, was being expanded to provide for follow-up reexamination of 20 per cent of the newborn to determine if there were any new findings at the ages of eight to ten months and to confirm previously identified abnormalities. Children who were within 1,000 metres of the hypocentre were identified and examined.

The study of outcome of pregnancies of mothers who were within 2,000 metres of the hypocentre was finally initiated and concluded just prior to my return to the US. In mothers who demonstrated signs of radiation sickness compared to mothers who did not develop such findings there was a significant increase in perinatal loss and some of their children had an abnormally shaped small head who were mentally retarded. The incidence of miscarriage, stillbirth and death during infancy was 43 per cent, seven times the incidence in a control group who were considered to have received no radiation. Of 16 children born to mothers with radiation signs, four had neurological abnormalities in contrast to one abnormality in the control group of 106 children whose mothers were not exposed to radiation. In the children of mothers who were within 2,000 metres, growth was delayed compared to the children of the control group, with significant reduction in mean height and head circumference. The evaluation of these data was difficult, owing partly to the possible effect of burns and partly to the indirect effects of haemorrhage, infection, and malnutrition.[23]

However, in an interdisciplinary laboratory investigation initiated at UCLA following my return, the effect of radiation alone revealed the marked vulnerability of the developing brain.[24] The brain lesions and neurological abnormalities were greater in the younger animals and the severity was a function of the radiation dose. Extensive laboratory studies undertaken by investigators here and abroad have substantiated these findings.

In Hiroshima and Nagasaki, subsequent studies revealed that the gestational stage of 8 to 15 weeks is when the developing brain is the most vulnerable to the radiation exposure resulting in microcephaly, mental retardation, and unprovoked seizure and showed a response which was proportionate to the dose.[25]

The ongoing Genetic Study at ABCC is the most comprehensive genetic study ever undertaken to determine the potential delayed genetic effect from exposure to the atomic bomb. Would there be any difference between children conceived subsequent to the atomic bombing effect and children of a suitable control population? Accordingly, some 76,000 pregnancies were evaluated representing over 90 per cent of the pregnancies in the two cities comparing the untoward pregnancy outcome (stillbirth, neonatal death, weight at birth and malformation). No significant differences were found. With the development of newer methods to assess mutations of chromosomal defects and biochemical alterations, no significant differences were observed. Nevertheless, after 50 years of follow-up in Hiroshima and Nagasaki, the various studies by no means rule out that some genetic damage was sustained, although any calculation of the exact amount is proving difficult. It is clear that genetic effects from these exposures are not as great as were once feared. Now the search for mutation at the DNA level was begun, obtaining samples from the exposed parents, their children and a control group. Permanent cell lines have been established to extend this inquiry with newer methods to identify genetic injury.[26]

The significance of these studies has been profoundly impressed on the families of Hiroshima and Nagasaki. In the initial phase of the study that lasted for six years, each of the 600 to 800 babies born every month in both cities were visited by the ABCC physicians and the parents were made to realize that the tragedy of August 1945 might extend to their child. These infants, now adults, who are still participating in the ongoing studies, are now parents themselves or hope to have families, and realize they may be tainted by the toxic radiation and often disclaim their identity and become fearful for their children.

In 1949 a young practising physician in Hiroshima, Dr. Takuso Yamawaki, came to ABCC along with Dr. Wayne Borges, a paediatric haematologist from Children's Hospital in Boston, to confirm the diagnosis of leukaemia among the survivors. With Dr. Jarrett Folley they were able to demonstrate that increased incidence of leukaemia occurred in the survivors within 2,000 metres of the hypocentre. Meanwhile, in Nagasaki, from among 65 children who had been among those closest to the hypocentre, two of the children developed leukaemia. These findings were not unexpected as leukaemia had been associated with radiation, notably among radiologists. But in the next four years an unexpected rise in leukaemia developed with the greatest increase among children, and with moderate radiation exposure the incidence was 30 times the normal incidence. In adults, leukaemia appeared much later. The findings are particularly significant when one considers that leukaemia is the commonest form of cancer in children.[27]

The discovery of leukaemia among the survivors set for what would become the largest research programme of its kind in the history of medicine. By 1957 more than 120,000 people in Nagasaki and Hiroshima were participating in the programme. The studies revealed that cancer is a major health effect of exposure to ionizing radiation. The female breast is the single organ most sensitive to cancer induction after exposure to ionizing radiation. Furthermore, it can now be added that, in young girls, risk of breast cancer, as in leukaemia, was greatest among the young. Those who had been under ten years of age when exposed had a risk five times greater than those 40 and older. Similar findings were reported for thyroid cancer. The study show that increases in eight other forms of cancer were attributable to bomb radiation: colon, lung and respiratory tract, ovary, salivary gland, skin (excluding melanoma), stomach and urinary bladder. The effect was greater in children, and the dose was the most important condition to each type of radiation induced cancer. The total number of cancers attributable to radiation induced cancer is not large and is not a major public health problem, but is understandably a vital concern for the surivors who have awaited the outcome these many decades. Because the lifetime consequences are uncertain for the 80 per cent of those still alive who were young at the time of the bombing, the observations of this group needed to be continued for another two decades or more.[28]

Estimates of the radiation dose received by the individual survivor are essential to measure the deleterious effects of radiation. Initial estimates of the immediate and delayed radiation effects were based on the distance from the hypocentre of the explosion and the survivor; continuing efforts to improve the dose estimates that each survivor absorbed followed. With collaboration of scientists at the National Laboratories at Livermore, Oakridge, Los Alamos, at Pacific Northwest Laboratory and other facilities with their Japanese counterparts, a reassessment programme was completed in1986; aided by the recent availability of high speed digital computer computation, it was possible to determine the best available estimate of the dose of radiation that is deposited in the body. Measurement of the neutron and gamma ray were obtained with the test bomb detonations, mock up of original bombs and simulated reactor outputs and how it varied with distance, and by the shielding provided by building and terrain. These results have been validated with measurements of neutron induced radioactivity in materials at varying distances near the hypocentre as well as from dosimetry measures of gamma ray in brick and tile archaeological objects. Because the bomb was exploded in the air, radioactive fallout was small and localized to a small area. Nearly all of the survivors in Urakami Valley were shielded substantially from the thermal pulse and the blast and nuclear radiation by structures and terrain and were accounted for in computing the radiation dose. Similar calculations were applied for the shielding by the body of underlying organ location relative to the direction of the radiation in determining the dose to these tissues for each individual in the study.[29]

The dosimetry obtained was also of particular value as it provided reliable comparative measures to assess the effects of large radiation dose exposure when thermal radiation and blast effect was not a factor, as obtained from radioactive fallout following surface detonation with weapons of tremendously greater yield in the Marshall Islands.

In 1957 a Special Committee on Radioactive Fallout of The American Academy of Pediatrics extended its inquiry into radiation hazards to children. One of my principal committee assignments was to update the findings of the ongoing investigation in Hiroshima and Nagasaki and the 15 megaton test weapon, almost a thousand times more powerful than the Nagasaki bomb, which was detonated in Bikini atoll of the Marshall Islands on March 1, 1954.[30]

6   ATOMIC TESTS IN THE MARSHALL ISLANDS

The medical problem in the immediate vicinity with the detonation of a megaton weapon in Bikini, the areas of damage would be similar to that of the kiloton weapons of Hiroshima and Nagasaki but, of course, magnified many times; and thus the number of mechanical, thermal and radiation injuries, from the instant penetrating direct radiation of the whole body with gamma rays and neutrons would be enormously increased. However, with the detonation of the megaton weapon near the surface at Bikini, the radioactive material is swept up into the cloud and an intensely radioactive fallout is deposited beyond the area of instant destruction creating a serious radiation hazard. The result is a comparatively localized area of contamination with the formation of a plume 30 to 40 miles wide and 200 miles long, contaminating thousands of square miles, resulting in the exposure of intensely radioactive fallout on sparsely populated atolls of the Marshall Islands. The Marshallese on some atolls were exposed to dangerous levels of radiation and were evacuated after two days of exposure. This fallout consisted of penetrating whole-body gamma radiation, irradiation of the skin and internal absorption of radionuclides from ingestion of contaminated food and water. The penetrating gamma rays caused radiation sickness with nausea, vomiting and diarrhoea within the first 24 hours and, after several weeks, caused depression of the white cells to dangerous levels most notable in children. The radioactive particles adhered to the skin causing 'beta ray' burns which in some instances caused deep lesions after a few weeks.[31]

The most serious internal exposure was that to the thyroid from radioiodines, which were deposited in the thyroid gland. The first indication of the delayed effect was the reduced growth of the children who were under the age of one at the time of exposure. Nearly all of the 16 children on the island (Rongelap) receiving the largest amount of fallout and who were ten years or younger at the time of exposure developed thyroid nodules, first observed after a delay of ten years following the exposure. Most of the same children also developed low thyroid function; and one developed a thyroid cancer.[32] Two of three persons who were in utero on Rongelap at the time of the exposure developed thyroid nodules, one of whom had a small head size.[33]

The dosimetry received considerable attention. On Rongelap Atoll a hundred miles from Bikini, the whole body radiation exposure was estimated to be 190(r). In the uninhabited northern end of Rongelap atoll 2,000(r) was delivered within the first 36 hours. In contrast the average dose of the survivors of Hiroshima and Nagasaki is estimated to be between 40 and 50(r). Further poignant travails of the Marshallese still attempting to seek refuge have been recently told by Dr. Robert Conard who led the medical survey for 28 years.[34]

The radioactive fallout following an underwater burst of an atomic weapon poses an extremely dangerous radiation hazard. An underwater burst of a 20 kiloton atomic bomb, similar to the weapon used in Nagasaki a year earlier, was conducted at Bikini, referred to as 'Operation Crossroad – Test Baker'. Naval vessels of every category, e.g. from carrier, battleship, destroyer, etc..., some obtained from former enemy countries and others obsolete vessels of the US Navy, were situated in the lagoon of Bikini atoll, approximately 25 miles long and 25 miles wide.[35]

'Nine ships were sunk and when the bomb was detonated underwater (at a depth of 200 feet)l the radioactive contamination of the ships not sunk was extreme and in many instances permanent; it could not be removed by any means'. The immediate effect of the detonation was a lethal radioactive mist about three miles wide even upwind, which developed under the great mushroom cloud of water and steam that formed immediately after the bomb exploded and drifted about ten miles downmind. Radioactivity was so high on the surface of Bikini Lagoon that for some hours it was not possible to go into the target areas beyond the periphery to examine the ships. The detonation created an initial wave almost a hundred feet high followed by waves of lesser height that travelled rapidly and innundated the beach and caused serious flooding; the depth of the innundation was sometimes twice as high as the approaching wave.[36]Dr. Stafford Warren, who had led the research teams at the sites of all previous blasts since 1945 concluded that, 'The only defence against atomic bombs lies outside the scope of science. It is the prevention of nuclear war'.

If the atomic bomb that exploded over Urakami Valley had been dropped instead at the head of the harbour in Nagasaki, there would have been no fiery inferno or the crushing blast in Urakami Valley; all the buildings, even the most humble home, would have been standing. But the harbour, the mountainous terrain and valleys of Nagasaki would have been enshrouded by the radioactive mist and drenched with rain droplets filled with radioactive particles that seeped into the crevices of each dwelling; and the inhabitants would not have realized that they were being enclosed in a cavern of radioactivity; but soon they would become ill with the symptoms of radiation sickness. The casualties would have been far more numerous than those that actually happened in Urakami Valley.

7 NUCLEAR WEAPONS AND HUMAN RESPONSIBILITY

In the Official US Government Report on the Development of the Atomic Bomb, authorized in August of 1945, Henry DeWolf Smyth, a physicist from Princeton University, wrote: 'In a free country like ours, decisions must be made by the people through their representatives. This is one reason for the release of this report. The people of the country must be informed if they are to discharge their responsibilities wisely'.[37] Yet nowhere in this volume are found even the names of Hiroshima and Nagasaki. Meanwhile, our government has not published an official account for the general public about the human toll of Hiroshima and Nagasaki or the Marshall Islands. Accordingly, John Dower commented, 'In the United States there has been an almost pathological aversion to what actually took place under the mushroom clouds'.[38] Now as the second generation of the post World War II generation emerges to inherit the nuclear legacy and its responsibilities, it is incumbent upon us of the preceding generation to develop measures to provide them with the facts of the nuclear issue.

NOTES

1. R. Ernest Dupuy, *St. Vith Lion in the Way: the 106th Infantry Division in World War II* (Washington: Infantry Journal Press, 1949).
2. See Richard Drinnon, *Keeper of Concentration Camps Dillon S. Meyer and American Racism* (Berkeley University of California Press, 1987). See also, *WWII Time Life Books: History of the Second World War, Holocaust* (New York: Prentice Hall Press, 1989) pp. 134–57.
3. Carmine D.D. Clemente and Donald B. Lindlsey, eds, 'Aggression and Defense Neural Mechanism and Social Patterns', *Brain Function*, Vol. 5. (Berkeley and Los Angeles: University of California Press, 1967). See also, John W. Dower, *War Without Mercy: Race and Power in the Pacific War* (New York: Pantheon Books, 1986).
4. See A.W. Oughterson, George V. LeRoy, Averil A Liebow, E. Cuyler Hammond, Henry Barnett, Jack D. Rosenbaum, B. Audrey Schneider,

Medical Effects of the Atomic Bomb. Report of the Joint Commission on the Effects of the Atomic Bomb in Japan, Office of the Air Surgeon NP–3041 United States Atomic Energy Commission, Technical Information Service, Oak Ridge, Tennessee, Vols 1–5, 1951, Vol. 6. Declassified 29 Dec. 1954; and see also, *Genetic Effects of the Atomic Bombs in Hiroshima and Nagasaki*, Genetic Conference, Committee of Atomic Casualties, National Research Council (June 24, 1947). 'J.V. Neel presents his plan for the Genetic Study in Japan', *Science*, vol. 106 (October 10, 1947), pp. 331–2.

5. L. Goldstein and D.P. Murphy, 'Microcephalic Idiocy Following Radium Therapy for Uterine Cancer During Pregnancy', *American Journal of Obstetrics and Gynecology*, vol. 18 (1929) pp. 189–95.

6. See Josef Warkany, *Congenital Malformations: Notes and Comments* (1309 pages) (Chicago: Year Book Medical Publishers, 1971). See also Josef Warkany and E. Schraffenberger, 'Congenital Malformations Induced in Rats by Roentgen Rays', *American Journal of Roentgenology and Radium Therapy*, vol. 103 (1947), No. 520.

7. British Commonwealth Occupation Forces: Headquarters QG/801/2/Accm., 5 March 1949. Subject: Use of BCOF Facilities by US personnel, (Distribution included The Director, Atomic Bomb Casualty Commission):

> para. 2. Japanese nationals or persons of Japanese extractions, except when the later are wearing the uniform of the United States Armed Forces, and except as stated in paragraph 6 below, cannot be permitted to enter or use any BCOF facility (e.g. bus service, housing, schools, etc.) para. 3. The following facilities are available to US personnel except as stated in para. 2 above- (a)-(e)
> S/D.G. McKenzie Lt-Col. For Brigadier, Principal Administrative Officer.

8. James N. Yamazaki, Physician-in-Charge, *Atomic Bomb Casualty Commission Nagasaki Annual Report*, January 1–December 30, 1950.

9. Ashley W. Oughterson and Shields Warren. National Nuclear Energy Series, Manhattan Project Technical Section Division VIII, Vol. 8, *Medical Effects of the Atomic Bomb in Japan* (New York: McGraw Hill Book Co., 1956).

10. Monica Braw, *The Atomic Bomb Suppressed: American Censorship in Japan 1945–1949* (Malmo, Sweden: Liber Forlag, 1986).

11. Masao Tsuzuki, 'Medical Report on Atomic Bomb Effects', The Medical Section: The Special Committee for the Effects of the Atomic Bomb, The National Research Council of Japan, January 1947. Translated into English 1953.

12. John Hersey, 'Hiroshima', *The New Yorker*, 1946.

13. A.W. Oughterson *et al. Medical Effects of the Atomic Bomb. The Report of the Joint Commission on the Effects of the Atomic Bomb in Japan,* Volume 1, Appendix 1, p. 24. Study of Atombomb Casualty, August 26, 1945, United States Atomic Energy Commission, Technical Information Service, Oak Ridge, Tennessee, 1951.

14. See Yoshimoto Okamoto, *The Namban Art of Japan; The Heibonsha Survey of Japanese Art*, translated by Ronald K. Jones (New York and Heibonsha, Tokyo: John Weatherhill, 1972 (English Edition)). See also John Z. Bowers, *Western Medical Pioneers in Feudal Japan* (Baltimore: The Josiah Macy Jr. Foundation, John Hopkins Press, 1970).

15. *Nagasaki 100, 1989 Nagasaki Municipal Centenniel*, Nagasaki City, 1989.
16. Raisuke Shirabe, 'My Experience of the Nagasaki Atomic Bombings: An Outline of Damages caused by the Nagasaki Explosion', Presented at the Nagasaki University Medical School at his 87th birthday celebration. May 17, 1986.
17. June 7, 1950 Symposium at the Nagasaki Medical College with particpation of the ABCC members. Chaired by Raisuke Shirabe, Professor of Surgery. Ed. James N. Yamazaki, Physician-in-Charge, ABCC.
18. Raisuke Shirabe, 'Medical Survey of Atomic Bomb Casualties (Nagasaki)', in W.S. Adams, S.W. Wright and J.N. Yamazaki, eds, *Military Surgeon*, vol. 113 (1953), p. 250. A more detailed hand written version of this report was given to RERF by Dr. Shirabe's family.
19. Atomic Bomb Casualty Commission, Nagasaki, Quarterly Report January–March 1950. James Yamazaki Physician-in-Charge, Tracer Laboratory Residual Radiation Field Study, p. 9.
20. Stafford L. Warren, 'The Role of Radiology in the Development of the Atomic Bomb', Chapter XXXVII in *Radiology World War II*, ed. Kenneth D.A. Allen, as a volume in the series Medical Department of the US Army in World War II, p. 886 (Surgeon General's Office, 1966).
21. *Stafford L. Warren, An Exceptional Man for Exceptional Challenges*, Vol. 2, Tape No. XIV Side 2, September 15, 1966, pp. 784–800. Oral History Program, Regents of the University of California, 1983.
22. Joseph C. Goulden, *Korea, The Untold Story of the War* (New York: Times Books , 1982).
23. J.N. Yamazaki, S.W. Wright, and P. Wright, 'A Study of the Outcome of Pregnancy in Women Explosed to the Atomic Bomb in Nagasaki', *Journal of Cellular and Comparative Physiology*, vol. 43 (1953), Suppl. 1.
24. C.D. Clemente, James Yamazaki, L.B. Bennet, R. McFall, and E.H. Maynard, 'The Effects of Ionizing x-irridation on the Adult and Immature Brain', in *Proceedings of the Second United Nations International Conference on the Peaceful Use of Atomic Energy* (Geneva: United Nations Publication, 1956) vol. 22, pp. 282–6. See also J.N. Yamazaki, L.B. Bennet, C.D. Clemente, 'Behavioral and Histological Effects of Head X-Irridation in Newborn Rats' in T.J. Hadley and R.S. Snyder, eds, *Response of the Nervous System, to Ionizing Radiation* (London: Academic Press), pp. 95–109.
25. James Yamazaki and William J. Schull, 'Perinatal Loss and Neurological Abnormalities Among Children of the Atomic Bomb', in *Nagasaki and Hiroshima Revisited, 1949 to 1989*, JAMA 264, No. 5 (1990), pp. 605–9.
26. Planning for the genetic programme began in 1946 and the data collection has been continuous since 1948. The 518 page anthology includes the principal investigations undertaken by the authors and their resident Japanese colleagues in Hiroshima and Nagasaki at the Atomic Bomb Casualty Commission Laboratories and its successor, Radiation Effects Research Foundation. It also reflects the evolution of the programme as it attempted to incorporate the new genetic technologies as they emerged. It is the most extensive genetic epidemiology ever undertaken. See James V. Neel and William J. Schull, *The Children of Atomic Bomb Survivors: A Genetic Study* (Washington, DC: National Academy Press, 1991).

27.   J.H. Folley, W. Borges, T. Yamawaki, 'Incidence of Leukemia in Survivors of the Atomic Bomb in Hiroshima and Nagasaki', *American Journal of Medicine* (1952), p. 311.

28.   From the 'Cancer Incidence in Atomic Bomb Survivors, Radiation Effect Research Foundation, Hiroshima and Nagasaki, Japan', ed. R.J.M. Fry, Supplement to *Radiation Research*, vol. 137, no. 2, 1994, pp. S1–S112.

29.   William C. Roesch, ed., *US-Japan Joint Reassessment of Atomic Bomb Dosimetry in Hiroshima and Nagasaki*, 11 volumes (Hiroshima: Radiation Effects Research Foundation, 1987).

30.   Conference on Pediatric Significance of Peacetime Radioactive Fallout. Sponsored by the American Academy of Pediatrics in conjunctions with US Public Health Service and the Atomic Energy Commission (James Yamazaki, co-chairman of the session on Radioactivity in the Individual), San Diego, California, March 14–16, 1966. Supplement to *Pediatrics*, vol. 4, no.1 (January, 1968), Part III.

31.   'Some Effects of Ionizing Radiation on Human Beings', in E.P. Cronkite, V.P. Bond, and C.L. Dunham, eds, *A Report of the Marshallese and Americans Accidentally Exposed to Radiation from Fallout and a Discussion of Radiation Injury in the Human Being*, United States Atomic Energy Commission, July 1956, AEC-TID 5385 (Washington DC, US Government Printing Office).

32.   Robert E. Conrad *et al.*, *A Twenty Year Review of Medical Findings in a Marshallese Population Accidentally Exposed to Radioactive Fallout*, Brookhaven National Laboratory Associated Universities Inc. BNL 50424, TID–5400 (Springfield, VA: Naval Technical Information Service, 1975).

33.   Wataru Sutow Personal Communication, October 29, 1979, M.D. Anderson Hospital and Tumor Institute, Houston, Texas. (W. Sutow was the pediatrician to the Marshall Island Survey: 91958–59, 1963–65, 1967–72. From 1948 to 52 he was Chief of Pediatrics ABCC, Hiroshima.)

34.   Robert E. Conrad, *Fallout: The Experience of a Medical Team in the Care of a Marshallese Population Accidentally Exposed to Fallout* (New York: Brookhaven National Laboratory Associated Universities Inc., 1992).

35.   Stafford Warren Papers 987, UCLA Special Collection, August 3, 1946. To Commander Joint Task Force (Vice Admiral Blandy) from Radiation Safety Officer (Stafford Warren). (Top Secret Declassified 6/8/65 AEC).

36.   *The Effects of Nuclear Weapons* (revised edition) (United States Department of Defence/United States Atomic Energy Commission, 1962), pp. 53–68.

37.   Henry DeWolf Smyth. *Atomic Energy for Military Purposes: The Official Report on the Development of the Atomic Bomb Under the Auspices of the United States Government 1940–1945* (California: Stanford University Press, 1989). (Originally published by the the United States Government in 1945.)

38.   James N. Yamazaki and Louis B. Fleming, *Children of the Atomic Bomb: An American Physician's Memoir of Nagasaki, Hiroshima, and the Marshall Islands,* with a foreword by John Dower (Durham: Duke University Press, 1995). Parts of this chapter are extracted and/or condensed from that book.

Index

Acheson, Dean, 216
Ahmed, Qazi Hussain, 285
Afghanistan (Afghan), 27, 110, 278–9, 289, 294–5
Algeria, 146, 324
Allison, Graham, 81–2
Almond, Gabriel, 274
American Academy of Pediatrics, 344
American Broadcasting Company (ABC), 212
American Nuclear Society, 195
Amrollahi, Reza, 319
Angola, 95
Anti-Ballistic Missile (ABM) Treaty, 3, 35, 175
Arabs (Arab states), 12, 16, 93, 198
Arab–Israeli conflict, 36, 38, 93, 262, 275
Argentina, 4, 11, 26, 34, 56, 59, 86, 97, 136, 146, 317–18, 324
Armacost, Michael, 189, 193
Asahi Shimbum, 188, 190
Aspin, Les, 165
Atomic Bomb Casualty Commission (ABCC), 334–6, 340–2
Atomic Energy Commission (US), 84, 197, 340
'Atoms for Peace' programme, 30, 186, 276
Aum Shrinrikyo, 130
Australia, 2, 59
Australia Group, 131
Azerbaidzhan, 166

Bailey, Kathleen, 20
Baker, James, 18
Bangladesh, 94, 274, 299
Baruch Plan, 203
Belgium, 86, 311
Blank, Stephen, 20
Beheshri, Ayatollah Mohammed, 314
Belarus, 6, 11, 17–18, 146
Bentham, Jeremy, 223–5

Berlin Crisis, 92, 150
Betts, Richard, 81
Bhabha, Homi, 82–3, 96, 272–3
Bharatiya Janata Party (BJP), 13
Bhutan, 2–3, 291
Bhutto, Benazir, 284, 286
Bhutto, Zulfikar Ali, 94, 268, 277, 279, 285, 299
Bikini atoll, 186
biological weapons, 2, 4, 7, 131–4, 137–8
Biological Weapons Convention (BWC), 2–4, 7, 32, 132–4
Black Sea Fleet, 166–7, 176
Blackett, Lord P.M.S., 273
Blix, Hans, 227
BNFL (UK), 194
Borges, Wayne, 343
Bosnian Muslims, 323
Botha, P.W.J., 95
Brazil, 4, 11, 26, 34, 56, 86, 97, 100, 135–6, 146, 194, 300, 324
Britain/Great Britain see United Kingdom
British Commonwealth Occupation Forces (BCOF), 335
Brezhnev Doctrine, 167
Brodie, Bernard, 262
Brown Amendment, 289
Bundy, McGeorge, 78, 111
Bury, Chris, 212–13
Bush Administration, 16, 29, 137, 165, 207, 213, 310, 313
Bush, George, 38–9, 225, 228–9, 279, 286
Buteyko, Anton, 161
Butler, Lee, 228

Cable News Network (CNN), 234
Camp David Accords, 36
Canada, 2, 6, 59, 82, 275, 289, 299, 301
Canadian Atomic Energy Agency, 251

Canberra Commission, 184–5
Carnegie Endowment, 236
Carter Administration, 27, 197, 278, 289
Carter, Jimmy, 25, 193, 227, 234, 288, 299
Castro, Fidel, 226
Center for Science and International Affairs (CSIA), 196
Central Intelligence Agency (CIA), 16–17, 131, 149, 227–8
Central Treaty Organization (CENTO), 93
Chad, 223
Chanda, Nayan, 226–7
Chari, P.R., 267
Chechnya, 166
chemical weapons, 2–4, 7, 12, 130, 134, 136–8
Chemical Weapons Convention (CWC), 2–4, 7, 12, 131–2
Chernobyl, 9, 165, 170
Chicago, University of, 221
Children's Hospital (Boston), 343
Children's Hospital Research Foundation (Cincinnati), 341
China (Chinese), 1, 3, 6, 10–17, 19, 26, 33, 37, 44, 46–8, 50, 54, 58–9, 61, 66–7, 69, 79–80, 84, 92–3, 96, 99–100, 108, 134, 141, 144–5, 174, 198–9, 201, 210–11, 216–17, 221, 230, 235–6, 244, 248, 252, 255, 273–4, 277–8, 285–306, 318–20
    relations with India, 13, 15, 79, 93, 273–4, 277–8, 285–306
    and North Korea, 210–11, 216, 221, 230, 235–6
    and NPT, 11, 26, 58, 141
    relations with Taiwan, 66, 92
Chornovil, Vyacheslav, 161
Christopher, Warren, 165
Chung-hee, Park, 219, 221, 250–1
Cimbala, Stephen, 164
Clausewitz, Karl von, 150, 210–11
Clinton Administration, 25, 142–3, 145, 165, 176, 230–1, 234–35, 245, 254, 280, 310, 313, 318–19, 324

Clinton, Bill, 18, 38–9, 223, 228, 230, 232–3
COGEMA (France), 194
Cohen, Samuel, 218
Cold War (Post-Cold War), 5, 7, 9–15, 18, 27–8, 30–1, 37, 41–5, 47, 50, 55, 58–9, 64, 68–70, 97, 101, 113, 140, 143–5, 149, 151, 183, 185, 202, 208, 225, 236–7, 243, 252, 260, 264, 280, 293–5, 305
Columbia University, 236
Commissariat l'Energie Atomique (CEA), 82–3, 96
Committee on Atomic Casualties, 334
Commonwealth of Independent States (CIS), 161, 165–7, 174
Comprehensive Test Ban Treaty (CTBT), 1–3, 5, 9, 11–12, 47, 69, 75, 141–2, 183–5, 198, 203, 284–6, 291–2, 297, 300
Conference on Disarmament (Geneva), 2–3, 47, 184, 186, 291
Conference on Security and Cooperation in Europe (CSCE), 162–3, 173
Conrad, Robert, 346
Conventional Armed Forces in Europe (CFE), 167
Cornell University, 193
Council on Foreign Relations, 228
counter-proliferation, 35, 102
Crimea, 162, 166–8, 171, 173–4, 176
Cuba (Cuban), 2, 95–6, 290
Cuban Missile Crisis, 92, 111, 149–50, 188, 262
Cumings, Bruce, 20
Czech Republic, 163

Davis, Zachary, 20
Debré, Michel, 78
De Gaulle, Charles, 78–9, 91–2, 301
Deguchi, 337
Dhanapala, Jayantha, 49
Doo-hwan, Chun, 217, 251
Dower, John 347
Dulles, John Foster, 214–16
Dumas, Roland, 18

Eerkens, Jeffrey, 312
Egypt, 36, 93, 101, 106, 134–5
Eighteen Nation Disarmament
    Committee (ENDC), 190, 274
Einstein, Albert, 39
Eisenhower Administration, 215, 276
Eisenhower, Dwight, 91–2, 186, 214
EURATOM, 54, 190–1, 193–4
European Union (EU), 163, 167, 175

Far Eastern Economic Review, 226
Feaver, Peter, 106–7
Fesharaki, Fereidun, 314
Flanagan, Thomas, 233
Folley, Jarrett, 343
Ford Administration, 27
Ford, Gerald, 218
Ford–Mitre Group, 193
Formosa Resolution, 92
Forsyth, Frederick, 196
Foucault, Michel, 224
France (French), 2, 5–6, 10–11, 33–4,
    44, 46, 50, 58–60, 63, 65, 67, 69,
    78–80, 83–4, 90–3, 96, 99, 108,
    141, 145, 192–3, 198, 251, 287,
    299, 311–12, 315, 317
    and NPT, 11, 58
    parliament, 83
Frankel, Benjamin, 93, 101
Fukuda, 193

Gallucci, Robert, 231
Gandhi, Indira, 267, 275, 299
Ganguly, Sumit, 20
Gelb, Leslie, 212, 228
Genda, Minoru, 192, 195
Georgia, 166
Germany (German), 2–3, 36–8, 44,
    57, 63–5, 67–70, 84, 86, 89–92,
    101, 112, 161, 173, 192, 194,
    196–7, 243, 255, 311–12, 317,
    319, 333–4
Gilpin, Robert, 63
Glenn Amendment, 278–9, 288
Glenn, John, 18–19
Goldstein, Avery, 64
Greenpeace, 198
Guam, 217, 228
Guatemala, 223

Guillaumat, Pierre, 82–3
Gujral, Inder Kumar, 284
Gulf Cooperation Council, 322
Gulf War (Desert Storm), 16, 25, 28,
    30, 32, 38, 103–4, 131, 133, 150,
    208, 212, 219, 222, 225, 236,
    294, 310, 318

Haiti, 144
Halperin, Morton, 81–2, 263
Haq, Zia-ul, 279
Harrison, Selig, 232, 236
Harvard University, 196
Hasan, Munawwar, 284
Hawaii, University of, 236
Heikal, Mohammed Hasanein, 311
Helsinki Treaty, 173
Hersey, John, 335
Hiroshima, 3, 6, 20, 41, 90, 152, 186,
    333–47 *passim*
Hitler, Adolf, 29
Holloway, David, 89
Holocaust, 93
Holovatyy, Serhiy, 161, 175
Hosakawa, Morihoro, 66
Hungary, 163
Hurd, Douglas, 18
Hussein, Saddam, 29, 33, 37, 102,
    133, 150, 197, 228, 237, 318

Il, Kim Jong, 207, 212, 235, 243, 247
Imai, Ryukichi, 20
India, 1–4, 6, 9, 11–15, 19, 26–7, 36,
    45, 48, 53, 65, 67–9, 79–83,
    93–6, 99–100, 108, 134–6, 144,
    146, 149, 184, 228, 248, 260–8,
    272–6, 278–80, 284–307,
    310–11, 319
    atomic test 1974, 3, 11, 65, 70, 81,
        94, 99, 274–5, 278, 287–90,
        297, 310
    relations with China, 13, 15, 79, 93,
        273–4, 284–305 *passim*
    and CTBT, 9, 12, 14, 184, 284–6,
        291–2, 297, 300
    Department of Atomic Energy, 272
    and NPT, 6, 11–14, 26, 67–8, 70,
        274, 281, 284–6, 290–2,
        296–8, 300–7

India *(Cont.)*
  nuclear programme, 82, 83, 96, 264,
    267–8, 272–6, 288–90, 297–301
    relations with Pakistan, 13, 36, 94,
      273–4, 277–8, 280, 284–307
      passim, 311
    political parties, 291
    Tata Institute of Fundamental
      Research, 272
Indochina, 92
Indonesia, 59
Indo-Soviet Treaty of Peace &
  Friendship, 277, 299
Institute for USA and Canada
  (Moscow), 174
Intermediate Nuclear Forces (INF),
  10, 297
International Atomic Energy Agency
  (IAEA), 12, 15, 26–7, 29, 42, 50,
    99, 109, 140, 145, 186, 190, 192,
    209, 221–2, 226–7, 229–32, 234,
    245, 249–50, 275, 289, 297–8,
    301, 319
International Institute for Strategic
  Studies, 188
Iran, 2, 4, 9, 16–17, 47–8, 62, 76, 81,
    96, 99, 102, 104, 112, 131,
    134–6, 146, 295, 310–24
  Atomic Energy Organization of
    Iran (AEOI), 311, 319
  Clerics' regime and policy,
    312–23
  Revolutionary Guards, 315, 317
  Shah's legacy, 311–12
  Tehran Nuclear Research Center,
    311–12
Iraq, 1, 4, 9, 12, 15–16, 29, 33, 35, 38,
    55–6, 62, 76, 80, 93–6, 99–102,
    104, 131–6, 146, 248, 257, 295,
    304, 310–11, 313, 315–18, 320,
    324
  chemical and biological weapons,
    131–3
  and Gulf War, 16, 104, 310
  nuclear programme, 76, 100,
    310–11, 318
  and NPT, 12, 15, 29, 62
  Osirak reactor, 9, 35, 101–2, 304,
    316

Iran–Iraq War, 96, 104, 313, 315–17,
  320, 324
Ireland, 38
Israel (Israeli), 1, 3–4, 6, 12, 16, 26,
    29, 35–6, 45, 80–1, 93, 99–100,
    102, 106–8, 110, 112, 134–6,
    144, 184, 255, 257, 262, 281,
    285, 289, 295, 300, 304, 306,
    310, 316
  accord with Palestinians, 12, 36
  conflict with Arabs, 36, 38, 93, 106,
    262, 275
  and CWC, 12
  and NPT, 11, 26, 281
Italy, 2, 86, 101

Jackson, Henry, 193
Jaffar, Jaffar Dhia, 100, 102
Japan (Japanese), 2–3, 5, 15, 28, 35–7,
    48, 53–4, 57, 60–71, 76, 84, 86,
    90, 101, 112, 144, 146, 183–204,
    209, 217, 228, 232–4, 243–4,
    246, 248, 251–3, 255, 257,
    333–47
  constitution, 187
  House of Councillors, 192
  Japan Atomic Energy Research
    Institute (JAERI), 190
  Japan Atomic Industrial Forum,
    193
  Japan Atomic Power Company
    (JAPCo), 190
  Japan Socialist Party, 192, 221
  Liberal Democratic Party (LDP),
    192
  National Research Council, 335
  and nuclear energy, 188–94,
    198–202
  and nuclear weapons, 185–8, 194–8
Jinnah, Mohammed Ali, 276
Joeck, Neil, 110
Jordan, 93

Kaguera, 338
Kaplan, Morton, 244
Karrubi, 322
Kashmir, 94, 149, 263, 280–2, 294–5
Kay, David, 99, 101
Kazakhs, 17

Kazakhstan, 3, 6, 11, 17–19, 142, 146
Kennedy administration, 4
Kennedy, Paul, 63
Khamenei, Ali Akbar, 322–3
Khan, Abdul Qadir, 286–7
Khan, Munir, 287
Kharrazi, Kamal, 321
Khomeini, Ahmad, 322
Khomeini, Ayatollah Ruhollah, 314–16, 321, 323
Kissinger, Henry, 218, 299
Korean Energy Development Organization (KEDO), 195, 246–8, 252, 254
Korean War, 33, 92, 150, 187–8, 209, 211–12, 214, 235, 338, 341
Koresh, David, 213
Kostenko, Yuri, 163
Kozyrev, Andrei, 166
Kratzer, Myron, 251
Kravchuk, Leonid M., 18, 159, 162, 169–171
Kuchma, Leonid, 161, 177
Kurchatov, Igor, 89–90, 96
Kurds, 38, 316
Kuwait, 16, 29, 35, 38, 150, 316, 318

Lacouture, Jean, 91
Lane, Christopher, 64
Lapp, Ralph, 84
Larus, Joel, 90
Lavoy, Peter, 20, 79, 83
Lawrence Livermore National Laboratory, 344
Lawrence, Robert A., 90
Lebanon, 2, 323
Lenin, V.I., 166
Lewis, John Wilson, 92
Libya, 2, 4, 9, 16, 33, 131, 134, 136, 291, 300, 306
chemical weapons, 131
relations with Pakistan, 16, 300
Limited/Partial Test Ban Treaty (LTBT), 2–3, 11, 188, 297
Litae, Xue, 92
London Guidelines, 203
London Treaty, 60
Los Alamos National Laboratory, 340, 344

Luck, General, 233
Lucky Dragon incident, 186
Luttwak, Edward, 174

Mahallati, Mohammed Jaafer, 321
Malaysia, 246
Manhattan Engineering Group, 340
Manhattan Project Technical Series, 335
Manning, Robert, 235
Marshall Islands, 344–5, 347
Matayev, Scitkazy, 18
Mauritius, 2
McNamara, Robert, 92
Mendès-France, Pierre, 91–2
Mendl, Wolf, 91
Meshkov, 168
Mexico, 59
Michigan, University of, 335
Miller, William, 161–2
Ministry of International Trade and Industries (MITI), Japan, 190
missiles, 17, 32, 66, 102, 134–6, 216, 230, 281, 296
Missile Technology Control Regime (MTCR), 2, 7
Modelski, George, 63
Mohajerani, Ayatollah, 16, 295
Mohan, C. Raja, 264
Mohtashemi, Ali Akbar, 321
Molotov, V.M., 90
Monroe Doctrine, 166–7
Mozambique, 95
Murtha, John, 228
Muslim League, 276

Nagai, Takashi, 337
Nagasaki, 3, 20, 41, 90, 152, 186, 222, 333–47 *passim*
Nagasaki University Medical School, 338
Nakasone, Yasuhiro, 192
Nakhleh, Charles, 20
Namkung, Anthony, 236
Napoleon, 177
National Academy of Sciences–National Research Council (NAS–NRC), 334–5

National Broadcasting Corporation (NBC), 233
Nazarbayev, Nursultan, 18
Nazi Germany (Nazis), 89
Neel, James, 335
Nehru, Jawaharlal, 93, 267, 272–3, 284
Nepal, 94
Netherlands (Dutch), 63–4, 86, 197
Newsweek, 232
New Yorker, 335
New York Times, 18, 210, 219, 229
Nietzsche, Friedrich, 224
Niger, 16, 300
Nigeria, 6
Nixon Administration, 213
Nixon Doctrine, 250
Nixon, Richard, 214, 293, 299
Non-Aligned Movement (NAM), 146
North Atlantic Treaty Organization (NATO), 28, 36, 43–4, 67, 91, 93, 160–4, 166–7, 169–70, 174–5, 177, 219, 285
Northern Ireland, 144
North Korea (Democratic People's Republic of Korea), 1, 4–5, 8, 12, 15, 17–19, 25–6, 29, 35, 55–6, 62, 66, 68, 76, 81, 96, 99, 102, 112, 134–6, 142, 144, 146, 150, 195–6, 203, 207–37, 243–9, 298, 324, 341
    and nuclear programme, 15, 25, 29, 66, 68, 76, 220–2, 226–8, 234–5, 243–7, 249–50
    and NPT, 12, 15, 19, 26, 62, 213, 228–30, 298
    relations with South Korea, 207–37 *passim*, 243–9 *passim*
    relations with US, 207–37 *passim*
    Yongbyong reactor, 15, 195, 220, 226, 234, 243
Nouri, Nateq, 322
nuclear disarmament, 11
nuclear free zones, 14, 59, 97
Nuclear Non-Proliferation Act (US), 194, 289
Nuclear Non-Proliferation Treaty (NPT), 1, 3, 7–10, 14, 17, 26–7, 31–2, 35, 41–2, 46, 48–51, 53–60, 64–6, 69, 75–7, 97, 99,

101–3, 105, 110, 113, 140–8, 151–2, 159–63, 169, 171–2, 183–4, 187–8, 190, 193, 213, 228–30, 234, 245, 248, 253, 263, 277–9, 281, 284–6, 290–2, 296–8, 300–7, 311, 319, 321–4
    Article I, 7, 42, 57, 298
    Article II, 7, 42, 298
    Article III, 42, 190, 297
    Article IV, 7, 43, 77, 151, 193, 298
    Article V, 7, 43, 77, 298
    Article, VI, 7–8, 10, 43, 46, 57, 141–2, 151, 184, 285–6, 297, 305
    Article VII, 43
    Article IX, 57
    Article X, 8, 298, 301, 306
    causes of proliferation, 75–113
    and the international system, 56–71
    assessments and prospects, 4–55, 140–52
    Review and Extension Conference (RevExCon), 25, 41, 45–8, 50–51, 53–4, 59, 66, 75, 140, 142–3, 183
Nuclear Suppliers Group (NSG), 54, 98, 100
Nunn–Lugar programme, 142, 164, 202
Nuremberg, 333
Nye, Joseph S., 193, 245, 248

Oakridge National Laboratory, 197, 344
Oppenheimer, Robert, 85
Organization for Economic Cooperation and Development (OECD), 199, 203
Organization of Petroleum Exporting Countries (OPEC), 275
Organski, A.F.K., 62
Oughterson, Ashley, 335
Overholt, William, 159, 165, 169–70

Pacific West National Laboratory, 344
Pahlavi, Shah Mohammed Reza, 17, 311–14
Pakistan, 1, 3–6, 9, 11, 13–19, 26–7, 33, 36, 45, 53, 68, 80–1, 94–5, 99–100, 108, 134–5, 144, 146,

149, 184, 197, 260–8, 276–81,
284–306 *passim*, 318
Jamaat-i-Islami, 284–5
Kahuta nuclear plant, 16, 286–7
and NPT, 6, 11, 14, 19, 26, 281
nuclear programme, 5, 13, 15, 17,
68, 94, 264, 272, 267–8,
276–9, 286–9, 304–6
Pakistan Atomic Energy
Commission (PAEC), 276
Pakistan Institute of Nuclear
Science and Technology (PIN-
STECH), 276
relations with India, 13, 36, 94,
273–4, 277–8, 280, 284–306
passim
relations with Libya, 16, 300
Palestine (or Palestinians), 12, 323
accord with Israel, 12
Park, Tong Whan, 20
Partnership for Peace, 161, 173, 176,
285
Paul, T.V., 20
Pearl Harbor, 192
Perle, Richard, 193
Perry, William, 161–2, 233
Pilat, Joseph, 20
Poland, 27, 101, 163, 173, 175
Polanyi, Karl, 223
Portnikov, Vitaly, 173
Portugal (Portugese), 64, 336
Posen, Barry, 107
Powell, Colin, 226
Pressler Amendment, 279–80, 286, 289

Quester, George, 109

Radford, 214–15
Rafsanjani, Ali Akbar Hashemi,
316–19, 321–2
Rathjens, George, 20
Ray, Dixie Lee, 197
Razuvayev, Vladimir, 166
Reagan Administration, 278, 289,
313, 316
Reagan, Ronald, 279, 288
Reiss, Mitchell, 82
Rhee, Syngman, 214–16
Rhodes, Richard, 89

Riscassi, Robert, 207
Rochester, University of, 341
Rockefeller Foundation, 236
Roosevelt Administration, 89
Roosevelt, Franklin, 89, 91, 96
Ruhani, Hasan, 320
Russia (Russian), 3, 6, 10, 17–18, 28,
33, 37, 44, 48, 54, 65, 67, 79–80,
107, 133, 141–2, 145, 150,
159–77, 196, 198, 202, 244, 252,
278–9, 285, 319–20, 336
parliament (Duma), 202
relations with Ukraine, 11, 18, 79,
159–77 *passim*
relations with United States, 44, 50,
141–2, 162, 168–70, 173
see also Soviet Union
Rutherford, Lord Ernest, 272

Sachs, Alexander, 89
Sam, Kim Young, 232
Sanger, David, 210
Saudi Arabia, 16, 135
Scheinmann, Lawrence, 83, 193
Schelling, Thomas, 263
Schmidt, Helmut, 194
Schull, 341
Seabord, Glenn, 195
Shah of Iran *see* Pahlavi, Shah
Mohammed Reza
Shahi, Agha, 277–8
Shastri, Lal Bahadur, 83, 267, 273–4
Shirabe, Raisuke, 338–9
Shiv Sena, 13
Shokhin, 166
Slovakia, 163
Smyth, Henry DeWolf, 347
Snyder, Glenn, 280
Sok-ju, Kang, 231
Solomon, Richard, 213
South Africa, 4, 11–12, 26, 55–6, 59,
80–1, 99, 108, 112, 136, 146,
196, 219, 318
nuclear weapons, 12, 95
South Korea (Republic of Korea), 5,
26, 28, 35–6, 66, 76, 80, 86, 96,
101, 144, 146, 193, 199, 201,
207, 209, 212, 216–17, 219–20,
231–2, 243–58, 306, 312, 341

South Korea (*Cont.*)
  nuclear programme and policy,
    243–54
  relations with North Korea, 207,
    209, 212, 216–17, 219–20,
    231–2, 243–58 *passim*
Soviet Union (Soviets/USSR), 3, 5,
    9–11, 13, 18, 20, 27–8, 30–1, 38,
    43, 53, 63, 65, 68, 78, 80, 84,
    89–90, 92, 95–6, 99, 101, 104,
    107–8, 110–12, 134, 142, 144–6,
    148, 150, 184, 186, 192, 195,
    203, 214, 216, 221–2, 228, 264,
    274, 285, 293, 295, 297–8, 315
  relations with United States, 30,
    43–5, 144–5, 148, 151, 264
  See also Russia
Spain, 63, 311, 317
Special Committee on Radioactive
    Fallout, 344
Sri Lanka, 49, 94, 295
Stalin, Josef, 89–90, 96, 166, 211
Stalinists, 210
Stilwell, Richard, 217–18
Strategic Arms Limitation Talks
    (SALT-I and -II), 2–3, 10, 58,
    285
Strategic Arms Reduction Talks
    (START-I and -II), 2–3, 10,
    17–18, 50, 101, 141–2, 159, 162,
    169, 175, 183–4, 195–6, 202, 285
Suh, Dae-sook, 236
Summers, Harry, 210
Sundarji, General K., 14
Sung, Kim Il, 207, 211, 213, 215–16,
    221, 226, 228, 234
Supreme Commander of Allied Forces
    (SCAP), 335
Sweden, 86
Symington Amendment, 278–9, 288
Syria, 2, 107, 134–5
Sziland, Leo, 89, 96

Tae-woo, Roh, 251
Taiwan (Republic of China), 5, 15, 66,
    86, 100, 146, 199, 306
Tajikstan, 19
Talleyrand, 177
Tanzania, 2

Taranger, Pierre, 82–3
Tarasiuk, 161, 173
Thayer, Bradley, 20
Thomas, Raju, 20, 94
Thucydides, 211
Threshold Test Ban Treaty (TTBT), 3
Tibet (Tibetan), 296
Trachtenberg, Marc, 111
Treaty of Tlatelolco, 97, 290
Tretyakov, Sergei, 319
Trilateral Commission, 198, 202–3
Trivedi, Vishnu, 274
Truman, Harry, 90, 334
Truman Administration, 211

Ukraine, 6, 11, 17–18, 28, 33, 36, 79,
    142, 146, 159–77
  parliament (Rada), 163, 169
  policy objectives, 159–65
  relations with Russia, 11, 18, 79,
    159–77
  and US, 160–1, 164, 172–3, 175–6
United Kingdom (Britain/England),
    2–3, 5–6, 10–11, 33–4, 44, 50,
    60–1, 63–5, 67, 78–80, 84, 86,
    89–90, 96, 108, 141, 190, 192,
    222, 274, 285
United Nations, 1–2, 4, 8, 37–9, 68,
    95, 102, 104, 140, 144, 150–1,
    161–2, 184, 198, 222, 230, 232
  Charter, 222, 237
  General Assembly, 2, 43, 151,
    184–5
  Secretary-General, 26
  Security Council, 8, 26, 29, 35, 47,
    60, 69, 144, 162
United States, 2–5, 8–11, 16–18, 25,
    28–30, 33–4, 36–9, 41, 46–51,
    53–4, 60–1, 63–7, 69, 75–6,
    78–80, 84, 89–92, 95–7, 101,
    103–4, 107–8, 110, 112, 133,
    136–8, 141–5, 148, 150, 159–65,
    168–70, 172–3, 175, 184, 188,
    192–9, 202, 208–37 *passim*,
    243–58 *passim*, 262–4, 274–5,
    278–81, 285–9, 292–3, 295,
    298–300, 303, 305, 310, 312,
    314–17, 319–24, 333–47 *passim*
  and alliances, 5, 28, 43

Atomic Energy Commission, 84,
197, 340
Congress, 17, 28, 92, 163, 278–9,
289
Defense Intelligence Agency, 314
Department of Defense (Pentagon),
25, 31, 35, 143, 159, 214, 216,
225, 229, 236
Department of Energy, 312
and Gulf War, 16, 37, 132–3, 208,
219, 222, 225, 236, 316, 324
and India and Pakistan, 274–5,
278–81, 285–9, 292–3,
299–300
National Security Council, 193,
214–15
and North Korea, 207–37 *passim*,
298, 341
and the NPT, 8, 10, 41, 46, 49, 65, 75
relations with Russia, 44, 50,
141–2, 162, 168–70, 172–3
Senate, 2–3, 91, 251
and South Korea, 243–58 *passim*
relations with Soviets, 27, 30, 43–5,
144–5, 148, 150, 264
State Department, 193, 214, 235,
245, 251, 303
and Ukraine, 160–1, 164, 172–3,
175–6
University of California at Los
Angeles (UCLA), 342
Usmani, I.H., 276

Vannikov, B.L., 90
Vaziri, Haleh, 20
Venezuela, 59
Visegrad Four, 175

Velayati, Ali Akbar, 321
Vietnam (Vietnamese), 243
Vietnam War, 211, 235, 292, 294–5
Vishwa Hindu Parishad, 13

Wade, James, 213
Walker, Richard 'Dixie', 217
Waltz, Kenneth, 64, 86
Warkany, Josef, 334, 341
Warren, Stafford, 340, 346
Warren, Shields, 335
Warsaw Pact, 95–6
Washington Naval Treaty, 60
Washington Post, 250
Watson, Edwin M.J., 89
Weber, Max, 210
Weech, Ashley, 334
Wilson, Woodrow, 144, 223
Woolsey, R. James, 131, 149, 228
World War I, 130
World War II, 36, 64, 71, 90, 150,
185, 211, 333, 347
Battle of the Bulge, 333

Yamawaki, Takuso, 343
Yamazaki, James, 20
Yavlinsky, Grigory, 177
Yeltsin, Boris, 142
Yi, Chen, 92
York, Herbert, 84
Young-Sam, Kim, 251
Yugoslavia, 173

Zedong, Mao, 92
Zimmerman, Peter, 99
Zhirinovsky, 146
Zlenko, 161